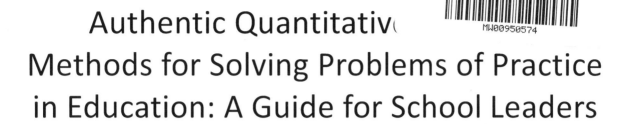

Authentic Quantitative Methods for Solving Problems of Practice in Education: A Guide for School Leaders

A Practical, Innovative, and Easy-to-Understand Approach to Using Quantitative Evidence to Improve Schools and Increase Equity

Version 1.0

Stanley Pogrow,
Professor of Educational Leadership and Equity
San Francisco State University

Professor Emeritus
University of Arizona

stanpogrow@att.net

Published by KDP Publications

Printed in United States of America

Library of Congress Cataloging-in-Publication Data

ISBN: 9798409108915

Authentic Quantitative Research Methods for Solving Problems of Practice in Education: A Guide for School Leaders:
A Practical, Innovative, and Easy-to-Understand Approach to Using Quantitative
Evidence to Improve Schools and Increase Equity

Author *Stanley Pogrow*

This book is available on *Amazon*

Cover Design by Stanley Pogrow

The New Exciting World of Quantitative Methods for Leaders

Quantitative evidence is becoming increasingly important to leadership practice. This textbook is the first and only quantitative methods textbook for educational leadership programs built around the newest quantitative methods for developing, presenting, and consuming evidence in ways that better inform leadership decision-making in schools.

These newer quantitative methods are far more intuitive and accessible to leaders than the traditional, mathematically complex, statistical methods—while also enabling better leadership decisions on how to improve schools and increase equity. *This creates the potential for quantitative methods courses and experiences that are dynamic and meaningful for students and educational leaders interested in improving education.*

However, that tends to NOT happen. Instead, students are made to learn from traditional statistics texts with high levels of technical jargon and mathematical formulae that is more disorienting to the vast majority than it is informative—and convinces them that they cannot master such methods and/or see no relevance to their work as leaders.

Furthermore, there is growing evidence that, while the traditional, rigorous, statistical methods that have dominated textbooks, research journals, and educational leadership programs, for the past 80 years are useful for laboratory basic research, they have largely failed to lead to improvements in practice in many applied fields, including branches of medicine and education. Indeed, these rigorous methods have tended to misdirect practice in education (see chapters 3-6). For example, there is growing evidence that most of the programs certified as being effective by the federal What Works Clearinghouse (WWC) which uses the highest traditional statistical standards, are NOT actually effective. It also appears that the school reform with the strongest evidence of effectiveness, and the most widely used to reform high-poverty schools over several decades, "Success for All," had not actually been effective. *The result has been sub-par education for the most vulnerable students that dashed the hopes of their parents that their children would experience greater success in schools.*

This means that leaders cannot assume that evidence-based practices will be effective in their schools regardless of how scientifically prestigious the source of the evidence is or how rigorous the methodology that was used to produce the evidence. Even more problematic is that there has been a trend for government to mandate that schools adopt those practices simply because they have been deemed to be "evidence-based" by some authority such as the WWC. When these mandated interventions do not produce benefits, the result in wasted opportunity to improve education, and increased cynicism towards research evidence by leaders.

At the same time, some of the evidence from those same sources are invaluable in guiding school improvement efforts. But which evidence? How can leaders differentiate and separate the valuable wheat kernels of evidence from the chaff? Such differentiation is one of the most important quantitative skills that leaders seeking to use evidence-based research need to develop. Relatedly, what should leaders seeking to engage in evidence-based practice do if they cannot find research that is likely to improve their schools?

It is time to push back on the assumption and the imposition that the rigorous methods that are valid for laboratory, PhD type basic research are valid, useful, and appropriate for conducting applied research in schools. This textbook focuses on alternative scientific methods that are referred to as "authentic quantitative methods."

Authentic quantitative methods emphasize alternative, and emergent scientific methods that are accessible to leaders and students, and that enable them to critically examine research evidence, and conduct their own research, to solve problems of practice. It will be shown that these authentic methods are more valid for using research evidence to improve schools and increase equity than the traditional methods.

Definition of authentic quantitative methods

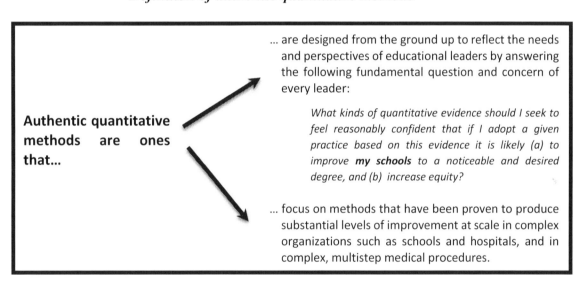

Authentic quantitative methods are ones that...

... are designed from the ground up to reflect the needs and perspectives of educational leaders by answering the following fundamental question and concern of every leader:

> *What kinds of quantitative evidence should I seek to feel reasonably confident that if I adopt a given practice based on this evidence it is likely (a) to improve **my schools** to a noticeable and desired degree, and (b) increase equity?*

... focus on methods that have been proven to produce substantial levels of improvement at scale in complex organizations such as schools and hospitals, and in complex, multistep medical procedures.

Traditional statistical methods and analyses generally do NOT meet these requirements. They emphasize the techniques that are useful for conducting research in controlled laboratory conditions, and for researching the effects of a single drug on the human body. However, when researchers use the same techniques to conduct research under real-world conditions in schools, more often than not their results tend to exaggerate the actual effectiveness of what they were testing—and thereby mislead practice. Such exaggeration is true *even when such research is published in the top research journals and highlighted by the major professional associations*. Such highly promoted evidence-based practices usually do NOT lead to actual improvements in the real world. Of course, when that happens researchers tend to blame practitioners rather than reexamining the methodology they are using.

Instead of blaming practitioners, it is critical to reexamine the methodologies used in educational research as schools are complex organizations in which myriad, ever changing interactive dynamics, are operating simultaneously—processes which cannot be adequately described via traditional statistical methods. Traditional statistics courses and textbooks simply do NOT meet the authentic needs of leaders who are NOT planning to become professional researchers or work in laboratories—but who are instead seeking methods of identifying, generating, and applying evidence that are more likely to actually result in improvements and increases in equity in their schools.

The primary goal of this textbook is to present the emergent quantitative methods that are more applicable to the complex realities of practice in schools. This unique textbook is designed to provide guidance on the types of critical evidence leaders (and leadership students) need to actually improve schools and increase equity—both as consumers of available research and as designers and evaluators of potentially better interventions. In addition, this textbook focuses on quantitative methods from the needs and perspectives of leaders and reformers (as opposed to professional statisticians) in the following ways:

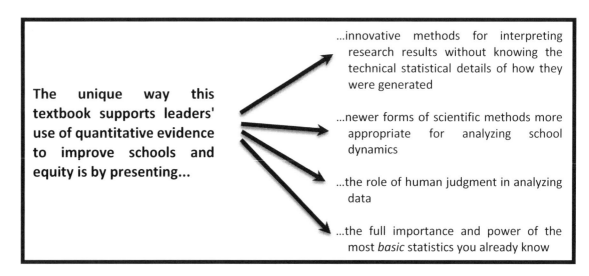

The **unique way this textbook supports leaders' use of quantitative evidence to improve schools and equity is by presenting...**

...innovative methods for interpreting research results without knowing the technical statistical details of how they were generated

...newer forms of scientific methods more appropriate for analyzing school dynamics

...the role of human judgment in analyzing data

...the full importance and power of the most *basic* statistics you already know

In other words, the most useful and dynamic methods for improving practice are the ones that do NOT require sophisticated methods. Indeed, it will be shown that the simplest statistics and methods are far more useful for informing leadership decision-making than had previously been acknowledged.

Figure 1 below illustrates the gap between the perspective of the types of evidence that leaders seek and need—as opposed to the traditional methods that statisticians/psychologists have imposed on education and educational leadership programs.

Figure 1 demonstrates that while there is an overlap between the two perspectives, there is a large gap in the types of evidence that leaders seek and the types of evidence that are provided.[1] This textbook will document the nature of these gaps. In addition, this textbook will focus primarily on those statistical methods that overlap and those that are unique to meeting the evidentiary needs of leaders. The good news is that the overlap, and therefore the most useful quantitative methods, are the simpler and more intuitive statistics.

---

[1] Davis (2008) is an excellent description in the differences between the evidentiary needs of leaders given the nature of real-world decision-making and how academicians view and produce evidence.

Figure 1
Divergence Between the Evidence Provided by Researchers and Leaders' Needs

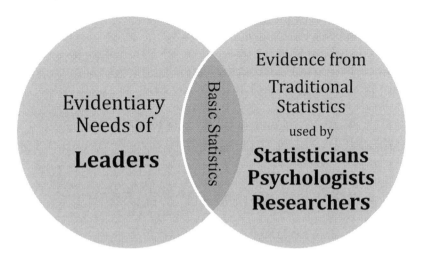

As a result, this text eschews the more sophisticated statistical methods that academic researchers and statistics textbooks tend to favor. It does not treat mathematical sophistication as an end in and of itself. As such, this textbook is NOT primarily a statistics text (though there are statistics). Rather, this text focuses on the newer, more authentic quantitative methods such as "improvement science" that are useful for actually improving schools and increasing equity.

Traditionalists will critique these newer methods as not being "rigorous" science. That is unfair and wrong!

The primary goal of science is to make accurate predictions about the nature of the real world. The fact that these newer authentic quantitative methods have been shown to produce much higher levels of improvement in the real world environment of complex organizations such as schools and hospitals, and even in some branches of medicine, than the traditional statistical methods. This makes them more scientifically rigorous for the applied research needs of educational leaders and clinicians in other fields. For example, these newer methods are credited with enabling obstetrics to save the lives of millions of premature babies and for major improvements in the delivery of health care. In addition, examples will be provided in Chapter 8 as to how these newer methods were used to solve problems of practice in education. Furthermore, it will be shown that the evidentiary standards of the newer methods in this textbook set more rigorous standards for making conclusions that an intervention is effective than the traditional methods.

Additional scientific credence to these alternative methods is evidence by their being published in prestigious scientific journals—including medical journals—most commonly under the rubric of *improvement science*. The key methodological recommendations in this textbook have also been published in *The American Statistician*, the flagship journal of the American Statistical Association (ASA), and in a variety of respected education journals.

So, the alternative methods presented in this textbook represent the best traditions of science— i.e., using scholarship, observation, and empirical data as evidence to better predict outcomes of actual effectiveness. Indeed, the predictions made by these authentic methods will often contradict the findings and conclusions made by researchers in top education research journals as to the effectiveness of a given practice. But rather than being problematic, such contradictions are healthy and necessary if the newer research methods are to provide better evidence for leadership decision-making.

An additional benefit is that these newer scientific techniques make the beauty and power of numerical reasoning intelligible and relevant to leaders and students. Stripping away the unnecessary mathematics and jargon of traditional statistical methodology makes the application of statistical methods and quantitative evidence far more accessible and useful for leaders. As a result, this textbook focuses on the few key statistical methods and data analysis techniques that produce the most authentic evidence for leadership decision-making processes.

Characteristics of authentic research methods

The authentic quantitative methods and uses of statistics in this text are those that leaders can directly apply to noticeably improve their organizations and increase equity. They are:

- Intuitive to leaders and students;
- Far less technical and generally rely on the simplest of statistical analyses;
- Allow for human judgment in the interpretation of data, and intuition in the process of scientific discovery;
- Dynamic, and take into account real world complexity and the many ways that schools differ from each other;
- Use rapid prototyping of new interventions and iterative forms of analyses to seek patterns of effectiveness across different contexts;
- Respectful of personal theories of action and informal methods for designing new interventions;
- Consistent with leadership and management theory and practice; and, most importantly,
- *More likely to result in better decisions by leaders as to what research, data, and analyses are likely to actually improve their schools.*

 The exciting news is that this is a good time to rethink how to teach quantitative methods in leadership programs given the emergent scholarship on alternative quantitative methods. These newer methods are superior and more valid for identifying effective practices for actually improving complex organizations such as schools and increasing equity.

The emergence of this new scholarship and methods means that it's time and necessary to reform quantitative methods courses in leadership programs—and opportunity to do so. It is time to stop using statistics textbooks in educational leadership programs and to switch these courses to the newer more authentic forms of quantitative methods. *The reality is that the longer education relies on traditional "rigorous" statistical methods to identify effective practices—the harder it will be to actually improve education and increase equity.*

A final advantage of this textbook is that unlike traditional statistics textbooks that are typically written by statisticians with little expertise or experience in actually reforming schools, this book reflects both this author's methodological expertise, as well as his expertise in education reform as both a scholar and successful reformer. The methods textbook reflects his large-scale success in working with leaders across this country to design and implement new interventions that improved their schools and increased equity. Such experience provided him with unique insight into how evidence needed to be used to shepherd an intervention from inception, design, redesign, evaluation, and adoption—to large-scale success. This experience also provided unique insight into the types of evidence that leaders sought, how they think about evidence, and why it is important that they do so.

The Design of This Textbook

This textbook is designed to replace the traditional statistics textbook in leadership programs and change what is taught in quantitative methods courses in leadership programs. It is time to end the monopoly that traditional statistical research methods have enjoyed, and recognize that they often mistakenly identify practices as effective and evidence-based when they were actually ineffective. Analyses and leadership decisions using the newer, authentic, quantitative methods highlighted in this textbook will generally produce more valid, findings that lead to better outcomes.

Most importantly, this is the first quantitative methods textbook written from the perspective of the types of evidence leaders need and seek to make valid decisions about how to noticeably improve their schools and increase equity—*as opposed to what statisticians and researchers (with no leadership experience) have deemed to be important for the past 80 years with little real evidence of their actual impact on improving practice.*

Key Methodological themes

- **The importance of the critical application of science, theory, and quantitative evidence to improve practice;**
- The power of numbers and the importance of leaders making authentic sense of numerical information and analyses;
- The importance of combining personal theories of action with academic theories;
- How to apply the simplest statistics and analyses to analyze the findings of the most mathematically sophisticated research and guide evidence-based decisions;
- The importance of leaders critically interpreting research findings are likely to benefit their schools—and how the independent conclusions or leaders will often differ from how researchers and statisticians generally interpret the findings;
- The importance of BIG benefits in research evidence for guiding decisions, and how to determine BIGness;
- How and when to apply human judgment in interpreting research findings and data;
- How to interpret the results of statistical tests and their criteria for guiding leadership decisions—and why the statistical tests are more important for informing decisions than the statistics themselves;
- How to find research evidence;
- The conditions under which leaders can trust and apply claims of evidence-based practices from traditional research methods—and when they should not—even if the research has been validated by the federal What Works Clearinghouse;

- How to design potentially breakthrough interventions and how to conduct action research to evaluate their effectiveness; and
- How to manage data flows in an organization and create a data infrastructure for supporting data-based decision-making.

Key goals

The key goal of this textbook is to present quantitative methods that are accessible to leaders and leadership students, and that are so authentic for improving practice that leaders will continue to use them in their subsequent practice to improve their schools. It is expected that the methods will enable leaders and leadership students to …

- Critically reflect about the implications of data and numerical outcomes in research, including:

  - Published research
  - Evaluations
  - Existing datasets at the state and federal levels
  - Data generated from one's own practice/action research

- Ask the right questions about the data needed to solve a problem of practice, and design a relevant data collection and analysis process;

- *Critically* use evidence to inform practice and make authentic decisions by discerning what evidence is likely to actually improve their schools; and

- Design innovations to solve problems of practice and design the needed real time analyses of their effectiveness as part of a continuous improvement effort.

Most of all, it is hoped that this textbook will start conversations among students, leaders, researchers, and leadership faculty, about rethinking most of the existing assumptions about the application of quantitative evidence to improve schools and increase equity.

General approach

This book focuses on the application of quantitative evidence in ways that are likely to improve one's schools and increase equity. It is based on the latest knowledge and demonstrates how authentic quantitative methods often yield very different conclusions than the recommendation of researchers and statisticians—and why the former often better predict real world outcomes.

At the same time, some traditional statistics and research methods remain valuable and are authentic. These statistical methods are presented in this textbook in a concise, pragmatic, and intuitive fashion on a need to know basis. In most cases the recommendations on how to apply these traditional statistics are novel—but scientifically valid.

This textbook also uses practical examples from many fields, humor, and case studies. There are also applied challenge questions at the end of each chapter (with solutions). These challenges enable students to see the relevance of the quantitative methods to their everyday world of practice, and their value in helping solve the dilemmas and problems they routinely face. Indeed, many of the authentic methods in the textbook have emerged from interactions with leaders at all levels and from leadership students. In addition, the intuitive nature of the methods encourages students' belief that they can and should master and apply them.

The textbook also provides some guidance on how to use Microsoft Excel to conduct the recommended statistical analyses. Excel was chosen because this is also a useful tool for administrative practice. As a result, a working knowledge of how to use Excel for research will also provide ongoing value for using Excel in administrative practice.

Most of all, the quantitative methods in this textbook are NOT presented as an academic exercise in learning statistical facts. Rather, the quantitative methods presented are ones that will continue to be relevant to leaders in their everyday efforts to use evidence to improve their schools and increase equity.

Structure/Overview

Part I (Chapters 1-2) The Authentic Role of Scientific Evidence and Theory in Improving Practice

Part I discusses the importance of science, scientific evidence, and theory for improving practice. It provides a more authentic way to link theory and practice that also values the theories that emerge from one's own experience.

Part II (Chapters 3-7) Authentically and Critically Analyzing Research Evidence

Part II discusses the methods researchers use to generate evidence and presents authentic methods that enable the typical leader and leadership student to critically analyze the most sophisticated published research evidence and data without having to develop new mathematical skills. The authentic methods enable leaders to function as independent judges of research evidence to determine whether claims of effective practices are indeed likely to improve *their* schools—and avoid adopting supposedly "evidence-based" practices that are NOT.

Part III (Chapters 8-10) Practitioner Initiated Research—Designing Innovative Practices and Action Research Data to Solve Problems of Practice

It is not always possible for leaders to find authentic research evidence for solving a given problem of practice. In such cases, leaders need to initiate a novel approach and generate their own evidence. This part describes how to apply the scientific and data analysis methods of the prior parts of this book to one's own research as a leader and/or student.

This part also describes how leaders can use improvement science to design their own innovative approaches to solve a problem of practice, and how to identify and analyze the types of real time data and summative evidence needed for a continuous improvement process, and how to evaluate their existing improvement and equity practices.

This part also provides key methods for leadership students to conduct original action research, or other degree culminating research projects, in graduate programs, such as conducting literature reviews.

Highlighting key technical terms and ideas

To help readers extract key ideas from the text, the following textual emphases are incorporated:

- Key technical terms are italicized and lower case, e.g., *sample of convenience*;

- The first time a technical term is defined it is bolded so that readers can quickly scan text to find the definition;

- Statistical measures/tests are italicized with the first letter in upper case, e.g., *Analysis of Covariance* (whatever that is), and is bolded the first time used;

 This graphic indicates a situation where leaders/students need to use human judgment in applying, conducting, or interpreting quantitative research for decision-making purposes.

The text inside this box is a case study

 Good news about opportunity to use research to improve practice

 This graphic indicates an important difference between the perspective of researchers and the perspective and needs of leaders

 Suggestions for using Excel

Key ideas to remember

Warning about a key problem to avoid

 Practical tip for leadership practice

Key Takeaways   This is a preview of the key ideas that the chapter will develop

Uses of This Textbook

This textbook is designed to be used *instead* of a statistics text in educational leadership programs. While it can be used as the quantitative text in an EdD program …

… there is a more in-depth version of this text by Dr. Pogrow, specifically for EdD programs. (See below) The EdD version is published by ICPEL and is available from Lulu.com.

As a result, this textbook is primarily intended for Masters level leadership and policy programs. This book can also be used as a resource by anyone seeking the latest ideas about research methods for improving practice in education—including all practitioners and policy makers.

What if a program only has a single research method course?

Sometimes Masters programs teach quantitative, qualitative, and mixed-methods research in a single course. While it is preferable for students to learn these methods in separate courses, if a Masters program has only a single course on research methods, it is best to combine this text with one on qualitative research—*as opposed to using a single text on mixed methods research*. The problem with available mixed methods texts is that the quantitative research part uses a very traditional approach. In addition, using separate texts for quantitative and qualitative research provides a more in-depth learning experience about each methodology.

In addition, the low price of this text (as compared to other quantitative methods texts) makes it feasible for use in a multi-purpose research course that requires the use of other materials.

Finally, the comprehensive nature of this text means that it can also be used across several courses—including introduction to research, conducting action research, and literature review (including critiquing research).

What if I want to learn mixed methods research on my own?

The same advice applies. You are best off with combining this textbook with a separate text on qualitative research.

About the Author

Dr. Stanley Pogrow is a leading authority on the application of innovative research methods for educational leaders and is a leader in bringing these more authentic methods to the field of educational leadership.

The author has taught quantitative methods at six universities over a 35-year period. This has given him a broad base of teaching, guidance, and research experience in a wide variety of contexts. Many of the methods presented in this book are ones the author developed to make research interesting, intuitive, and relevant to practice for his students.

Dr. Pogrow is also a highly successful school reformer. He developed and directed the Higher Order Thinking Skills (HOTS) project for Title I and Learning Disabled students in grades 4-8 in approximately 2600 schools across the U.S. serving ½ million underserved students. He discovered that implementing such a large-scale reform required the use of alternative research methods that provided timely feedback. The resultant research methods that were developed out of necessity were largely responsible for the unique success of the HOTS program—and provide the basis for many of the novel research methods presented in this textbook.

As such, this experience, and the work of others who have used similar methods, have demonstrated that the use of these alternative research strategies provides a way to develop substantially more effective approaches to improving educational equity.

Finally, Dr. Pogrow welcomes comments, suggestion, and reactions to the book on his blog: *leadership-quantmethods.blogspot.com* or privately at *spogrow@sfsu.edu*

Acknowledgements

I would like to thank Maxwell Yurkofsky (Radford University), Karen Moran Jackson (Soka University), and James Fox (Salisbury University) for serving as reviewers. Their critical analyses made this book much better than it would have been otherwise.

I would also thank Christopher Tienken (Seton Hall) for sharing his insights and the many recommendations he made in the development of this book. Wayne Padover provided valuable insights for shaping the chapter on action research.

I would also like to thank the sublime Deborah Sherman for her astute proofreading, as well as Yisroel Shaw.

Most of all, I want to thank the many students and leaders who have shared their ideas about evidence-based decision-making and their experiences with me over the course of the past decade.

PART I (Chapters 1-2)
Using Scientific Evidence and Theory to Improve Practice

Introduction to Part I

Part I of this book describes the nature of scientific evidence and its importance for improving practice. Chapter 1 shows how the fundamental nature of scientific evidence is the mediator between belief, quantitative data, theory, and practice. Chapter 2 discusses how quantitative research is conducted.

Part I also:

- Provides a way to end the contentious theory vs. practice debate. Such debate is dysfunctional and represents a fundamental misunderstanding on both ends of that spectrum. It provides a proactive way to better relate the concepts in a more authentic fashion that values the perspective, needs, and insights of both leaders and researchers.

- Places the interpretation of quantitative analysis in the context of the nature of science and the critical importance of evidence, and will show how to best evaluate and use the evidence in quantitative research as the basis for leadership decision-making, and

Chapter 1

The Authentic Role of Scientific Evidence and Theory in Improving Practice

There are many misunderstandings as to what science, scientific evidence, and theory are—and how they relate to practice. All too often professors view theory in mystical terms and the fountain of truth, while practitioners often view theory as idealistic notions that have little, if anything, to do with the pragmatic, real world they experience every day. Some view science as an inscrutable process conducted by people in lab coats who know little about what happens in schools, while others believe that school practitioners can and should engage in scientific research. Some view science as an unbiased process that produces findings that are necessarily true, while others feel that its methods are highly biased and that many scientific findings are wrong. Some think that science cannot provide meaningful findings for schooling which is a far more idiosyncratic and diverse process as compared to medicine, while others believe that it is possible to discern scientific principles in social processes such as leadership. Some believe that numbers and numerical outcomes are too limiting a description of what is happening when leaders try to improve schools and increase equity, while others believe that numbers are as essential to describing what happens in schools as they are to describing the physical world.

It turns out that there is some truth in ALL of these positions!

So, before we can critically examine what evidence-based practice is and how to determine what scientific evidence is most useful for informing leadership decision-making, we need to step back and examine (a) what the nature of science is, (b) how it generates knowledge, and (c) the role of theory in that process. It is also important to understand what science is not.

It is especially important to examine these issues at this point in time given that the use of scientific evidence is now viewed as critical for improving practice and educational outcomes and equity. The *Every Students Succeeds Act* (ESSA), which is the largest federal education program for k-12, requires the use of evidence-based practice. The federal government also established the What Works Clearinghouse (WWC) to apply the best scientific methods to determine which practices "work" and could thus be considered evidence-based. WWC's methods were also used to determine which new research proposals should be funded. It is also important to examine whether education has benefitted from this scientific effort to identify effective practices—and if not why not?

As a result, this chapter provides a background on the fundamental nature of science and the role of scientific evidence. It then uses these frames as the basis for relating research, theory, and practice. But the whole process of scientific quantitative methods centers around the use of the most powerful symbol of all—"numbers."

The Importance and Power of Numbers

If a picture is worth a thousand words, a number is worth a million words. Numbers are powerful symbols. A single number, with only slight variation, determines whether life as we know it can exist on earth or any planet (e.g., the percentage of oxygen in the atmosphere). A salary increase of 2% versus 5% can have a dramatic impact on one's everyday living. Numbers are powerful symbols that impact most of the decisions we make in daily life, whether it is the cost of goods when shopping, budgeting, or whether it is describing the status of one's health. When students tell me that they are not good at quantitative analysis I always point out that they are constantly doing that in their everyday lives—e.g., buying a car.

A single number can also encapsulate complex dynamics in organizations that would require many words to adequately describe. A single number representing the degree of profit or loss tells us many things about the health and functioning of the organization. There are also numbers that tell us many things about the status of educational organizations and how well they are functioning.

While much of what we do as educators and leaders involves understanding emotional needs and responding to them with acts of caring and kindness, increasingly educational leadership decision-making revolves around the analysis of numbers— hereafter referred to as quantitative analysis. A variety of pressures, including accountability movements, business pressures, and pressure from the research community to make education function more like medicine in making evidence-based decisions—as well as the general desire to improve schools and the educational success of all students, all have contributed to dramatically increasing the amount of quantitative data and analysis involved in leadership decision-making. The fundamental push is to use the best scientific quantitative evidence to make leadership decisions as to the types of practices schools should adopt to improve educational outcomes and increase equity.

However, the focus on scientific evidence to guide decisions is relatively new in education—and in society overall. Relying on scientific evidence remains controversial and often misunderstood. Therefore, this textbook focuses on the nature of science and quantitative evidence.

The Nature of Science

Science is a relatively recent invention. Science evolved as a way to better understand the physical world around us by those who did not want to rely on conventional, largely religion-based tenets as explanations. The approach was to rely on observations, systematically record those observations, and put forth explanations of what seemed to have been observed. These basic explanations of systematically recorded observations are called *theories*.

Theories need to be related in some way to the observations and the recorded data. Often more than one set of explanations, i.e., theories, can emerge from the same observations, while in other cases observations defy reasonable explanations for decades and raise more questions than they answer. Ary, Jacobs, and Razavieh (1979) further note that good theories explain the "why" of the observed events and data and should be expressed in the simplest form possible. They note *"A theory that has fewer complexities and assumptions is favored over a more complicated one."* In other words, when someone presents a seemingly pompous and complicated theory, it probably is not a very good theory.

However, there are times when theory is NOT based on observation but on mathematical conjecture. For example, Einstein predicted the existence of black holes from his equations—long before any observations of them were made. However, that is very advanced physics, and in education most theories are made on the basis of observations.

The records of the systematic observations are typically called ***empirical data***. *Empirical data* can be *quantitative*, i.e., numerical data, or *qualitative* data relying on descriptive language. An example of the latter would be keeping a journal of observed behaviors of animals over time, or in the case of a classic anthropological study of educational leadership, Wolcott (1973) kept an observational log of the workday life of a principal. Research often combines the two types of empirical data in what is called mixed-methods research. While this book focuses on the measurement and application of quantitative data, it is important not to reject sound research based on qualitative empirical data.

Desired characteristics of theories

Sherlock Holmes reportedly said:

> "It is a capital mistake to theorize before one has data."

Good theories organize a wide variety of empirical data into a succinct proposition from which testable predictions can be derived and tested. Consider, for example, tectonic plate theory—i.e., that earth's crust and upper mantle are made up of a series of moving plates. There were many predictions that could be made from this theory involving a wide range of phenomena including where earthquakes and tsunamis occurred, and the distribution of plants and animals around the earth. Other powerful theories are natural selection (which explains the evolution of species), relativity, gravity, etc.

Good theories are also ones in which the predictions have been carefully tested and confirmed. Sometimes it can take 35 or more years from the time a theory is proposed till progress can be made in measurement instrumentation to begin to test the theory's predictions. This has recently been the case with two major theories in physics, with new evidence about the existence of the hypothesized Higgs boson and for cosmic inflation theory. The latter theory states that inflation was the primary process that occurred right after the Big Bang that led to the current structure of the universe.

Figure 2 below describes the traditional conception of science and the relationship between empirical data, theory, and the testing of predictions that are implied by a given theory. A test of a given prediction leads to a conclusion that the theory has either (a) been corroborated for now, (b) falsified, or (c) the results are not definitive either way. If the findings falsify, i.e., contradict the theory, then you need to start the cycle over again with better empirical observations that lead to a new or modified theory. However, even when theories have been corroborated over time with replicated results, new empirical data and/or new ways to test a given prediction tend to lead to ongoing modifications of even previously corroborated theories. In other words, the process of developing and testing a theory (via its predictions) is an ongoing dynamic process of rejection, refinement, and creation.

Figure 2
The Traditional Conception of Science and the Relationship Between Empirical Data and Theory

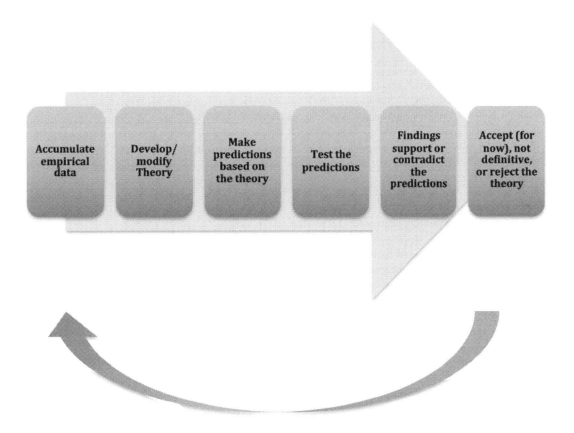

At this point it is hard to find theories in education that are as encompassing as those that have emerged in recent years in the physical sciences or that have led to the types of successful interventions that have been produced in medicine. At the same time, there are some education theories that have emerged that seem to have been supported by quantitative research and that have many implications for practice, such as Vygotsky's (1978) "Zone of Proximal Development." This theory states that over the longer term academic achievement is increased by challenging students above their current developmental level. I suspect that as we learn more about how the brain functions some new major education theories will emerge. However, it is not clear what the catalyst will be for developing better theories for the social processes in education, e.g., theories for improving teacher satisfaction or for developing better forms of interaction among students of different races, etc.

Not all statements are theory and not all forms of knowledge generation are scientific. For example, a **philosophical statement** is something that is *believed* to be true. A philosophic statement or **normative** belief is not expected to be empirically tested—nor can it be. For example, a belief in God, or a particular religion, is a philosophic statement of faith. You believe or you do not. It cannot be proven empirically to be valid or false. Statements such as (a) God exists, (b) God is on our side, (c) a sunset in Hawaii is more beautiful than a sunset in Arizona, or (d) schools should develop the full abilities of all students, are all philosophical statements of belief. A belief that a piece of music or a painting is beautiful is a reflection of one's aesthetic sense. These statements and beliefs are essential elements of what it means to be human—but they are not theories because they cannot be tested empirically.

Cleary, religion, philosophy, social norms, and aesthetics are all valuable ways of thinking and seeing the world. Philosophers also seek to develop explanations of how humans interact with each other and with the world around them. Religion also has explanations of the physical world. However, these ways of thinking about physical reality and social processes are NOT science.

This is not to argue that science is better than philosophy, religion, or aesthetics—only that it is different and that the difference is important. Nor are these different ways of thinking necessarily incompatible. Many scientists are deeply religious and others are very musical. Indeed, conceptions of education practice should start with philosophical propositions about equality, fairness, and democratic participation. However, this book is focused on applying scientific quantitative research to help better achieve such philosophical goals.

Science is distinguished from these other ways of knowing by one specific requirement—that theories need to be derived from empirical data and provide predictions that can be empirically tested to determine whether or not they are *false*. If the predictions are proven to be false, the theory is rejected. But suppose the predictions come true. Does that mean the theory is true? NO!

Why can't a theory be proved to be true? Consider Einstein's theory of relativity. So far it has met all the empirical tests that have been designed to date. So it *seems* to be true. However, as our knowledge of the universe increases and our instruments become more precise, it is always possible that someone will design a test in the future in which the empirical results contradict the theory of relativity. At that point the theory will be deemed to be false. Till then all we can say is that there is a substantial amount of evidence to support the theory, or that the theory has been corroborated by all experiments conducted to date, or that there is credible supporting evidence.

6

There is no such thing as absolute truth in science or quantitative research! We can only say that something *appears to be true* to a certain level of *probability*.

When my students hear science does not provide certainty there is an audible gasp. I think the gasp means that their expectation that science and quantitative methods provide a haven of certainty in a very uncertain world has been deflated.

So when creationists say that the theory of evolution has not been proven to be absolutely true—they are right. *But that is true of everything in science.* The notion of "scientific truth" is a misnomer. The only question is whether all the evidence gathered to date about predictions emanating from the theory of evolution have supported the theory—and the answer to that question is a resounding YES!

Over time, as evidence accumulates, science can lead to findings which are so very likely true that they can be trusted and acted upon.

Much of the discussions in subsequent chapters deal with trying to determine the amount and type of scientific evidence needed for leaders to trust that if they act upon the evidence their schools will likely improve.

Resistance to science

Given the relative newness of science in human history, many of the early scientists who made some of the most important discoveries were rewarded for the knowledge they produced by being imprisoned or killed by the Church. The most famous case was Galileo who was imprisoned for his belief that the sun, not the earth, was the center of the solar system. Less well known is the case of Giordano Bruno who was burned at the stake in 1600 for proposing that the sun was just another star in a universe; one of an infinite number of other stars with orbiting planets. These theories directly conflicted with key religious teachings of the time about the nature of the universe.

Nor has science denialism been limited historically to religious authorities. Science and scientists can also run afoul with the whims of tyrants. Lysenko was a Soviet agronomist who opposed genetics (Krugman, 2020). But Stalin liked him and scientists who disagreed were sent to labor camps or executed. Soviet agriculture was based on Lysenko's scientifically discredited ideas.

People continue to deny scientific evidence on issues such as global warming and human evolution when it runs counter to a variety of cultural-based beliefs—most notably religion and political orientation (Pew Research Center, 2013; Kahan, 2014). We have seen science denial in the response to the COVID-19 pandemic by some leaders around the world—and even a U.S. President where warnings by scientists as to the dangers were treated as fake news.

However, there are consequences to science denialism. Refusal to apply modern genetics led to the disastrous famines of the 1930s in Russia. Recently, countries with leaders who disparaged the advice of scientists on the existence and handling of the coronavirus experienced catastrophic death rates.

Science denialism continues today in education with fights over the teaching of evolution in science, though fortunately this disagreement plays out only in bitter political fights about state science standards and textbooks—without anyone being burned at the stake.

That does not mean that science, or more accurately, the science of the moment, is always correct. Scientific findings, conclusions, and theories often shift over time. Indeed, scientists are trained to be skeptical of any new finding. The primary imperative in science for any new finding to overcome this skepticism is to try and *replicate* important findings—i.e., for others to verify the finding in subsequent research. It is only when researchers other than the one making the original claim can produce the same results in a separate study that the finding can be considered to be likely to be true.

A recent example of replication is the effort to develop a COVID-19 vaccine. This was the first time that a messenger RNA approach was used to develop such a vaccine (as opposed to the traditional vaccine which provides a mild dose of the infection). Pfizer was the first to report an efficacy rate of around 95%. Normally such an astounding result would have been considered to be too good to be true. However, shortly thereafter Moderna similarly reported that their independently developed variant of a messenger RNA COVID-19 vaccine produced similar results. This essentially was replication evidence, or confirmation, of the effectiveness of the messenger RNA approach.

The drive to seek *replication* is the primary defense against research error or outright scientific fraud. When leaders seek evidence that a practice has been effective in a variety of settings they are seeking evidence of replication. If other, independent, researchers cannot replicate the published results of an important study the finding is probably NOT valid. Indeed, problems with replication will play a major role in the recommendations for alternative research methods in subsequent chapters.

The Reflective Nature of Science and Quantitative Analysis

While science is different than religion, philosophy, or aesthetics, that does not mean that it is sterile or devoid of reflective human thought. As the amount of data that could be collected by scientists grew, increasingly sophisticated statistical analyses were developed to organize the mass of numbers collected, and/or to make sense of whether the numbers did or did not support a particular theory. However, regardless of how advanced the statistics are, the results often raise more questions than they answer. For example, consider the following finding by Reardon (2013):

> The black-white achievement gap was considerably larger than the income achievement gap among cohorts born in the 1950s and 1960s,

but now it is considerably smaller than the income achievement gap.
(p. 11)

What are we to do with such a finding that differences in income levels are now a more important determinant of differences in student performance than racial differences? Does this mean that we should ignore issues of race in designing new approaches to? Should we only try to understand how poverty affects achievement independent of race? Why did this shift occur? Does it mean we can only improve education if we dramatically reduce or eliminate child poverty? The state-of-the-art statistical procedures used in this study do not eliminate the need for human reflection in interpreting/applying the findings for educational leadership decision-making and for future studies.

In addition, quantitative research cannot be the sole basis for leadership decision-making. Personal philosophy and changing societal norms play a big role. For example, when I first moved to California 40 years ago, caning (spanking with a stick) was a common discipline practice. Candidates for school leadership positions in some communities who did not overtly support caning were at a disadvantage as they were viewed as being soft on discipline. REALLY! However, societal mores changed as did school practice in the vast majority of states. Part of this change resulted from quantitative research that showed that positive reinforcement was better at promoting behavioral change and academic achievement than negative reinforcement. Today any administrator who caned a student, or engaged in any type of corporal punishment would probably be arrested in most states.[2] As this is being written we are going through another transformation. Due to equity concerns we are moving away from zero tolerance and aggressive discipline policies. As a result, research is being repurposed to determine the best alternative ethical approach.

The Importance of science

Science is important because it breaks down common assumptions about the "real" world; be it the world of nature, the world of everyday life, or the world of professional practice. As we grow older, the number of things we think we 'know' increases. We become less likely to question them. However, science teaches us that many of the things that we 'know' are actually wrong. Here is a simple test based on the best scientific evidence at this time. See how well you do in the following true false test.

1) The shortest distance between two points is a straight line.
2) A particle cannot be in two places at the same time.
3) Nothing in our universe has ever traveled faster than the speed of light.
4) Time always runs at the same speed.
5) Most of the violence in the US is committed by those with mental illness.
6) The more talent a basketball or football team has the higher the level of performance.

---

[2] As of 2021, 19 states still allowed corporal punishment in schools. HR 1234 was introduced in Congress in 2021 to eliminate such punishment, but as of this writing it has not passed.

7) Telling classic moral tales such as "Pinocchio" and "The Boy Who Cried Wolf" reduces the incidence of lying in children.

Sorry, but all the statements appear to be false under the current state of scientific knowledge.[3]

Finding out that something we always assumed to be true is not, or something we always assumed to act a certain way does not, changes our perspective and opens up the potential for discovering new and better approaches to solving key problems.

Ingrained beliefs also exist in education and in our everyday practices that we assume to be correct. Consider the following two examples of very counter-intuitive scientific findings. The first example is Vygotsky's theory of the "Zone of Proximal Development" described earlier. This theory and the supporting evidence indicate that for most students who are struggling, rather than dumbing down the curriculum or gearing it strictly to their developmental level, educators should do the opposite and gear instruction at a higher level.

The second example of a counter-intuitive conclusion comes from my own research that deals with accelerating the performance of students from low-income households who are struggling in grades 4-8. What do you think is the best way to accelerate their learning?

Provide extra help in the content area they are struggling with,
...or...
Develop their general critical thinking skills.

The dominant belief is that the best way to help students from low-income households who are struggling in grades 4-8 is to provide additional assistance in the content objectives they are struggling with. If students are having problems in math problem solving, the dominant belief is to provide more math problem solving help. This intuitive belief has been the basis of federal and state supplemental help initiatives in

---

[3] The following is an explanation for why each of the examples is false: (1) Over large distances it becomes apparent that the shortest distance between two points is a curve, which is why airplanes fly great circle routes as they are the shortest points between two destinations. (2) Under quantum theory a particle can indeed be in two places at once. (3) Under Einstein's theory nothing can travel *through* space faster than the speed of light, but under the theory of inflation, the boundary of the universe itself traveled faster than the speed of light when the universe was first formed. (4) The rate at which time progresses is affected by the speed at which one is traveling. (5) According to Friedman (2014) only 4% of overall violence in the US is committed by those with mental illness. Most violence is committed by those under the influence of drugs or alcohol. (6) Swaab et al. (2014) found that talent facilitates performance—but only up to a point, after which the benefits of more talent in sports such as basketball and football decreases as intra-team coordination suffers. However, in sports such as baseball that has less team coordination, the higher the talent the higher the performance. (7) According to Lee, et al. (2014), telling children stories about the negative consequences of lying contained in the classic children's tales did not reduce the incidence of lying. However, telling them the story of George Washington and the cherry tree, which emphasize the positive consequences of telling the truth, did reduce lying.

both progressive and conservative periods since the passage of Title I in 1965.[4] Relatedly, much has been published by cognitive scientists arguing that developing general thinking skills (also called critical thinking skills) is ineffective and that the only way to improve math or science problem-solving is to provide extra help in math or science problem-solving (e.g., Willingham, 2007).

However, my own large-scale research has shown that this highly intuitive approach of providing extra content-based help, regardless of whether its basic skills or problem solving help, is largely ineffective after the third grade with students born into poverty. So what does work? Surprisingly, the alternative approach of providing intensive general thinking development—i.e., learning how to think abstractly, divorced from the formal content of the classroom/subject content—is far more effective in raising content test scores. The conventional wisdom and existing research are simply wrong.[5] Low-income students generally do NOT benefit equally from content-specific problem solving instruction to their full intellectual potential until they have internalized key general thinking instincts—such as generalization. This theory, called *The Theory of Cognitive Underpinnings*, is very counter-intuitive. How is it possible that NOT providing additional help in specific reading and math content could produce greater gains on end-of-year tests for disadvantaged students in grades 4-8? This counter-intuitiveness is why almost everyone disagrees with this theory. Some disagree because they (mistakenly) view it as a "deficit model."[6]

In terms of the scientific process, the counter-intuitiveness and the non-acceptance does not mean that this theory is wrong. The only way to tell is to look for patterns in data and observations, and to study testable predictions. In terms of patterns of date, *The Theory of Cognitive Underpinnings* provides a powerful explanation as to why little progress has been made in reducing the eighth grade achievement gap since 1988, and suggests an alternative approach that might be more effective. In addition, here is a testable prediction:

> *If the Theory of Cognitive Underpinnings is correct then the combination of the Common Core and trying to help struggling low-income students simply by providing extra help in content problem-solving will NOT work and will actually exacerbate achievement gaps in grades 4-8.*

---

[4] While everyone is on board with *always* relying on the content-based approach as a supplemental improvement strategy, The only historical disagreement has been whether such content-based help should focus on providing extra emphasis on basic skills (conservatives) or on problem solving (progressives).

[5] There are very specific conditions under which intensive general thinking can accelerate the learning of educationally disadvantaged students after the third grade. Presenting the conditions, and the reasons why general thinking development works, is beyond the scope of this book. Those interested can read some of my articles (Pogrow, 2004; Pogrow, 2005).

[6] It is not a deficit model because the work has shown that children born into poverty have the same intellectual capability as any other. This theory simply posits that if we redirect available funds to provide an intensive intervention to develop their innate general thinking abilities they will then in fact blossom academically. It is not a deficit in the children, but a deficit in the types of intervention we provide to them after the third grade.

One of the challenge questions at the end of this chapter provides an opportunity for future cohorts of students to examine the validity of this prediction.

 Another human element that is critical to science is "skepticism." Science advances because someone becomes skeptical that dominant ideas and beliefs are actually true. This is what fuels new theories and innovations of thought and practice. Scientists are very skeptical of new theories or new evidence, and do everything they can to discredit them. Remember, scientific truth is all about proving theories of the moment to be false. This skepticism is important because it forces proponents to do the hard work of testing the theory and accumulating a wide array of supporting evidence.

A key problem in the use of science in education has been that both academicians and practitioners have been more likely to accept the theories of the moment than the physical sciences communities—hence the churning of popular theory in education and the related churning of what constitutes best practice. As caring individuals, educators often gravitate towards theories they want to be true or because it makes intuitive sense to them. But as just discussed, our intuition can be wrong.

To be fair, even the medical profession has periodically been sucked into acting on the basis of a popular notion instead of evidence. The medical profession wanted to believe that it was possible to manage pain without producing addiction. This lack of scientific discipline led to the opioid crisis.[7]

Within professions, science is seen as an important sign of a commitment to protecting a given field from taking inappropriate action that may cause harm, or from wasting resources in pursuing agendas that have no provable benefits. Education is no different. Education leaders are bombarded by proposals for new practices. For example, Carpenter (2000) surveyed one professional education journal between 1987 and 1997. He counted 361 reform proposals that seemed to be "good ideas"—in just a single journal. He also noted that many of these proposals are accompanied by claims that evidence has shown them to be effective. Such claims often get repeated and promoted by professional organizations. It all sounds very intuitive and convincing. Yet Carpenter also notes that all these reform proposals resulted in few gains. Science and its reliance on empirical data are critical for helping leaders make data-based decisions on which (if any) of the multitude of good ideas they are bombarded with, or claims of evidence supporting the ideas, are likely to in fact improve their school(s).

The Importance of quantitative data and tools

As previously discussed, quantitative data are the critical basis for generating a theory and for testing the predictions of that theory.

Some of the most useful data for generating theories and evidence-based practice/policy recommendations are ones that describe the current and historical state of practice and outcomes. There are many datasets at the federal and state levels that

---

[7] Lembke (2016) documents the extent to which the medical profession was sucked into supporting the increasing use of opioids without real scientific evidence, and how all the medical regulatory safeguards that were supposed to protect the public went along for the ride.

researchers and leadership students can access to ask questions such as: What has been the trend of the achievement gaps since the 70s? At which grade levels do these gaps contract or widen? What is the distribution of students/faculty/administrators in different regions by race? What are the best predictors of students going on to postsecondary study? How many students who enter the community college assigned to remediation courses succeed and make it into credit-earning courses? How many students earning advanced degrees are first-generation? Are US students doing worse on international comparisons than previously? Is my school/district doing better or worse than other demographically similar schools in their state.

My experience is that once students (and leaders) start looking into the raw data in these datasets they are generally surprised by what they find. (Chapter 4 provides some examples of how to find important datasets.) This then provides opportunity for discussing why students were surprised by the data and why they think that this is the state of practice. Once students start trying to answer these questions they are essentially forming theories.

One such example of a surprising finding that emerges when looking at the actual data of the achievement gap over time is that while there was great reduction in the Black-White and Hispanic-White achievement gaps from the early 1970s to 1988, the gap has remained pretty much the same since then. Why? Answering this question begs for theory generation, and many such theories have been put forth (Brookings, 1998). As a professor I always like to hear the theories of my students.

Such *primary sources* of data are also important for responding to general accusations that some politicians like to make that American education is declining. (Primary source refers to accessing and referring to the actual data in a dataset or published article, as opposed to *secondary sources*, which are quotes from others who characterize what they think the data indicate.) Indeed, the use of these datasets are so important for identifying genuine needs and problems of practice in education, or for justifying theories and approaches for solving them.

Skills in working with quantitative data are also of increasing importance now that we are in the era of big data. For better or worse, the world is increasingly awash with quantitative data of all types, and the ability to manage and utilize such data is increasingly valued. Increased pressures for accountability and equity are forcing school leaders at all levels to (a) analyze quantitative data, (b) determine and communicate their implications for school improvement, and (c) develop a plan and support for school improvement based on the results.

Dealing with loads of quantitative data is not just important for school leaders, but also for the students in their schools. Good jobs throughout society increasingly require the ability to process and utilize quantitative data produced by sensors and 'smarter' machines that are becoming more prevalent in most areas of production. This is the world that graduating students are already facing. This is true for today's auto repair technician who needs to interpret the quantitative data emanating from the many computer systems within each car, to assembly line workers. Thirty years ago, when employers complained that schools were not adequately preparing students they were generally referring to habits of mind such as showing up on time. Today, when employers talk about habits of mind they are seeking more advanced 21st century characteristics such as collaboration and critical thinking. When they talk about a "skills gap" they are complaining about how graduates do not have the quantitative skills needed to figure out how to direct the types of sophisticated machines that are contributing to a renaissance in American manufacturing, or how to interpret and problem-solve the quantitative data emanating from these machines in order to make needed adjustments.

Quantitative tools and analysis also provide great potential for improving practice. Consider the example described by Tullis (2014). New York City Public Schools had a nightmarish logistical challenge of trying to accommodate its 75,000 eighth grade students' choice as to which of the city's 426 high schools they wanted to attend. The top students were able to get their top choice, but almost half of the other students got no match at all for any of their multiple choices. Once the city adopted a quantitative allocation of preferences model that had been used to match graduating medical students with hospital residencies, the number of unmatched students immediately dropped from 31,000 to 3,000, and roughly half of all students got their first choice. While not a perfect solution, this quantitative allocation produced a major improvement that reduced the anxiety of the vast majority of students and parents—as well as that of principals.

At the same time, education is about nuanced, complex social interactions among individuals with a wide variety of cultural perspectives. There is always the danger that reducing these processes to sets of summary numbers can gloss over and be insensitive to the importance of these cultural perspectives in shaping outcomes.

The importance of cultural perspective in data analysis is best captured by Walter and Anderson (2013) in their book *Indigenous Statistics: A Quantitative Research Methodology*. They characterize the use of largely census statistics to describe Indigenous populations in the following way "…many of these data, as they currently exist, tend to constitute Indigenous peoples as deficient and that these portrayals can, and do, restrict and inhibit other ways of understanding…Indigenous peoples" (p. 16). However, instead of conventionally using such concern to bash quantitative methods and argue that only qualitative research can do justice to understanding Indigenous populations, they then proceed to develop a set of alternative statistical approaches that are in accord with Indigenous worldviews and that "…demonstrate that quantitative methodologies reflect aspects of our contemporary selves every bit as Indigenous as those of qualitative methodologies" (p. 16).

Good News

The lesson of *Indigenous Statistics* is that quantitative methods are not monolithic, dogmatic, or repressive—but that they can be tailored to represent different cultural perspectives and needs.

Similarly, this textbook is geared to helping students and leaders adapt to the cultural differences between the evidentiary experiences, incentives, and needs of researchers/statisticians versus those of leaders. It is a rethinking of how to critically analyze, generate, and use quantitative evidence to produce results that better characterize the strengths, realities, and specific needs of school leaders seeking to help all their students.

14

The Role of Theory in Educational Practice

What Is theory?

Within the scientific method, theory is the intermediary step between empirical observation and reaching a conclusion. Putting forth a theory is the start of a process of testing whether it seems to be true. *In other words, theory is a means to an end— not an end in and of itself.*

In addition, much of what is ascribed to theory in education is not the way theory is used in physics. The eminent physics theorist Lisa Randall (2005a) notes:

> These [elementary] particles, and the physical laws they obey, are components of what physicists call a theory—a definite set of elements and principles with rules and equations for predicting how those elements interact. When I speak about theories ...I'll be using the word in that sense; I won't mean "rough speculation", as in more colloquial usage. (p. 66)

It seems that much of what passes for theory in education (and social sciences in general) is more a colloquial use of ideas as opposed to ideas grounded in empirical data.

This is not intended to diminish the importance of theory in education. As data and experience with a particular phenomenon or set of phenomena increases it becomes increasingly difficult to understand what is fundamentally going on: i.e., what the common denominator is that links all the data. Then one day someone has a flash of insight that unifies and makes sense of all the myriad individual pieces of bits of information.[8] This insight will be concise and precise so that it leads to a series of predictions that can be tested. Research can then proceed to test the theory; i.e., its predictions and the field can consider taking advantage of the theory's implications.

But can leaders rely on theory? Sebastion Jung, one of the nation's leading theoretical neuroscientists, recently noted (Gorman, 2004):

> Theories and speculation can be around for half a century or a century
> without going beyond, without becoming real science.

This was his way of explaining why he was switching from theoretical work back to conducting basic experiments to generate more data. He felt that at that point there was

---

[8] Sometimes these flashes of insight are so revolutionary that they change everything, the so-called paradigm shift (Kuhn, 1970). It became fashionable for a while in the 80s for anyone proposing a new theory in education to refer to it as a paradigm shift. Such claims tended to be hyperbole since paradigm shifts tend to occur *at most* only once or twice a century in any scientific field.

a need for better data about how the brain works before better theories could be developed. In addition, Hubbard (2015) notes that theory is subordinate to the production of and analysis of data, and that more Nobel prizes have been awarded for generating novel forms of data than for positing theories.

Remember

Valid theories do not exist without data. Theories evolve from looking for patterns in data. The research scientist looks through formal reports of phenomena and data sets to try and discern a pattern. The practitioner also seeks to find some coherent patterns in the flood of events they are exposed to every hour of the day.

There are many sources of data from which theories can be constructed. Physicists construct theories from patterns of debris resulting from the collision of proton beams. Social scientists construct theories from patterns as to the causes and effects of key historical events or from excavations. Education researchers develop theories from patterns in large data sets about schools and students, and from previously published research. Similarly, education leaders evolve theories from patterns in the consequences of the dozens of decisions they make every day and from their observations of human behavior. Indeed, leaders' theories may even be subconscious ones—though, as will be seen later, they can be made conscious.

But what should a leader do when they are exposed to a theory developed by others. Should the leader trust the theory—i.e., make a decision on the basis of that theory? How can one know whether there is sufficient evidence to support that theory? Above all, it is clear that a leader cannot wait around for half a century to begin to find out how valid that theory is because there are lots of decisions that have to be made today.

Leaders vs Researchers

The role of theory in practice is highly contentious. Most conceptions of the critical role of theory for improving practice have been written by academicians. Thousands of such articles have been written. Generally, such articles draw on philosophical and theoretical perspectives along with drawing parallels to how theory is used in the physical sciences. Such articles then generally berate practitioners for (a) being atheoretical, (b) not understanding the role and importance of theory, and (c) being remiss in not basing their practice on the latest research and theory. Finally, such articles generally conclude that the practice of education will not improve until practitioners develop a greater appreciation of theory and more systematically incorporate it into practice.

In turn, practitioners often come to view theory as something amorphous, highly general and overly simplistic that does not really describe the realities that they face, and that cannot inform most decisions that they make.

Who is right? Can this difference in viewpoint be bridged? YES!!!! But it requires a new conception of the role of theory.

A new conception of the role of theory in leadership decision-making

Instead of taking the sides of the academicians in this often "failure to communicate" debate as to the value of theory in improving practice, the following is a new framework to try and gain clarity; one that accepts that both sides are right and wrong.

The reality is that ALL thoughtful leadership decisions are in fact made on the basis of theory.

This reality includes the dozens of decisions that leaders must make every day. For example, an irate parent marches into a school and demands to see the principal. A successful principal has dealt with this situation many times. The principal then decides to handle the situation in a particular way based on the belief that this approach will produce a particular type of outcome based on prior experience. For example, the principal may have learned that the best approach is to invite the parent into the office and offer him/her a cup of coffee. Such a theory that is based on accumulated experiential data is called a "**personal theory of action**". The principal is not making a decision on the basis of a coin flip, a prayer, or an emotional reaction—but on the basis of a carefully honed theory, even though that theory does not have a formal name and will never be published. At the same time, this theory may also be based on considerable evidence. As previously noted, every episode in the hectic day of leaders is a datapoint, and depending on the amount of experience, there may be more data underlying a "personal theory of action" than a published theory.

When academicians talk about theory, they are talking about the specific theories that are discussed in the research articles that they read: hereafter referred to as "**academic theories**".

Both "personal theories of action" and "academic theories" fit the fundamental definition of "theory", i.e., a proposition put forth for the purpose of empirically testing whether it appears to be true—or is clearly false.

Academic Theory vs. Personal Theories of Action

The two types of theories leave us with a whole series of questions such as: Is "personal theory of action" or "academic theory" better for supporting improvements in practice? Which type of theory should leadership programs emphasize? Which types of academic theories are best for preparing education leaders? Should the emphasis be on leadership theory, learning theory, social justice theory, critical race theory, etc.?

Both "personal theories of action" and "academic theories" have advantages and limitations.

Advantages of academic theory

There are a number of *advantages* to academic theory. Often academic theories consider more factors than typical personal theories of action and many have been honed over decades with convincing evidence. Many academic theories have undergone extensive scrutiny by many individuals other than the originators. At times academic theory can also deal with novel issues that the practitioner community has not yet addressed and for which most practitioners have not yet developed "personal theories of action" or even considered important to think about. In such cases academic theory can change leaders' perceptions, or spark a sense of social consciousness, that causes them to recognize that a problem exists and that they need to explore approaches for solving it—which then in turn informs the development/evolution of a personal theory of action. An academic theory can also spark a leader's creative insight that inspires the implementation of a new service or intervention.

Another advantage is that academic theory often has a history. Seeing how key theories related to an issue evolve over time provides an intellectual perspective about how professional thinking and evidence has changed and hopefully become more valid and applicable. Such historical changes in a given academic theory over time highlights the importance of constantly rethinking one's own perspectives on practice. For example, Piaget's groundbreaking work on the development of cognition in children, which viewed cognitive development as a predetermined stage by stage developmental process has given way to more fluid theories of intellectual development such as Vygotsky's (1978) theory of the "Zone of Proximal Development" described earlier. In addition, there is experimental data confirming Vygotsky's theory. This evolution of academic theory provides practitioners with a way of accelerating the development of their students beyond what one would expect from Piaget's work. Knowing about this evolution in academic theory to a more fluid conception of cognitive development can potentially inspire leaders to push for more advanced approaches to instruction for students who are struggling. The push for increasing participation in *advanced placement* courses at the high school level can be seen as one way of operationalizing Vygotsky's theory.

In addition, knowing that an academic theory was tested and proved false can prevent a leader, or in some cases the entire field, from adopting a specific practice.

Finally, the general nature of academic theories in education means that they can be applied to a wide variety of situations.

Limitations of academic theory

Clearly, professors favor academic theory. As a professor I know that this is our stock in trade. However, there are problems and limitations with the application of academic theory. A big problem is that the educational research and academic communities tend to take as given that practices based on academic theory are better than those that are not. This is reflected in a variety of ways in academic program standards, funding agencies, and research journal editorial standards. *However, there is absolutely no empirical evidence that education practices and decisions based on academic theory produce better results than those that are not.* If basing practice on academic theory provided such a compelling advantage there would be evidence by now. As a result, the idea that theory improves practice needs to be considered at this time as a belief/bias, or at best a theory with little or no evidence, as opposed to being a scientifically validated proposition.

Warning

Existing published articles on the relationship between academic theory and practice tend to idealize and overestimate the value of theory in general, as well as the currently popular theories in education, while ignoring the lack of underlying evidence. Therefore, one should be cautious about the value of many of the theories typically taught in colleges of education for actually improving practice in the real-world.

The misunderstood complexity of applying academic theory to practice is further reflected in the few instances where academicians who specialized in a class of theory, such as theories of organizational change or theories of teacher training, decide to actually put their knowledge into practice. The results have never been encouraging. As a personal example, a number of years ago I was in competition with another professor for major funding from a prestigious foundation for a new approach to teaching mathematics. The other program was funded on the basis that it was better grounded in theory (which it was). However, I knew that my approach was better designed and had a better chance of working based on preliminary results and my earlier successful work. Alas, despite generous funding the other program never worked and disappeared as soon as the funding ended.

Personal experience aside, there is little research comparing the extent to which interventions based on the best academic theory and research as recommended by academic experts yield better results than those implemented by practitioners. Quite the contrary! Consider the following gold-standard quality research studies funded by the U.S. Department of Education. Burdumy (2009) found that the research-validated programs recommended by reading experts did not produce better results than what randomly selected schools were already doing, and one intervention, 'Success for All', did worse. Garet, et al. (2011) found that the best, longer-term professional learning/development that math education experts could design for randomly selected schools did not increase the math performance of seventh graders. *This suggests that the applicability of the current state of academic theory and research to school improvement is more limited than academicians admit and does not necessarily provide a clear advantage over how leaders currently make decisions.*

There are other problems with trying to apply academic theories in education. The number of academic theories in education seems to be constantly mushrooming and passing in and out of style quickly. The vast majority of theories are never tested and are thus simply discussion pieces to determine if one agrees or disagrees with them. When theories are tested and the results are positive, there is almost never any effort to replicate the findings. Many theories are widely disseminated in the academic community simply because they reinforce existing normative beliefs or favored philosophies. In other cases, practices based on highly general academic theory turn out not to work: e.g., the effusive praise approach of the mid 80s. The problem of relying on untested theories is not limited to education. In discussing the state of theory in psychology, Meehl (1978) noted that:

> ...most so-called "theories" in...psychology (clinical, counseling...community, and school psychology) are scientifically unimpressive and technologically worthless...Most of them suffer the fate that General MacArthur ascribed to old generals – They never die, they just slowly fade away. In the developed sciences, theories either tend to become widely accepted and built into the larger edifice of well tested human knowledge or else they suffer destruction in the face of recalcitrant facts and are abandoned...But in fields like...social psychology, this seems not to happen. There is a period of enthusiasm about a new theory...and then people just sort of lose interest in the thing and pursue other endeavors. (p. 806-807)

This approach to theory is not science and is not likely to improve practice.

Another problem is that while academic theories in the hard sciences often provide very detailed and specific predictions, the theories in education and the social sciences tend to be more general in nature. For example, *Frame Theory* talks about how people's perceptions of proposed ideas differ sharply. While this does have implications for practice in terms of knowing that implementation of new ideas is more complex than previously understood, there is not enough basic research done around that idea for it to have any detailed predictive power. So Frame Theory does not help us understand what types of people are most likely to view an idea a certain way, or what the range of perceptions around an idea are likely to be. In addition, many academic theories are so general that they border on philosophy, as opposed to science, and offer few predictions that can be tested or clues as to how to implement them in ways that are likely to be effective.

Conversely, developing effective interventions requires more than a general theory. My own experience is that there is often only a very limited set of parameters of implementation for which a given intervention will be effective from among an almost infinite set of possibilities. Unfortunately, education theories and research seldom provide specific implementation parameters—e.g., the amount of the intervention that is needed, how it should be delivered, specifics of how it should be implemented included the training needed, etc.

In other cases where the parameters of effectiveness are known, the political system will not allow them to be put into effect in such a way as to take advantage of that knowledge. For example, consider the research on the effects of reducing class size on student achievement. A synthesis of 77 studies by Glass and Smith (1979) found that for class size reduction to have an effect it needs to be reduced below 20 students per teacher. Finn and Achilles (1999) found in experiments with class size reductions in Tennessee that classes of 13-17 students produced large benefits; particularly for disadvantaged students. Together the studies indicate that there are large achievement gains for educationally disadvantaged students if they are in a class of about 15 students for three years. This type of specificity meets Randall's criteria for what a theory is.

So what happened in this unusual case where the parameters of effectiveness were known? Alas, when California implemented class size reduction statewide political expediency intruded. Instead of focusing the funds on high poverty schools, the state funded such reduction in *all* schools to make it more politically palatable. This had two major drawbacks. First, including all schools made the program so expensive that the number of grade levels funded was limited, and as soon as the state experienced recession the program was dropped. Second, this created so many new positions in the higher SES schools that there was an exodus of experienced teachers from the lower SES schools. Indeed, during this period I talked to several principals of low-SES schools who indicated that they had no certified teachers at any of the critical grade levels—which negated whatever benefits could have been expected from having smaller classes. A classic example of the "*lord giveth and the lord taketh*."

Other academic theories that come to the fore do have some evidence but no one can figure out how to take advantage of them. For example, consider Gardner's (1983) theory of Multiple Intelligences. It was one of the predominant theories taught in colleges of education in the late 80s and early 90s. It clearly points to the possibility of reorganizing instruction to tap into the range of intelligences that students possess; particularly those who are struggling with the predominant mathematical-logical form of thinking that is emphasized in schools. However, a number of notable efforts to design schools based on tapping into multiple intelligences were never able to demonstrate increases in achievement. As a result there is less emphasis on this theory today. Of course, that does not mean that the theory of multiple intelligences is incorrect, or of no utility, or that someone will not in the future figure out how to take advantage of what is known about multiple intelligences.

All of the above problems are exacerbated by education's short attention span for any given theory before a new set of theories is brought forth to vie for our attention and we shift our focus. This is theory as fashion. Science, on the other hand, will spend half a century trying to find a way to validate and/or apply a theory. Conversely, some education theories that continue to be widely cited and taught have never been empirically tested.

To be fair, it is harder to develop significant academic theories in education than the physical sciences. The physical sciences deal with complex, but stable processes. The speed of light or the gravitational force does not change (…as far as we know). On the other hand, people change all the time. So developing theories about teacher behavior or student learning, particularly grand unifying theories, is much more difficult. Indeed, some argue that the principles of science cannot be applied to the social sciences in general and education in particular. For example, postmodernists believe that the nature of human behavior is not subject to fundamental laws, as the physical world appears to be. This philosophy believes that all decisions and behavior reflect individual motivations and power relationships that are NOT uniform OR systematic.

While there is some truth to the post-modernist philosophy, it is clear that it is indeed possible to develop valid theories in the social sciences and education. It is just hard to do so. Locke (2007) provides examples of theories that have stood the test of time in organizational management such as *Bandura's Social Cognitive Theory* (Bandura, 1986), and Miner (2003) lists 73 theories of organizational behavior considered to be important by academicians.[9] But developing such theories requires great persistence and hard work. Haig (2013) estimated that it takes social scientists anywhere from 3 to 30 years of generating and reflecting about data in order to be able to develop a theory to explain a phenomenon of interest.

This finding that it takes a long time span to develop a theory mirrors my own experience. I was able to demonstrate systematic effects in accelerating the learning of Title I and Learning Disabled students on a large scale and then develop a theory to explain the results. It took about 14 years for me to begin to understand why the approach was working and the conditions under which it was working. I was then able to develop a grand theory that encompassed students from a wide diversity of racial backgrounds and settings—from isolated bush schools in Alaska and the Navajo reservation, to the teeming inner city schools of Detroit and barrio schools in Tucson. This suggests that (a) it is clearly possible to develop powerful theories in education, and (b) developing such theory in education not only requires extensive amounts of time, but it probably cannot be a grand theory; i.e., a theory of everything as physicists try to do. In other words, my *Theory of Cognitive Underpinnings* does not make universal claims about all forms of learning for all types of students at all grade levels.

So it is feasible to develop powerful, but limited, theories in education around very specific processes. The problem with theory in education, and why it is misunderstood, is that the theories seem to come into favor and then disappear quickly without ever being truly tested. Research journals encourage this churn by favoring submissions based on novel theories. Also, the architects of theories try to gain the attention of the profession by posing them as grand theories; i.e., new paradigms. An example of how exaggerating the importance and validity of a given theory damages and inhibits progress is the competing theories about the best way to teach reading. The intense political conflict between the competing theories of phonics and whole language obscures the likelihood that there is no one best way to teach reading across all grades and types of students. By refocusing research and our expectations for what we can scientifically discover, and looking instead for interactive effects in how to teach reading by grade, types of students, different mixes of types of instruction, etc. we can develop theories that are less grand, but ones that are valid and useful for designing more effective practices.

Despite all these limitations, there is clearly value for leaders and leadership students to learn and know some key academic theories and to engage in the intellectual process of exploring the practical implications of those theories. That should be a rite of passage in any leadership program. Indeed, the moment of discovery of some academic theory that strikes a resonant chord in a student, or that makes you want to think more deeply about a problem you are dealing with, or when you realize that it explains something that you have been puzzling about, are all wonderful moments of discovery. At the same time, the limited evidence associated with most education theories means that there is little justification for requiring that all/most leadership decisions have an academic theoretical basis or justification.

---

[9] The fact that these theories are considered important does not of course necessarily mean that they have a strong evidentiary base, nor does it necessarily mean that they would be useful for managers/leaders.

Advantages of personal theories of action

The key advantage of "personal theories of action" is that they are highly specific and detailed. They enable leaders to deal with a wide variety of issues efficiently. Personal theories of action provide a lot more of the detailed information needed to determine the specific parameters involving implementing new approaches, such as how to schedule them, how to build support, how much effort and amount of service to provide, etc. Personal theories of action are consistent with the expression "God is in the details," and implementation details determine the success or failure of most interventions.

In addition, a mindset to consciously develop personal theories of action can lead one to become more inquisitive, and reflective—which can in turn lead to better practices.

Limitations of personal theories of action

When "personal theories of action" do work, the leaders are often not conscious that they are using a specific theory in making related decisions. In addition, the specificity of these theories limits their applicability—partly because they are missing a key characteristic of a good theory already discussed. The previously described principal's "personal theory of action" for dealing with an angry parent does not meet Ary, Jacobs, and Razavieh's (1979) criterion that a good theory explains "why" it works. So while that theory has utility at this point, not exploring the fundamental principle of human behavior that causes it to work means that the principal may not be able to extend the approach to additional situations—e.g., how to handle distraught students and teachers—and/or the boundaries wherein a given theory is not likely to be effective.

Warning

However, the key limitation of "personal theories of action" is what Kahneman (2011), a Nobel Prize winner, discusses as "narrative fallacy".[10] Narrative fallacy is that people (a) construct stories about past events that are flimsy, (b) exaggerate the consistency of evaluations, and (c) exaggerate the role of skill and underestimate the role that luck (i.e., random variation) played in the outcome. He notes that people build the best possible story available to them, and if it is a good story they believe it.

The underestimation of the effect of luck in success at a given task, and attributing the outcome to one's skill or strategy, is well documented in the social psychology literature. For example, Langer and Roth (1975) showed experimentally that early success in a game of *pure chance* caused individuals to (a) believe they were better at the task than others, (b) exaggerate the initial success in their own minds, and (c) expect more future success. They conclude that: "It appears that the motivation to see events as controllable is so strong that the introduction of just one cue, a fairly consistent sequence of wins…is enough to induce an illusion of control over the task of coin flipping even in sophisticated subjects" (p. 955). This means that a given "personal theory of action" may be an illusion.

---

[10] The origin of the phrase is ascribed to Nassim Taleb, author of *The Black Swan*.

Indeed, it is possible that personal theories are highly influenced, not by successful patterns of experiences, but by implicit biases—e.g., certain "types" of students cannot think at a high level. When no creative effort is put forth to develop such thinking skills, the bias becomes a self-fulfilling prophecy. The fine line between self-fulfilling prophecies and personal theories of action is that the former is not based on an effort to solve a problem or produce improvement. This fine line is why it is critical for leaders to periodically step back and reflect about why they have made the key decisions they made over the recent past.

The difficulty in constructing valid "personal theories of action" not only applies to leaders trying to make sense of the seeming chaos of daily practice, but also to highly respected management gurus who develop narratives as to what distinguishes successful companies from unsuccessful ones. Examples of such narratives of the practices that produce successful companies are found in well-known publications such as *In Search of Excellence* (Peters & Waterman, 1982), *Built to Last* (Collins & Porras, 2004) and *Fortune Magazine's* list of most admired companies. Fortunes are made by gurus disseminating these narratives to both business and education leaders. However, Kahneman notes that studies have found that the difference in profitability and stock returns of companies identified as successful compared to unsuccessful companies declined to almost zero after the lists were published.

A number of scholars have put forth explanations as to why it is often so hard for leaders to replicate past success. Langer's (1989) work on mindlessness shows how people often rely on distinctions drawn in the past in a routinized manner and do not recognize how new distinctions are possible and/or necessary. In addition, James March, the co-developer of the field of organizational theory, points out that in general leaders who are highly successful in one setting tend to fail when they move on to another more prestigious position (March & March, 1977; March & March, 1978). He points out even if one does not underestimate the effects of luck; luck still plays a major role in success. March (2014) notes that "a substantial portion of success in any one year will depend on "luck" and is relatively unlikely to be repeated." A farmer's success or lack thereof is dependent on the variability in the amount of rain, and the success of a leader is dependent on variability in the economy, and the success of educators is dependent on variability in a whole host of factors such as a board election that he/she cannot control.

So the reality is that it is hard to develop valid "personal theories of action" that are applicable to future or different events and that we come to believe too strongly in the highly specific narratives that we create. This works against individuals when new circumstances arise—particularly in the absence of a broader theoretical sense such as that provided by academic theory against which individuals can assess their specific "personal theories of action".

Also problematic is that there is a very fine line between a personal theory of action and one's intuition. However, intuition by itself can be highly misleading. If you look back to the examples earlier in this chapter, your intuition probably led you to answer most of the questions incorrectly. *Science is at its best when its findings contradict our intuitions, which then frees us to explore new frontiers of theories and ideas.* The evidence-based idea that birds descended from dinosaurs is very counter-intuitive.

Similarly, many of our intuitions about student needs and best practices are wrong—but discovering counter-intuitive substitutes open up opportunities for improvement!

Another problem with "personal theories of action" is that it is hard to determine how generalizable anyone's theories are and whether they will be equally effective if other leaders use them—or even if they will be equally effective if the same leader uses them in another context. Which, and whose, personal theories of action should be taught and disseminated? Even worse, a leader can develop a strong ego attachment to his/her personal theories of action, and there is always the potential for an organization to atrophy if the same theories of action continue to be followed and transmitted without careful analysis of their effectiveness or of alternative ways of handling key situations.

So which type of theory Is better?

Is a leader's "personal theory of action" or an existing academic theory better? It depends. Neither type of theory is better or worse. *How good a given theory is depends on the quality of evidence underlying the theory.*

Academic theories without real evidence are likely to be wrong or passing ships in the night—regardless of how prestigious the individual who has put forth the theory or the number of times it is cited. Some of those advocating applying academic theory to practice seem to forget that theory is a midpoint in the scientific process, not an endpoint. Theories need to have some basis in data and subsequent confirming evidence before the scientific community takes them seriously. For example, the theory of inflation in physics describes what happened trillionths of a second after the big bang. The theory came partly from data that showed that all areas of the observable universe have the same temperature. This could only happen if all the matter poured out of the big bang at the same time and at inconceivably high rates of speed. The underlying data were so compelling that an army of physicists spent 35 years trying to confirm or modify that theory.

The point is that there is no clear apparent benefit to applying academic theory to practice in the absence of evidence that confirms the theory and that practices based on it produces *noticeable* improvements in practice.[11]

Similarly, "personal theories of action" without evidence beyond a few anecdotes are really war stories that are as likely to lead to bad practice as good decisions. Anecdotes, testimonials, intuitions, or isolated examples do NOT constitute evidence. For example, consider the earlier example of a principal engaging an angry parent. Clearly, a repeated pattern of incidents wherein the strategy was effective constitutes evidence. For it to be considered a valid theory, information needs to exist as to the outcome from a repeated series of such encounters and what the results were, and how consistently the desired results occurred. For it to be considered as a valid theory of practice as opposed to a "war story", data, formal or informal, are needed as to whether the practice demonstrably (a) resulted in fewer complaints to the central

---

[11] The criterion that improvement be noticeable is an important one. Chapter 3 will show that a substantial portion of research evidence in top journals that show an intervention to be effective is doing so on the basis of benefits that are NOT noticeable.

office and board by parents, (b) improved attendance and achievement by the children of those parents, and/or (c) increased the amount of parent volunteers in the school and PTA participation. If a "personal theory of action" has such data it can be considered part of science. From the perspective of good practice, it is important that leaders consistently test and reconsider/modify their personal theories of action by periodically examining the data associated with a given practice.

To sum up, the general nature of most academic theories is both a limitation and advantage. The limitation is that it may provide little guidance to leaders on how to make the myriad of highly detailed decisions needed to implement a recommended practice—where getting even one of the details wrong can negate its effectiveness. At the same time, the advantage of general academic theory is that it can help leaders relate their theories of action to broader contexts and thereby enable them to better adapt their "personal theories of action" as circumstances and needs change.

In the same vein, the specificity of personal theories of action can be both an advantage (solving a particular problem in a specific context) and a disadvantage (limiting their ability to adjust their practice to a new context).

Regardless of whether we are talking about "academic theories" or "personal theories of action", the key is the type, quantity, and quality of empirical evidence supporting the theory.

Remember

However, all things being equal, personal theories of action are probably better and necessary for leaders in the short run, while good academic theory probably helps expand the decision-making horizons of mobile leaders in the longer run.

There is, however, a better way to integrate the two types of theories!

Integrating Academic Theory With Personal Theories of Action

The best approach is to figure out ways to combine both traditions of theory generation in the pursuit of better practices to solve fundamental problems of practice. This is the goal of a new research tradition, *Improvement Science*, which is discussed in Chapter 8.

Another way to integrate the two types of theory and research is to enable leaders and leadership students to make their "personal theories of action" explicit. This is best done by having them realize that they do have theories about human behavior and learning, and then getting the students to articulate them. Once students have done that the next step is to ask them to speculate on "why" their theory works. The door is then open for them to reflect on how their theory can be expanded to include other circumstances they encounter and in doing so come to realize how academic theories and research is relevant for enriching their own theories. So, while the previously discussed principal's personal theory of action theory has utility at this point, it has greater potential if the principal can figure out "why" it works in this situation. If the principal can then extract some fundamental principle of human behavior that causes it to work he/she can then use this insight to extend the approach to additional situations; e.g., how to handle distraught students and teachers.

When I ask a class of leadership students to reflect about and verbalize one personal theory of action they use I initially get puzzled looks. However, after 20-30 minutes of small group discussion theories start to emerge. Then an interesting variety of ideas begin to emerge. The next step is to ask them why they think their theories work. More puzzled looks and then exciting hypotheses begin to emerge.

The following is an example of a dialogue that I had with a female assistant principal when conducting such an exercise:

Assistant Principal:	My personal theory of action is that when a student gets referred to my office for fighting, I reassure them that we will talk things through and that everything will be okay. However, it works better for girls if I wait longer to have the follow-up chat, and then have them sit longer afterwards before sending them back to class, than I need to wait for boys.
Professor:	That is an interesting theory. "WHY" do you think your approach/theory works?
Assistant Principal:	Perhaps there are differences in the rate at which anger hormones/neurons subside between girls and boys.
Professor:	That is a very interesting theory. Coincidentally I have just come across some research with adults that supports your theory. Let's try to find that research. It may be that we have to look into research in biology.
Assistant Principal:	Wow!
Professor:	Now that you have read the academic work, can you think of ways to further refine your approach? Can you think of other situations in your practice that you can apply this knowledge to?

Good News

This type of process develops mutual respect for each other's basis for developing knowledge and theory. Leaders and leadership students develop a deeper appreciation of the role of academic theory and research in developing better practices, and becoming more reflective practitioners who understand the strengths and limitations of their own theories of decision-making. Professors develop a deeper appreciation of the thoughtfulness and originality of their students' approaches to solving problems.

Summary of Key Points

The nature of science

- Science is driven by data from observations and formal research—as opposed to opinion or belief;

- Science cannot prove something to be true with 100% certainty;

- A key principle is the importance of replicating research findings and thereby accumulating evidence that a given finding is probably true; and

- While science is not all knowing, and can at times reach conclusions that are later disproven, science denialism—i.e., ignoring scientific findings with strong evidence—usually has dire consequences.

The nature of theory

Theories emerge by discovering patterns in data. Once a theory is posited the validity of its predictions are systematically tested. The desired characteristics of any theory are that…

- It provides a precise/specific/detailed proposition to explain collected data and/or observed phenomenon;

- It provides testable important predictions;

- There is related evidence that one or more of the predictions have come to pass; and

- It explains "why" things work the way they do.

Theories that do NOT have a track record of having their predictions successfully tested are not likely to improve practice to a greater extent than what thoughtful practitioners are already doing—regardless of how prestigious the individual is who posited it, or how often it is cited in the professional and academic literatures.

The dichotomy between theory and practice is artificial. All actions by thoughtful leaders are based on theory. Indeed, the experience of leaders are data. The real issue is the dichotomy between academic theory and "personal theories of action". In addition…

- Both academic theories and "personal theories of action" have advantages and limitations; and

- It cannot be assumed that academic theory is more valid or valuable in a given circumstance than "personal theories of action", or that basing practice on academic theory necessarily results in better practice.

Current conceptions of the use of theory need to be updated to…

- Recognize both academic theory and the "personal theories of action," of successful leaders; and
- Do a better job of considering the state of evidence as the primary determinant as to which theories should be relied on (though philosophic preference will also always play a role).

Of course, if evidence is the key to understanding which theories to trust to improve practice, this raises the following questions:

➢ What is good quantitative evidence for the purpose of informing leadership decision-making?

More specifically…

➢ What constitutes authentic quantitative evidence for leadership practice—i.e., evidence such that if leaders act on it they are likely to see a noticeable improvement in their schools?

These questions will be addressed in subsequent chapters.

Challenge Assignments

1. Social Reproduction Theory developed in 1976 states that education institutions replicate the patterns of social, cultural, economic positionality that serve to perpetuate the status quo. Is this theory true or false?

   To answer this question what specific types of data would you look at?

   a) List two variables.
   b) If this theory is true, make a prediction as to what the trend/pattern would have been with these two variables since 1976?
   c) If this theory is false predict what the trend in these variables would have been to date?
   d) The ideal would be to then examine census data and longitudinal results from sources such as census data, some of the primary sources of data listed in Appendix B.

2. Pick a theory that you are interested in. Then do the following:

   a) Find some empirical research that supports the theory,
   b) Make two specific predictions from the theory that have implications for student and/or teacher development, or for school improvement, and
   c) Try to find empirical research that either supports or refutes your prediction.

   For example, if you are interested in critical race theory, you can find lots of research about the prevalence of racism. When it comes to making a prediction it might be something like: (1) that students of a given ethnicity learn better with an ethnocentric curriculum, or (2) a school with a leadership and staff that reflects the ethnic makeup of the school performs better than a similar school in which the leadership and staff do not, or (3) ...., etc.

   (If this book is being used as a class text this exercise can be done as a class project in which a few theories are selected and the students divide into groups to respond to the challenge.)

3. Think about your own practice. Think about a recurrent issue that you deal with successfully, and think about your "personal theory of action" for dealing with it.

   In thinking through one of your personal theories of actions, please do not confuse "personal actions" with "personal theories of action." For example, a statement such as: "I make sure to respond to every email I receive before the end of that schooldays." That is an *action* you take.

   The corresponding *personal theory of action* is something like: "People get upset if their email is not responded to promptly, therefore I ...<action>..." or "A quick response to a concern increases the likelihood that individuals will feel that their voice has been heard and considered, and will thus be more likely to accept my position on the matter of concern, therefore I ...<action>...."

   (**Recommendation for FACULTY:** This challenge is effective as a small group activity in which individuals start to consciously assess what a key "personal theory of action" of theirs is and share it/them with each other. This activity helps bring their theories out of the closet of the subconscious. They can then reflect whether the "personal theory of action" is consistent, ignored, or not consistent with the academic theories and research they have learned in the program to date—and what the overlaps and differences are.)

4. Some politicians are claiming that public education is declining and failing in order to promote their own "reform" agendas. What evidence would you seek to refute that perspective? Be as specific as you can as to subject areas, time duration, and specific outcomes you would gather data on.

Answer to Question #1

Possible variables would be:

> Graduation rates for minorities.
> Social mobility of minority graduates; i.e., what percentage move up in economic class based on income

If the theory is true it would tend to predict that (a) the graduation rate for minorities would stay low over time, and (b) the level of minority graduates reaching middle/upper class status would not increase.

There are also other possible variables.

It is also expected that different groups in a class will come to different conclusions as to how to best determine whether the theory is correct, as well as different conclusions as to whether the data they have collected support or refute the theory. The key point is that such debate is a valid reflection of the process of science—wherein skepticism and debate slowly, over time, lead to a consensus on how to best determine whether a theory is false and/or whether it is false.

Chapter 2

Scientific Evidence and the Evidentiary Needs of Leaders

The goal of evidence-based practice is for leaders to use scientific evidence to make decisions. How well does the scientific process for generating evidence match up with the evidentiary needs of leaders—particularly the need for evidence that supports authentic decision making? This chapter discusses the nature of "evidence" from the perspective of the authentic needs of leaders and how science goes about generating evidence.

Leaders' Need for Authentic Evidence

The key organizing construct for this textbook is authentic quantitative analysis and the search for authentic evidence. The key authentic need of leaders considering whether to use specific evidence to support decision-making is:

What kinds of quantitative evidence should I seek to feel reasonably confident that if I adopt a given practice, or make a decision, based on this evidence it is likely to improve my schools and increase equity?

Remember

While many think that science is necessarily sophisticated mathematical formulas, Chapter1 showed that science is about providing *accurate* predictions. Sophisticated statistical methods that conclude that practices are effective which subsequently do NOT actually produce noticeable gains in real world practice—are NOT good science—regardless of how mathematically sophisticated the statistical formulas are or how widely they are accepted by the research community.[12] Indeed, it will be shown throughout this text how the simplest quantitative methods that use basic math, and even human judgment, can lead to better predictions of whether interventions will lead to noticeable improvements in practice than the current wave of complex statistical methods and criteria prized by research journals.

When simple methods make more accurate predictions of real world results, they are better science.

---

[12] Hossenfelder (2018) documents how even in physics, researchers can get so carried away by the beauty of innovative and sophisticated mathematical techniques that they get caught up in building quantitative models that this becomes an end in and of itself without regard to whether the models accurately predict how the physical world works.

There are many ways that leaders should, and do, use quantitative evidence. However, to truly benefit from quantitative evidence generated by existing rigorous research methods and sophisticated statistical analyses, leaders need to be judiciously skeptical as much of the evidence about effective practices generated from such research does not translate into actual real world improvement. Leaders need to be proactive in exercising independent analysis and judgment to determine which subset of the available quantitative evidence is authentic—i.e., most likely to meet their improvement and equity needs.

Leaders use of Evidence

There are four main ways that leaders use quantitative evidence.

1. Determine the current status of organizational performance including equity;
2. Search for evidence of an effective practice that can improve performance;
3. Evaluate whether an internal improvement effort has been effective; and
4. Monitor in real-time the progress of an improvement effort.

Determining the current status of organizational performance including equity

This type of evidence involves collecting and analyzing results for a variety of organizational outcomes such as staff morale, attendance, reading scores, etc. It involves knowing both the status quo of a variety of measures and knowing the trend— e.g., has it been improving or declining over the recent past—and by how much and at what rate. This type of analysis often involves comparing current organizational performance to how other demographically similar schools/districts are performing.

These types of quantitative analyses often reveal organizational problems, particularly if results are declining, not meeting improvement goals, or lower than the performance of other similar schools/districts. When a problem is documented, the next steps are identifying the causes, setting improvement goals, and developing strategies for achieving the goals.

Equity is typically determined by analyzing gaps in performance between different ethnic, racial, income status, and special education subgroups. The now defunct federal No Child Left Behind (NCLB) law was the first to require schools to break down results for the different subgroups and demonstrate improvements across all subgroups. Reflecting heightened concerns about increasing equity in education outcomes as a form of social justice, states are requiring demonstrating the ability to engage in gap analysis as part of obtaining certification.

Search for evidence of an effective practice that can improve one's organization

Scientific evidence that practices/interventions/programs are effective are usually found in published research. Research published in journals that have *blind peer review* are considered to be of higher quality than those that don't. Blind peer review means that those reviewing the proposed article or book do not know who the author(s) is so they are not biased in their judgments either pro or con by knowing the author.

Practitioners generally find out about recent research from two main sources. The first and most common is via the newsletters and websites of their professional association which highlight what it considers to be the research findings that are the most relevant for its members. A second common source of research evidence of effective practices is the federal What Works Clearinghouse (https://ies.ed.gov/ncee/wwc/). The purpose of the What Works Clearinghouse (WWC) is to set rigorous scientific standards for evaluating what research on effective practices is scientifically trustworthy, and then gives the equivalent of the Good Housekeeping Seal of Approval in the form of indicating which practices have evidence that they work. Practices that have met its standards of having evidence of working are organized by content area. Such practices are then said to be "evidence-based."

So, *in theory*, leaders can scan the recommendations of the WWC or their professional journals to identify a practice that has been deemed to be evidence-based that they feel has potential to improve their schools and/or solve the identified problems. Indeed, the current federal Every Student Succeeds Act (ESSA) passed in 2015 requires that the federal monies be spent on evidence-based practices.

Warning

The caveat "in theory" is used because, as subsequent chapters will demonstrate, there are problems with the scientific criteria used to determine whether a practice is actually effective.

Another source of information about effective practices comes from presenters at professional conferences, and conversations with other leaders who claim to have found a way to deal effectively with the same problem. Such information is typically considered to be anecdotal reports as opposed to scientific evidence. Such information has not been independently assessed. Furthermore, just because it has worked elsewhere there may have been extenuating circumstances. A final source of information about effective practices is salespeople—though they are probably the least reliable source.

Leaders vs Researchers

When examining published research on an effective practice that you may want to consider for your schools, the size of the benefit reported in the research is a key consideration. One of the big disconnects between researchers and leaders is that researchers will often settle for significantly less benefit in the outcome in order to conclude that a practice is effective than what leaders would like to see before accepting that the practice was truly effective. That is why there is a major emphasis in this textbook on critically examining the amount of benefit actually documented in the research, along with simple methods for doing so.

Remember

A key element in accepting scientific evidence of any kind is whether the evidence has been replicated in another study. Until someone else can produce the same result in an independent research effort, researchers and leaders should be skeptical of the reported finding—including evidence supporting a claim that a given practice is "evidence-based."

The issue of replication—i.e., independent verification of research evidence—will be a critical one in the forthcoming chapters.

Evaluate whether an internal improvement effort has been effective

Once schools adopt a practice to improve overall performance, or reduce gaps, or solve a problem, the next step is to evaluate whether the effort has been effective. Districts often conduct evaluations as to the effects of the new practice. Evaluations of outcomes are often referred to as a *summative evaluation*, and are typically conducted by a district's research office. In addition, when considering adopting a new practice a pilot study is often conducted—i.e., an evaluation on a small scale—to determine the extent to which improvement goals were met. Depending on the results of the pilot study leaders may then decide to expand the use of the innovation or cancel its use.

The statistical methods used in evaluation can be very similar to those used in published research to determine the effectiveness of any intervention. The big difference is that published research determines progress and/or success of a practice at other schools, and an evaluation refers to studying outcomes at one's own schools.

Monitor in real-time the progress of an improvement effort

Once a new practice is adopted there should be periodic checks on the quality of implementation. This is often referred to as ***formative evaluation***. Formative evaluation is often thought of as qualitative analysis in which efforts are made to interview key staff as to how individuals feel about how the implementation process is unfolding. However, quantitative analysis often plays a key role in formative evaluations; particularly for interventions that require periodic data checks, such as midterm grades or daily attendance, or that require real time sharing of progress reports across different individuals in an organization. For example, an effort to increase the number of students sending out college applications requires constant monitoring of information flows between counselors, teachers, students, and key leaders on basic quantitative metrics such as: (a) how many and which students have seen counselors, (b) how many students have filled out at least one application, (c) the number of additional credits students need so that they become eligible to apply for college, etc.

Having, and sharing, such quantitative data on an ongoing basis will enable all parties to engage in ongoing cooperative proactive action that will likely result in better outcomes as opposed to waiting till the end-of-the-year ***summative evaluation*** to see whether more students have applied to college than prior years. Of course, setting up the technology and creating a culture of sharing data across organizations is for most districts an innovation in and of itself, and can potentially enhance the effectiveness of other new practices. This relationship between the technical and social aspects of data sharing are discussed further in Chapter 9.

Characteristics of Quantitative Evidence

Science has specific processes for generating quantitative evidence. Determining how well it fits with the evidentiary needs of leaders requires understanding the nature of scientific evidence and how it is generated.

What is scientific evidence?

We all have different thresholds as to the amount and types of evidence that we desire to convince us to take action on a wide range of decisions such as shopping and investing. The same is true for making decisions in our educational leadership practice. Science also sets a variety of standards of acceptable evidence for supporting conclusions, just as the legal system sets standards for determining verdicts and judgments.

When most students start a course in quantitative research they expect that the payoff from using numbers will be an unambiguous indication what is right and what path should be taken. Alas, that is not the case. In the previous chapter it was noted that *you can never prove something to be completely true.*[13] As a result, science makes judgments on the basis of probabilities. Statistics can only determine the probability that something is true in the specific context in which a given study was conducted. The only way we can know if the results or the original research were valid, and or whether the results will hold up in another context, is if a series of independent replication studies find the same results. The more studies that reach a similar conclusion the more likely that the findings can be trusted and have wide applicability—especially in your schools.

Knowing that the probability of something being true is never 100%, what probability do you want to see that a research finding may be true before you decide to take action on the basis of that finding? For example, everyone is familiar with the reporting of election polls: e.g., Candidate A is ahead by a certain amount with an error of plus or minus 3 percentage points. Suppose that Candidate A is ahead by 50.5% to 49.5%, with a 3 percentage point error. Would you bet a lot of money that Candidate A is actually ahead? Probably not. The margin of error means that Candidate A's actual

---

[13] The only time you can prove something to be true is in a mathematical system. For example, in high school Geometry you proved things to be true. However, in this mathematical system you are proving things to be true based on specific assertions/assumptions that other things are true. In other words, if certain things are assumed to be true then other things can be proved to be true. However, this is merely a logical system that is not a description of how the real world operates or of the scientific process.

score ranges from a possible 47.5% of the vote, i.e., being behind, to 53.5%, i.e., more comfortably ahead. (This range of possible outcomes is called the *Confidence Interval* in statistics.)

If, however, the poll shows Candidate A garnering 52.5% of the vote, we would be pretty confident that he/she actually has more than 50%, even though it is still possible that the actual result could be less than 50% for him/her (as low as 49.5% at the absolute bottom of the *Confidence Interval*). We would be even more certain of Candidate A polled at 54%, because even in the worst-case error scenario, he/she would still be above 50%.

Nor is there a standard of absolute certainty in law, even for the purpose of awarding the death penalty. The standard is "beyond a *reasonable* doubt". This recognizes that someone can always construct a very far-fetched alternative scenario to explain away the most obvious incriminating evidence since the jury, judge, and lawyers did not actually witness the crime. In civil cases the standard is "a preponderance of evidence". This is clearly a lower standard. The difference in the standards of evidence explain why even though prosecutors could not get a jury to convict O.J. Simpson of murder, the plaintiffs won in civil court and were awarded damages. But what is "a reasonable doubt" or "a preponderance of evidence"? These clearly involve judgment.

We have the same issue in education. What should the standard of evidence be for leaders to decide that something is likely to improve their schools? This will be a major methodological consideration in upcoming chapters.

Remember

Since a statistical procedure cannot tell us with certainty what is true or predict with certainty what will happen, this uncertainty is generally referred to as *statistical error*.

Evidence vs anecdotal reports

There are many claims of the success of a practice or a school in the popular press, in professional newsletters, presentations at professional conferences, and by salespeople. By themselves these do NOT constitute evidence of success. They are considered to be *anecdotal reports*. Such anecdotal reports may be true or self-serving claims. Such reports are NOT considered to be evidence of effectiveness or to have any scientific credibility. To be considered evidence the claims would have to be verified by a third party, then systematically studied using the types of research techniques discussed in subsequent chapters. At the same time, recurring anecdotal reports of success can be an important stimulant to getting researchers to test the claims. If the claims are supported by subsequent research, the anecdotal reports become an important source of scientific discovery.

Leaders should not take anecdotal reports at face value—regardless of how famous or important the individual making the claim is. If a leader is interested, he/she can explore further by checking the claims of success against other data such as state reports, and talk to a variety of individuals within the school or district. But as with scientific reports, leaders should seek evidence of replication or confirmation from independent sources. Such conformation could be in the form of other schools/districts reporting similar benefits, or indications that the benefits have persisted across time. However, this would still not be considered to be scientific evidence. It is also important to understand that leaders speaking about claims of success resulting from a given practice may be receiving perks from the organizations that market or distribute the associated products.

How to Find Research Evidence

The main sources of research evidence are:

- Published studies;
- School district evaluations;
- Datasets at the federal, state, and local levels; and
- Organizations that rate research evidence such as the What Works Clearinghouse (WWC).

Scientific evidence is generally thought of as formal studies published in research journals, and studies conducted by professional associations and policy institutes such as RAND. Such studies on a topic of interest or a specific intervention are generally found by searching scholarly databases such as Google Scholar (scholar.google.com) which is available to the public, and a database available at a university library such as JSTOR. In terms of the latter, you will not be able to use it unless you are a current student. In addition, in most instances Google Scholar will only provide abstracts of the article. However, you can tell from the abstract whether a study will be interest to you. Indeed, you can usually eliminate the vast majority of potential studies by just looking at the abstracts. Then if Google Scholar does not provide access to the actual study, you can contact a friendly professor or a current student to get you a copy of the most interesting articles.

In addition, many prestigious foundations, and university and private research organizations provide free access to their studies.

Internal evaluation studies conducted by school districts can also be considered to be scientific evidence. While such evaluations typically are not as statistically sophisticated as studies published in the top research journals and have little standing in the academic community, my own research has found that evaluations produced by school districts can at times be more valid and authentic than evidence of effective practices produced in the top research journals.

How to find relevant published studies

Leaders typically find out about the latest applied research in professional newsletters, while students will encounter them in coursework. However, it is equally important for leaders seeking to apply evidence for making a critical decision, or students seeking evidence for a term paper or action research project, to conduct their own search for relevant studies—and to critique them.

Usually, searches for relevant studies will be conducted using a library database/index. The specific methods for conducting searches in databases for to find published research of interest are described in detail in Chapter 10's section on the literature review. Methods for critiquing research studies' findings are contained in Chapters 4-7.

Finding school district evaluation studies

Studies of an intervention you are considering by a school district evaluation office are usually not published. However, you can often find reference to them in professional newsletters or professional conferences. As with published studies, it is important to read the actual study. Usually school district evaluation offices are willing to share such studies once they are officially released by the district.

How to find and apply relevant datasets

Another type of useful scientific evidence are data. You can often learn a lot from raw data. For example, the process of continuous improvement discussed in Chapter 9 requires a continuous flow of relevant data which are used to make real time decisions.

In addition, Appendix B lists sources of primary datasets at the federal, state, and local levels from which leaders can easily extract key data about their community and the performance of their schools. In addition, some of the datasets have easy to apply tools that you can use to easily generate custom reports. Chapter 4 provides an example of using such a tool in the National Assessment of Educational Progress (NAEP) to conduct a gap analysis of the relative performance of Black girls versus White girls.

Avoid the recommendations of the WWC

The last and least useful source of scientific evidence is, surprisingly, organizations that use scientific criteria to determine which interventions have strong evidence of effectiveness. The most prestigious such source is the federal What Works Clearinghouse (WWC). Unfortunately, as will be shown in subsequent chapters, its recommendations are NOT reliable. You will be better off finding the key studies on your own and then applying the recommended scientific criteria in Chapters 4-7 to determine whether the evidence in the research is authentic—i.e., likely to improve your schools and increase equity.

Concerns about evidence-based practice

What type evidence standard should education use to judge that a given practice or program is effective? There are a lot of terms tossed about to give a patina of science and evidence to claims about the effectiveness of practice. Examples include: (a) best practice, (b) scientifically based practice, (c) validated practice/program, (d) evidence based practice/program, (e) NCTM based practice, (f) effective schools practice, (g) reform based practice, etc. One hears tons of speakers at professional conferences proclaim: *"We know what works, if only we ..."* Speakers and writers also like to claim *" Research shows that..."* Usually (but not always), when I check I am not able to find the convincing research evidence that the speaker/writer claimed existed.

A good rule of thumb is that when someone says *"We know what works"*— they are selling something!

In reality, claims of actual evidence are loosely applied—even for nationally promoted reforms. Most reforms and standards in education come about from panels of experts putting forth their recommendations. These reforms represent the best thinking of experts and advocates on the assembled panels. But are they truly based on impartial scientific evidence or a preponderance of such evidence? Usually not! There is usually little or no formal evidence validating the effectiveness of the specific reforms being recommended. Rather, the proposed reforms represent the preferences/ideals of the panel members.

Nor are panel recommendations generally field-tested over a 3-5 year period before they are rolled out nationally. The argument is always that there is such a crisis that everyone needs to adopt the reform right away. The result is usually that the reforms do NOT work. It is only afterwards that we see how little evidence there was for them in the first place—though the advocacy groups rarely admit that fact and prefer to blame practitioners for poor implementation.

Consider the following two examples on the right of widely advocated and implemented national reforms without convincing scientific evidence:

- The mathematics standards reform developed by the National Council of Teachers of Mathematics (NCTM) that everyone was required to implement in the mid-90s; and

- The Common Core Standards led by the Council of Chief State School Officers (CSSO) and the National Governors Association (NGA) that many states have adopted.

NCTM
Consultants fanned out all over the US to provide assistance to schools and districts, and thousands of articles were written extolling the standards and providing advice on how to implement them. The only research that I know of that claimed to show that the reforms actually worked for students were studies by Boaler (2006), and Boaler and Staples (2008) who studied three high schools in California, two that used conventional approaches to teaching mathematics, and a third with a pseudonym of Railside, that used a reform based approach. These studies, funded by the National Science Foundation, claimed to have found that while the students entering Railside were demographically poorer and lower scoring, they ended up doing better in mathematics after two years in the reform classes than the students at the other schools. Math educators and government officials all over the US hailed this research as evidence that NCTM reform was working. However, this could not be considered convincing evidence since it only involved a single school and no one else replicated such a finding. Even worse, a group of researchers (Bishop,

40

Clopton and Milgram, downloaded 2012 from the web) figured out which school Railside actually was and found that Railside's state math ranking was in the bottom 10% of all schools in California with similar demographics. So even this single school was NOT a success. Ultimately there was no evidence for the NCTM standards either before the national rollout or during the reform period. Now we are rushing into common core math and reading.

Common Core

The common core website assures us that the standards are evidence-based. However, a review of all the "evidence" by Tienken (2011) showed that NONE of the studies cited were empirical. In other words, the common core standards are based on opinion—not scientific evidence. Indeed, if education really wanted to be a more science-based profession, a good starting point would be to insist on replicated trials of proposed reforms to gather evidence as to whether they actually provide an advantage, and under what conditions they are effective and can be implemented with fidelity—before they are promoted nationally.

Warning

The absence of actual scientific evidence in many of these national reforms is a cautionary warning that leaders seeking to use evidence to improve their schools need to apply due diligence and examine claims of scientific evidence critically—regardless of how well supported they are by "experts" and professional associations.

Good News

There is indeed a great deal of valid and useful scientific evidence that leaders should incorporate into making decisions.

But this takes us full circle back to the questions of:

- What constitutes appropriate types and levels of evidence to support *evidence-based decision making*?
- Under what conditions should leaders ignore claims that a practice is evidence-based on the basis that the research does not provide authentic evidence?

In order to answer these questions, we must take a step back. Clearly, it makes little sense to talk about the standards of legal evidence without knowing anything about how a trial is conducted. Similarly, in order to talk about the quality of quantitative research evidence in education, one needs to understand how the process of quantitative research is conducted.

Most importantly, the methods presented will enable you to easily discern which research evidence is likely to benefit your schools without developing extensive statistical skills.

How is Scientific Evidence Generated?

Basic vs. applied research

Research is categorized as *applied* or *basic*. **Basic research** studies the fundamental nature of key processes and seeks to find out "why" or "how" something happened— e.g., How does the brain work? How does human motivation develop? Why do people believe what they do? How are attitudes formed? **Basic research** investigates the fundamental nature of things or processes.

Applied **research** investigates whether something works or how to solve a problem. It is generally intended to be immediately practical.

There is always a tension in government and companies as to what percentage of research dollars should be allocated for *basic* research vs. *applied* research. While *applied* research usually produces greater short-term benefits, and the benefits of basic research are longer term, both types of research are needed for any field or profession to advance. *Basic* research breakthroughs provide the basis over the longer term for a pipeline of new discoveries and for new and better products and treatments.

Consider the following recent medical experience that illustrates the relationship between *basic* and *applied* research.

Hepatitis C was routinely spread by blood transfusions because science did not know it existed even as recently as the 1980s. Once this virus was discovered the search for a cure was on. *Correlational* research established that a combination of Interferon and Ribavirin eliminated the virus in some people. Medicine did not know how or why it worked. However, the *correlation* between the use of the drug and the result was sufficient for these drugs to be FDA approved and prescribed to those suffering from Hepatitis C. Determining the right dosages, and which types of individuals the treatment worked for, was *applied* research. However, this drug regimen did not work for a large percentage of those afflicted, and it had major side effects.

Fortunately, approximately 30 years after the discovery of the Hepatitis C virus in the blood supply, and approximately 20 years after finding correlational benefit to using Interferon and Ribavirin, *basic* research on the interaction of the virus with different proteins in the cell established that this virus needed a certain type of protein to survive. Medicine was then able to use this *basic* research to develop a new class of drugs that eliminated this protein. Experimental trials then determined that the new drugs were highly effective at ridding the body of the virus with virtually no side effects. So knowing the *causal* mechanisms enabled the creation of new drugs that are highly effective.

Another recent example of the fact that the development of the messenger RNA COVID-19 vaccines—i.e., applied research—resulted from 30 years of research into the nature of RNA molecules—i.e., basic research.[14]

These examples illustrate that it can take medicine, or any scientific endeavor, decades to understand *causal* factors from *basic* research to make it possible to produce new and better drugs and treatments (applied knowledge). Conversely, the treatments of mental illnesses, such as bipolar, have suffered because of the lack of breakthroughs in the basic research as to the causes of the disease. So, for example, lithium is known to help with bi-polar disorder (applied research), but it is not known why—or what to do if it does not work. More *basic* research on brain functioning is needed.

Education struggles to make *basic* research breakthroughs. Examples of *basic* research include trying to understand (a) the nature of disabilities, (b) how the brain operates to support the processes of remembering, learning and perception, and (c) how belief systems develop and affect behavior.

Applied research in education has focused, among other things, on the search for more effective interventions and schools, and better implementation of effective practices. Major advances in *applied research* are tied to advances in basic research, as *applied* research is often based on implementing the implications of *basic* research. So, for example, some key design elements of my successful Higher Order Thinking Skills (HOTS) intervention for Title I and Learning Disabled Students were based on *basic* research on how the brain stores information.

At the same time, this book focuses (only) on research methods for *applied* research designed to improve schools and increase equity. The methods are designed for use by, and the unique/specific evidentiary needs of, school leaders and educational policy makers—NOT researchers seeking *basic* research breakthroughs. That is why many of the recommendations of this textbook are very different than the typical recommendations of statistics textbooks.

Types of research

There are three basic types of quantitative research used to generate applied evidence are:

1. Descriptive analysis;
2. Relationship research; and
3. Experiments.

Descriptive analysis provides summary data about the status of a single variable, such as the data on the racial composition of students in ones' schools.

---

[14] For the fascinating history of how pieces of basic research came together over time to lead to the mRNA vaccine, see Kolata and Mueller (2022) and Isaacson (2021).

Relationship research examines the interactions between two or more variables. For example, such research would examine the relationship between race and performance, or the relationship between race and economic status on performance, and which has a stronger relationship. A popular type of relationship research in the 90's and earlier this century was to examine the relationship between leadership practices and school performance.

Experimental research seeks to determine what happens when an intervention or innovation is used. It is a more activist form of research than relationship research, though relationship research is often the basis for deciding to conduct a specific experiment. For example, we know that there is a relationship between student self-esteem and academic performance. Experiments would seek to determine what happens when schools implement practices to increase self-esteem. Unfortunately, education leaders and policymakers (and advocates in the research community) often mistake relationship research for evidence of impact. So, for a while it was very popular for schools to implement practices to increase students' self-esteem based on relationship research before there was any experimental evidence as to whether such an approach was effective. (It wasn't.)

Experiments usually involve comparing results from an experimental sample that receives an intervention and a similar comparison group, referred to as a *control* group, that did not. Sometimes there is only an experimental group and results are compared from before it received the intervention to after.

The role of statistics

All forms of quantitative research generate/analyze lots of numbers. Statistics is the science concerned with designing a methodology and tools for systematically collecting and organizing the numbers, and then analyzing and synthesizing the data into a series of findings and conclusions. The final step is to present the findings in a way that makes the methodology of producing the results, and the results themselves, understandable for the intended audience. The two most common methods for presenting evidence include tables of numerical outcomes and pictorial representations of the numbers in the form of graphs and charts.

Each of these steps has a series of methods and conventions that have been established over time and accepted by the scientific community as best or preferred practice. However, there is no single standard that all fields use for accepting evidence that a discovery has been made. Physics has a more stringent standard for statistical evidence that a discovery has been made than the social sciences. The medical community uses a different methodology to test the effectiveness of medicines than most applied research in the social sciences. In addition, the criteria that a discipline considers to be valid evidence of a discovery can change over time. As this is being written, there is a movement to reconsider some of the most sacrosanct standards of scientific evidence and a search for alternatives (more on this later).

The major concern of this textbook is the scientific statistical methods and standards that are, and/or should be, used in education to accept evidence that a practice is effective—and in particular, to identify the characteristics of authentic evidence that indicate that a practice is likely to improve *your* schools and increase equity.

Remember

At the same time, it is important to remember that research evidence and statistics canNOT provide an absolute signal that something will *definitely* improve your schools. Quantitative results are expressed in probabilities—not certainties—regardless of how mathematically sophisticated the methods are. However, what you can do is look for key clues in the research results that indicate that the intervention in the research is LIKELY to improve your schools in noticeable ways. Finding and interpreting these clues is the focus of the next four chapters.

Summary

This chapter has discussed (a) how leaders seek to use quantitative data, (b) the nature of scientific evidence, and (c) the basic ways that such evidence is generated.

What is the fit between leaders' needs for evidence and how scientific evidence is generated? The next four chapters will discuss the opportunities and cautions for how leaders can and should use data and the three types of quantitative evidence to support authentic decision-making—i.e., how to use research evidence in ways that are likely to improve their schools and increase equity.

Authentically and Critically Analyzing Data and Research Evidence

Part II describes how to analyze research evidence critically from the authentic perspective of whether acting on the basis of the findings and data is likely to result in a noticeable improvement in practice and equity at your schools. It provides easy to follow guidelines and principles on how to make authentic judgments of research findings—even for the most mathematically sophisticated articles published in the top research journals. Best of all, these authentic principles do not involve learning or interpreting complicated mathematics.

These principles apply equally to analyzing…

- Published research;
- Evaluations of practices in your schools; and
- Action research you conduct as a leader or leadership student.

Part II introduces new methods for determining whether quantitative evidence is authentic—most notably:

- The power trio of statistics
- The importance of BIGness in research results;
- The importance of analyzing actual results as opposed to relative results,
- Applying the new statistical tests of practical benefit and potential practical benefit; and
- The value of eyeballing data outcomes

Part II will also show how these authentic methods diverge from the typical conclusions and recommendations by researchers and statistics textbooks, and why these newer methods are more valid for leadership decision-making. It will show how researchers typically interpret evidence that a practice is effective can over-estimate its likely real-world effectiveness. In other words, just because the research community has certified a practice to be evidence-based does not mean that it is likely to improve your schools—or even that it was ever effective in a real-world sense in the first place.

Remember

Avoiding the supposedly effective practice of the moment is as important a leadership decision as identifying a practice that is truly effective and likely to improve your schools.

At the same time, some research evidence that a practice is effective is indeed authentic. How can one identify such research? Part II will provide accessible and intuitive tools that leaders can use to determine which evidence-based practices are *in fact* likely to improve their schools. Indeed, finding evidence that a practice is likely to improve your schools is a joyous discovery.

The authentic principles of how to analyze quantitative evidence in Part II are accessible to the typical leader and leadership student because they bypass the technical and statistical details that unnecessarily complicate the interpretation of quantitative evidence for leadership decision-making. While sophisticated statistical procedures and their technical mathematical details and interpretations are impressive scientific achievements and a triumph of the human intellect, that does not mean that they are necessarily the best way to answer the types of questions that education leaders ask, and to help solve the immediate problems they are facing. Indeed, it will be shown that the more technically complicated the research methodology is, the less likely it is that the findings will be useful to leaders—or even that the findings of effectiveness are correct. Instead, Part II will show that the simplest statistics are the most powerful and relevant. This is as true for published research—as it is for action research that you conduct as a graduate student or evaluations you conduct as a leader.

Remember

The simplest statistics are the most important ones regardless of whether you are analyzing others' research or conducting your own.

Part II is organized around establishing a set of principles for analyzing whether quantitative evidence is likely to be authentic. These principles are then elaborated and used to critically examine the three most common types of applied research—descriptive, relationship, and experimental research.

The recommended techniques ignore the sophisticated statistics and myriad technical details in the research. Instead, the techniques rely on extracting only a few key sub-results/numbers from the most basic statistics that leadership students and leaders already know, and the methods provide easy-to-follow and intuitive criteria for interpreting these numbers.

Chapter 3

Initial Principles for Analyzing Quantitative Evidence

This chapter is a starting point for describing the key principles that will enable leaders and leadership students to critically determine the authenticity of available research on effective practices. These principles are needed because many (but not all) of the practices that research has found to be evidence-based have not turned out to actually improve real-world practice. Which research evidence can be trusted by leaders? These principles provide easy to apply guidance that leaders can use to identify which evidence is authentic—i.e., likely to improve their schools and increase equity.

Initial principles

Several of these basic principles were hinted at in the first few chapters and will continue to be added to and elaborated in subsequent chapters.

 Remember

These principles apply equally to ALL research evidence, regardless of whether it is published in top journals, program evaluations conducted by schools/districts, produced by professional associations, studies presented by salespeople, or your own action research.

Principle #1—Always seek replication/confirmation of a research finding

Replication of an important research finding by independent researchers is the fundamental way that science validates evidence. Replication occurs when a different and independent researcher repeats a previously published study and finds the same result. Such confirmation lends credibility to the original finding. However, if the new research is not able to replicate the original finding, the original finding is NOT considered to be valid evidence.

Unfortunately, conducting a replication study is not considered to be as academically prestigious as original research. Therefore, top journals tend not to publish replication research. For example, Makel and Plucker (2014) found that only 0.1% of all published articles in education were replications, and Makel and colleagues (2016) found that only 0.5% of published articles about special education were full replications. In addition, the lack of replication studies is not unique to education. It is a widespread problem across the disciplines.

Concern about the lack of published replication studies led to efforts by research groups in a variety of disciplines to try and replicate the research that was the most influential in shaping practice. Keep in mind that the studies they attempted to replicate were published in the top research journals and among the most widely cited as scientific evidence for a given practice.

What percentage of the important studies do you think were successfully replicated? The results in the table below shocked the research communities.

Table 3.1
Percentage of Studies Whose Findings did not Replicate by Discipline

Discipline	% of Findings that did NOT Replicate [15]
Psychology	More than 60%
Oncology (cancer research)	89%
Economics	72%

Table 3.1 illustrates that the majority of the most influential research findings documenting effective practices in a variety of fields could NOT be replicated—and thus were probably not valid findings, and that the original evidence misdirected practice. What does this say for the vast majority of research studies on effective practices where no effort was made to see if they replicate?

Table 3.1 also illustrates that the problem of questionable research evidence on effective practices is a widespread problem. The lack of replicability in oncology research shows that even research findings in laboratory medical research can be problematic. The lack of replicability in experimental research in psychology is also a warning sign for education given the enormous influence that educational psychology has had in defining the desired characteristics of scientific evidence for education.

Kraemer (2016) found similar replication problems in psychiatry and Ioannidis (2005) in biomedicine.

Warning	The failure of a substantial portion of influential applied research to be able to be replicated under laboratory conditions means that most of the evidence-based practices tested in the original research will NOT replicate in real-world practice and will NOT improve schools and increase equity. Those who adopt such practices will end up wasting time, energy, and money with nothing to show for it.

---

[15] The citations for the replication studies in this table in the order in which they are presented are: Open Science Collaboration (2015), Begley and Ellis (2012), and Ziliak and McCloskey (2004).

The failure of a large percentage of influential applied research to replicate in subsequent independent tests or in practice is referred to as "the replication crisis."

To make matters worse, Garcia and Gneezy (2021) found that published papers in top psychology, economics, and general interest journals that FAIL to replicate *are cited more than those that replicate*. This difference in citation does not change after the publication of the failure to replicate. The willingness to publish and cite such studies are attributed to their being more interesting to the audience.

There is also a replication crisis in education research on evidence-based practices. The Investing in Innovation (i3) federal program initially funded 67 interventions whose evidence of effectiveness met the stringent scientific criteria of the federal What Works Clearinghouse (WWC). The goal of the funding was to expand the use of these "evidence-based programs." Fortunately, the i3 legislation mandated a follow-up evaluation of the effects of the expanded use of these interventions—which was in effect a replication study. Guess how many of the 67 produced actual benefits to the schools that adopted them? An analysis of Boulay, et al.'s (2018) findings from the follow-up evaluations shows that only 9 of the 67 produced any indication of benefit and *only 4 produced noticeable benefit for the schools* that adopted the interventions. In other words, the vast majority of schools that adopted these evidence-based practices saw no discernable benefit.

If you adopt an evidence-based practice whose evidence has not been able to be replicated, your schools are not likely to see any improvement or increase in equity from its use.

This is NOT a criticism of science or the use of quantitative evidence. What it does mean is that there are problems with some of the statistical criteria used by researchers to identify effective practices in a variety of disciplines—including education. (These problems, and how to identify them, will be discussed in Chapters 5-7—as well as how to identify evidence-based practices that are in fact likely to noticeably improve your schools and increase equity.)

The good news is that some of the research did replicate and provide substantial benefits. In addition, there are other sources of research about successful practices that can be used to try and find evidence of replication besides formal replication studies or articles in the top research journals.

If you are interested in seeing what research exists for a specific program or type of practice, e.g., small groups, you should start with Google Scholar and see what you can find. Additional sources of research studies are:

- Reports from school district research offices[16];

---

[16] Most larger districts have research offices that conduct evaluations. If you hear of a school/district that claims to have experienced success with a specific practice, see if there is a report produced by the district's research office.

- Research reports from non-profit policy organizations such as
  - RAND Corp (rand.org)
  - Mathematica (mathematica.org)
  - Manpower Development Research Corporation (mdrc.org);
- Federal National Center for Educational Statistics; and
- Research centers at universities in your state.

Warning

Unfortunately, you should avoid the recommendations of the federal What Works Clearinghouse because, as previously discussed, the vast majority of the programs they vetted did not replicate.

But the key questions are:

- Why did some scientific evidence replicate in follow-up studies while most did not?

- Are there any clues in the evidence that leaders can use to anticipate whether an intervention is likely to produce replicable benefit in their schools?

The answer to the second question is a resounding YES!

The purpose of the next three chapters is to answer these questions and recommend specific alternative statistical criteria that leaders can apply to research to see which studies and findings are authentic —i.e., likely to replicate into noticeable benefit in their schools—regardless of what the research concluded.

Principle #2—The greatest threats to the validity of quantitative evidence are:

- **Researcher bias;**
- **Statistical error; and**
- **Confounding variables.**

Researcher bias—When researchers engage in multiple activities within research they tend to bias results. For example, if the individual who designs the new practice also collects and analyzes the evaluation data, that is a highly biased research process. It is even more biased if that same individual also designs the materials that will be used to collect the data. Ideally, individuals who are independent of the developer of the practice would conduct all the other research processes, with each step done by different individuals. This is why, for example, medicine uses a double blind experimental method wherein neither the medical personnel administering the medication, nor the individuals in the sample, know whether a given individual is receiving the experimental medicine or a placebo (e.g., a sugar pill). This eliminates the possible bias wherein the person giving the experimental medication can be more encouraging (even subconsciously) to those receiving the actual medicine to try and produce a positive reaction.

51

When conducting research or a program evaluation, different individuals should independently conduct the different steps in the research process.[17]

Sub-principle 2.1—The more a single individual or organization is involved in all the different steps in a research study, the greater the degree of bias there is, and the less trustworthy the findings are.

Statistical error—This is a bit of a misnomer as it does not mean that the statistician made a mistake. It is best thought of as *uncertainty* about a reported result, and/or the difference between reality and the statistical result. As previously mentioned, statistical procedures work on probability not certainty—so there is always some statistical error inherent in the mathematical procedures. Statistical error is why the definition of authentic research talk about determining whether a research result is *likely*—as opposed to certain—to improve ones' schools.

Statistical error is made explicit when a political poll announces that the percentage of the voters favoring a certain candidate is 52%, +/- 3%. The plus or minus of possible outcomes is statistical error. The degree of error can be reduced by polling more individuals—but it cannot be completely eliminated. At the same time, the goal of research is to try and minimize statistical error.

In addition, the error inherent in any one statistical procedure compounds as more procedures are conducted to arrive at a result. For example, if one designs a questionnaire with 20 items, and then analyzes each item separately, the likelihood that any one finding is wrong is high because of the compounded errors. Alternatively, one should consolidate the results from similar items into perhaps two summary measures. Reducing the analysis to consider only two items (instead of 20) will produce two findings that are less likely to have been caused by error and that are therefore more trustworthy.

Given the uncertainty/error inherent in any statistical procedure, the more statistical procedures that are conducted within an analysis, the greater the degree of statistical error—i.e., uncertainty—in the resultant evidence.

Alas, the latest statistical methods prized by research journals emphasize increased complexity with multiple, complex statistical manipulations to arrive at a conclusion. For all the statistical sophistication, the degree of statistical error is problematic and raises questions about the validity of the resultant research conclusions.

---

[17] To be fair it is not always possible for each step to be conducted by different individuals. I ended up summarizing the research about my Higher Order Thinking Skills (HOTS) program because I was not able to recruit other individuals to conduct the research or secure funding for such an effort. At the same time, all the studies were conducted by the district research offices, and I simply reported the same results that they passed on to their state departments of education. So there was some independence in the data analyses.

Sub-principle 2.2—The more statistical procedures that are conducted in a study, the less trustworthy any one finding is.

Confounding variables—Just because a variable appears to cause a particular outcome, it may actually be a different, hidden variable causing the outcome. Such hidden variables are called confounding variables. For example, suppose a school adopts a new reading program and test scores go up. At first glance it would appear that the new reading program caused the increase and is therefore effective. But wait! Could something else have coincidentally caused the gain? Perhaps the school's boundary changed and the makeup of the student body changed and the newer students were better readers. Perhaps, a new, better principal, or new better teachers, were hired that year and that is what is causing the increase.

In this example, boundary changes or new personnel are possible confounding variables.

In analyzing research it is important to anticipate and account for possible confounding variables. In this study, the researcher should report on whether these and possible other confounding variables could have accounted for the outcome. This can be tricky because not all potential confounding variables are obvious. When the researcher can account for and eliminate confounding variables—i.e., explain and produce evidence why they were not a factor in producing the results—then it is likely that A caused B—or in this case that the new reading program was in fact the variable that caused the improvements in reading.

On the other hand, if there is in fact a confounding variable moderating the relationship between the reading program and increase in reading scores, then other schools that adopt the same reading program will NOT benefit from its use.

The most common way to account for a possible confounding variable is to simply document why it could not have impacted the outcome. In the above example, the researcher could simply have noted whether (a) there had been any school boundary changes or changes in the characteristics of students, (b) whether a new principal had been hired, or (c) whether significant staff turnover had occurred. Another way to account for a possible confounding variable is by controlling for its possible effects. This more complicated process will be demonstrated in the next chapter.

Remember

Just because there is a *relationship* between two variables (as indicated by a correlation), in this case a new reading program and reading scores going up, that does not mean that one *caused* the other. *Causation* is a more definitive process than a *relationship*. Causation can only be determined by demonstrating that the outcome was not affected by any confounding variable.

Given the differences between establishing that a relationship exists and documenting causation, there are separate research methods for each. (Relationship research is discussed in Chapter 5, and establishing causation is discussed in Chapter 6.) Indeed, there are times when merely establishing that a relationship exists is the best that you can do.

Sub-principle 2.3—To determine *causation* it is important to eliminate the possible effects of (all) possible confounding variables. (The statistical methodology for doing so is discussed in Chapter 6.)

When examining a research finding, always try to think whether the research accounted for possible confounding variables.

Principle #3—The most convincing evidence that a practice is likely to improve your schools is research that demonstrated BIG benefits.

(Chapters 5-7 discuss how to use the statistical test of *practical benefit* to determine whether a BIG benefit has occurred.)

First of all, wanting to see research that documents BIG benefits for the experimental schools before you would consider adopting that practice is common sense. You do not make decisions in real life based on very small differences. For example, you would not buy a car because it got one mile more per gallon than the one you have. You would want to see much BIGGER improvements in gas mileage to entice a change. In addition, the fact that the reported research was conducted in schools other than your own means that you cannot know for sure that you will see the same benefit in yours. So why would you take the risk and spend time and money if the best benefit you can hope for is very small—and where even that is not guaranteed.

There are many examples where societal innovations were not adopted because the benefits were not BIG enough. Everyone is familiar with the standard QWERTY keyboard. But there is another keyboard standard, the Dvorak keyboard. While the Dvorak is easier to learn and offers a 25% improvement in typing speed, it was not adopted because the significant benefit it provided simply was not a big enough improvement to warrant everyone giving up what they were used to and had invested in. Similarly there was slow adoption of the early bulky cellular phones, but once the iPhone appeared, it offered so much benefit that it quickly displaced landline use.

In other words, innovations that do not provide BIG benefits tend not to be adopted. Similarly, educational leaders should not be expected to voluntarily adopt a new educational practice that doesn't provide a BIG benefit.

Furthermore, there is now evidence that when research finds small benefits from the use of a practice the finding is NOT likely to replicate in subsequent research—if a replication study is conducted. This means that there probably never was any actual benefit—despite the researcher's claim of having proven its effectiveness.

Indeed, the recent replicability research, discussed earlier, has found that a key predictor that the findings will NOT replicate in follow-up research was small benefits in the original research. Open Science Collaboration (2015) concluded that size of the benefit mattered and a key predictor that the research would replicate in subsequent research was the finding of a large benefit in the original research. Ioannidis, the co-director of the Meta-Research Innovation Center at Stanford (METRICS), is scouring the bio-medical literature to determine which studies can be trusted. He has concluded that the smaller the benefit in any scientific research the less likely the research findings are true (2005).

A final reason why small benefits should NOT be trusted as evidence that a practice is effective is that the statistical error may be larger than the benefit. For example, would you bet money on Candidate A winning an election if an election poll showed that he/she had 50.2% of the vote (small advantage) with an error of +/- 7% (large error)? The correct conclusion from such data would NOT be that Candidate A is ahead, but that the election is too close to call. Similarly, if evidence of an effective practice is based on demonstrating a small benefit, chances are that the error is larger than the benefit—particularly in highly sophisticated research that includes many statistical procedures.

> **Sub-principle 3.1**—Leaders should generally ignore evidence of effectiveness if the research only demonstrated a SMALL benefit from the use of a practice—and should usually avoid implementing the practice analyzed in the research.

(The few exceptions to this principle—i.e., where small ESs can be useful—will be discussed in Chapter 6.)

Conversely, the BEST predictor that the research will replicate in subsequent research and in real-world practice is BIG benefits in the original research (assuming that the research has been conducted in a non-biased fashion).

Giving more credibility to research that documents BIG benefits is consistent with the economists Ziliak and McCloskey's (2004) *theory of economic significance*. This theory states that the size of benefit matters in the utility of research findings, *and that imprecise findings of big benefits are more important for real-world impact than being able to precisely predict a level of small benefit.*

Warning

Unfortunately, as will be shown, educational research is focused far more on the precision of research evidence than by the size of the benefit. Indeed, it all too often accepts precise research documenting small benefit as evidence that a practice is effective—which is probably a major factor in explaining why so much education research evidence does NOT replicate.

But how do you determine whether a research finding indicates that a BIG benefit occurred?

Principle #4—The BIGness of the benefit found in experimental is NOT determined by analyzing the results from the statistics—e.g., t-test, F-test, etc. Rather, the benefit is found by analyzing the statistical tests used to determine the importance of those results.

There are actually two components to statistical analysis. The first is the array of statistics themselves, with esoteric names such a chi-square, t-tests, logistic regression, etc. There are literally hundreds of statistics, each with a variety of technical details and options. (See Appendix A for a detailed listing of common statistics and the uses of each.)

The role of these statistics is to bring clarity to the implications of a large array of data. They do so by mathematically reducing the array of data to a single number, or series of numbers, accompanied by a letter—e.g., $F=2.45$. There are also t, z, Z, r, R statistical outcomes. *But what the heck do these resultant numbers mean? What does F=2.45 mean in any practical sense?* Does it indicate an important result? Does it mean that an intervention is effective?

Answering these questions requires a way to interpret the result from the statistic. Bringing clarity to the statistical result involves a second component of statistical analysis—the statistical test. A ***statistical test*** is applied to the number(s) generated by the statistic to determine their importance or significance.

For example, suppose the doctor tells you that your blood pressure is 130 over 85. That does not tell you anything by itself. Nor are you interested in the technical machinery that produced the outcome number. It is only when you are given the criteria for how to interpret that outcome number that you can understand its application to your life. Once the doctor gives you the scientific criterion that more than 120 over 80 and less than 140 over 90 is considered normal, then you as a non-medical specialist can make sense of the outcome number. In this case you would conclude that things are normal.

Similarly, the statistical test and its criteria are used to understand the importance of a statistical result.

Conveniently, there are only two widely used statistical tests, and they are the final arbiters of the importance of the results across almost all statistical results. In other words, regardless of what statistic is used, the key to understanding the importance of the results comes down to interpreting one or both of the following widely used statistical tests:

- Statistical Significance—i.e., p value
- Practical Significance based on Effect Size (ES)

(This two stage process of statistical analysis, *statistical output + statistical test*, is depicted in the cartoon at the end of this chapter.)

As a result, instead of needing to know all the arcane complex mathematics associated with the myriad of available statistics, the key for leaders to determine the authenticity of research evidence lies in simply analyzing the results of a few statistical tests.

 Good News	Learning how to interpret the results of the few universal statistical tests is a far more manageable, bottom-line, process than trying to learn a massive array of statistics and their technical details—as depicted by the intrepid investigator in the cartoon at the end of this chapter.

 Beware	Unfortunately, statistical significance and practical significance tend to exaggerate the importance of the statistical results.

As a result, Chapter 6 will introduce the new statistical test of ***Practical Benefit*** to replace both of the existing ones. Practical benefit is a more authentic statistical test in that it provides better guidance for leaders as to whether the benefit indicated by a statistical analysis is BIG enough to likely result in improvements in their schools. *So in the end, all of the technical machinations will be arbitrated by the results of a single statistical test*—which is what leaders should focus on to determine the authenticity of the research for improving their schools.

Using These Principles in Your own Action Research

These principles are equally relevant for critiquing published research as they are for guiding your own action research as a leader and student as described in Chapter 10). You should apply these same principles to your own action research—e.g., a program evaluation or a gap analysis. You similarly need to be careful in your own research about the effects of bias, statistical error, and confounding variables. The keys to avoiding these problems in your own action research are to be reflective about your findings, and to seek alternative possible explanations for them. In addition, be careful not to overstate your conclusions in terms of the benefits that you claim to have found, or to claim that you have "proven" something.

Additionally, in your own research you will be the one conducting the statistical analysis before you can apply the above principles to analyzing the results. But which statistic to use? Appendix A provides an easy to understand method for determining which statistic to use depending on the circumstance of the research.

In other words, there is no need to learn about the details of a wide array of statistics. You only need to learn the statistic that is most appropriate for your research. Then once you have collected your data you can plug into a software program such as Excel to conduct the appropriate statistical analysis.

Using Excel

In recent years Excel has made great strides in its statistical analysis capabilities through its *Analysis ToolPak* add-on. (When using Excel it is important to have the latest version, especially Mac users.) It is also fairly easy to learn how to conduct the statistical analysis of choice using Excel via YouTube and other online sources.

There are a variety of sources for learning to use Excel and its statistical capabilities.[18]

Summary

This chapter has put forth some initial principles for critically analyzing quantitative evidence that document an effective practice. The final elaboration of these principles will be presented in Chapter 7.

Evidence-based practice is essential to improving practice. However, not all scientific evidence of effective practices is created equal. It now appears that a majority of evidence of effective practices does NOT replicate—even scientific evidence published in the top research journals. Non-replicable practices will generally NOT translate into improvements in your schools—no matter how prominent the claims are that the practice is evidence-based. This problem is compounded by the fact that no attempt is made to replicate the majority of research evidence.

Therefore, it is necessary for leaders to engage in judicious analysis of the scientific claims that a practice is evidence-based and look for clues in the research to anticipate whether it would have replicated and/or is likely to improve their schools.

Using Excel

The replication studies did find that some research DOES replicate and such research has potential to improve your schools and increase equity.

In addition, the replication studies provided a key clue as to what leaders can look for in order to have confidence that evidence they are considering is likely to in fact replicate to produce benefits in their schools. ***The key predictor is whether the research found evidence of BIG benefits from the use of a given practice.***

Determining the size of the benefit does not depend on any advanced knowledge of statistics, but on an understanding of how to interpret the two most common statistical tests (plus the new test of Practical Benefit). To develop such understanding, the next

---

[18] Recommended resources for learning to use Excel are (a) *Smart Method* books by Mike Smart—either Mac or Windows version, and (b) free videos on YouTube.
https://www.youtube.com/watch?v=k1VUZEVuDJ8

Recommended resources for learning to use Excel statistical capabilities are: *Excel Statistics: A Quick Guide* by Neil Salkind, and *Excel Dashboards & Reports for Dummies* by Michael Alexander. Another helpful all-around text is *Excel Data Analysis for Dummies* by Paul McFedries.

three chapters will discuss how to determine whether these statistical tests have documented a BIG benefit,

The next three chapters will also describe how to apply the above key principles of data analysis to identify which quantitative evidence is likely to improve your schools and increase equity—for the following three types of quantitative research:

- **Descriptive**
- **Relationship**
- **Experimental**

Two-Stage Analysis Process

Statistics   **Data**

Pearson R, Spearman rho, Gamma Kendall,   *6668044-0 8733339 3833992*
Chi Square, Phi, Cramer's V, Multiple Regression,   *3535 63379 83732 42009*
Discriminant Analysis, ZZ Top, t test,   *08585858 342982 221198 73304840*
Mann-Wilcon Sign, McNemar, ANOVA,
Kruskal-Wallis, Friedman,
Cochran Q, Mann Whitney U, Wilcoxon

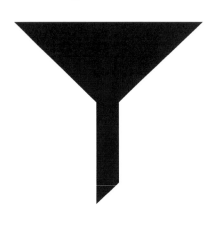

Stage 1 Statistical Output   e.g., t=3.25, F= 6.25/Tables

Stage 2 Apply Statistical Test

Statistical Significance   P < .05 *
Practical Benefit (See Chapter 6)   ES = .15

Chapter 4

Analyzing Data Using Descriptive Analysis

🔔 Key Takeaways 🔔

Descriptive analysis describes the key characteristics of a set of data collected about a sample of individuals or events. It simply indicates the current status of whatever is being sampled or studied and does not try to explain how or why the results are the way they are.

In most conceptions of research, descriptive analysis is considered the stepchild of real research and is viewed as the lowest ranking form of research. However, in terms of informing leadership decision-making, descriptive analysis will become the *most* important form of research.

The most common statistics use in descriptive research are:

- **Mean (e.g., average)**
- **Median**
- **Standard deviation**

In addition, these three, simple-to-understand statistics are so important and useful that they are hereafter referred to as the *power trio of statistics*. Indeed, when used in combination they are central for making authentic sense of all forms of research.

In terms of equity, descriptive research is often used to conduct gap analyses—e.g., determining how much difference there is in student performance based on race, sex, and/or other demographic variables. In addition, histograms can be used to visually describe the distribution of values to make it easier to spot anomalies or sub-patterns within the data that may reflect inequities.

This chapter also introduces:

- The **law of actual end result** as being critical for leaders to make independent judgments of the likelihood of research claims of an effective practice to improve their schools and increase equity within the schools. This law applies to all types of research and, together with the power trio of statistics, enables leaders to critically analyze the most sophisticated journal articles;

- How to **control** for the possibility that a third, confounding variable may be causing a gap based on race and sex—with using as an example determining whether the achievement gap between Black and White girls is caused by different levels of poverty; and

- The difference between using research evidence to demonstrate that a **relationship** exists versus establishing that a practice **caused** an outcome.

The Importance of Descriptive Analysis

The start of scientific analysis involves collecting some data or analyzing existing data. Quantitative data are usually developed (a) from repeated observations of some social or physical phenomenon, (b) by conducting a survey with a questionnaire or other instrument, (c) by testing, or (d) by automatic electronic monitoring of transactions.

The data collection process will generally produce hundreds, thousands, or millions of numbers. This is the *raw data*—i.e., unprocessed numbers. How does one make sense of such a raw mass of numbers?

The first step is descriptive analysis. Descriptive analysis describes the most salient characteristics of the accumulated numbers, which typically describe a sample (i.e., a group of individuals), the characteristics of a variable or an outcome. For example, the sample might be data about students in a school, district, or state—or books checked out of a library. Descriptive analysis can be as simple as determining the total enrollment of a given school, or as complex as determining the characteristics of a subset of all students, such as how many students entering all public universities in the nation are first-generation students.

Descriptive analysis is used to describe the current status of some sample, variable, or outcome. It will tell a leader how their students are currently performing in reading, or how students were also performing in the recent past so as to indicate the degree of improvement. It can also be used to determine whether there are differences in performance for different types of students, such as males versus females, which is typically referred to as *gap analysis*.

The statistics used in descriptive analysis are the most basic ones—such as counting the size of the sample, and the frequency of each value, percentages, averages, and standard deviations for each variable or characteristic.

Descriptive analysis canNOT be used to (a) determine how the results got to be that way, (b) examine relationships between the variables, or (c) make predictions. So, for example, if one conducts a survey of a sample of voters' preferences between two candidates and reports the percentage of voters favoring each candidate, that is *descriptive analysis*. However, the moment any effort is made to use that data to project how all voters (i.e., the population) will vote, or why voters favor that candidate, or how to best change their mind—answering those questions requires the forms of research that will be discussed in the next several chapters. Descriptive analysis can determine the amount of a gap in students' performance, but not *why* it exists or *how* it can be reduced. As a result, descriptive analysis is considered to be the most basic form of research.

However, that does not mean that descriptive analysis is unimportant. Aside from the obvious fact that knowing how many students you have in your school affects your funding, descriptive analysis is the fundamental starting point of the scientific process. You have to know the "what is" before researchers can get to the more prestigious stages of forming theories of "How and Why" things are the way the descriptive data indicate they seem to be—and then test the predictions of those theories.

Remember

And while the most common forms of descriptive analyses are usually simply counting the number of students or transactions, determining averages and variations of distributions, or listing the characteristics of individuals or objects in the sample—such analyses are the foundation for every other type of research.

Furthermore, the basic statistics used in descriptive analysis are the keys to (a) analyzing the authentic outcomes of the more sophisticated forms of research discussed in the next few chapters, and (b) enabling the average leader to determine whether the findings of the most sophisticated quantitative research are likely to improve their schools and increase equity.

The types of numbers/values

The most fundamental unit in quantitative analysis is the individual number/value. There are three main types of numbers:

- Regular numbers, also called Interval Data;
- Rankings, where numbers reflect a place in a set of values listed in order, also called Ordinal Data, e.g., percentiles, or where a "3" means that you are the third tallest in a class; and
- Categories of things, also called Categorical Data, where the values can be letters—e.g., letter grades or the letters A, C, G, and T to represent the basic chemicals of the human genome—or words; e.g., short, medium, and tall.

When using categorical data you conduct quantitative analysis about letters and words—e.g., what percentage of the population is tall.

There is also a fourth type of value widely used in research called a z value, which will be discussed further in Chapters 5-6.

The type of number used in any research study plays a key role in determining which statistic is used. (see Appendix A). However, the discussion going forward in this chapter will focus on analyzing interval data.

The Power Trio Statistics (Mean, Median, Standard Deviation)

The most important descriptive statistics are (a) the Mean or Average, (b) Median, which is another measure of average, and (c) the Standard Deviation or Variance. (Hereafter the terms Mean and Standard Deviation will be used as they are more common in the literature.) These three statistics are so important and fundamental to everything that they are hereafter referred to as the power trio of statistics.

Indeed, the power trio is all you need to know to assess the practical benefit of any research regardless of how mathematically sophisticated it is and how prestigious the research journal is! It is also important to know how these three descriptive statistics interact with each other.

The Relationship between the Mean, Standard Deviation, and Median

The statistic we are most familiar with in our everyday experience is "Average." We constantly want to know whether something is above or below Average. In the aftermath of a drought we want to know if this year's rainfall is above or below Average for this time of year. We want to know if our schools are above Average. We want to know whether our child's height and weight are "normal" for a given age level.

The reason why Average is such a powerful and comfortable statistic for even the math phobic is that it gives us a yardstick in the form of a single number that is considered to be the most representative value among the myriad numbers that have been gathered. For example, when trying to figure out if your child's height is normal for his/her age, you could obtain a printout of all the heights of all children in the U.S. at that same age of the past 50 years. However, this would produce a list of hundreds of millions of numbers which by themselves would be overwhelming rather than helpful in determining whether your child's height is normal. The alternative is to obtain the Average of all those numbers and compare your child's height to that single number. Which is easier? Obviously, the use of the Average statistic is easier.

It is interesting to note that in this example we are equating the Average value of the height of each individual child born over the past 50 years to indicate what is normal. Seeking the norm is generally true whenever we find the Average of anything—be it rainfall or children's heights. Stated differently, the Average is usually considered to be the most representative single value for a collection of numbers.

As a result, the Average is the most powerful, general, and widely used statistic in research and everyday life. Alas, statistics has to make things more complicated so it uses the term "Mean" instead of "Average," so hereafter this book will use the term "Mean".19 In addition, the collection of individual numbers/values from which the Mean is calculated is called the distribution of numbers.

The Mean is such a powerful tool for making sense out of a mass of numbers that most of the advanced statistics used in experimental research in the top research journals focus on the relative difference between the Means of each group. It makes sense that if we are to compare the performance of two groups, each with a large number of members, that we would compare the most representative value of each. However, in certain circumstances the Mean result for a group of scores can be misleading. For example, consider two communities, each of which has 10 families. Using Table 4.1 below, which of the following two communities is richer?

---

[19] The **Mean**, or the *Average*, is calculated by adding all the numbers together and dividing by the number of numbers.

64

Table 4.1
A Comparison of the Average Family Income in Two Communities

	Community A	Community B
Mean Family Income	$111,925	$36,349

Clearly, the answer is Community A. But is Community A really the wealthiest? We cannot know for sure until we look at the distribution of individual incomes in each community. Table 4.2 below has a distribution, i.e., a listing, of each family's income in each community.

Table 4.2
A Distribution of All Incomes by Community

Income of Each Family in Community A	Income of Each Family in Community B
12,200.00	39,000.00
11,000.00	28,800.00
11,600.00	42,000.00
16,500.00	38,500.00
19,245.00	33,200.00
17,000.00	46,000.00
9,000.00	28,000.00
14,800.00	37,000.00
7,900.00	34,890.00
1,000,000.00	36,100.00

After eyeballing the two columns do you still think Community A is the wealthier one? Probably not. Why not?

The problem is that reducing the set of numbers in Community A to a single value ignored the nature of the diversity within those numbers and allowed a single value (one of the community members) to skew the results. This example shows that we cannot ignore the diversity, or to use the statistical term, the degree of variation, within each set of numbers—any more than we can ignore the diversity within a group of individuals. Clearly, the more diverse a given set of numbers is, i.e., the greater degree of variation, the less representative the Mean is of all the numbers. The unrepresentativeness of the Mean is particularly exposed in a case such as this where you have an unusually different value, hereafter referred to as an "outlier". The Mean is particularly non-representative when all the outliers are on one side of the Mean. So in this case Community A has an outlier with an unusually high income, and this single data point biased, or skewed, the Mean sharply upwards. As a result, the Mean for Community A was not representative of that community as a whole which was in reality very poor.

What this means is that the more diverse, or spread out, a set of numbers are, and the more imbalanced the extreme scores (if any) are, the less representative the Mean is of all the scores.

Of course, in this case with a distribution of only 10 numbers we can easily eyeball the data and determine that Community A is actually poorer. However, suppose there were 10,000 families in each community. Your eyeballs would revolt against trying to make sense of 20,000 numbers. As a result, we need a statistic that can measure how diverse or spread out the scores are and how balanced such variation is. The Standard Deviation is the most widely used measure of how spread out a set of values for a variable are.20

Remember

The larger the divergence of scores from the Mean—i.e., the higher the Standard Deviation is relative to the Mean—the less representative and more misleading the Mean is.

Table 4.3 below adds the Standard Deviation to Table 4.1

Table 4.3
The Mean and Standard Deviation of Family Income in Two Communities

	Community A	Community B
Mean Family Income	$111,925	$36,349
Standard Deviation	312,059	5,537

Table 4.3 shows that the Standard Deviation of the individual incomes in Community A is very large relative to the Mean, so much so that it is actually bigger than the Mean, while the Standard Deviation for Community B's scores are much less than the Mean. This indicates that the Mean is NOT representative of family income in Community A—but is for Community B.

When the Standard Deviation is large relative to the Mean a different statistic needs to be used to represent the central tendency of the distribution of values. The Median, which is the middle score of the distribution, is the most widely used alternative way to determine the most representative score. The Median is calculated by listing in numerical order all the individual numbers, in this case the income of each family, and selecting the one in the middle. Since there is an even number of scores in this case, the midpoint would be in the middle of the 5th and 6th scores. In the case of Community A, it would be the midpoint of 12,200 and 14,800, or 13,500. Table 4.4 shows the difference between the Mean and Median scores.

---

[20] The **Standard Deviation** indicates how much variation there is in the distribution of all scores relative to the *Mean*. It is actually the average deviation of each score from the *Mean*.

66

Table 4.4
The Mean and Standard Deviation of Family Income by Community

	Community A	Community B
Mean Family Income	$111,925	$36,349
Median Family Income	13,500	36,550

Clearly, for this distribution of incomes the Median is the more representative score and clearly indicates that in fact Community B is the wealthier one. This example illustrates that when the Standard Deviation is large in comparison to the Mean, then the Median is usually the more accurate statistic—i.e., the more representative value. (Note how different the Mean and Median are for Community A.)

Principle #5—Always first examine the Mean, Standard Deviation, and (if needed) the Median of any distribution. This power trio of statistics is fundamental.

Remember

Sub-principle #5.1—Rule Of Mean-Median Differences: When the Mean and Median are very different, trust the Median, or at the very least explore the nature of the distribution of individual numbers.

This sub-principle also explains why the average (i.e., most representative) home price in a geographic area is reported as the *Median* price. The *Median* is used because there are usually a few exceptionally expensive homes that are sold whose prices are vastly different than the price range of the vast majority of homes sold. These few outliers inflate the *Mean* price and make it too unrepresentative. Therefore, the price of the home in the middle of the distribution, i.e., the *Median*, is used.

Another example where Mean and Median are at odds is the discussion of whether American households have benefitted from the economic revival that started in June 2009 through 2014. *Mean* household income is up. This seems like a positive. However, Irwin (2014) cites an analysis of census data that shows that during this recovery period the *Median* family income actually dropped. This reflects the situation of the widening income gap where a few have benefitted disproportionately from the rising economy, but that most households are experiencing declines in income. (This real-world example is eerily similar to the made up earlier example of family income in Communities A and B.)

Now let's apply this knowledge of the relationship between *Mean, Standard Deviation*, and *Median* to education research. Consider a study to determine whether a new practice increases the mathematics performance of 5th graders. Suppose that by the end of the year the *Mean* math score of the experimental group is 5.9, and the comparison Group A's end of year *Mean* math score is 5.46. Which group did better?

We cannot say which group of 5th graders did better until we know the Standard Deviation for each group. For example, consider the following distribution of scores from the experimental and comparison groups in Table 4.5 below.

Table 4.5
A Distribution of All Students' Scores in Each Group

Scores of Each Student in the Experimental Group	Scores of Each Score in Comparison Group
3.1	5.9
3.5	5.3
4.1	3.7
4.7	5.1
3.8	5.1
4.3	5.3
4.1	5.2
4.9	6.2
11.3	6.1
12.4	7.1

The *Mean* of the experimental group is larger, but eye-balling the data of individual student performance, which group do you now think did better? **Which group do you think has the greater *Standard Deviation*?**

Cleary, the experimental group has a higher *Standard Deviation* as two of the experimental students had high outlier scores. However, on balance the comparison group clearly did better—even though it had the lower *Mean* score. Table 4.6 illustrates that the *Standard Deviation* of the experimental group is indeed large relative to the *Mean*. Therefore, the comparison between the groups should be done based on the *Median* score—which shows that the comparison group did better. In other words, the correct conclusion is that there is no reason to adopt the experimental intervention—even though the experimental group had a higher Mean score.

Table 4.6
A Comparison of the Mean, Standard Deviation and Median of the Math Scores by Group

	Experimental Group	Comparison Group
Mean Score	5.9	5.46
Standard Deviation	3.3	0.9
Median Score	4.3	5.3

In other words, distinguishing between whether the *Mean* or *Median* is the appropriate statistic to use has real-world consequences. Simply knowing that the experimental group had a higher *Mean* score does not necessarily mean that it actually did better. If the *Median* was the appropriate statistic then the experimental group may have in fact done worse. In such a case it would be a mistake for leaders to adopt the new practice.

The key analytical question then becomes:

> How big should the *Standard Deviation* be in order to indicate that the *Median* should be used as the most representative statistic?

Alas, there is no formal rule. The earlier example of community wealth shows that in Community A the *Standard Deviation* is so large that it is bigger than the *Mean*. On the other hand, while the *Standard Deviation* of the scores for Community B is by itself a large number, it is much smaller than the *Mean*. So we can conclude that when the value for the *Standard Deviation* is small relative to the *Mean*, that the *Mean* should be used. If the *Standard Deviation* is almost as large, or larger, than the *Mean*, *then the Median should be used.*

You can use common sense to determine whether a *Standard Deviation* for either or both of the groups is large relative to the *Mean*. I tend to want to see a *Standard Deviation* that is a third, or less, than the *Mean*. In the case of the math scores just discussed where the *Means* were 5.9 and 5.46, I would want to see a Standard Deviation of at most 1.5—i.e., a third of the *Mean*—to have confidence in the *Mean*.

The basic rule is that when in doubt, calculate and examine the *Median*, and apply the basic rule of Mean-Median differences.[21]

Warning

Ironically the most advanced forms of statistical analyses tend to do calculations based on the Mean. In other words, in situations where the most representative statistic is not the Mean, the sophisticated mathematics and tables may be producing invalid results. In particular, be very suspicious of research, or summaries of research, that report just *Means* without indicating *Standard Deviations*—and if needed, the *Medians*.

Why the *Power Trio* of Statistics is Critical for ALL Research

Remember

Regardless of how sophisticated the research method and statistical analysis is, making authentic sense of the results—i.e., how likely is it that the results will improve your schools—comes down to knowing the *Means* of the results, and whether it or the *Median* is the most representative value of the target sample based on the size of the *Standard Deviation* relative to the *Mean*.

---

[21] As an alternative, there may be cases where it makes sense to drop an outlier score. For example, if you find out that a student who did not answer any questions on the test had a parent die the day before, it would make sense to drop that student's score. Clearly, whatever reason is given for dropping an outlier has to be applied equally to each group and should be applied with great caution and disclosed. In addition, the researcher should inform the reader of the scores both before and after an outlier is dropped.

The subsequent chapters will continue to demonstrate the importance of this power trio of statistics for interpreting the authentic usefulness of ALL types of research—without knowing any advanced statistics or mathematics. The figure below demonstrates the flexibility and many uses of the power trio of statistics. Indeed, you can use the power trio to conduct all the major types of analyses that are critical to leadership decision-making.

Uses of the Power Trio

While most of these uses of the power trio will be discussed in upcoming chapters, the next part of this chapter will demonstrate one of the uses—eyeballing power trio results to determine the degree of equity.

The bottom line is that the power trio of statistics is a powerful, easy-to-use tool that leaders can use to determine the authenticity of any type of research evidence for improving their schools and increasing equity—even the most mathematically sophisticated published research.

Using Excel

You can easily calculate the power trio descriptive statistics for any dataset in Excel. You can find the power trio (plus dozens of other descriptive statistics and variations) listed under the INSERT menu, and then select "Function." The power trio are listed as: AVERAGE, MEDIAN, and STDEV.

Descriptive Analysis of the Distribution of Values

While in the above two examples of community wealth and reading scores it was easy to eyeball the actual numbers and figure out what was going on, how does one handle a more typical situation where there are thousands of families in a community, or even hundreds of thousands, and millions of students? Trying to eyeball the numbers and make sense of them would cause a massive headache. While you can reduce the enormous amount of data to the overall *Mean*, *Median*, and *Standard Deviation* of the numbers, there are many cases where sub-patterns within the set of numbers can convey important information. For example, there may be a concentration of low income homes in one area of the community.

So there is an important middle ground between (a) examining thousands of numbers to look for sub-patterns/groupings, and (b) reducing them down to a single number— e.g., *Mean or Median*. This middle ground involves looking at how the numbers are grouped—specifically, how the values are distributed across the range of values.

Why analyzing the distribution of values is important for equity

Sometimes the most important insights come from within a subset of the overall data. For example, knowing the *Mean* for a school increased does not tell how different groups of students are performing, or whether there are large numbers of students lagging badly. So, as important the *Mean* or *Median* statistics are, they do not reveal any inner patterns within the data. Equity concerns mean that it is not sufficient to just look at Means/Median, but that it is also important to look at how the results are distributed across different types of students.

For example, if a new program increased the overall average but only a small percentage of students benefitted, is it effective? Is a program effective if the average went up but none of the below average students progressed? The distribution of what happened within the overall result is important for supporting additional improvement and equity. Schools often focus such distribution improvement analysis on the extent to which an approach raised borderline students above a given cutoff score, and/or the extent to which the bottom third or quarter performing students moved up into the next level grouping. The latter distribution analysis should also characterize which types of students are progressing and which are not.

Analyzing the distribution of values

There are two tools that provide a way to look for sub-patterns within a large set of numbers. These tools provide information on the frequency with which various values occur with an overall set of numbers/values.

The first tool is a *"frequency table."* So for example, if in Boston, 515 families earned between $35,000-45,000, and 720 earned between $75,000-85,000, that section of the *frequency table* would look like:

Table 4.7
Example of a Frequency Table of the Income Distribution of 1235 Families

Family Income Level	# Of Families (Frequency)
Below $35,000	0
$35,000-45,000	415
$45,001-59,999	70
$60.000-74,999	30
$75,000-85,000	520
Above $85,000	200

However, the most helpful way to understand the nature of the distribution of values is to see it visually. A **histogram** is a chart that indicates how often each score occurs.

Histograms are designed so that the vertical axis (y axis) represents the number of values that fit in the given value/range of values on the horizontal axis (x axis). The x axis can either be interval, ordinal, or categorical data.

For example, consider the histogram on the right from the Math Is Fun website which shows the distribution of the heights (in centimeters) of all the orange trees in an orange grove—i.e., how many of the trees are of a specific height.

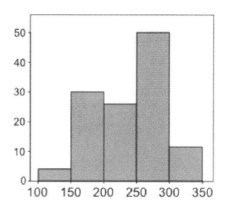

This *histogram* shows that this grove had 30 trees that ranged from 150-200 centimeters in height, and that the most frequently occurring tree (n=50) was 250-300 centimeters tall.

Below is another histogram indicating the number of schools nationally (vertical axis) that have different percentages of students "Eligible for Free and Reduced Lunch" (horizontal axis)—ranging from 0 to 100% such students.

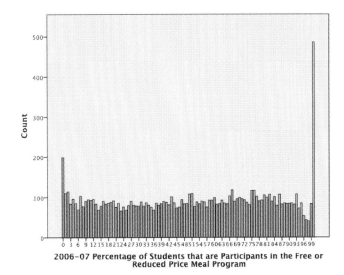

2006-07 Percentage of Students that are Participants in the Free or Reduced Price Meal Program

What does this histogram suggest about the distribution of poverty in schools?

<<...Think for a minute...>>

The most important bar is the rightmost bar. It shows that there are a large number of schools with unusually/extremely high concentrations (98-99%) of students living in poverty.

What statistic would be more representative of the percentage of free and reduced lunch in American schools—the *Mean* or *Median*?

(ANSWER: The *Median* because the rightmost bar skews the results.)

Given the skewed distribution, using the *Mean* would under-estimate the actual severity of the concentration of poverty in schools.

How to break up the categories of values on the x axis of histograms is somewhat arbitrary. In the first of the above histograms, the scores (i.e., heights of the trees) were broken out by steps of 50, whereas in the second histogram the percentages of students in poverty were broken out for every single value between 1 and 100. Alternatively, categorical values could have been used for the x axis in the first histogram—e.g., short trees, medium, tall, very tall.

The second *histogram* also indicates that there are extreme outlier values—particularly on one side of the graph. This will be a foreshadowing that the *Standard Deviation* will be very high and that you will need to use the *Median* value.

However, the big takeaway from this histogram is not what the most representative statistic is, but the graphic evidence of the almost total absence of economic integration in a large number of schools. It is shocking to see the disparity highlighted by the large numbers of schools without any students born into poverty, and an even larger number of schools where virtually ALL students were. This inequity would be masked if the only data generated were the power trio of statistics. Therefore, the first step in descriptive analysis is to generate a histogram.

	Before you calculate any statistics, it is important to develop a histogram of the data and eyeball the results for any important patterns within the overall dataset.

Understanding the distribution of scores in your schools, as well as in key subgroups, is a key aspect of leadership. If the *Mean* of a school's performance has increased that does not mean that all segments of the distribution of scores—i.e., all the subgroups of students—increased. You would want to know, for example, whether the performance of the special education students lagged. The distribution/histogram will show what percentage of those students lagged, and what percentage were extreme laggards. It will also show what percentage did well. The same questions can be asked of students of color.

Histograms of the numbers of students who achieve a given score in each sub-group is a quick way to see whether a particular subgroup is lagging, and to visually see the degree of inequity—particularly when the bars for each subgroup are superimposed on the same graph using different colors for each subgroup.

So, understanding the nature of the current status of how a school is doing or the degree of inequity requires looking at more than a single statistics such as the *Mean* of all scores. Rather, it requires an understanding of the interplay of a variety of statistics, most notably the power trio, and the nature of the distribution/histogram of results across and within subgroups. So, as important as the *Mean* is, relying entirely on it is too reductionist an approach for characterizing a set of numbers—as it can be misleading for all the reasons and examples given earlier. Therefore, it is recommended that you generate a histogram and reflect about the nature of the distribution before looking at any statistics.

Once you understand the interplay of the distribution/histogram of values together with the power trio statistics as to what the current status of some measure is, the next step is to try and understand why it is the way it is—which then leads to ideas about how to improve the results. The former involves the development of theory, and the latter involves seeking evidence-based practices using the more advanced quantitative methods discussed in the next two chapters. In other words, quantitative research done right is a much richer and reflective process than its critics would have you believe.[22]

The normal distribution

Different types of social phenomena often produce different distributions of results, which produce histograms with different shapes. For example, in the histogram of tree

---

[22] Advocates of qualitative research like to criticize quantitative research as being reductionist—i.e., reducing complex phenomena to a single number. First quantitative research is much more sophisticated than that and requires reflection about several types of numbers simultaneously. In addition, generating or using evidence to develop recommendations for practice is reductionist to some extent—regardless of whether qualitative or quantitative data are used. For example, qualitative research generally relies on only one or two examples of evidentiary quotes or events to support the conclusions of the researcher—which is itself reductionist. This is not an argument against qualitative research. It is simply to point out that the criticism of quantitative research as being reductionist is often overstated.

height, most of the results were towards the middle of the distribution. Conversely, in the histogram of the number of schools with different percentages of poverty, most of the schools were at either end of the distribution—i.e., schools with almost no poverty or schools where almost all students were born into poverty. The shapes of the histograms of these different phenomena are very different.

One of the most important distributions in education is the ***normal distribution***. Its histogram graph is referred to as a bell-shaped curve. Its shape is displayed below. The normal distribution describes the distribution of scores on an intelligence test, heights of human beings, and other social phenomena.

Illustration of a Normal Distribution

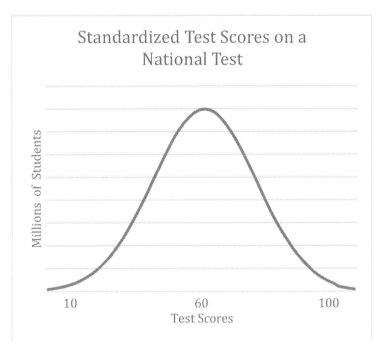

You can tell from the shape that the majority of student scores are at the middle of the distribution, with the most at the highest point which is the *Mean* of all the scores. In addition, a normal distribution is uniform on both sides of the *Mean*—i.e., there are equal number of individuals on either side of the *Mean*. As a result, the *Median* will be the same as the *Mean*.

In a *pure* normal distribution almost 70% of the students will score within 1 standard deviation of the mean. So, for example, the *Mean* score on intelligence tests, which is a normal distribution, is 100 and the standard deviation is 15. This means that close to 70% of those tested will score between 85 (1 standard deviation below) and 115 (1 standard deviation above). Relatively few receive scores at the extreme ends of the distribution.

In addition to describing many social phenomena, the normal distribution is also important for determining which statistic to use in more advanced forms of research.

Appendix A shows how certain statistics are selected on the basis of whether the distribution of scores for a given variable is normal.

In many cases, determining whether a distribution is normal can be made by understanding the context of the results being studied. For example, if we collected data on how many minutes before the start of a movie people arrived at a theater, the distribution probably would not be close to normal since most people would arrive very close to the start of the movie with only a few arriving more than 30 minutes before the start of the movie. That is clearly not going to be a normal distribution since most of the scores would be at the very low end of the distribution (as opposed to the middle). In addition, while the earlier histogram of the tree heights is closer to being a normal distribution than the histogram on the concentration of poverty in schools, is it sufficiently close to be considered a normal distribution? Indeed, most distributions are not a perfect normal distribution.

The best way to tell whether a distribution can be considered close enough to normal to be considered a normal distribution is to calculate a statistic called "skewness." *Skewness* indicates whether the distribution is "leaning"—i.e., whether a disproportionate number of scores are on one side of the distribution, and in which direction it is leaning. A *normal* distribution has a Skewness of 0. If the Skewness is less than -1 or greater than +1 it is leaning too much for it to be considered a *normal* distribution.

Using Excel

You can easily calculate the skewness of any dataset in Excel. Go to the INSERT menu, select "Function" and then select SKEW.

Of course, before you can develop a distribution of data values, you need data. The most important source of data are primary sources.

Descriptive Analysis Using Primary Source Data

What are primary source data?

Research starts with data and the most important type of data are primary source data. *Primary source* data are data and analyses that are produced directly from a research effort—usually produced either by a researcher who has conducted a published study or by organizations that collect data and produce reports based on that data. This is in contrast to reading someone's description of what someone else's data or data analysis revealed—which is referred to as a *secondary source* of evidence. So, for example, when someone writes about historic trends in the achievement gap without analyzing the original dataset, or cites what someone else said about the achievement gap, these are secondary sources.

My own experience is that when I or my students fact-check a secondary source with primary source data, the secondary source is usually misstating the actual data and/or result to varying degrees.

Primary source data is the best source of evidence about the status of some phenomenon of interest to leaders. Looking at these datasets one can determine the answers to questions such as the degree of improvement, size and changes in performance gaps, whether the number of students who are homeless or on free and reduced lunch are increasing, etc.

In addition to data collected by the researcher in published research, there are increasing amounts of *primary source* data collected at the state and national levels by government agencies, foundations, professional associations, and research centers. Such data depositories are increasingly available to leaders, researchers, and citizens to access and analyze—and are increasingly used as evidence to recommend policies and practices.

How to find primary source data

Appendix B lists a wide variety of sources of primary source datasets and descriptive data that are useful for leaders and leadership students.

For non-researchers the data are usually made available as descriptive statistics. For example, many states publish descriptive results of the *Mean* performance of every school and district. Such descriptive data are used by many groups—e.g., real estate agents seeking to interest clients in a listing based on the data about the quality of the neighborhood school. In some cases the raw data are made available to researchers to conduct follow-up analyses. Primary source data are a tremendous resource for evidence on the current state of education locally and nationally, as well as for historic trends. In addition, census data gives education leaders precise data about the characteristics of their community.

Importance of primary source data

Why are primary source data critical? Consider the following example.

> One of my students identified the key problem for his/her action research as being that a certain subgroup of Asian American students were doing poorly—contrary to the belief that all Asian Americans do well in school. The evidence was that he/she quoted someone who was supposedly an expert in the field as saying that this subgroup was not doing well. I asked the student to provide primary source evidence that this subgroup was doing poorly. The student refused. Since I was unfamiliar with this subgroup, I was curious and went to a variety of sources and was able to find several that broke out the national performance for this subgroup. It turns out that this subgroup was actually doing quite well.

The unfortunate lesson from this example is that since this student's research was premised on a question and assumption that was simply not true, the findings are worse than useless—they are in fact misleading practice and are demeaning to students of this heritage and their families.

Clearly, using primary source data to make your key points is a higher standard of evidence than relying on secondary sources. Indeed, the latter really is not really evidence. In addition, one of the most exciting discoveries that you can make as a student is to find a new insight from analyzing existing primary source data and developing an original conclusion. You may also discover that what scholars believe the original data demonstrated, or what they believe a key scholar theorized—is wrong!

In addition, reliance on *primary* sources is not just appropriate for data and research results, but also for citing philosophic perspectives. Wherever possible you should NOT rely on a secondary source as to what a particular text or individual argued. Rather, you should go to the original source and decide on your own what the real meaning/intent of the original author was.

Indeed, many of the recommended decision-making techniques in the next two chapters are a result of my rereading a classic text written in 1988 and discovering a key point that statisticians had overlooked. This point enabled the development of the statistical test of practical benefit presented in Chapters 5-7 that makes it possible for leaders to easily judge the authenticity of research results.

Primary source datasets are also valuable for researchers. For example, if a state database lists the percentage of free and reduced lunch students and average score on the state test for each school (descriptive analysis), then it is easy for a researcher to conduct an analysis of the relationship between the two variables.

Another valuable resource for researchers is longitudinal federal surveys that follow samples of students over time. An example is the National Longitudinal Study of the 8th grade cohort of 1988 which follows this sample of students throughout the next phases of their lives. Researchers can then analyze the raw data for changes over time in whatever fashion they desire.

Perhaps confusingly, when a researcher conducts a reanalysis of an existing dataset, it is called a ***secondary analysis***. However, once that analysis is conducted, the results are considered to be a primary source since that represents a result produced by the researcher.

Leaders should always seek out primary sources of data as the basis for decisions or for determining the extent of a given problem. Primary source data provide leaders with a comparative basis to see how their schools are performing as compared to others in a region and/or to determine the extent of achievement gaps in their schools. In addition, some of the state and federal datasets provide tools that make it easy for leaders and leadership students to extract relevant data and conduct their own secondary analyses to answer the specific questions they are interested in. An example of such a tool to conduct a national gap analysis is described in the next section.

Conducting Gap Analyses

Given current concerns about inequity, gap analysis—i.e., describing differences between different subgroups based on race, sex, parent's education level, household income, disability, etc.—becomes an important tool for identifying the degree and types of inequities that exist. Gap analysis also informs leaders as to which subgroups of students are underperforming and need additional help. The now defunct federal *No Child Left Behind* law recognized the importance of reducing performance gaps by requiring schools to meet minimum improvement goals for ALL subgroups—i.e., it was not enough to improve the school as a whole if the Latinx students did not improve.

Indeed, gap analysis is considered to be so important that some states now require candidates to demonstrate the ability to conduct such analysis on certification exams for leaders and teachers.

The fact that a gap exists is NOT necessarily a problem. At any point in time there will ALWAYS be differences between groups that are caused by chance. It becomes an equity problem when the gaps are large and *systemic*. Systemic means that the direction of a large gap remains the same, and does not appreciably narrow over time. So it's NOT enough to simply indicate that a gap currently exists. You need supplementary information to answer the following questions:

1. **Is the current gap large?**
2. **What is the historical trend—has the gap previously existed, and if so has it been decreasing over time?**

If the answer to both of these questions is "yes," that means that the gap is large and has not narrowed over time—so, chances are that the gap is being caused by some *systemic* problem that needs to be addressed.

In order to illustrate the use of descriptive statistics to conduct gap analysis, the following example makes use of one of the primary source dataset in Appendix B— the federal dataset of the National Assessment of Educational Progress (NAEP), more commonly known as *The Nation's Report Card.*

Overview of NAEP

NAEP tests are generally administered to a sample of students in each state in grades 4, 8, and 12 every 4 years in a variety of content areas. NAEP results are reported as both raw scores (listed as *scale scores*) and as categorical scores (listed as *achievement scores discrete*). Categorical scores are the percentage of students achieving Advanced, Proficient, Basic, and Below Basic levels. A great deal of data is collected about each school and student which are then summarized by state, some urban districts, and by different student characteristics. This makes NAEP a tremendous reservoir of primary source data that can support a wide variety of improvement and gap analyses.

An example of the importance of NAEP data is that the NAEP state level categorical results have been used to determine how rigorous a given state's end of year test is. In many states, the percentage of students achieving proficiency on the state test has been much higher than the equivalent performance of the state's students on the NAEP test. In such cases the state test is viewed as being too easy. Such disparities in the quality of state tests led to the pressure for national standards—which was the impetus for the common core standards and associated tests.[23]

The specific descriptive analysis about to be discussed was brought to me by one of my doctoral students. She was a Black woman who felt that schools had not been responsive to her educational needs in the early grades. She felt that this experience was a sign of systemic racism. She wanted to confirm whether what she experienced was a more systemic problem, and therefore wanted to know how widespread the problem of the underperformance of Black girls is nationally at the elementary and middle school years, and what the gaps are.

She found a great deal of research and discussion in the literature on gaps in overall Black student performance versus Whites, and in the overall performance of girls versus boys. But she was having trouble finding *primary source* research on the gaps between Black girls versus White girls. She was seeking more specific gap data that analyzed the two variables (race and sex) simultaneously, instead of the existing research that looked at each variable separately.

So we went to the NAEP website. The website provides lots of reports with descriptive gap and improvement analyses over the many years that NAEP has been administered. However, while these NAEP reports are comprehensive, these reports also broke out the variables of sex and race separately—not together. Fortunately, NAEP enables non-statisticians to easily specify the descriptive analysis they are looking for with whatever combination of variables they are interested in, and the system will produce the result. This capability is provided by NAEP's *Data Explorer*.

Determining the Black girls versus White girls reading gap

In order to make the gap analysis manageable, she asked *data explorer* to:

- Report on 8th grade reading scores in public schools across the U.S.;
- Compare the reading gap in the reading tests administered in 2011 and 2019 (to test whether the gap has been systemic, as per gap criterion #2 above); and
- Produce the results in terms of the scale scores as opposed to categorical scores.

In order to replicate the process she engaged in to obtain the needed analysis, go to the NAEP website. The easiest way to do that is to:

Google "nations report card" and click on the main heading (Nation's Report Card). Then…

---

[23] The two national tests used to measure mastery of common core skills are the Partnership for Assessment of Colleges and Courses (PARCC) and Smarter Balanced.

1. **Select** *Data Explorer* **(currently listed under the "Data Tools" menu).** This brings you to the Main Data Explorer.
2. **Select a Subject.** *Reading*
3. **Select a Grade.** *8*
4. **Select a jurisdiction.** *National public*

5. **Select** *Enter Main Data Explorer*

6. **Under SUBJECT-YEAR-GRADE-SCALE tab, choose** *2019* and *2011* **for year**, and *composite scale* **for scale**
7. **Under the VARIABLE tab, check** *Race/ethnicity using 2011 guidelines, school-reported* **(Uncheck** *ALL***)**
8. **Check** *Gender*
9. **Skip to the STATISTIC tab and choose** *Average Scale Score*
10 **Click on** *Create Crosstabs* (Currently listed under the VARIABLE tab)
11. **Click** *Race/Ethnicity***, and** *Gender*
12. **Enter a name of your choosing for the report**
13. **Click on** *Create*
14. **Click on** *Submit*
15. **Close the** *Crosstabs* **window**
16. **Click on** *Create Report*
17. **Click on** *Show Report Data*

The result is the following table.

Average scale scores for grade 8 reading, by gender, and race/ethnicity using 2011 guidelines, for 2019 and 2011

			Male	Female
Year	Jurisdiction	Race/ethnicity	Average scale score	Average scale score
2019	National public	White	266	277
		Black	238	250
		Hispanic	246	256
		Asian	277	290
		American Indian/Alaska Native	244	254
		Native Hawaiian/Other Pacific Islander	247	257
		Two or more races	259	273
2011	National public	White	267	277
		Black	242	253
		Hispanic	248	255
		Asian	272	282
		American Indian/Alaska Native	248	257

Native Hawaiian/Other Pacific Islander	245	258
Two or more races	260	273

This table clearly has more numbers than are needed. However, one of the most important quantitative skills for leaders is picking out the key numbers from complicated tables. Take a few moment to highlight or circle the four key numbers in the table for determining whether a Black Female-White Female gap exists, and whether it is systemic.

The four key numbers are:

277, 250, 277, 253

If you organize these four numbers, you get the following summary table:

Table 4.9
Eighth Grade NAEP Reading Scores of Girls in Public Schools by Race

	White Girls	Black Girls	Gap
2019	277	250	27
2011	277	253	24

Keeping in mind that a grade level of achievement that approximately 10 scale points equals one year of achievement, what are the answers to the two gap questions.

1. **Is the latest gap substantial?** (Yes)
2. **What is the historical trend—has the gap previously existed, and if so has it been decreasing over time?**
   (The gap has not only persisted over time but has even gotten slightly larger— therefore, it appears to be *systemic*.)

Indeed, determining that the gaps between *Means* in the above table is large is an example of reaching a decision by *eyeballing* a descriptive statistic. There was no need for any statistical tests to reach that decision. There will be more discussion of eyeballing data as a legitimate research technique in subsequent chapters.

But what is the *cause* of this large systemic gap? My student felt that the cause was systemic racism. Was it?

I suggested that before she could conclude that racism is THE cause of this gap, she should dive deeper into the data to rule out other possible confounding variables as a *cause* of this longstanding gap. (The previous chapter described a confounding variable as a hidden one that is actually the cause of something.)

Controlling for the Effects of a Confounding Variable

A key element in any type of data analysis is to look more deeply into a dataset and not settle for any initial finding. There may be some other underlying factor, or confounding variable, that is the hidden main reason for the initial finding. One should always search for alternative underlying effects and confounding variables. A key process for digging deeper into data is to ***control*** for how other variables may be affecting the result produced by the initial analysis. Controlling for the effects of other variables is the best way to avoid settling for a superficial and possibly misleading initial data analysis.

Remember

Indeed, the process of going deeper into an initial analysis by controlling for the possible effects of additional confounding variables is so important that it will be a key emphasis in all subsequent methodology chapters.

In this case study, the most likely candidate for a confounding variable among the variables provided by NAEP is "Eligible for the National Lunch Program" which is more often referred to as "Free and Reduced Lunch." In other words, an alternative hypothesis could be that Black girls do worse because they are more likely to come from low-income homes. In that case, poverty, not race would be the more likely cause of the systemic gap.

Fortunately, my student could test whether this alternative explanation was true by controlling for the effects of poverty in the relationship between race and reading achievement by analyzing the three variables of race, sex, and poverty simultaneously.

A simple way to control for the effects of a possible confounding variable

The easiest way to control for the possible effects of a confounding variable is to limit the analysis of the main/initial variables to only those students who experience the potentially confounding effect—in this case, poverty. This can be done by asking the following research question?

Is there a reading achievement gap between White girls and Black girls who live in poverty?

Asking this question and thereby limiting the analysis *only* to girls who exist in poverty is a way to ***control*** for the effects of the possible confounding effect of different degrees of poverty.

The NAEP variable of eligibility for the national lunch program is a way to distinguish those who live in some degree of poverty versus those who do not. So we can control for the effects of this third variable of poverty by comparing the performance of the most relevant, single value of the third variable—in this case by comparing the scores *only* for those Black girls and White girls who are eligible for the national lunch program—i.e., those who receive free and reduced lunch. In other words, we are ignoring those girls who do NOT receive free and reduced lunch because that subgroup is not relevant to the question being examined.

If the reading gap between Black and White girls who receive free and reduced lunch remains as bad as the more general gap documented in the previous table, then we can be pretty confident that the systemic gap is NOT resulting from different degrees of poverty—and would provide support for my student's theory that the reading gap is being caused by systemic racism.

Fortunately, NAEP's data explorer allows one to expand beyond the previous two variable analysis and combine a third variable. So my student…

- Modified the original gap analysis report request by adding in the variable of *eligibility for free and reduced lunch program*;
- Analyzed the resultant report that combined these three variables; and
- Found the cells in the resultant table that showed the results for the Black girls and White girls that were eligible for the national lunch program.

Do you think that there was still a systemic gap after controlling for the possible confounding effects of different degrees of poverty?

(HINT: The answer is "yes.")

You are encouraged to conduct the analysis of controlling for the effects of poverty on your own and reach your own conclusion as to whether the results still indicate a systemic gap among only girls who are eligible for the national lunch program. Challenge Question #1 at the end of this chapter provides tips to help you conduct this analysis. Does your analysis support the theory that this achievement gap is a result of systemic racism?

Five caveats to the above gap analysis:

1. **Black girls are as academically and intellectually capable as White girls— or any other category of students—when provided with appropriate learning environments.**[24]

2. The problem of inequities in education outcomes is not limited to Black girls. You would also find systemic gaps for males and for other ethnic groups, as well as for special education students;

---

[24] This conclusion is based on my 26 years of working with the HOTS program which included a significant number of Black girls. (For a summary of this research see Pogrow (2004; 2005))

3. There are other relevant variables that you might want to control for such as the alternative NAEP measure of *socio economic status* such as "parental education level;"

4. The values in the above tables are *Means*. You would find that the standard deviations are relatively small so the Means are the appropriate representative measure for the gaps; and

5. The fact that such large gaps persist despite decades of education reform and the use of supposedly evidence-based practices calls into question the validity of much of research evidence that the reforms and practices are based on—and the methods used to produce that evidence.

(The latter is the impetus for the recommended alternative ways of analyzing evidence in the next several chapters.)

Remember

The important lesson is that when analyzing data one always needs to think of alternative possibilities and explanations for the initial conclusion that is reached. Dig deeper! Conducting a more in-depth analysis often involves bringing an additional variable into the analysis, and then controlling for the effects of the additional variable.

In this case race was more important than economic status in generating the systemic reading gap. (See Challenge Question #1.) However, if the gap had disappeared for all girls who received free and reduced lunch, that would indicate that poverty was more important than race.

This method of controlling for the effects of a possible confounding variable has the advantages of:

1. **Being intuitive;**
2. **Not requiring sophisticated knowledge of math or statistics**—only how the use of the power trio; and
3. **Enabling the quick testing of a variety of possibilities and scenarios.**

While three is really the maximum number of variables that one can simultaneously look at, digest, and make sense of using this method, this simple method can be used to control for the most obvious possible confounding variable. In addition, other possible confounding variables can be controlled for separately.

If the situation were to arise where you need to analyze more than three variables at a time or you are not sure what the key *confounding* variables might be and want to test a large number of possible combinations, the next chapter discusses the statistical tool of *regression analysis*. Regression analysis is a more mathematically sophisticated way to control for the effects of several possible confounding variables simultaneously.

Key Tip

In most cases I have found the simpler method described above for controlling for the effects of a possible confounding variable to be the most useful—as compared to the more sophisticated methods in the next two chapters.

Exploring NAEP to answer questions of practice

Remember

The most important research skills that leaders need are the ability to (a) ask the right questions about the state of practice in their schools, (b) identify the specific types of data needed to answer this and other questions, and (c) explore the results and their implications for making decisions about how to best improve practice.

Exploring NAEP data is a way to develop the skills of trying to pose questions, identify the needed variables, gather the needed data, and then apply the power trio to make judgments about trends in school performance and equity.

While creating the first report in NAEP involves a lot of steps, once you have created your first result you can then shorten the process of creating new reports of your own choosing by selecting...

- **Edit criteria**
- **Create New Report**

Selecting "edit criteria" lets you quickly change any of the factors immediately and see the effect on the outcome. Either way you can then quickly change some or all of the entries and quickly create your next report. So for example, if you wanted to see what the gap would be between Black and White girls based on categorical scores, keep everything the same as the example just discussed, but change the **STATISTIC** option to:

...Achievement levels discrete...

The results in 2019 would indicate that:

- 41% of White girls were rated as proficient (at grade level) while only 17% of Black girls were
- Only 14% of White girls were rated as below basic while 40% of Black girls were

This is a different view of the gap which in some ways is even more dramatic and intuitive than examining the raw scale scores.

Hopefully you will want to test other outcomes and comparisons at different grades, different subjects, ethnicities, or gaps between public and private schools, or determine the extent of the gaps between those with and without identified disabilities and whether they are narrowing over time, etc. Data explorer is a very flexible tool and is a great way to get used to interpreting and creating sub-tables and charts/graphs.

In addition, you are encouraged to explore many of the other sources of primary data listed in Appendix B, such as census data. Census data are a great way to learn about the characteristics of the community your schools reside in.

While these other sources may not have analysis tools built in such as *data explorer*, you can copy the key results that interested you into Excel and easily apply the *power trio* to them, and create histograms and other types of charts/graphs (see below).

While you will quickly develop the skills to conduct descriptive analyses with primary source data, you will discover that there are many analyses that you can conduct. Therefore, it becomes important to prioritize which analyses are the most important.

Conducting Improvement Analysis

The law of actual end result

The degree of improvement is most often communicated as a percentage increase or as a percentage rate of increase. The use of percentages has the advantage of being easy to communicate and understand. However, it can be extremely misleading. Suppose for example you see a report that a district used a new instructional technique and increased its graduation rate 50% over the past 3 years. That sounds impressive. And it may be. However, in order to truly understand whether this, or any, gain is impressive, you need to know what the actual end result is. Hereafter, this principle is referred to as the *law of actual end result.*

Principle #6—The *law of actual end result* states that:

The only way to understand whether a published research finding generated in other schools is authentic—i.e., likely to improve your schools—is to know what the *Mean*, *Median*, and *Standard Deviation* of the actual end result was for the research subjects (only) was **at the end of the study**—as opposed to a relative change over time for the research subjects, or a relative difference between groups or things.

In other words, you first have to know how the research subjects (only) actually did on their own **at the end of the experiment**.

For example, suppose the graduation rate in a study was originally 2% of students graduating. A 50% increase would mean that 3 years later only 3% of the students were graduating. This is a terrible actual end result—one that does not bode well for a leader who decides to adopt this practice for his/her schools. However, if the graduation rate was previously 50% and it then increased 50%, the new graduation rate at the end of the experiment—i.e., the actual end result—would be a graduation rate of 75%. That would indeed be a substantial improvement and we could reasonably conclude that the practice was successful and worthy of adoption (assuming that your existing graduation rate was substantially lower than 75% at the time).

In other words, while a published finding which showed a relative improvement of 50% sounds impressive, you cannot judge whether the intervention was successful until you know the actual final percentage of the students who ended up graduating—i.e., the *actual end result.*

In other words, the report of relative progress (pre vs. post result) was NOT the actual end result. The degree of progress was a *relative* comparison. How the students who were the subjects of the experiment actually performed **at the end** of the three years is the *actual end result.*

Key Tip

Leaders should apply the *law of actual end result* to any research finding, regardless of whether it is published in a prestigious journal, a claim made at a conference, or by a salesperson. This law is a leader's best friend to avoid adopting a practice that on the surface appeared to be successful and evidence-based—but in reality was actually a failed practice—as evidenced by the actual end result. If you cannot find in the research how the students or schools actually ended up performing, *then you can assume that they probably did not do all that well.*

Unfortunately, published research often relies on presenting only the relative comparisons. Here are some examples:

Relative Statement	Critical Analysis	Needed Actual End Result Info
School A adopted a new reading program and performed significantly better than School B that did not.	*How well did school A actually end up performing?*	**Did school A end up doing well? Did it out-perform your schools?**
After adjusting for initial differences in reading levels, School A, using the new TBA reading program, performed significantly better than School B.	*How well did school A actually end up performing without the initial adjustment?**	**(same as above)**
There is a significant positive relationship between students' grit and their academic performance.	*How strong was the relationship (r = ___)?*	**How often did knowing students' grit level predict their academic performance (r x r = ___)?**

- Adjusted scores are not *actual* scores

While the *law of actual end result* seems obvious, you will discover in subsequent chapters that researchers, professional associations, and salespersons often do not report the *actual* end result and prefer to report *relative* results. *Indeed, it will be seen in the next two chapters, that the more mathematically sophisticated the analysis and scientifically rigorous the methodology, the less likely it is that the research reports actual end results.*

In addition, the law of actual end results is very robust for leaders as it applies to any statistical analysis discussed in this textbook (or any other)—regardless of how mathematically sophisticated the methodology is.

It is critical that you bypass all the sophisticated mathematical description of research results and ask the simple question: *But how did the students actually end up performing using a familiar metric?*

It is easy to apply the *law of actual end result.*

Caveat: This is NOT an argument against leaders or researchers reporting *percentage increases* as a metric for *their* schools' performance. Indeed, the easiest way for a leader to communicate the degree of improvement to a community is to report a percentage increase in some desired outcome. However, such a statistic should always be accompanied by the actual end result.

Consider the time span

A final issue in improvement analysis is to determine the time span you want to analyze. In the above gap example the decision to use the time span 2011 to 2019 was arbitrary. It might be that a different time span might make the gaps appear to be larger or smaller. There is no best rule for what time span to analyze.

Generally, leaders will use whatever time span that makes the degree of improvement appear to be the largest. An extreme example of the time span making a complete difference in perception of success occurred when I was at the national conference of the largest urban school districts. The award for the urban superintendent of the year went to an individual who in his second year had produced substantial gains on test scores. I then looked up the district's data and noticed that the prior year, the superintendent's first, the scores had gone down an equal amount. So the reality was that there had been no growth during the superintendent's tenure. However, restricting the time span made it seem like a major success had occurred.

Practical Tip

Timing is important. The best advice is to move into a new leadership position the year *after* a new district or state test is initiated. Test scores almost always go down the year after a new test is initiated partly because of unfamiliarity with how to best prepare for it. However, after the initial experience the test scores usually go up the next year. So if you are hired the second year after a new test you will get off to a good start and be considered to be a successful turnaround leader.

A wonderful source of data of improvement trends for education across the US is a special component of NAEP—the Long Term Trend Assessment. This assessment has followed the performance of 9-, 13-, and 17-year old students since 1971 (reading) and 1978 (math) to 2012.[25] You can also apply data explorer to this dataset. To do so…

    1. Go to *Nations Report Card*
    2. Click on Data Tools and Choose *Data Explorer*
    3. Click on *Enter Long Term Trends*
    4. Choose the *subject, age, years, variables* of your interest

This historical dataset reveals the extent to which the waves of reform have actually produced improvements in outcomes—or not. One interesting finding is that achievement gaps shrank dramatically in the 70's and most of the 80's, but started to rewiden after 1988. The reason for this rewidening is a matter of debate among scholars.

The time span of analysis also plays a role in assessing student progress, especially subgroups that are lagging. Schools typically evaluate progress from the fall through the spring. However, that is not sufficient. Research with Title I students showed that they made progress every school year—yet fell further and further behind. This was partly due to summer loss, and the higher requirements of the test in the following year. The best way to get a better sense of whether they are progressing relative to grade level expectations is to conduct a spring to spring evaluation.[26]

---

[25] The difference between the NAEP Long Term Trend (LTT) dataset and the regular NAEP dataset is that the LTT tests and variables have remained unchanged over time whereas the regular NAEP has made adjustments over time. Unfortunately, not all LTT variables have been tracked since the beginning. For example, English as a second language has only been tabulated since 2004. While LTT is a tremendous historical resource, unfortunately it was last administered in 2012.

However, a newer different dataset for longitudinal analysis, the Stanford Education Data Archive (SEDA) produces trend analyses of reading language arts and math in grades 3-8 starting in the 2008-09 school year. Unlike NAEP which used the same national test over time, and reports results in grade equivalents for schools, districts, counties, and states, SEDA equates the results from the different state tests. See the description of SEDA in Appendix B.

[26] You can also use a Fall to Fall testing schedule but that captures more the effect of summer loss than the contribution that schooling made to students' progress.

Communicating the Results of Descriptive Analysis

Once an analysis has been completed, how should a leader communicate the results to a school board, the community at large, or to the press? Presenting a large array of numbers is usually not the best way to create an understanding of the key findings and garner support for resultant decisions based on the data. Two key methods to communicate quantitative findings are to create **summary tables**, and develop **charts and graphs**.

Creating summary tables

In the above example about the NAEP reading gap, the original table generated by data explorer with all the data would just have confused the audience. Instead, using a summary table is a great way to focus the viewer's attention on the key pieces of data. An example of a summary table is Table 4.9 that presented just the most relevant gap results.

Key elements of an effective summary table are brevity and focus. The title of the table and the headings of the rows and columns are critical for helping the reader quickly understand the meaning and importance of the table. Good titles, such as the title in Table 4.9 above, have the following characteristics:

1. **The title is very specific**, indicating that the scores are on the NAEP test and includes only public schools; and
2. **The title uses the term "by"—e.g., by race—to indicate the variable by which the data are being broken down/categorized in the table.**

Try to keep this title format in all the tables you create.

Developing charts and graphs

As previously demonstrated, tables are a great way to reduce a volume of numbers into a simple and easy-to-understand display of relevant data. However, to the extent that a picture is worth a thousand words, charts/graphs are a way to pictorially present the results of descriptive analyses that makes it easy to visualize the results. The use of charts/graphs is one of the best ways for leaders to communicate school performance to the public, particularly improvement data. (The histograms displayed earlier are examples of charts.)

Among the many different types of charts, the ones most widely used by leaders are:

1. **Pie chart** for visually indicating the part that each type of object or individual comprises of the whole/total. A pie chart might be used to visually indicate what the percentage of (a) teachers are by race, (b) revenue are by source, or (c) expenditures in each category, etc.

2. **Line chart/graph**, for showing continuous changes in a variable over time. It is typically used to show improvement visually over an extended period of time and at different points in time. Several variables or lines can be displayed in the same graph. For example, if you wanted to track monthly attendance over the course of a school year you would use a line chart/graph. In addition, you could display the monthly attendance of subgroups, such as special needs students, on the same line chart/graph by using different colored lines or dotted lines.

    The line chart/graph below shows a comparison of COVID-19 cases in the US and European Union.

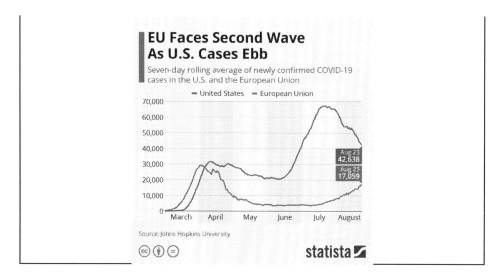

3. **Bar chart**, for illustrating a comparison at a given point in time, or change over a few points in time.

    For example, the figure below uses a horizontal bar chart to show how the target district, the lighter grey bar, compares to similar ones in terms of the percentage of students who met state standards in science. (The vertical line is the median result for all districts in the state.) The chart clearly shows that the target district is doing relatively well in grade 5 compared to other similar districts, but not as well in grade 8. This helps a district prioritize its improvement effort.

A Comparison of the Performance of Similar School Districts on the State Science Tests in Grades 5 and 8.

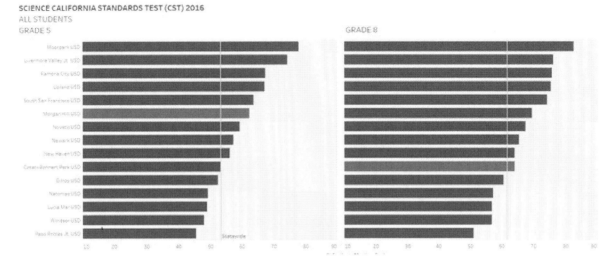

Where do your students stand on state test outcomes in science?

SCIENCE CALIFORNIA STANDARDS TEST (CST) 2016
ALL STUDENTS

Source: **School Wise Press**, Inc., a consulting company specializing in helping districts assess its performance and progress relative to other districts that have similar demographics.

While this bar chart of science results in different districts is horizontal which is easy to read, bar charts can also be vertical as is often the case for Histograms. When using a vertical bar chart to show values over time, the horizontal labels on the bottom of the graph denote the time period/dates, and the labels on the vertical left hand side of the graph denote the quantity being measured.

The bar chart is also good for displaying the values for the various categories of a variable at a point in time or over a few periods of time. For example, the bar chart could be used to display the number of teachers, administrators, and paraprofessionals in a district in each of three years.

Using Excel

Excel can easily convert data into a wide series of charts. To access the charts click on the **INSERT** menu, and then select **Chart**. A list of the available chart types will then appear. Highlight the data you want to be charted, and then select the type of chart you want.

Remember

A picture is worth a thousand words. Charts and graphs are basically a way to conve data into pictures.

If you are interested in learning more about the many different types of charts/graphs, and how to use them to better communicate the story behind the numbers and analyses in ways that are intuitive to your community, two recommended books are:

- *Storytelling with Data* by Cole Knaflic

- *Data Visualization & Presentation With Microsoft* Office by Valerie Sue & Matthew Griffin

Summary of Key Ideas and Evidentiary Needs of Leaders

Summary of key ideas

This chapter discussed:

- **The Power Trio fundamental statistics of *Mean, Median,* and *Standard Deviation,*** and the key idea that when the Standard Deviation is large relative to the Mean, the Median is probably the most representative value for the set of numbers in the dataset;

- **The importance of generating histograms to get a sense of the nature of the distribution of scores, and the characteristics of a normal distribution;**

- **The Law of Actual End Result**—Leaders should always seek to determine what the actual end result was from the use of a practice and not settle for relative outcomes such as a comparison to some other outcome or degree of progress;

- **How to tell if a gap is systemic**—i.e., it is large and has not narrowed over time;

- **How to conduct basic gap and improvement analyses;**

- **The uses of primary datasets and the importance of primary data;**

- **How to determine causation**—to conclude that A caused B you have to show that all possible alternative factors (confounding variables) that could have affected B did not have any effect;

- **The importance of controlling for the effects of possible confounding variables;**

- **How to control for the effects of a third variable on an outcome** by limiting the search only to individuals with the desired characteristic on the third variable; and

- **BIG benefits in research evidence is a key determinant as to whether adopting that practice will likely improve your schools and increase equity.**

A key focus of the next two chapters is to provide specific guidelines as to how leaders and leadership students can determine whether the findings of quantitative research and claims of effectiveness have in fact documented BIG benefits.

The evidentiary needs of leaders versus researchers

The introduction to this textbook noted that there is a limited overlap between the types of quantitative information that leaders need and how researchers and statisticians use statistics. Based on the ideas presented in this and the previous chapters, the key area of overlap so far are:

- The importance of statistical tests
- Applying the power trio of statistics

However, the next several chapters will show that the data needs of leaders and the evidence provided by researchers begin to diverge sharply.

As a result, the remainder of this text will focus on the application of these overlapping concepts and on leaders' divergent evidentiary needs. As the next several chapters discuss other forms of research, additional overlapping and divergent elements will be added to this graphic. For example, it will be shown how leaders' need for evidence that documents BIG benefits is a divergence.

Updated Principles of Data Analysis

This section lists the principles of data analysis discussed to this point. The shaded ones are those added in this chapter.

CAVEAT: These principles apply equally to analyzing published studies and evaluation studies conducted by schools/districts.

Principle #1—Always seek replication/confirmation of a research finding.

Principle #2—The greatest threats to the validity of quantitative evidence are (a) researcher bias, (b) statistical error, and (c) confounding variables.

> ***Sub-principle 2.1***—The more involved a single individual or organization is in all the different steps in a research study, the greater the degree of bias there is, and the less trustworthy the findings are.

> ***Sub-principle 2.2***—The more statistical procedures that are conducted in a study, the less trustworthy any one finding is, and the greater the statistical error.

> This is why all the adjustments that are made in experimental research analysis (see Chapter 6) are problematic—particularly if there is a small difference between the groups.

> **Sub-principle 2.3**—To determine *causation* it is important to eliminate the possible effects of (all) possible confounding variables.

Principle #3—The most convincing evidence that a practice is likely to improve your schools is research that demonstrated BIG benefits from the use of a practice.

> **Principle 3.1**—Leaders should generally ignore evidence of effectiveness if the research only demonstrated a small benefit from the use of a practice—and should usually avoid implementing the practice analyzed in the research.

Principle #4— The BIGness of the benefit found in experimental research is NOT determined by analyzing the results from the *statistics*—e.g., t-test, F-test, etc. Rather, the benefit is found by analyzing the *statistical tests* used to determine the importance of those results—e.g., p value and effect size.

Determining the desired level of BIGness for relationship research is described in Chapters 5 and 7, and for experimental research in Chapters 6 and 7.

Principle #5—Always first examine the Mean, Standard Deviation, and (if needed) the Median of any distribution. These three statistics are fundamental and the *Power Trio* of statistics.

> **5.1—Rule of Mean-Median Differences:** When the *Mean* and *Median* are very different, trust the *Median*, or at the very least explore the nature of the distribution of individual numbers using a histogram.

Principle #6—The *law of actual end result for the research subjects.* The only way to understand the authenticity of a research outcome for improving your schools is to know what the actual end result was for the research subjects (only) *at the end of the study*—as opposed to a relative change over time for the research subjects, or a relative difference between groups or things.

In other words, you first have to know how the experimental subjects actually did on their own at the end of the experiment.

Challenge Questions

1. **Determine whether there is a gap between White and Black girls who are eligible for the national school lunch program, and is this gap systemic, and does poverty or race appear to be the key factor in this gap.**

   a. Is there a gap between White and Black Girls controlling for whether they are eligible for the national lunch program (free and reduced lunch)? More specifically, is there a gap between Black girls and White girls who receive free and reduced lunch?

      HINT: To use data explorer to answer this question, and conduct the analysis with the additional (control) variable of eligibility for the national lunch program, repeat the same process used in the example in the chapter with the following changes to steps 8-11:

      8. **Click on** *Gender* **and choose** *National school lunch program eligibility*
      9. **Skip to the STATISTIC tab and choose** *Average Scale Score*
      10. **Click on** *Create Crosstabs*
      11. **Click** *Race/Ethnicity*, *National school lunch eligibility*, **and** *Gender*

      This will produce a table with 3 variables. Limit your analyses to the values associated with the category of "Eligible" for the school lunch program, as a way to control for the variable of poverty —i.e., you will just be considering students living in poverty.

      Find the key numbers in the table, and create a summary table of the gaps between Black and White girls for the two years being considered.

   b. Is there still a gap between Black and White girls when controlling for the effects of poverty, and does it appear to be substantial and systemic—and why?

   c. Comparing this table with the one in the chapter, does the gap appear to be primarily because of race or poverty—and why?

2. **Find a question that you are curious about exploring within data explorer that involves either determining whether there is an improvement trend or a systemic gap in some subject area and grade level. Write out your question, conduct the analysis/highlight the key data, and present your conclusion based on the data.**

3. **Use another one of the sources of primary data in Appendix B to explore some other dataset of interest to you.** (One option that is popular with my students is to access census data to determine racial and economic makeup of their communities, and the changes over time.)

4. **Consider the following post from a research group's blog about Denver Public Schools, which has been receiving a great deal of national press for its reform effort. Is the evidence presented about the success of schools a relative or absolute measure? Do you find the evidence presented convince you that Denver has made major progress and that it is a district that leaders should visit for ideas to bring back to their school(s)?**

Evidence Matters: Proving Whether School Reforms Make a Difference for Kids

WEDNESDAY, OCTOBER 9, 2013

When people lament that innovation is not possible in "regular" districts—ones that are overseen by elected school boards and working with active teachers unions—we at CRPE often point to Denver Public Schools. We're not alone in noticing Denver—cities around the country have heard about its energy, new ideas, and solid implementation. Last year alone, more than a dozen city teams visited Denver to try to bring some of its ideas back to their own communities.

Denver has produced results. During Boasberg's tenure, … over four years, 68 percent of new charter schools and 61 percent of new innovation schools exceeded the district median in student growth…

5. You find out in a publication that a school put in a new counseling program and as a result graduation rates increased 60% (or the odds of graduating were increased by almost two-thirds). Assuming that the cost is not an issue and that there are no moral objections—should you adopt the program?

6. If only 12 of the students in your high school's 300 entering freshman class were graduating in four years, what would be your minimum improvement goal for adopting a new intervention or set of interventions to increase the graduation rate over the next two years?

Answers to the Challenge Questions

1. The new table produced by data explorer is more involved, but extracting the key numbers will lead to the following table:

   a. Eighth Grade NAEP Reading Scores of Girls in Public Schools Eligible for the National School Lunch Program by Race

	White Girls	Black Girls	Gap
2019	264	245	19
2011	265	250	15

   b. There is still a substantial gap. The gap also appears to be systemic since the gap has increased over this span of time.

   c. Based on comparing the results in this table and the earlier summary table 4.9, controlling for the effect of poverty did reduce the gap somewhat, but that reduction was largely because White girls who were eligible for free and reduced lunch did worse than those who weren't. However, Black girls did pretty much the same as in the other table (i.e., it did not matter whether or not they came from poverty).

   As a result, the conclusion is that:

   > The reading achievement gap between Black and White girls remained large and systemic even after controlling for the effects of poverty. This finding *supports* the theory that this gap results from systemic racism.

   (The word "supports" is used since—given the discussions in (a) Chapter 1 about the nature of science, and (b) this chapter about causation—we cannot definitively conclude scientifically that this evidence *proves* that systemic racism has *caused* the gap.

   For example, the variable of "eligibility for the national lunch program" is a very imprecise measure of poverty as it includes a range from those who are desperately poor with many other risk factors to those close to the poverty line. A more precise measure of the degree of poverty is not available in this dataset. Therefore, differences in the degree of poverty could be another confounding variable.

   At the same time, it would be disingenuous based on this evidence to deny that race and racism plays a role in this gap.)

2. and 3. Have fun exploring data and datasets.

4. This is a report of <u>relative</u> growth. The article never tells you what the actual growth rate was and what the absolute level of performance of the charter or innovation schools were, or what the

achievement gaps were between the high poverty charter and innovation schools versus the regular schools, or even why the *Median* growth was used as opposed to the *Mean* growth rates.

By the way, leaders typically report relative improvements to their community. There is nothing wrong with that. What is being criticized is when a school or district claims that it is being unusually successful for the purposes of gaining national attention and convincing other leaders to see how it is being successful. Under such a scenario, an outside leader would be foolish to consider the district as being successful based strictly on such evidence and would be well advised to NOT visit that district.

5. It depends. The data provided is only about relative growth. If originally there were only 10 students graduating, another 60% would only lead to 16 graduating. Is that an acceptable actual end result? Probably not. However, if for example, 120 out of 250 were graduating, a 60% increase would end up with another 72 students graduating, or 192. That seems like a noticeable improvement and a desirable end result.

6. There is no best answer.

Chapter 5

Applying Relationship Research Evidence

🔔 Key Takeaways 🔔

Relationship research is the first of two types of *inferential* research. (The other type, *experimental* research, will be discussed in the next chapter). The primary goal of inferential research is to reach a conclusion whose findings apply to the world at large—i.e., apply beyond the specific individuals or organization that were the subjects in the research.

When leaders adopt a practice in their schools that research has shown to be effective, they are *inferring* that their schools will see the same benefit. Will they? That depends to a large extent on the key characteristics of the research including:

- The nature of the sample used in the research including its size, and how similar the context of the schools in the research is to their schools; and
- How BIG the benefit was that was shown in the research.

The goal of relationship research is to determine how the variation in one variable is related to changes in one or more variables. Establishing a strong relationship enables leaders to better predict how a change in one variable is likely to result in a change in another. So, for example, if research finds that a healthy lunch program is related to an increase in students' mental health, that predicts that other schools that implement such a lunch program will see an increase in their students' mental health. The next question is how well does the relationship predict mental health increases. For example, if the relationship accurately predicts an increase in only 2% of students the costs may not be justified. On the other hand, if it accurately predicts an increase in 25% of students it might well be justified.

At the same time, relationship research does NOT determine whether the changes in one variable *caused* the change in the other. The relationship could just have been happenstance in a particular situation and was caused by some other hidden confounding variable that does not exist in your situation. (Causation can *only* be established by experimental research.) As a result, relationship research can provide useful clues as to what might be a successful improvement strategy—but not causal or conclusive evidence.

The focus of this chapter is to understand:

- The different types of relationship research;
- How to interpret the results of relationship research from a leadership decision-making perspective—i.e., how much predictability has been established; and
- The conditions under which relationship research can be used to inform leadership decision-making.

Introduction to Inferential Research

Inferential research means that the research is conducted with a sample, and the results are intended to generalize to the larger population of individuals or organizations that are similar to those in the study. So if research is published that shows a particular method to be effective, or that a relationship exists, the inference is that the findings will also apply to your schools, students, or staff.

An evaluation you conduct in your own schools may or may not be inferential. If the research is conducted directly in the schools where the results will be applied it is an evaluation—but not inferential research. At the same time, if you conduct an evaluation about the effects of a program in one school and then based on the results you decide to expand it to others based on the findings, that is inferential research.

Most inferential quantitative research examines either (a) relationships between variables, or (b) comparisons of how one or more experimental groups that have received one or more novel approaches do in relation to a comparison/control group that usually receives a conventional approach. The first type of inferential research is **Relationship Research**, which is discussed in this chapter, and the second type is **Experimental Research**, discussed in the next chapter.

Most published quantitative research, particularly in top journals, is inferential research. In addition, the vast majority of evidence supporting *evidence-based* or *best* practices is from inferential research.

Inferential research is much more sophisticated methodologically and mathematically than the descriptive analysis methods discussed in the previous chapter. However, a high degree of mathematical sophistication does NOT guarantee that the evidence of an effective practice is trustworthy or likely to improve your schools. Given that scientists are trained to be skeptical about research claims, particularly ones whose findings have not been replicated, the same should be true for educational leaders. This is particularly important given the evidence for the lack of replicability of a majority of evidentiary claims as discussed in Chapter 3. So it is essential for leaders to critically assess evidence around the effectiveness of a practice they are interested in considering.

But how can leaders critically analyze evidence based on sophisticated mathematics? While it is impossible for the non-mathematician/statistician to learn the intricate details of inferential research, there are a series of non-technical clues that the typical leader and leadership student can use to independently critically assess the evidence provided by such research to determine whether a given practice with evidence of effectiveness is likely to improve their schools and increase equity—or even whether there was in fact actual evidence of its effectiveness in the first place *regardless of what the researchers claim in summary and conclusion sections of published research.*

While leaders should indeed seek to adopt evidence-based practices, it is equally important for them to NOT adopt a practice based on evidence that is not authentic—regardless of how intense the pressure is from government or from peers. Every time schools around the country adopt a practice that has been designated as being evidence-based, or as best practice, that does not replicate into subsequent, noticeable improvements in practice, the result is years of wasted improvement opportunity and money—and the schools failing a generation of needy students.

A classic example of such damage has been the widespread adoption of the 'Success for All' reading reform program over several decades because the research community believed that it had strong evidence of effectiveness. However, my research in 2000-2002 (Pogrow, 2002) documented widespread failure, and almost two decades later Boulay et al. (2018) similarly found that it was not improving schools. A review of the extensive evidence supporting the program would reveal that none of it was authentic. Those thousands of schools that adopted the program in the interim likely were disappointed.

This means that if leaders are going to use research evidence they need to conduct an independent analysis of the authenticity of the evidence—regardless of how much an intervention's effectiveness is hyped by the research and professional communities. Such a critical analysis should consist of:

- **Examining the original evidence itself using the clues that will be provided**;
- **Scouring the literature to find contrarian evidence** (which existed in the case of the Success for All program); and
- **Evidence of successful replication** of the research by independent researchers.

As a result, this chapter and the next one will focus on setting forth a series of practical guidelines that leaders can apply to examine the evidence and differentiate the conditions under which inferential research findings that a practice is effective are likely to in fact improve their schools and increase equity. These clues will be emphasized instead of the sophisticated statistical details of inferential research methodology. Indeed, it will be shown that the more sophisticated the methods, the less likely it is that the results are authentic.

Introduction to Relationship Research

There are two general types of relationship research evidence.

- **Correlation** to show the extent of a relationship between two variables, including *partial correlation* which examines the correlation between two variables **controlling** for the effects of a third variable; and
- *Multiple correlation* or *regression analysis* for determining (a) which variable in a set of variables best predicts an outcome, and/or (b) the extent to which the combination of a group of variables is able to predict an outcome.

Correlation Research

Bracey (2006) explains that a correlation is the answer to the question: "*As one variable changes, how does a second variable change*" (p. 76). Expressed from a leadership perspective, the question becomes: "How well does knowing one or more variables enable me to *predict* the value of another variable that I am interested in?" For example, how well does knowing how much home construction is going on in my district enable me to predict changes in enrollment in my school(s).

Measuring the size of the relationship between two variables

There are two ways to determine the size of the relationship between two variables. The first is to use a statistic for determining the correlation between two variables such as the Pearson correlation or Spearman correlation listed in Appendix B. The statistic produces a number that indicates the size of the relationship, together with a sign that indicates the direction of the relationship. Correlations are usually designated with the letter "r."

Correlations between two variables can be positive or negative and have an *r* value between +1 and -1. A positive correlation means that both variables move in the same direction so that as one variable increases the other also increases, or as one decreases the other also decreases. In other words, if both variables decrease, that is still a positive correlation. A negative correlation means that the variables move in opposite direction— i.e., as one variable increases the other decreases.

For example, the correlation between temperature and the sale of winter clothes is negative, because as one variable goes down (i.e., temperature), the other goes up (i.e., sale of winter clothes). On the other hand, the correlation between parents' income and their children's GPA is positive because as one goes up the other also goes up, and as one goes down the other also goes down. So the sign of the correlation only indicates the nature of the relationship, while the number by itself (regardless of the sign) indicates how large or strong the relationship is.

Remember

While in regular math -.45 is smaller than +.2, in this context where the minus sign only indicates a direction, a correlation of -.45 indicates a much stronger relationship than a correlation of +.2— because the number by itself is larger.

Correlations (r) are valuable to leadership decision-making because of their ability to predict the value of one variable knowing the value of another. For example, it would be very useful to identify a variable that could predict in the first grade which students will end up very behind by the third grade, in order to provide those students with more intensive early interventions. As a result, the following discussions focus on using correlations to make predictions.

Prediction is a fundamental leadership decision-making process. There are many things that school leaders and researchers would like to be able to predict with increasing accuracy. The closer the value of r is to +/- 1, the stronger the relationship is and the more useful the resultant predictions are to leaders. Leaders would like to be able to predict next year's enrollment, the likely performance of students on next year's end-of-year test, what effect the adoption of new interventions will have on their school(s), etc. In addition, whenever leaders select an intervention to use in their school(s) they are predicting that its use will improve some critical outcome. Researchers would like to develop better ways to predict the effectiveness of teachers, students' response to interventions, etc.

A correlation of +1 indicates a perfect relationship such that knowing the value of the first variable we can accurately predict what the second one will be 100% of the time. In this example, if we could identify the right variable and there was correlation of + or − 1 with third grade reading scores, we could accurately predict beforehand which students would be severely falling behind in the later grades.

A correlation of zero means that knowing the value of the first variable will *never* accurately predict the value of the second.

In reality, human nature is extremely variable and complex and, therefore, correlations are almost never 0 or +/-1. Correlations are generally somewhere in between—i.e., a decimal such as .32 or -.29. An r that is a decimal indicates that knowing one variable you can only predict the value of the second variable some of the time. The size of the decimal (number part only) indicates how often you can accurately predict. A key question that will be discussed later on is:

> *How much predictability is desirable for leaders as an incentive to apply correlation evidence—or stated mathematically, how large a decimal is desired for it to have a level of predictability that would be useful for leaders?*

In big data analysis research usually explores all the possible relationships in a large number of variables in order to see which ones have a strong relationship. The results are typically displayed in a *correlation matrix*. Consider the following example of a correlation matrix in the table below which explores the relationship between school characteristics and how principals spend their time. The numbers in the table are the correlations. So, for example, the correlation between the % of FRPL (free and reduced price lunch) students and the time principals spent developing the educational program time is .204. Note that the correlation is positive. This means that the greater the percentage of students living in poverty in a school, the more time principals spent developing the educational program. At the same time, the correlation between prior math achievement and the time principals spent on developing the educational program is negative (-.183). How would you interpret that relationship, and does it make sense? (Answer is in this footnote.[27])

---

[27] Since a negative correlation means that the values go in opposite directions, this correlation indicates either (a) the higher the prior math scores the less time principals spend developing the educational program, or (b) the

Such a matrix provides a quick way to explore what relationships may exist among a series of variables, and thereby provide guidance on which relationships to focus further and deeper analysis on.[28]

Table 5.1*
Descriptive School Characteristics and Correlations Between Characteristics and Principals' Instructional Time Use, Overall and in Several Specific Categories

School Characteristic	Sample Statistics		Spearman Correlations					
	Mean	Standard Deviation	Total Instructional Time Use	Coaching Teachers	Developing the Educational Program	Evaluating Teachers	Classroom Walkthroughs	Required or Nonrequired Teacher PD
School enrollment	716	447	−.273**	.115	−.145	.071	−.258**	−.038
% FRPL	69.7	21.8	.270**	−.107	.204*	.121	.213*	.141
% Black	33.8	33.7	.173†	.047	−.008	.093	.120	.153†
% Hispanic	54.8	30.4	−.148†	−.084	.076	−.101	−.098	−.110
% High school	37.1	48.4	−.256**	.008	.003	−.044	−.235**	−.074
% Middle school	28.2	45.1	.017	−.005	−.093	.060	.064	−.025
% Elementary school	34.6	47.8	.237**	−.007	.078	−.016	.178*	.095
Prior math achievement[a]	−0.029	0.420	−.225*	.041	−.183*	−.185*	−.131	−.218*
Prior reading achievement[a]	−0.030	0.439	−.214*	.043	−.198*	−.166†	−.144	−.211*
n of schools	127							

* Grissom, J.A. et al. p. 437. (2013). Effective Instructional Time Use for School Leaders: Longitudinal Evidence From Observations of Principals. *Educational Researcher*, 42,433-444.

The second related way to determine the nature and strength of a relationship is to generate a scatterplot and examine the data visually. A *scatterplot* produces a set of dots on a graph, with each dot representing the value of the first variable and the corresponding value of the other variable for a single case/individual. The computer then does some calculations to produce the straight line that passes through the most points on the graph. The more points the line touches, and/or the closer the points are to the line, the larger the correlation—i.e., the stronger the relationship. So, for example, if the correlation between two variables is +1, which never really happens, all the dots would align perfectly in a straight line sloping upwards. A correlation of -1 would result in a series of dots aligned into a straight line sloping downwards. In a less precise relationship, the dots are more scattered. The smaller the correlation, the more scattered the dots.

The following scatterplots illustrate the relationship between the pattern in the scatterplot and the size and direction of the corresponding correlation.

---

lower the prior math scores the more time principals spend developing the educational program. Both interpretations make sense.

[28] More typically, a correlation matric will have the same variables listed vertically and horizontally—i.e., it will show the inter-correlations between a single set of variables.

Correlation between the Percentage of Students Receiving Free and
Reduced Lunch and the School's 2006 Base Academic Performance

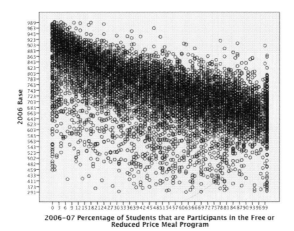

In the above scatterplot the pattern of concentrated dots is a fairly well defined straight band sloping downwards so it is a negative relationship. However, the band is somewhat wide so a straight line drawn through it would miss many of the dots. This means that it is not a perfect correlation; i.e., -1. In this case the correlation coefficient $r = -.549$; which is a pretty strong correlation.

At the same time, there are times when the dots do not even come close to forming a straight-line pattern. The less that the dots align along a line and instead form a more circular pattern the closer the correlation is to zero. For example, consider the following *scatterplot* that shows the relationship between the average value-added assessment score that a given school obtained in 2009 and the score for that same school in 2010 (Baker, 2013). Each dot represents a school, and this *scatterplot* represents the results for all schools in Ohio during that period.

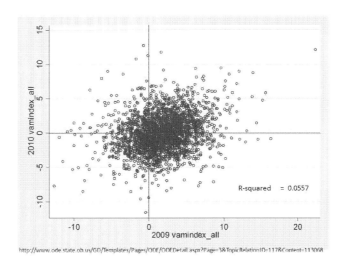

In this case the scatterplot indicates that the *correlation* would be close to zero. What conclusion can you draw from this relationship? The answer is in this footnote.[29]

However, regardless of how carefully you measure the strength of a correlation between two variables —i.e., the strength of the relationship—it does not tell you anything about what is causing the relationship. In the absence of knowledge about causation, even a large correlation can be an illusion that misleads practice.

What is the difference between correlation and causation?

In order to understand the difference between *correlation* and *causation*, consider the following example:

> Willingham (2007) notes that there would be a high positive correlation between the consumption of ice cream and the number of crimes on a given day. Clearly, eating ice cream does not *cause* individuals to commit crimes.
>
> The related rise in both variables is actually *caused* by a third variable, i.e., high temperatures. Therefore, banning ice cream sales would not reduce crime.

As previously explained, causation means that it has been determined that no possible confounding variables contributed to a given relationship. Clearly, there was a confounding variable in this ice cream example so the relationship was NOT causal. It would clearly be folly to adopt a policy to reduce crime by banning ice cream sales.

Here is an education example to illustrate the difference between correlation and causation.

> A district adopts a new reading program and the reading scores go up. There is clearly a positive correlation between implementing that program and the reading scores. However, did the new intervention *cause* the scores to go up?
>
> We cannot tell without further analysis. Perhaps at the same time the district boundaries changed, or perhaps several new high-end developments opened up that changed the districts demographics and this new demographic would actually have done better under the original program. As such, we cannot be sure that there is *causation*.

The significance for leadership decision-making is that if the new reading program was NOT the cause for the increase in reading scores in the research, if you adopt the program for your schools it is unlikely that test scores will increase.

---

[29] There is virtually no relationship between a given school's average value-added score from one year to the next which suggests that there was no value in the value-added assessment of school performance in Ohio. It means that the assessment is not measuring a school's effectiveness.

Conversely, it is possible, but probably rare, to find relationships wherein causation operates within the two variables and you only need to determine the direction of the relationship. For example, Pearl and Mackenzie (2018) illustrate the difference between relationship and causation via the phenomenon of a rooster crowing when the sun rises. This is a very strong relationship. However, the rooster crowing does NOT cause the sun to rise. Trying to get the rooster to crow earlier will not cause the sun to rise earlier. However, the sun rising does cause the rooster to crow. When the sun rises earlier late in the summer the rooster will crow earlier. So in this case causation is contained within the two variables of the relationship, but only in one direction.

In both cases, the relationship between ice cream and crime, and the rooster crowing and sunrise, the simple fact that there is a positive relationship does NOT mean that you can *assume* that increasing one variable will increase the other. (The next chapter will discuss how to tell when one variable will *cause* an increase in the other variable.)

Knowing that something *causes* something else to happen is a deeper level of knowledge, and provides a higher level of predictability as to the likely outcome of a decision based on that knowledge—as opposed to just knowing that a relationship exists. If you know that A causes B to happen, then if you adopt intervention A, or design an intervention around A, it is very likely that B will occur. Conversely, simply knowing that a correlation indicates that there is a relationship between A and B makes it less certain that implementing A will lead to B. The relationship may have just been happenstance or work in the opposite direction.

Nor is causation limited to being an abstract statistical concept. It has major application to a wide set of human experiences. For example, causation has major applicability in law. In the George Floyd murder case, a key element of the legal arguments centered on whether the cop placing his knee on George Floyd's neck was the *cause* of his death, or whether there were contributing factors, such as heart problems, carbon monoxide poisoning or drug use—i.e., confounding variables—that *caused* his death. All these factors were clearly present, but which one was the primary *cause* of his death? The jury had to weigh this evidence and decided that the knee to the neck for more than nine minutes was the *cause* of death.

Another problem with interpreting correlations is that they can indicate a relationship when there isn't one. If you collect data on lots of variables and check for correlations among the variables, some will show significant *correlations* with each other just by happenstance without there being any meaningful relationship. For example, there might be a correlation between the number of books in the public library and the number of strawberries sold at the local farmers market. So what? That is a spurious result.

Spurious correlations result from *data analysis sub-principle #2.2*. This principle states that the more analyses one conducts, in this case correlations, the more likely it is that compounded statistical error will produce false or useless results—i.e., spurious correlations. As a result, the first step in looking at any correlation is to ask the simple question:

Does this relationship indicated by the correlation make any sense?

Problems with using correlation as evidence for decision-making

On the surface, taking action on the basis of the correlation between ice cream sales and crime seems silly. Surely no one would try to reduce crime by suppressing ice cream sales. However, unfortunately, education has not only made the equivalent mistake of engaging in large-scale reform on the basis of a correlation as if it was causation—with dire results—it has done so many times. Examples of such misdirection based on correlational evidence of a relationship include:

- The effective schools movement in the '80's;
- The self-esteem movement in the '90's; and
- The enhancing grit movement in the 2000's.

The effective school's movement resulted from research that showed a relationship between schools being unusually effective and having some common characteristics—such as intensely focusing the school's energy and resources on promoting academic skills and frequently monitoring student progress. As a result, consultants spread out across the US training school leaders on what the characteristics of effective schools were and how to implement them. It was expected that implementing these characteristics in schools would cause them to become more effective. This was undertaken on a national basis before there was any research to see whether implementing such characteristics actually led to more effective schools. It turns out that it did not.

In the '80s and early '90s, educators used the positive correlation between self-esteem and academic performance to establish workshops on a large scale throughout the US on the importance of, and methods for, enhancing the self-esteem of low-performing students. They assumed causation—i.e., that increases in self-esteem led to increases in academic performance. It wasn't until many years later that it became apparent that this strategy was not working—and that increasing self-esteem does NOT *cause* an increase in academic performance. The self-esteem movement then became the poster-child for conservative criticism of education fads.

In the 2000s a reported correlation between grit and academic achievement led to a national push to develop the grit of low-performing students. Poor academic achievement was attributed to a lack of grit. Once again, there was no evidence that efforts to increase grit led to academic improvement—or even that the methods actually increased students' grit.

In all the above cases, the movements based on correlations failed and resulted in a large waste of time and monies—with no benefits for needy students.

Why has education continued to jump on bandwagons based on findings of correlation and accept them as valid predictors of outcomes without any research demonstrating such results? Usually, the relationships make intuitive sense and fit into professional ideals or, in the case of grit, it fit into prejudices. In addition, there is a deep-felt

110

professional desire to improve outcomes and equity—which makes the profession susceptible to simplistic ideas. The rationale for jumping on bandwagons is that the need for progress is so dire that there is no time to waste in putting the new "evidence" to use. Of course rushing implementation without subsequent evidence of the expected outcomes ends up wasting lots more time and ends in disillusionment.

In addition, it is easy to confuse relationship with causation when trying to solve a pressing problem. Consider the following example.

My experience as a professor is that while my students understood the difference between *correlation* and *causation* on a conceptual level, the minute it was cast into a managerial decision-making context the difference between the two receded in their minds. For example, right after presenting the difference between *correlation* and *causation,* I would tell my class about a study at the community college level that found that there was a *positive correlation* between whether students attended the first orientation and whether they were likely to complete the program. Those who missed the orientation were significantly less likely to complete a program than those who came. I would then ask:

> "If you were a leader at that institution, what practice would you adopt as a result of this study?"

I would be dismayed when students would respond unanimously that they would establish an effort to get students to the first orientation. Of course, the answer I was looking for was that since the result was a *correlation* there should be no change in practice based on just that result, since to make an effort to get students to the orientation based on that result would imply *causation*. Chances are that something else was *causing* students not to attend the orientation, and this something else might also be *causing* them to fall behind in their studies. So it was not likely that there would be any substantial increase in program completion from trying to increase turnout at the first orientation.

On second thought…there may have been merit in the students' recommendation. Stay tuned…

Why is correlation evidence important?

So, if evidence based on relationship research has had such a bad track record of misdirecting education reform, why spend time learning about it? First of all, it is verrrrrrry difficult to prove causation. (The primary method for proving causation in education research will be discussed in the next chapter.) Second, there are circumstances in which *correlational* research can be highly useful for leadership decision-making and for improving practice. For example, relationship research was used as the basis for solving one of the great plagues in history—Scurvy! For hundreds of years scurvy was the major cause of disability and mortality among sailors on long sea voyages. It was discovered that those who ate oranges and lemons did not develop scurvy. While a relationship such as this may be discovered by chance, and at the time no one knows why the relationship exist or what the underlying cause is, that does not make a relationship such as this any less valuable to leaders. Ship captains thereafter added lots of citrus fruits to their cargo which solved the problem of scurvy.

Why did it work? It wasn't until much later that Vitamin C was discovered, and that scurvy was *caused* by a Vitamin C deficiency. However, not knowing causation did not negate in the interim the value of the relationship evidence for protecting sailors.

In this case, the captains who were early adopters based only on relationship evidence made the right decisions.

The fact is that many valuable practices in medicine and business are based on correlations. Indeed, a great deal of clinical medicine is based on *correlational* data. *A substantial portion of clinical trials in medicine to establish causality or demonstrate the degree of effectiveness and safety of treatments occur as a result of initial supportive relationship/correlational data.*

For example, someone tried a drug on a prison population to see if it would reduce smoking and discovered that while it did not reduce smoking it did result in weight loss. Similarly, the earlier examples of using interferon for hepatitis C or oranges for scurvy were based on large correlations—i.e., you could predict almost 100% of the time that if someone ate citrus fruit they would NOT get scurvy. So in all these cases the correlation evidence could be used as the basis for treatment—even though it was not known at the time what *caused* the benefit.

Furthermore, as you will learn in the next chapter, causal research conducted in schools has not been very helpful. But even if it was, leaders do not have the luxury of ignoring an important correlational result while waiting for *causal* research to pay off 30 years down the road—if ever.

While statisticians currently tend to be dismissive of correlation evidence as inferior to causation, the fact is that correlation evidence has historically been of tremendous value to scientists in a variety of disciplines and to leaders. Indeed, Pearl and Mackenzie (2018) showed how until about 40 years ago statisticians celebrated correlation as the preferred form of evidence and dismissed the value of causal evidence. Correlation evidence remains important because in most cases correlation evidence may be all that is available to leaders to try and solve a problem. So the critical issue for leaders is:

> *Under what conditions can correlations be trusted to provide a basis for decisions that are likely to improve schools and increase equity?*

There are a series of factors that leaders and researchers can use to determine whether correlation evidence will identify a practice that is likely to be effective—even by potential early adopters who are considering taking a chance on the evidence.

Factors impacting the applicability of correlation research

Determining whether a relationship makes sense and is useful evidence for leadership decision-making is a function of the following five elements:

- Whether the relationship is linear;
- Whether the variables are actionable;
- Whether there are obvious confounding variables;
- Whether the direction of the relationship is one-way; and *most importantly*
- **The BIGness of the correlation.**

Is the relationship linear?

While a correlation of zero normally indicates that there is no relationship, there is one situation where in fact a correlation that is close to zero can be masking a very strong relationship. Consider the following graph of one of the most famous hypothesized relationship in the social science literature. This graph, referred to in the literature as the inverted U curve, shows the hypothesized relationship between arousal, i.e., stress, and performance. (Downloaded from http://en.wikipedia.org/wiki/Yerkes–Dodson_law#mediaviewer/File: HebbianYerkesDodson.svg). This is called a *curvilinear/non-linear relationship* for obvious reasons.

The Hypothesized Relationship Between Stress and Performance

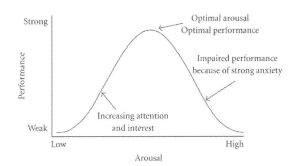

QUESTIONS:

1. How would you interpret this pattern of dots in a scatterplot?
2. Suppose almost all of the individual dots were on (or close to) this curved figure, does this graph indicate a strong relationship or a weak one?

Answers are provided in this footnote.[30]

The reason why the Pearson correlation would be zero is that any straight line between any of the hundreds of points would only touch two of the points. This would cause

---

[30] (1) As stress increases performance increases up to a point, and once the stress goes beyond a certain point performance starts to decline. In other words, some stress is good—too much stress is bad. (2) This is a strong relationship because all the points are aligned in a very specific curved line graph, i.e., a clearly non-linear pattern. Conversely, no matter how you drew a straight line, the largest number of points the straight line could touch would be 2 (out of the hundreds of points). So any linear calculation of the correlation would produce a correlation of zero. This small r would mask the existence of a strong relationship—albeit a non-linear (curvilinear) one.

the computer to conclude that there was NO relationship between arousal and performance.

In other words, when research reports a correlation, it is most often (unless otherwise noted) using a statistic that conducts straight line analysis, and is a **_linear statistic_**. So, a *correlation* of '0' typically means that there is no *linear* relationship between the variables (…but there may be a curvilinear one). But if the relationship is linear, the scatterplot will show the dots aligned in such a way that they form a shape that parallels and touches a straight line—which in turn indicates that as one variable in a relationship changes, the other changes in approximately the same proportion throughout the range of values.

However, not all relationships in education, or life, are that simple. For example, when a student has a growth spurt in height or learning in one year that is a non-linear change. Throughout one's life the relationship between age and height is NOT linear, nor is the relationship between age and language acquisition. The above relationship between arousal and academic performance is another example of a non-linear relationship since the relationship changes depending on the amount of stress. There is a very strong relationship—just not a linear one.

Consider the following research finding related to the ideal number of daily steps for older women. Lee et al. (2019) found that women in their 70s who completed 4,400 steps a day reduced their risk of premature death by 40% as compared to who only completed 2,700 or fewer steps a day. The risks continued to drop for those completing more than 5,000 steps a day, but there was little addition benefit from completing more than 7,500 steps a day.

QUESTIONS:

1. Is this a positive or negative correlation?
2. Is the relationship between the number of daily steps taken and the reduction in the risk of premature death a linear or non-linear relationship?

The answers are in this footnote.[31]

Another example of a non-linear relationship is the reliance on basic skill development to help accelerate students born into poverty who are falling behind. My research shows that while a dominant basic skill approach works to increase equity in grades K-2, by the fourth grade, as the curriculum becomes more sophisticated, this approach inhibits learning and the students fall ever further behind—thereby increasing inequity.

---

[31] QUESTION 1: It is a negative correlation, because as the variable of "number of steps" goes up, the other variable "risk of premature death" goes down.

QUESTION 2: It is a non-linear (curvilinear) relationship, since the relationship between the number of steps and the reduction of premature death changes at the different levels of stepping—i.e., the risk of premature death drops dramatically early in the range of values for stepping, then drops less dramatically after 4,400 steps, and does not drop further after 7,500. If it was a linear relationship, then the reduction in premature death would stay approximately the same for each increased level of stepping.

So the nature of this relationship changes dramatically as students get older and the same treatment produces very different results at the different grade spans. This is also sometimes called an **interactive relationship**.

The easiest way to tell if a correlation close to zero is masking a strong non-linear relationship is to examine the scatterplot. Without the scatterplot one would conclude that there is no relationship between stress and performance. However, the above scatterplot shows that there is a very strong non-linear relationship between these two variables, one that has major implications for education. This non-linear relationship would have predicted the failure of movements such as the self-esteem or effusive praise reforms of the 80s or of any intervention designed to relieve *all* academic stress on students—because some stress is essential for improving performance.

EXCEL does NOT calculate a non-linear correlation. However, once you observe a strong non-linear relationship in the scatterplot, an advanced statistical package such as SPSS or R can then calculate a non-linear correlation. This will result in a much larger value of r than that produced by a linear statistic such as a Pearson Correlation. Conversely, in the above example of schools in Ohio, there is no relationship, linear or otherwise.

Actionable variables

Variables in relationships can be classified as either actionable or non-actionable. Actionable variables are ones that leaders can manipulate. For example, if there is a positive correlation between the amount of time students spend reading and achievement, the first variable is actionable as leaders can take action and increase the amount of time spent reading. If, on the other hand, research finds that there is a relationship between the percentage of racial-ethnic minority students in a school and math achievement, leaders cannot change the race of their students. So in these examples, reading time is actionable while race is not.

Generally, a correlation in which both variables are non-actionable does NOT provide evidence for how to solve a problem—though it can provide some descriptive useful information on the extent of a problem. For example, if there is a very strong negative correlation between the percentage of minorities in a school and math achievement, this evidence can be used as a call to action to institute policies at the state or national level to reduce the number of schools with very high percentages of minorities. Indeed, if you look back at the histogram in Chapter 4 of the percentages of low-income students in schools, you can see the large numbers of schools with very high levels of poverty and the next largest concentration of schools with little or no poverty students. However, that relationship evidence does NOT help leaders of a high poverty school develop a specific improvement strategy.

Clearly, it is a social injustice that one's zip code determines the type of school environment they experience. At the same time, given my work in high poverty schools, I know that it is possible to substantially increase reading and math scores of the vast majority of students in such schools. So the types of correlations that are most helpful to leaders seeking to improve their schools are ones with large positive correlations between some type of intervention—i.e., an actionable variable—and academic, behavioral/emotional, or social gains.

Remember

> The most useful correlations for proactive leadership decision-making are ones where at least one of the variables is actionable.

Obvious confounding variables

When looking at any correlation that is of interest for possibly being the basis of taking any action, it is critical to brainstorm whether there are any likely confounding, hidden variables, that impact or are responsible for, or *causing*, the correlation. The previously discussed correlation between ice cream sales and crime is not a real relationship as they both reflect the effects of hot weather. So when looking at any correlation it is always important to play devil's advocate to see if it is masking some other relationship.

It can be difficult to spot a confounding variable. For example, the existence of a confounding variable was probably responsible for the failure of the effective schools movement. It could be that these schools' effectiveness could have been caused by the chance or deliberate coming together of unusually talented teachers and leaders. However, no study of highly effective schools ever considered unusually talented individuals as a possible characteristic.

If I may be permitted a sports reference, there was an analogous situation in basketball. The Chicago Bulls basketball team enjoyed extraordinary success using the triangle offense. It produced six National Basketball Association championships between 1991 and 1998. The principles of this offense were known. When the new coach of the Phoenix Suns decided to implement it, his team lost every game and he was quickly fired. The triangle worked because of the unusual confluence of a transcendent basketball player and leader in Michael Jordan (and later Kobe Bryant), and a Zen master coach in Phil Jackson.[32] Pushing this analogy a bit further, the "effective schools movement" was the equivalent of every school adopting the triangle offense. We rarely acknowledge that there are also transcendent teachers and Zen-master leaders in education, and that when they come together they can accomplish things that others cannot. Transcendent teachers and leaders could well have been a confounding variable in those highly effective schools.

Relatedly, in any school that I have ever seen where the principal turned it around, that principal worked diligently to get rid of ineffective teachers. That factor never appears in the studies of school effectiveness. In other cases the schools started from scratch with the principal given wide discretion in the hiring of teachers. This has little applicability to the typical school.

---

[32] A final irony is that even Phil Jackson could not make the triangle work without the right players. This led to his being fired in 2017.

So in the end, there is no rule for how you identify a likely confounding variable. Sometimes there are clues in the literature or prior scientific knowledge, and other times it is simply common sense or general knowledge. If there are any obvious possible confounding variables it is best to ignore the correlation.

Direction of the relationship

If there are no obvious confounding variables, there are times when it is possible to determine which variable in the relationship is the dominant one—i.e., the variable that is likely leading to the change in the other variable. (The term "likely" is used because we can never be 100% sure.) Consider the positive relationship between cancer and smoking. Chances are that smoking is the dominant variable—i.e., that smoking leads to increased rates of cancer—as opposed to the alternative that increased rates of cancer lead to smoking (…despite the protestations of the tobacco companies). Another way of thinking about this relationship is that smoking is causing cancer—not the other way around. So this is what is referred to as a ***one-way correlation*** since we can tell the direction of the relationship.

On the other hand, consider the positive relationship between self-esteem and academic success. For almost a decade the education profession assumed that this was a one-way relationship in which increasing self-esteem led to increases in academic performance. As a result, the profession took large scale action on that basis by implementing approaches that were designed to increase self-esteem. The basic approach was to provide effusive praise for everything that students did, tried to do, or said. This did NOT increase academic achievement because the relationship was a ***two-way correlation.*** It was just as likely that increases in academic performance led to increases in self-esteem. Under this latter interpretation of the relationship there would have been no reason to expect that the self-esteem movement would be successful. We subsequently realized that the latter interpretation was indeed the more likely one. In the meantime, this misinterpretation of research evidence resulted in a decade of failed efforts to improve the academic performance of under-represented students.

The self-esteem movement described above is an example of the danger in developing policy based on *two-way correlations*. Does the positive relationship between self-esteem and academic achievement indicate that increasing self-esteem increases academic achievement or that increases in academic achievement results in increases in self-esteem? Educators assumed it was the former direction, but it was probably the latter—which is why the self-esteem movement turned out to be folly. It was the equivalent of trying to make the sun rise earlier by training the rooster to crow earlier.

Unfortunately, it is all too easy to incorrectly assume that a *correlation* is a *one-way* one and take action on that basis, when it is in fact a *two-way* one. Consider the following example:

There is a positive *correlation* between calorie intake and one's weight. This has almost universally been interpreted as a *one-way correlation*—i.e., that an increase in caloric intake increases one's weight. The solution thus has been seen as increasing one's willpower to resist the temptation to eat and to eat less. There are lots of products and diets sold that claim to help reduce one's food intake. There is, however, lots of data that show that this approach has limited success. An article in the *Journal of the American Medical Association*, Ludwig and Friedman (2014), comes to the counter-intuitive conclusion that the correlation actually works in the other direction—that increases in weight *cause* us to get hungrier and to eat more. The *causal* mechanism is hypothesized to be that the fat in the highly processed foods we eat is not used to meet the energy needs of the body and is simply stored, causing the body to determine that it needs more calories—which triggers the impulse to eat more. Clearly, this hypothesis explains *why* the "increasing willpower" solution pushed by the diet and fast-food industries have little effect and suggests a very different set of policy initiatives which limit the use of certain ingredients in processed foods.

As another example of how it can be difficult to determine whether a relationship is one- or two-way, let's go back to the relationship between the number of steps women over 70 take and the risk of premature death. Which is it? It depends. If the researchers did NOT control for initial differences in the health of the individuals, then it is a two-way, because it is possible that the sicker ones who were more prone to premature death did not have the energy to walk very far on a daily basis. However, if the researchers DID control for differences in initial health status—and it appears that they did—then it is a one-way because the only direction that makes sense is that the walking led to the decline in premature death. (What is clear from this study is that there is no scientific basis for setting a walking target of 10,000 steps per day.)

Practical Tip

One-way correlations can be useful evidence for supporting leadership decision-making. However, before basing practice or policy on a correlation *it is critical to make sure that it is NOT a two-way correlation*—and/or there is no outside confounding variable.

The BIGness of the correlation

Once you know the size and direction of a correlation, the next step is to determine its BIGness—i.e., how important the relationship is for increasing the predictions of outcomes. Since correlations between two different variables are almost never exactly 1 or 0, they are almost always some decimal in between 0 and 1 and will always seem like a small number. If you look at correlations such as those in Table #2 they all seem small.

How BIG should the decimal be to consider the relationship to be important for leadership decision-making? Under what conditions is the decimal BIG enough to provide an incentive for leaders to consider it as useful evidence for informing a decision?

There are two approaches for interpreting the BIGness—i.e., importance—of a correlation:

1. Statistical significance
2. Predictiveness (r^2)

(1) Statistical significance

Data Analysis Principle #4 states that: The BIGness of the benefit found in a research study is NOT found by analyzing the *statistics* used—but by the *statistical tests* used to determine the importance and amount of benefit of the statistical outcomes.

The most widely used statistical test, by far, is **statistical significance**. In fact, virtually every statistic in Appendix A other than logistic regression uses *statistical significance* to determine the importance of the result.

Statistical significance is a test that indicates the probability that the result produced by the statistic did not occur by chance and indicates some real world effect. If the probability is at least 95% certain that the result did not occur by chance, then the result is said to be statistically significant. In testing for statistical significance, the researcher first posits a **null hypothesis**—i.e., that there is no relationship. Then the statistic tells you whether there is a 95% chance that the null hypothesis is wrong so that it is likely that the relationship did NOT occur by chance and that it is real. However, the fact that the null hypothesis is rejected does NOT mean that there is a BIG or important relationship.

If this seems like a convoluted process—it is! Hubbard (2015) cites the following example from Berkson (1942) that illustrates the artificiality of the null hypothesis thusly:

> In the null hypothesis schema we are trying only to nullify something…But ordinary evidence does not take this form. With the corpus delecti in front of you, you do not say, "Here is evidence against the hypothesis that no one is dead." You say, "Evidently someone has been murdered." (p. 65)[33]

The finding that a correlation is statistically significant is typically indicated in published research by one or more asterisks following the correlation. One asterisk (*) indicates that it is 95% certain that the result did not occur by chance, and it links to the expression below the table, $p<.05$. That means that the probability that the result did occur by chance is less than 5% or less than 5 chances out of 100.

Two asterisks (**)means that we can be 99% certain that the relationship did NOT occur by chance, and that links to $p<.01$ — i.e., there is less than 1 chance out of 100 that the result did occur by chance.

---

[33] To be fair, there is in fact an analogy of the null hypothesis in real life. Defendants are assumed to be innocent (null hypothesis) until a prosecutor can marshal enough evidence to convince jurors to reject that hypothesis.

Three asterisks (***) indicate even more likelihood that the result did NOT occur by chance, p<.001—i.e., there is less than 1 chance out of 1,000 that the result was caused by chance as opposed to being a real relationship.

So the convention that is followed in the social sciences is that as long as the probability that any statistical finding, in this case correlations, did NOT occur by chance is 5% or less, it is considered to be *statistically significant.*

If you look back at Table 2, most of the decimals are NOT followed by any asterisks. That means that those correlations were NOT statistically significant. Six of the decimals had two asterisks, which means that it is very likely that the relationship was not caused by chance. So under conventional analysis, these would be considered to be the most important relationships in the dataset.

Remember

While researchers and professional associations consider a relationship or intervention that is *statistically significant* to be important or effective, that is highly misleading for informing leadership decision-making. The reality is that statistical significance does not tell you anything about whether the outcome was of any practical benefit—or even whether there was a strong relationship.

There are many problems with the use of statistical significance which will be discussed more fully in the next chapter. The biggest problem is that if the sample is large enough trivial benefits can be statistically significant. Statistical significance tells you nothing about how BIG the benefit was. So if a certain type of car was found on average to get 1 mile per gallon more than another one, that difference could end up being statistically significant—but that is not likely to be a big enough difference to cause people to switch cars. Similarly, a finding of statistical significance should NOT be the basis for leaders to adopt a new intervention or for researchers to claim to have shown that the intervention was effective.

Even more misleading is when findings of statistical significance end up being listed as "significant" in abstracts and conclusion sections of published research. Professional associations then use that evidence to trumpet the call that research has found evidence of a "significant" improvement or relationship from a given practice. Converting a technical finding of "statistical significance" to a conclusion that relies on the colloquial, everyday use of the term "significant" is misleading— though it is done routinely in research journals. (Professional newsletters then trumpet that the research had found a "significant" benefit.) A research finding that something is statistically significant, and a finding that is significant, are two different things. Statistical significance does NOT mean that something "significant"—i.e., of major importance— occurred.

The bottom line is that *statistical significance* does NOT tell you anything about how BIG or important the relationship is.

Practical Tip

So, rather than explain the methodology of *statistical significance* in more detail, the recommendation is that leaders should ignore any finding based on *statistical significance,* or any claim that a relationship, or any research finding, is significant.

Indeed, relying on *statistical significance* has been blamed for much of the failure of research across disciplines to replicate. As a result, in 2018 the American Statistical Association called for researchers to stop using it as the basis for reaching conclusions about effective practices—and some journals have started refusing to publish findings based solely on findings of statistical significance.

Another problem in the era of big data is that computers can spit out tons of correlations—but the more correlations that are calculated the more the possibility of errors is compounded. If you look 100 times for correlations between variables you risk finding, purely by chance, about five bogus correlations that appear to be *statistically significant*—even though there is no actual meaningful connection between the variables (Marcus & Davis, 2014). Harris (2107) reported that of all the correlations between specific genes and a disease in tens of thousands of research papers, only 1.2 percent of these turned out to be truly positive results.

Remember

Ultimately, the only thing that a finding of *statistical significance* tells you is that probably something other than nothing occurred. That does NOT mean that something "significant" occurred.

Fortunately, there is a better method for determining how BIG or important a relationship is based on the value of (r) produced by the correlation statistic—a method that is based on how predictive the result is. Predictiveness is a better method given that, as discussed in Chapter 1, a key goal of science is to develop accurate predictions.

(2) Predictiveness (r^2)

A better approach to determining BIGness of a correlation is to determine how well it predicts what is likely to happen. The better that a correlation can predict an outcome the more valuable that evidence is to leaders. Fortunately, we can convert the value of the correlation (r) into a measure of the predictiveness of the relationship. When you square r, which means multiplying r by itself (r x r or r^2), the result indicates the predictiveness of the relationship. r^2 tells you how accurately you can predict the value of one variable knowing the value of the other.

Suppose r = .2. That would probably show up as a statistically significant correlation. Using some simple arithmetic, if r = .2, r^2 is .2 x .2, or .04. (Note that when you square a decimal the result is a smaller decimal than the original.)

The final step in determining the degree of prediction is to convert the squared decimal, in this case .04, to a percent, which indicates the percentage of cases when you can make an accurate prediction. To convert the decimal .04 to a percentage, move the decimal point two places to the right, and the result is 04 or 4. This means that one variable explains 4% of the variation in the other variable, or that if you try to predict the value of one variable knowing the other, you will be right 4 times out of 100. *Who cares?* In other words, an *r* of .2 cannot be said to be of any practical value for leadership decision-making.

The r^2 of the earlier scatterplot relating teacher scores from one year to the next in Ohio was .0557. This means that if you try to predict the scores that a teacher will produce next year knowing what his/her results were this year—you will be right 5.57% of the time. This means that you cannot really predict what the teacher ratings will be from one year to the next, which in turn means that, unless teachers typically undergo massive changes in the quality of their teaching, the method used to produce these school ratings is flawed and the ratings are misleading.

Since squaring a small decimal produces an even smaller one, r has to be very large to begin with in order to produce an r^2 that provides a useful level of predictiveness. Of course, this leads to the obvious question of:

> *How big should an r be to conclude that the relationship is potentially meaningful for informing practice?*

Alas, there is no accepted criterion. Therefore the best way to arrive at any type of recommendation is to work backwards and ask the question:

> What is the minimum increase in predictability that most leaders would seek to consider it worth their while to consider taking action based on evidence of a relationship?

There is no research to use as a basis for answering this question. So, a reasonable starting point is to posit that an increase in predictability of 15% is a useful improvement. For example, if a leader could accurately predict which first graders will be falling substantially behind by the third grade by another 15%, that would seem to be somewhat useful. (Obviously, that would be a minimum and leaders would desire even more predictability.) So what r would be needed to produce an r^2 of .15? That would be an r—i.e., a correlation—of .39. This is calculated by squaring the r of .39, or .39 x .39 = .1521, which is 15.21%

Remember

A BIG correlation will be considered to be one that is at least + or - .39.[34] For example, -.3 is too small, but -.45 is a BIG (albeit negative) relationship.

Note that none of the correlations in Table 5.1 approach that size. Therefore, the conclusion is that none of them represent a BIG or important relationship in any practical sense—i.e., none of them represent authentic evidence.

---

[34] Clearly, setting the lower boundary for a correlation to be considered as having practical importance at .39 is arbitrary. However, all the criteria of statistical tests are arbitrary. For example, setting the minimum certainty for statistical significance at 95% is arbitrary. Why should something that is 95% certain be considered statistically significant while 94% certainty is not? The 95% threshold is not God-given. Rather, it is simply an arbitrary threshold that social scientists have agreed to as a standard. On the other hand, physics demands much higher levels of certainty to claim a discovery. For now .39 seems to be a conservative criterion as it may turn out that leaders would want the minimum set even higher.

Beware

Large correlations are rare in research—though they do exist. As a result, researchers eager to claim important discoveries will continue to try and convince leaders to rely on smaller correlations which the researchers claim to be "significant." Avoid that advice! Act only on the basis of BIG correlations when they appear.

Indeed, advice to take action based on small, "significant" correlations can be dangerous. Consider the following example.

One of my Black students felt that the push for developing the grit of low-income students was discriminatory and not valid since his experience was that surviving in such neighborhoods required lots of grit so that low grit was not an explanation for poor academic performance. I encouraged him to review the literature on the relationship between grit and academic achievement and determine the size of the correlations. He found the size of the correlations to be trivial. This was contrary to the claims of the advocates. Nor could he find any evidence that efforts to increase grit actually increased grit or academic performance. In other words, there was no evidence to support the national movement to develop students' grit.

This example illustrates why it is important for leaders to examine the actual size of the correlation on their own. The fact that there are few BIG correlations makes it easier for leaders to quickly review a set of correlations and pick out those results that truly indicate an important relationship and ignore those that do not—regardless of how many asterisks there are, or whether the researcher concludes that there is a significant or strong positive relationship.

Beware

While correlations can provide important evidence for leadership decision-making, it does so only under the specific conditions just described. When the profession jumps on bandwagons—such as the self-efficacy, effective-schools, and enhancing grit movements—based on correlations that violate these conditions, the result is a major misstep by our profession that misdirects efforts to help needy students for as much as a decade.

Using Excel

To **create a scatterplot**, use the INSERT TAB in the main menu, choose "Chart" and then select "X Y (Scatter)".

To calculate the correlation "r" use the FORMULAS tab in the main menu, and select "Insert Function." Excel has several functions for **calculating the correlation** between two sets of values.. PEARSON, finds the correlation between two sets of numbers, and CORREL finds the correlation of a ranked set of numbers (in the absence of a function for calculating the SPEARMAN correlation coefficient).

(See Appendix A for more details on how to choose which correlation to use.)

Partial Correlation—Control Method II

In all types of analyses it is important to control for the possible contamination of results from the effects of *confounding* variables. In Chapter 3 we controlled for the possible confounding effects of differences in poverty on the comparison between race and the reading scores of girls on NAEP. In that case we controlled for the differences in poverty via the technique of *exclusion* or creating a *homogenous sample*—i.e., only considering the results for Black and White girls living in poverty.

We have the same need to control for a possible confounding variable in relationship research to accurately interpret the importance of evidence based on correlation. You always have to be on the lookout for the possibility that another confounding variable is affecting or controlling the relationship between two variables. In other words, while knowing the direction of the correlation is important, that is not helpful if the correlation itself is resulting from the action of another confounding variable.

For example, consider the correlation between smoking and lung cancer. Once this correlation was known, some scientists argued that this was not sufficient evidence to conclude that smoking *caused* lung cancer because of the possibility that there was a gene that predisposed individuals to both smoke and to get lung cancer. If there was such a confounding variable, then reducing cigarette smoking would have not had any more benefit on reducing lung cancer, any more than stopping ice cream sales would have on reducing crime in the earlier example.

Fortunately, there is a statistical method for controlling for the effects of a third confounding variable in a relationship—and that is **partial correlation**. So, for example, if we revisited the earlier example of the positive correlation between eating ice cream and crime rates, if we conducted a *partial correlation* on that relationship controlling for the effects of temperature, the resultant r would be close to zero.

There are similarly many instances in education where it makes sense to control for the effects of a third variable in a relationship. For example, you might want to examine the relationship between teacher morale and salary controlling for years of experience, or the relationship between ethnicity and GPA controlling for SES status.

Alas, there is no function in Excel to easily calculate the partial correlation. You would need to use a more specialized statistical package such as SPSS.

Regression Analysis

While correlations and partial correlations are able to describe relationships between 2-3 variables, complex relationships can involve the interaction of more variables. For example, maintaining a successful marriage consists of balancing a large number of variables. Similarly, there are probably more than three variables that enable someone to be a high quality teacher. To analyze such a complex multi-faceted relationship, researchers continually try to identify the mix of variables that will best predict a desired outcome—e.g., determining the mix of variables that can best predict who will be an outstanding teacher.

The statistic for analyzing relationships between and among a larger number of variables at the same time is *multiple correlation* or *regression analysis*. Discussions of regression analysis can get very technical very quickly as there are many different types such as regression-discontinuity analysis that are extremely complex. Therefore, the discussion here focuses on the most fundamental form of regression analysis— *ordinary regression*.

Regression analysis is a powerful prediction tool that is used in two ways. The first is to determine how well a set of variables, called *independent* or *predictor variables*, can predict an outcome or *dependent variable*. Mathematically this is expressed as how much variation in the outcome or dependent variable can be predicted by several predictor or independent variables. The second way that regression is used is to determine which predictor/independent variable(s) has the most unique influence on the outcome/dependent variable.

For example, leaders and/or researchers might want to know (a) which predictor/independent variables best predicts a community college's success in transitioning their students to 4-year institutions, or (b) whether race or income best predicts achievement gaps.

If you wanted to determine the effects/impact of Race and SES on Student GPA, Race and SES would be the predictor/independent variables, and Student GPA the dependent variable. Determining which variable is the dependent variable depends on the context. If you are trying to determine the effects of a leadership style on teacher attitudes, then teacher attitudes is the dependent variable. If you are trying to determine the effect of teacher attitude on school morale, then teacher attitude is the independent variable.

An example of multiple correlation or regression analysis that has been widely studied is the effort to determine which variables have the most impact on predicting a teacher's ability to raise students' achievement scores. In this case Teacher Success would be the dependent variable, and there could be a whole host of independent variables such as: Teacher's Undergraduate GPA, Years of Experience, GPA in Education Courses, Number of Extracurricular Activities in College, Quality of University Attended, etc. So far the research has not been able to establish a strong relationship between these variables. This lack of relationship either means that there is no predictable consistent relationship, or that the right independent variable(s) have not yet been identified and researchers have not been sufficiently creative in considering alternative possible predictive variables.[35]

---

[35] At one lecture I attended on multiple correlation/regression, the professor was talking about his research that was attempting to explain how offspring decide whether to maintain the tradition of church attendance they were raised in. None of the *independent* variables were providing much clarification of the decision. Then he had a hunch and added in the variable of "How Far the Individuals Moved Away from Their Parents" when they left

Conversely, there are regression analyses that do find strong relationships. A study by Tienken and Wolfe (2014) used more precise census data broken out by district boundaries to predict the percentage of students scoring proficient on the New Jersey state test in reading and math over a three-year period. They studied a sample of districts using a variety of SES related census (independent) variables. The regression analysis showed that the independent SES census variables were able to accurately predict the number of proficient students in each district (dependent variable) with 64-84% accuracy.

This study showed that the types of school variables that leaders can act on account for less than half of the variation in the dependent variable—i.e., how many students scoring at the proficient level (dependent variable). This finding shows that schools and leaders should not be given 100% of the blame under an accountability system for not achieving desired levels of achievement. At the same time, these regression results indicate that there is still a substantial minority amount of variation in outcomes not explained by demographic variables that schools can potentially impact.

This study illustrates an important value of regression analysis. Too much of contemporary debate is of the either-or, yes-no variety. Regression analysis provides precise insight into the extent to which various factors relate to outcomes. So while demographic factors were the majority determinant of outcomes, leadership practices also had a minority, but still substantial, impact.

Remember

The power of regression is that it takes us away from absolutist positions of either/or, important/not important—to *how important* is each, or how *much* does each contribute to a desired outcome, and how can we best apply each to contribute to an overall outcome.

In a regression equation the importance of each independent variable is indicated by a coefficient or parameter. For example, consider the following hypothetical regression equation of results from a make-believe study examining the relationship between the predictor/independent variables of Salary, Years of Experience, and Height on the outcome/dependent variable of Teacher Satisfaction.

Teacher Satisfaction = .013(Salary) -.005(Years of Experience) + .001(Height) +.025 (Sex) +12 36

In this case .013, -.005, .001, and .025 are the regression coefficients. This means that for every dollar that salary increases, Teacher satisfaction goes up .013 (holding years

---

home. It turned out that this *independent* variable was a major explainer of whether they continued to attend church, i.e., the farther away they moved, the less likely they were to attend church. The point of this example is that sometimes intuition in selecting the *independent* variables to include in the *regression analysis* can produce major research payoffs. When, as in this case, the obvious variables are not highly correlated with the *dependent* variable, in this case teacher effectiveness, some leap of intuition is probably needed to identify a more predictive independent variable. (Perhaps looking at how far away from home the university they attended might be a more predictive variable. Who knows?)

[36] I apologize. I promised that there would be no formulas in this book but this one exception seemed necessary.

of experience and height constant). This does not seem to be very exciting. You would want to see a much larger regression coefficient to have an appreciable impact on teacher satisfaction.

While in theory such equations can inform leaders as to what types of interventions they should prioritize if a variable has a large regression coefficient, in reality, the most important variables often turn out to be ones that the leader has no control over—i.e., are non-actionable—such as the sex or the poverty level of students.

Using z scores

When trying to determine which predictor/independent variable is more important, it is critical to convert all the numbers to some common metric. So, for example, if you are trying to determine whether family income is more important than High School GPA or IQ in predicting college freshman GPA, family income has the largest numbers—but it might not be the most important factor. So all numbers are converted into standard deviation scores, or z scores.

So, thinking back to the discussion of distributions and descriptive statistics in Chapter 4, suppose the distributions were as follows:

- Family income, Mean =50,000, Standard Deviation (SD) = 10,000
- High School GPA, Mean = 2.0, SD = .5
- IQ, Mean = 100, SD =10

A student who had the following values:

- Family income = $45,000
- HS GPA = 2.0
- IQ = 110

These numbers would be converted into standardized or z scores, and the values entered into the computer for that student would be:[37]

- Family income = -.5
- HS GPA = 0
- IQ = +1

(In other words, Family income was 1/2 SD below the Mean, HS GPA was 0 SD below the Mean, and IQ was 1 SD above the Mean.) When all the values are transformed to z or standardized values, the regression coefficients are called standardized coefficients. Standardizing the coefficients is valuable since the resultant coefficients indicate the relative importance of each variable in predicting the results for the dependent variable. For example, if the final regression equation was:

---

[37] Since a z score represents the amount of standard deviation units from the *Mean*, the calculation for converting a raw score to a z score is simply to subtract the score from the *Mean* and then divide by the *standard deviation*. So the calculation for the student's z score for the variable of *family income* would be: (50,000-45,000)/10,000 = .5. The same process was used for calculating the z scores for the student's HS GPA and IQ.

$$\text{Freshman GPA} = .31(\text{Family Income}) - .15(\text{HS GPA}) + .002(\text{IQ}) + 3.8$$

That would mean that Family Income had twice the importance on predicting Freshman GPA than did HS GPA (which was negatively related), and that IQ had no real impact. Indeed, many research reports would conclude at this point with statement such as:

- Family income had the biggest impact on Freshman GPA; or
- Family income had twice the impact of high school GPA.

But there are two problems with these conclusions. First, family income is not an actionable variable. Indeed, this could be used as an excuse for believing that there is nothing that leaders could do to increase the GPA of under-performing students and thereby perpetuating inequities. The second problem is that the regression coefficients are meaningless if the combined effect of the (three) independent variables do NOT actually predict Freshman GPA.

Practical Tip

Before you pay attention to the effects of any of the independent variables or the regression coefficients, you need to know that the equation as a whole provides a useful level of prediction of the dependent variable—in this case Freshman GPA.

In other words, knowing that Family Income has twice the impact on predicting Freshman GPA is of little value if the combination of variables does not predict Freshman GPA very well. Just knowing it has twice the impact is a relative analysis instead of presenting the actual end result (data analysis principle #6). So it is critical to first determine how well the combination of independent variables actually predicts Freshman GPA.

Determining how well the combination of independent variables actually predicts Freshman GPA is determined by the size of the correlation of the combined effects of the independent variables with the dependent variable. This correlation is usually indicated as R. From what you know from the earlier discussion about correlation, guess how you determine how well the combination of independent variables predicts Freshman GPA?

Yes! R^2.

So if the R is .26, how well does the combination of the three independent variables predict freshman GPA?

.26*.26 = .0676. Converted to a percentage that is 6.76%, which rounded off would be 7%.

So this relationship would only predict Freshman GPA about 7% of the time. Not very useful. So in this case knowing that one variable was twice as important than the other in contributing to the overall prediction does not help very much since the overall predictability of the relationship is too small to be useful. At this point the researcher needs to go back to the drawing board, drop IQ because it is not contributing to the relationship and add some other variables into the analysis, and recalculate R.

So the data analysis principle of Bigness would, as with correlations, indicate that an R of .39 would be the minimum value to consider the result useful for leadership decision-making. But suppose R is greater than .39 but…

- None of the variables are actionable?; or
- There is an actionable variable, but that variable does NOT contribute much to R —i.e., the overall prediction.

In both cases these results would still not be useful for a school leader (though they might have implications for national social policy).

On a more positive note, if R is greater than .39, and there is an actionable variable, there is the potential for the result to be valuable for school leaders—if that variable makes an important contribution to R as indicated by its standardized coefficient (z score). How large should the z score of the actionable variable be? It turns out that the z score is the same as a measure of BIGness called Effect Size (ES). (ES will be explained in the next chapter.) As per the recommendations for ES in the next chapter, the standardized coefficient of the actionable variable should be at least .3 to .5 depending on context, such as the grade level, that the research was conducted at.

In other words, there are three conditions for determining whether the results of a regression analysis is useful for leadership decision-making—i.e., has potential practical benefit. To be useful, a regression must have:

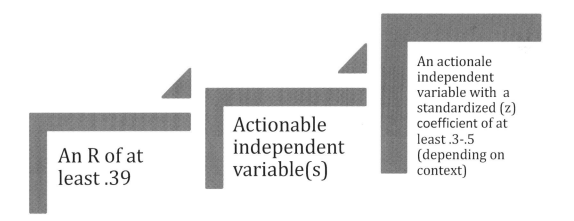

An R of at least .39

Actionable independent variable(s)

An actionale independent variable with a standardized (z) coefficient of at least .3-.5 (depending on context)

To be useful a regression should meet all three conditions. Few do! You can quickly eliminate most regression results with the first criterion. Then for those results that meet the first criterion, subject them to the next two. This will quickly eliminate from consideration most regression studies **and let you focus on the few that remain**.

Unfortunately, in many cases research does not report the standardized z coefficients, and instead rely on the *statistical significance* of the regular coefficients. Alternatively, results may be reported in relative (as opposed to actual) terms such as: Variable A was the most predictive of all the predictor/independent variables. *Ignore all such results.* The data analysis principle #6 of seeking the actual end results indicates that simply because it is the most predictive does not mean that it actually predicts very much. What does it actually predict? If its z score is less than .3-.5 (depending on context), it does not predict enough to warrant consideration.

Practical Tip | An easy way to spot that the findings from a regression analysis is based on statistical significance is to look at the key tables reporting the results from the regression analysis and see if they have lots of asterisks (*, **, and/or ***) next to the numbers in the table.

Finally, it is possible to calculate the error associated with the resultant prediction for the outcome/dependent variable and express it as a range of values which is called the confidence interval. However, in most cases the confidence interval does not help clarify decisions.[38] So it is recommended that you stick with the three step process for analyzing the practical benefit of regression analysis described above.

So, while regression is a powerful, important, and sophisticated statistical tool, when all is said and done most regression results will not stand up to the three step analysis in the graphic above—but those that do have important implications for leaders.

Logistic Regression

A type of regression analysis that is increasingly being used in educational research is ***Logistic Regression.*** Logistic regression is a statistical method used to examine the impact of a series of variables on an outcome that has two possible conditions; e.g., trying to predict which students graduate (yes/no), which teachers leave the profession, (yes/no), or which patient gets cured of an illness (yes/no). Hereafter, this two-value type of variable is referred to as a ***binary*** or ***dichotomous*** outcome/dependent variable.

The use of logistic regression has increased in education research given that many outcomes are dichotomous; i.e., something happens or it does not. It is also widely used in medicine—e.g., vaccines. Someone either gets hospitalized with an illness or does not.

Logistic regression has some mathematical and practical advantages over regular regression—as well as some disadvantages. For now, the application of this methodology to education is evolving and the results at this point cannot yet be said to have been demonstrated to provide results that are replicable, valid, or that have practical value.

---

[38] Clearly, the wider the confidence interval the less useful the results are for leadership decision-making as you are not sure what to believe. For example, a prediction that the likelihood that it will rain today is between 25 and 75% may be statistically correct but offers no useful guidance on whether you should bring an umbrella.

As a result, it is recommended for now that when the dependent variable is a *dichotomous one—e.g., trying to predict whether a student will graduate*—you should use the regression method of ***Discriminant Analysis*** (see Appendix A).

Factors impacting the applicability of regression research

Determining whether a regression analysis result provides useful evidence for leadership decision-making is pretty similar to that of correlation research, as follows:

- Regression is generally looking for linear relationships though there are some software packages that will try to identify curvilinear relationships;
- For regression to be useful for leadership decision-making, at least one of the independent variables needs to be actionable;
- It is important to include possible confounding variables in the regression;
- The direction of the relationship is predefined in the sense that regression is analyzing the impact the predictor/independent variables are having on the dependent variable. So it is always a one-way analysis;
- **The BIGness of the relationship**—i.e. the regression outcome (R) and the coefficients. As with correlations, the importance of a regression relationship should NOT be determined by the evidentiary criteria of *statistical significance*.

> The importance of a regression should be determined first by its predictive capability (R of at least .39), and second by the standardized coefficient of an actionable variable. at least .3 to .5 depending on context, such as the grade level, that the research was conducted at. The recommended specific value for the specific context is the same as those for the effect size recommendations in the next chapter.

Unfortunately, in the vast majority of cases, evidence produced from regression analysis is analyzed in terms of *statistical significance*—both for R and the regression coefficients. The tables in regression studies are filled with tiny numbers with lots of asterisks attached to indicate a significant finding. This makes the importance of each "significant" predictor/independent variable seem more important than it actually is. (As previously mentioned, *statistical significance* does not tell you anything about how BIG a benefit the results indicate.)

When findings do report the amount of benefit from the regression evidence it usually does so in relative terms—e.g., the variable that had "the most" impact on Freshman GPA was _____. However, this relative representation of the outcome violates data analysis principle #6. It does not tell how much impact that variable actually had. It could have been trivial. Once again, it is probably exaggerating the importance of the finding.

The fact that it is rare to find this level of R in published research makes it easier for leaders to identify the few pieces of research evidence that are likely to help improve their schools and increase equity.

Using Excel

> The Excel Analysis ToolPak has a linear regression tool. The closest non-linear tool is the GROWTH function which lets you make a prediction of a future outcome which allows for **curvilinear/exponential** growth.

How Leaders can use Correlation and Regression Evidence to Inform Decisions

While correlations or regressions do not indicate causation, they can still provide valuable guidance for leaders. However, the conditions under which they can are either ignored in most quantitative texts, and/or they are merely dismissed as an inferior type of analysis as compared to experimental design that can determine causation.

Therefore, the right type of relationship research finding can be an important source of evidence for deciding on trying a new intervention to improve schools and increase equity—as long as some fundamental principles are followed by the profession and individual leaders.

Don'ts

The profession *as a whole* should NEVER EVER take large-scale action on the basis of relationship research in the absence of experimental evidence (see next chapter) that demonstrates noticeable benefits from applying the relationship research.

Individual leaders (and the profession) should generally ignore:

⇨ Findings of important correlations or regressions based on *statistical significance* regardless of how many asterisks there are in the tables in the research with a small r (e.g., the research on "grit"), or regressions with small R—i.e., less than .39;

⇨ Reports of findings of "significant" relationships in abstracts/summaries of research articles, media reports, and syntheses put out by professional associations—such language is merely shorthand for statistical significance;

⇨ Reports of findings of a positive relationship without indicating the specific size of the correlation—such language by itself does not indicate whether the relationship was BIG;

⇨ Correlations based on a two-way relationships (e.g., the research on self-efficacy); and

⇨ Correlations and regressions that did not take into account confounding variables—e.g., the research on effective schools).

As has been shown, violating these rules has had devastating consequences for education.

Do's...for using relationship research evidence

In order to avoid the situation previously described where education used correlational data to establish training and interventions to increase students' self-efficacy or grit to no avail, relationship data (correlation or regression) should only be used as the basis for educational decision-making if the following conditions are in place:

⇨ The correlation/regression is BIG—(r or R greater than .39), and *one-way* with an actionable variable, with no obvious confounding variable;

⇨ For regression, if, and only if, R is greater than .39, then see if any standardized coefficient of an actionable variable is at least .3 to .5;

⇨ Ideally, the correlation is replicated in another study (ideally by a different researcher), and/or there is experimental research documenting the effects of implementing the actionable variable (as discussed in the next chapter);

⇨ The relationship makes sense and a leader feels that it is worth it to experiment with an intervention based on the evidence.

Admittedly, the last recommendation is judgmental. However, after looking at the numbers, there are times when judgment comes into play. That is okay as long as a leader knows that he/she is engaged in an experiment and with the understanding that there is no evidence that it is likely to work.

Judgment/
Decision

For example, let's go back to the earlier example where I chastised students for recommending that leaders should implement an effort to increase turnout at the opening orientation session as a way to improve completion rates based on a positive correlation between the two. True, it is probably a two-way correlation which mitigates the likelihood that increasing turnout will increase the rate of completion. However, on second thought, if the correlation is large, and the leaders do not have any better ideas for increasing completion rates, there is nothing wrong with trying this approach given that the cost is probably low. Indeed, the leaders may have an idea based on local knowledge of how to better increase turnout at the initial orientation and how to use that participation to gather valuable information on how to parlay that data into increased completion rates to a great extent than occurred in the original research.

However, it is important for the leaders going into this experiment to realize that there is no corresponding experimental evidence and that the prediction from this correlation does not mean that more students will actually complete. So it would be important for the leaders to monitor the results and if there is no visible improvement in completion rates *then it becomes essential to quickly shift course and try something else.*

Of course, if this contained experiment works—i.e., there is a substantial increase in completion rates—then others should feel comfortable trying the approach.

> In essence, someone trying to increase turnout in the opening orientation is like the *second* boat captain who decided to put citrus fruits onboard based on the experience of the first.

So, while the above checklist of "do's" and "don'ts" provides guidance as to the conditions under which it is prudent for leaders to take action based on a correlation, and to apply the recommended numerical guidelines of BIGness, there is a place for human judgment to conduct individual experiments on a limited basis. However, such individual experimentation should occur within an understanding of how to interpret correlation and regression evidence. Most importantly, in the absence of individual researchers conducting formal experiments (as discussed in the next chapter) with replicated results to see whether this, or any, given approach works, no state or federal government agency, or professional association, should recommend or mandate that institutions implement this or any other approach. It is always best to wait to scale an approach until there is authentic evidence of actual end result success—particularly for students of color and those born into poverty.

At the same time, that does NOT mean that only experiments conducted by researchers, and those designed to prove causation, are the only type of experimental evidence that can inform the profession. Individual leaders who make a judicious decision to act on the basis of authentic relationship evidence to adopt a new practice can be the ones who establish the initial experiments to demonstrate the effectiveness of this practice. Leaders can conduct program evaluations and if the approach turns out to be clearly effective, they can inform other leaders of the success of this approach, who can in turn repeat the experiment. This informal bottom-up rapid prototyping approach to experimental testing of an approach by practitioners based on relationship evidence is widely used to improve health care in the US and in the medical field of obstetrics.[39] If such networked prototyping works for captains and obstetricians, it can work for education leaders.

However generated, it is critical that there be convincing experimental results in a variety of contexts before the profession adopts a new practice based only on relationship results.

Summary

Regression and correlation research can be more important sources of evidence for improving practice than generally acknowledged by the research community. However, correlation and regression need to be applied very carefully.

This chapter has identified the conditions under which relationship research evidence can be considered to be authentic and major contributors towards improving practice. This chapter has also shown that when these conditions are violated there are major negative consequences for the profession. At the same time, these negative consequences can be avoided if leaders use the principles put forth in this chapter to

---

[39] You will discover in Chapter 8 that this approach to practitioner initiated research is called ***improvement science***.

examine relationship evidence more carefully before adopting or promoting a "solution." Avoiding promoting reforms that fail also requires that the research community be more judicious in the analysis of relationship evidence as opposed to either demeaning such evidence or hyping evidence based on small values of r, R, and standardized coefficients.

Clearly, most correlation and regression evidence cannot meet the criteria put forth in this chapter for applying relationship evidence. So what? It just makes the available correlation and regression evidence that can meet the criteria more valuable and easier to identify. Leaders and the profession can then focus on the few pieces of relationship evidence that do have major potential for improving schools and increasing equity.

Remember

Under no circumstances should the profession move forward to adopt a practice at scale based on relationship research in the absence of experimental evidence that demonstrates clear benefits on a small scale as a result of acting on such evidence.

It is important that individual leaders NOT jump on a bandwagon and follow the herd if the underlying relationship evidence does not meet most of the criteria put forth in this chapter for judging the authenticity of relationship evidence—regardless of what the research community claims.

The next chapter will describe various types and uses of experimental research. It will focus on how to identify authentic evidence and critically analyze claims of effectiveness based on experimental evidence. It will also discuss how gold-standard research methodology seeks to prove causation, and the extent to which such methods have produced useful evidence for improving schools and increasing equity.

Challenge Questions

1. **Hakim (1998) found that in a sample of 707 non-smoking, retired Japanese men, age 61-81 who were physically healthy enough to walk, the death rate over 12 years was twice as much among those who walked less than a mile a day as compared to those who walked more than two miles a day. This is after controlling for the effects of age, physical condition, and alcohol consumption.**

   However such data are relative results. You would need the additional information of the actual end results. In that respect it turns out that in the group that walked less than a mile, 43% had died, and for those who walked at least 2 miles a day, only 24% had died. Based on this evidence,

   (a) Is this a positive or negative correlation/relationship?
   (b) Is this a one-way or two way correlation/relationship?
   (c) Does walking more per day cause people to live longer?
   (d) Would you advise Japanese men to walk more than two miles a day once they retired?
   (e) Would you advise non-Japanese men to walk more than two miles a day once they retired?
   (f) Do you find this evidence convincing enough to make you decide to increase the amount of walking you do once you retire to at least two miles a day if you were physically able?

2. **Creighton (2007) notes that when research on the relationship between cigarette smoking and cancer started almost 60 years ago the initial research revealed only a very small relationship, and that the studies' findings contradicted each other. Over time, with better designed studies that have larger sample sizes, we now know that there is a very strong relationship.**

   What are some of the uncontrolled confounding variables that may have misled the earlier research and/or inhibited the quality of the research design?

3. **Interpret the results in the table below.**

   Use common sense to (a) indicate what leadership recommendation (if any) you would make based on this hypothetical data, and (b) what is another obvious *confounding* variable that is not controlled for?

   Mean reading performance of third graders by SES and Age (young vs old) at which they started kindergarten.

	High SES	Low SES
Young	3.1	2.9
Old	3.3	2.6

4) Pick a relationship between variables in education, or life, that you think is a…

    a. Non-linear (curvilinear) relationship

    b. Positive relationship

    c. Negative relationship

5)   Pick an outcome/dependent variable that you are interested in improving. State what this variable is. Then make a list of the four specific (*independent*) variables that you think have the most impact on this outcome. Include at least one specific variable that you can take action on as a leader.

_____

_____

_____

_____

Answers to Challenge Questions

1. **Clearly there is a strong relationship between walking more than two miles a day and living longer. Even though the actual value of the correlation—i.e., r— is not reported, the clear predictive benefit from the relationship in terms of increased longevity suggests that the value of r would be high—i.e., close to 1.**

   (a) It is a positive correlation because both variables work in the same direction—i.e., the more you walk the longer you live.

   (b) It is a one-way relationship. It is clear that walking more per day is associated with longer life.

   > **NOTE:** Interestingly, if the relationship was NOT miles per day, but total miles walked, it would probably be a two-way correlation as it would be possible to interpret the data that the longer one lives the more total walking they have done.

   (c) There was some control in the study for possible confounding variables. If upon closer examination of the study it would seem that the researchers adequately controlled for all the likely confounding variables, then it would be fair to assume that the extensive walking caused an increase in longevity in retired Japanese men.

   (d) Given how BIG the relationship is, and that the researchers controlled for the effects of age and health, it is reasonable to conclude that Japanese men would be well advised to walk more than two miles a day once they retired.

   (e) You can argue both ways. Technically, the sample in the study was only Japanese men. So it is fair to argue that there is no evidence that men of other ethnicities/nationalities would experience the same longevity benefits and that such research should be conducted. On the other hand, in the absence of any evidence that non-Japanese men experience the health benefits of exercise differently than Japanese men, it would seem to be reasonable to expect that the longevity benefits of walking more than two miles a day would apply to non-Japanese men.

   > **NOTE:** This exemplifies how interpreting quantitative evidence involves not just the data but also human judgment.

   (f) Even though I am not Japanese, as a male I personally find it convincing and, once I retire, I will try to make sure that I walk the equivalent of at least two miles at least 5 days a week. If I was a female, I would also probably do it based on this evidence.

2. **There are many possible answers.**
   Some of the obvious confounding variables would be (a) who conducted and/or supported the research: i.e., how impartial was the research, (b) health differences between the groups: i.e., if you limit the sample to only old very sick people you will not see much difference between smokers and non-smokers, (c) the quality of tests to detect cancer; i.e., if the early tests did a poor job of detecting cancer then smokers would seem to be healthier than they actually were, and (d) the sample might have included a disproportionate number of light smokers, or a disproportionate number of folks who had only smoked for a few years, etc.

3. **There are several ways to respond.**

(a) Basically, high SES students do better than low SES students, but the main effect in this hypothetical data is that low SES students do better if they enter kindergarten younger rather than older. The implications for leaders are that they should encourage low SES parents and caregivers to enroll their children in kindergarten at a younger age, and/or use a low or lower cutoff age for admitting low SES students into kindergarten.

(b) A *confounding* variable could be that the results were affected by whether students had remained in the same school for all three years. There are probably other potential *confounding* variables that you can think of.

4. **These are discussion questions to reflect upon. There are no right or wrong or best answers. examples of possible answers would be:**

   a. Curvilinear relationship—assigned homework and school performance. Up to a point homework probably helps, but after a point it puts too much pressure for almost no added learning benefits. There is certainly a curvilinear relationship between the amount of homework assigned and parents' sanity.

      Another example is medical expense and age. There are high expenses when one is born and in the earliest years and these costs decline as one gets older till later in life when costs start to rise again.

   b. Positive relationship—helping people and the amount of smiling one does in a day.

   c. Negative relationship—eating vegetables and one's weight: i.e., the more vegetables you eat the less you will weigh.

5. **There is no right or wrong answer.**

Chapter 6

Applying Experimental Research Evidence

Introduction to Experimental Research

Experimental research is the activist form of research. It is the form of research where you test whether an approach or specific intervention that you think is likely to work actually does work. Conducting experiments is a fundamental scientific process to test whether predicted outcomes actually occur. This is as true for testing the effectiveness of medicines as it for educational approaches.

In an experiment you consciously manipulate the environment by actively and selectively applying the intervention/practice/approach being tested. The setting can be a laboratory setting (basic research), or in districts, schools, and/or classrooms (applied research). The individuals being studied are typically student, teachers, and/or leaders.

The goal of *experimental* **research** is to determine the changes in the experimental group(s) that receives the new intervention as compared to a comparison /control group that does not (hereafter, the term comparison group will be used). The goal is to see which group does better over time. The main *independent* variable is whether a group did or did not receive the intervention. Ideally, the two groups are *initially* the same in all respects, so that any difference in outcomes is likely the result of the intervention being tested. In the most rigorous experimental designs it is possible to go a step further and even determine whether the differences in outcomes were *caused* by the new intervention.

Alternatively, an experiment may involve only one group that is studied over time. In this case the group receives the experimental treatment sometime during the timespan of the study to see if there is any resultant change from before the treatment was applied until after. For example, a group of students with a history of misbehaving could be provided with positive reinforcement. Then an analysis could compare the number of discipline referrals that same group experienced before the intervention to the number afterwards.

Sometimes, particularly in basic-research studies of behavior of a small number of individuals, the intervention may be started and withdrawn several times over the course of the study. (This is also referred to as a multiple baseline design.) The goal is to see if the individuals revert to their original status when the intervention is withdrawn and then improve when it is reestablished. This type of design is often used to study the effects of different approaches to motivating or disciplining a student.

An experiment can also have two or more experimental groups each trying a different new approach. The goal is to determine which experimental intervention works best, and whether either does better than the comparison group.

In laboratory-based experimental research the comparison group is generally given a popular conventional intervention. In school-based experimental approach, the main focus of this chapter, the comparison group generally engages in business as usual.

Experiments are conducted to test a wide range of innovations from complete comprehensive programs to improve a specific content area, to more general approaches for improving staff development, classroom management, etc. Hereafter, these will all be referred to as *interventions*.

The prior chapter showed how advocating a national reform such as *self-efficacy* or effective schools on the basis of relationship research often leads practice astray as they turn out not to be effective in an activist mode—i.e., implementing the intervention in ineffective schools turns out to NOT make them effective. As a result, a decade of reform effort tuns out to not make any difference.

Similarly, a laboratory basic research experiment that is conducted over the course of a few days that finds that developing self-efficacy has a positive outcome does NOT mean that a school-based intervention to increase self-efficacy will lead to improvements. While basic research provides important clues as to what *might* work in schools, you cannot conclude that an intervention to increase students' self-efficacy will in fact lead to improvements until applied experimental research is conducted to see whether it does.

The focus of this chapter is on experiments that are *applied* research—i.e., testing whether implementing an approach in a school setting leads to noticeable improvements or increases in equity. However, as explained in Chapter 1, there is a role for laboratory types of *basic* research—i.e., experiments to develop basic knowledge about the nature of learning and social interaction. Indeed, many of the ideas for *applied* experiments come from the findings of *basic* research.

Often ideas for experimentation come from theories or from evidence produced by the types of relationship research discussed in the prior chapter. For example, if it has been shown that there is a BIG relationship between self-esteem and academic achievement, the next step is to conduct an experiment in which practices designed to increase the self-esteem are applied to some students/classrooms/schools and not to others. An analysis would then be conducted to determine whether the experimental group that received the treatment to enhance self-esteem ended up doing noticeably better than those who did not—i.e., the comparison group.[40]

---

[40] Not all approaches to enhance self-esteem are likely to be equally effective in actually increasing self-esteem. Therefore, it is important to first have some basic experimental evidence that the specific approach being used to enhance self-esteem in school settings actually increases it, before using that specific approach in any applied experiment to determine the effects enhancing self-esteem has on school outcomes.

In other words, a finding of a strong relationship is a passive form of evidence, while the results of experiments are an activist form of evidence that indicates what happens when you take direct action.

As a result, the profession should not promote the large-scale use of interventions based only on relationship evidence without first conducting experiments to determine whether systematically applying the approach suggested by the relationship research produces the predicted benefits. It is one thing to know that unusually successful schools have a strong focus on instruction which is a relationship finding—and another to determine whether actively implementing an intervention to train staff in low-performing schools to be more focused on instruction actually leads to noticeable improvements in those schools.

Experiments can be conducted by researchers and by schools/districts. The experiments by researchers are designed methodologically to produce results that have wide generalizability—i.e., the results can be applied to a large percentage of schools. In addition, the most advanced form of experimental methodology can even determine whether the intervention *caused* the outcome. On the other hand, experiments by schools/districts tend to be program evaluations designed to inform their local improvement efforts.

How to find experimental evidence

Given the importance of experimental research, and that it tends to represent a small percentage of overall studies that one finds in general searches, you may want to do a targeted search to find the existing experimental studies on the topic you are interested in. To do so, when you search academic databases such as Google Scholar, Proquest, JSTOR, etc, add descriptors/keywords such as "experiment," or "experimental design."

So, for example, if you are interested in "culturally relevant pedagogy," and want to see if anyone has conducted experiments to test the impact of using such a curriculum. you would search on:

"culturally relevant pedagogy" AND "experimental design"

This will identify experimental studies where researchers tested the use of instruction that emphasized culturally relevant pedagogy to study its impact on outcomes. Did the students who were exposed to such an intervention perform noticeably better than those who did not?

If there are no experimental studies, that creates an opportunity for you to conduct such an experiment. If there are experiments in the use of culturally relevant pedagogy but the students did NOT do better, can you think of a better way to implement the concept? If the answer is YES, then conduct a new experiment using your approach.

The techniques for finding experimental, and other, evidence is described in greater detail in Chapter 10 in the literature review section.

Overview of experimental methods, application, and analysis

Experimental research tends to be the most technical. As a result, this chapter is quite long. It presents experimental methods as a journey through four sections. The good news is that at the end, you will be able to analyze the authenticity of the most mathematically sophisticated experimental evidence without needing complex statistical knowledge. You will only have to apply a few simple rules.

In the first two sections of the journey you will learn:

Section 1—Methods for Conducting Experiments
Section 2—Methods for Analyzing the Results of Experiments

This is the background technical information about the why's and how's of experimental research.

However, the next section, Section 3, is verrrry non-traditional—but it is of critical importance to leaders. It turns out that the very technical and arcane elements of experimental research often are used to exaggerate the actual benefits documented in the research. This is true regardless of how prestigious the source, or how rigorous the methodology. In such cases, findings that a practice is evidence-based will NOT replicate in real world practice and will NOT improve your schools or increase equity. Indeed, it will be shown that this is a widespread problem and probably a key reason why the results from the adoption of evidence-based practices have had little proven effect on educational outcomes.

The purpose of is not to demean research and researchers. Rather, it is done out of recognition that when leaders adopt what they have been told and do not see the expected benefits, that can only lead to cynicism about academic research.

Section 3—How Rigorous Statistical Analysis of Experiments Often Misleads Practice

Caveat emptor![41]

It is therefore critical for leaders to exert independent, critical judgment about evidentiary claims of effectiveness from experimental outcomes in order to identify those examples of evidence which are in fact authentic. The goal is not to demean research, but to avoid the cynicism that inevitably results when leaders adopt an evidence-based program and do not see the expected results. That is the goal of the next section.

Section 4—Implications for Practice: How to Identify Authentic Experimental Research Evidence.

---

[41] Latin for *buyer beware.*

Section 4 provides practical, easy to apply, rules for how leaders can judge the authenticity of the findings of experiments—i.e., identify experimental evidence that is likely to improve and increase equity in their schools. Rules will be provided to enable leaders to determine whether the benefits in the experimental results are BIG enough to warrant their adopting the approach that was tested.

The most important takeaway for leaders in this Section (and chapter) is to learn the simple method for applying the new statistical test of *practical benefit* for identifying experimental results that are likely to benefit their schools. Any leader can easily determine the *practical benefit*, and its stepchild *potential practical benefit*, of any experimental research for their schools.

While this is a long chapter, Section 4 is the one that is most directly relevant to leadership practice and decision-making. Sections 1-3 serve to provide the background and rationale for the methods in Section 4. So, it is suggested that you get a sense of the key ideas in Sections 1-3, and focus most carefully on Section 4.

Section 1—Methods for Conducting Experiments

Different ways of conducting experimental research affect the degree to which one can be confident that the intervention *caused* the outcome. The more confident we can be that the research design was of sufficient quality to establish *causation*, the more confident leaders can be that if they adopt the intervention they will experience in their schools the same benefit that was documented in the research. *Causation* means that the intervention or process being studied was directly responsible for the outcome by eliminating the possibility that the observed relationship was impacted/caused by an external confounding variable not included in the study.

For example, a confounding variable that can determine whether test scores go up or down that have nothing to do with any reading program is changes in district boundaries (scores can go up or down depending on how the school's demographics change). Other possible confounding variables are changes in the cut scores on a state test (cut scores usually go down which increases the percentage of students passing), installation of a new test (scores go down), and the year after the installation of a new test (scores go up relative to the first year).[42] The ideal experiment is one that would eliminate the possibility that all these confounding factors impacted the outcome so

---

[42] Confounding factors can produce misleading results that have national visibility. Bracey (2006) reports on what happened in Prince George's County in Maryland when it became the national showcase for raising test scores and dramatically reducing the achievement gap. It was done by the combination of *confounding* factors which included: (a) a state test that had not changed so that over time the schools became adept at teaching the test items, (b) a test that was easy to pass, and (c) leadership that promoted an over-emphasis on test prep. The results were impressive. Alas, the moment the test was changed, the district's results plummeted, and the gaps reappeared with the scores of African-American students falling to as low as the 18th percentile. Clearly this national "success" had nothing to do with improvements in teaching and learning. When the superintendent left for a position in another state he was unable to replicate this "success" and was fired.

that we can be confident that whatever benefit occurred was solely a result of the new reading program.

True-experimental, Randomized Controlled Trial (RCT)

As mentioned in the previous chapter, statisticians largely ignored causality until approximately 40 years ago but now it dominates. Researchers in most disciplines including education now view evidence of causality as the primary goal of research and tend to dismiss findings from research that use less rigorous methods that cannot prove causality. While a number of methodological tools have been proposed for establishing causality, the dominant method used for testing medicines and educational practices is the **Randomized Controlled Trial (RCT)**.[43] RCT is often referred to as the **gold standard** of research.

Gold-standard RCT research usually…

- Is conducted in real time;
- Uses random sampling;
- Incorporates large samples;
- Uses validated measures for collecting data; and
- Conducts sophisticated multivariate statistical analyses on the data.

The importance of RCT experiments: Establishing causation

A true experiment starts with a pool of participants who are then randomly assigned to either the experimental or comparison group. Random assignment means that neither the researcher nor participants determine which group the participants are placed in and that each participant has an equal chance of being assigned to either the experimental or comparison groups. Participants are assigned to a group via numbers generated randomly by a computer.

For example, the recent efficacy tests for the COVID-19 vaccines were clinical studies in which individuals were randomly assigned to an experimental group which received the vaccine or to a comparison group which received an injection of a placebo. The placebo is a solution which has no medical benefits—e.g., salt water. A placebo is used to eliminate the psychological effect that someone gets better simply because they believe they have received a powerful medicine. So everyone got an injection of something. In addition, this was a ***double-blind*** study. It is called double blind because neither the participants nor those providing the injections knew who was in the experimental or comparison group, or whether the shot being administered to any given individual was the vaccine or the placebo.

The benefit of having the medical personnel not know what was in the injection they were administering eliminates the possible bias in showing greater concern towards

---

[43] Other methods that have been proposed for establishing causation have been path analysis, and Pearl and Mackenzie (2018) have proposed using causal diagrams of Bayesian networks. Both of these methods are technically complex and rarely used, and are therefore beyond the focus of this book.

the person receiving the vaccine and that such concern could have healing effects. In addition, having the participant not know whether he/she was receiving the placebo controls for the **Hawthorne effect**. The Hawthorne effect is where the novelty of being a research subject and the increased attention from such participation leads to temporary increases in performance, thus artificially enhancing the result for the experimental group. However, in this case all the subjects are participating equally in the research as no one knows whether they received the vaccine or the placebo.

In addition, the sample was large so that the random assignment theoretically insured that any other human factors that could influence the effects of the vaccine were equally distributed between the two groups.[44] In other words, it was likely that there were equal numbers of people of color, older individuals, individuals with high blood pressure and other health problems, etc. in the two groups.

There are two more types of confounding factors that RCT methodology is particularly good at controlling for:

- *Regression to the Mean*, which is the tendency of extreme scores to move to the middle regardless of what happens, so that very low performing students will improve regardless. This is also why unusually tall parents will usually have children who are shorter than they are.

- *Maturation*, which is growth that occurs simply as a result of the passage of time that can be confused with the effects of the independent variable. This is particularly problematic in single group designs.

So random selection is a powerful way to simultaneously control for the possible effects of many confounding variables. This is (in theory) superior to the earlier control methods—i.e., restricting the sample to individuals who possess the key confounding variable in Chapter 4 and *partial correlation* in Chapter 5—which could only control for one or several confounding variables.

As a result of the benefits of random selection, the gold-standard double blind RCT methodology serves to ensure, to the extent that is humanly possible, that any improvement in COVID-19 health outcomes between the two groups was *caused* by the vaccine.

Applying RCT research in education

RCT methodology has also been widely applied in education. Traditionally, it consisted of short-term experiments often conducted in a lab by psychologists. It was only in the early 1990s that the work of Ann Brown (1992) convinced educational psychologists of the importance of shifting experimental research from the lab to the classroom/school in order to get more valid findings as to the impact of the research in

---

[44] While in theory random assignment eliminates confounding differences between the experimental and control groups, there is scant evidence that findings from experimental research differ when random assignment is not used. Lipsey and Wilson's (1993) summary of 302 meta-analyses found no difference between studies that used random assignment and non-random designs.

the real world. As a result, much of the applied experimental educational research shifted from being conducted in a lab setting where the treatment was provided by the researcher or associates under controlled conditions, to actual school/classroom setting where the novel treatment/intervention was delivered by the actual teachers/administrators/counselors. Hundreds of RCT education studies have since been conducted in school settings.

While RCT designs are the most prestigious type of gold-standard studies, conducting such research in school settings is more difficult than testing the effects of a medicine in human beings. Education occurs in very complex organizational settings which imposes its own confounding effects. Schools differ in many respects, as do classrooms, teachers and students. While studies to test the efficacy of a new vaccine can incorporate a sample with tens of thousands of participants, it is impossible to conduct experiments on tens of thousands of schools or classrooms. As a result, randomization cannot control for most differences between organizations as it does on human subjects in medical trials.

In addition, it is hard to get schools to agree to be assigned randomly to a treatment or placebo. If schools believe in the value of the intervention being tested they would want to be placed in the treatment group. Nor is it usually possible to provide a placebo. A placebo would mean that you spend the same amount of money in control schools to get them to adopt a practice that is known not to have any educational benefits. So RCT experiments in education typically randomly assign participating students, classrooms, or schools to be in the experimental or control group. The experimental group gets some new treatment, and the comparison group gets…nothing. The comparison groups go about business as usual.

Of course, this is NOT pure RCT. The fact that more monies are being spent in the experimental schools to implement the intervention is a major confounding factor.

The bottom line is that it is virtually impossible to control for all confounding variables in the chaotic world of schools. As a practical matter, RCTs are very expensive, take a long time to conduct, and by the end of the study the original conditions have changed. For example, a 5-year study of the effectiveness of a textbook is pretty useless since by the time the study has been completed several new editions have been released.[45] In addition, it is impossible to maintain the initial random assignment over the course of a study. There is student attrition, student and teacher reassignment, principals leave and new ones are hired.[46]

As a result of these and other problems, Ginsburg and Smith (2016) concluded that all the validated RCT design research of all the math programs certified as effective by the federal What Works Clearinghouse (WWC) are not useful for guiding practitioners' decisions. Gopal, and Schorr (2016, June 2) argued that RCT analysis is

---

[45] During that same time period 3-4 replication studies could have been conducted at much lower cost using the rapid prototyping research techniques in Chapter 8.)

[46] Finklestein, et al. (2010) is an example of a study that demonstrates how difficult it is to maintain the original design in RCT research.

unlikely to be helpful because the types of interventions that are easily studied within rigorously controlled experiments are probably too simplistic to solve complex problems. Bryk, Gomez, Grunow, and LeMahieu (2015) of the Carnegie Foundation have also critiqued the usefulness of RCT approaches in education.

In addition, the upcoming section on BIGness of results will show that the results from RCT research generally do not find beneficial outcomes.

Even medicine has moved away from this type of rigid experimental design for testing complex medical procedures that integrate multiple components that interact under real-world clinical conditions. This type of experimental research is called *Pragmatic Trials* (Ford & Norris, 2016). Carroll (2018) describes the rationale for, and approach of, Pragmatic Trials as:

> Promising health studies often don't pan out in reality…Research participants are usually different from general patients; their treatment doesn't match real-world practice; researchers can devote resources not available in most physician offices.
>
> Moreover, most studies, even the gold standard of randomized controlled trials, focus squarely on causality. They are set up to see if a treatment will work in optimal conditions…But what we also need are studies that test if a treatment will work in the real world — if they have effectiveness… A pragmatic trial seeks to determine if, and how, an intervention might work in practice, where decisions are more complicated than in a strictly controlled clinical trial.

Pragmatic trial experimental methodology appears to be a better fit for determining the effectiveness of education interventions than the current reliance on RCT methods. At the very least, education research needs to stop advocating reliance on RCT because "that is what medicine uses." Only *some* medical research relies on RCT—i.e., that which tests individual medicines—which bears little resemblance to the methodological issues and problems of conducting experiments in schools.

So while using RCT to test medicines is a major intellectual achievement that produces major health benefits, it appears to have limited applicability for education.[47] It is probably time to recognize that it is impossible to control for all possible *extraneous* variables in chaotic and complex organizations such as schools and hospitals. This means that it is virtually impossible to establish causation in real-world testing of educational interventions (though RCT is of tremendous value in basic research on the

---

[47] Researchers are starting to use advanced relationship models such as Regression-Discontinuity (RD) analysis as an end around to the logistical problems of establishing and maintaining an experiment. Researchers are claiming that the ex post facto RD analysis can simulate the use of random assignment and provide estimates of causal effects. At this time it is a tremendously complex methodology that few understand, and that has so many assumptions and options that provide the potential for error and misleading findings. At the same time, the underlying theory of this approach is fascinating and provides the potential for RD to be a valuable tool.

nature of learning and brain functioning, and a wide variety of fundamental psychological and social behaviors[48]).

 Good News | Fortunately, there are simpler methods for conducting experiments which can provide useful evidence for leaders even in the absence of evidence of causation. These are generally referred to as quasi-experimental research.

Quasi-experimental research

Quasi-experimental research is a more practical form of experimental method for education. Its two main characteristics are:

- It does NOT use random assignment; and
- It does NOT have to be conducted in real time. It can (but not necessarily) include analysis of an experiment and data collection processes ex post facto—i.e., after they have occurred.

Since quasi-experimental design does not require random assignment it is easier to set up the research process. So, for example, if a researcher finds four schools that want to try a new intervention, he/she can use all of them as experimental sites and then find four schools that are somewhat similar in key characteristics as the comparison schools. So the comparison schools can have the same percentage of students living in poverty, similar average test scores, etc. Similarly, it can select students, leaders, and/or teachers who agree to participate in the experiment, and then use others as the comparisons. Assignment to groups is done as a matter of convenience as opposed to using random assignment to determine which schools or individuals are in the experimental group.

Unlike true experiments in which the researcher initiates and operates the experiment, including assigning the groups, data collection and analysis, in real time, quasi-experimental research can involve analysis of data from an experiment ex post facto (after it has occurred). In *ex post facto research* the researcher may or may not have initiated the experiment or even established the groups. Indeed, the experiment may already have occurred and the data collection process previously completed by the school, district, state or federal agency prior to the start of the new research effort. Then the researcher goes back to determine the results, and what factors and relationships existed that might explain the results. Researchers might also conduct follow up interviews to determine how school personnel reacted to, and implemented, the intervention.

Researchers are also increasingly using state or federal databases to conduct ex post facto research. (See Appendix B for examples of such datasets.) The research that my student engaged in, that was described in Chapter 4, to determine the relative reading

---

[48] Basic research on the nature of brain functioning and memory was critical to the design of my successful Higher Order Thinking Skills (HOTS) intervention. Chapter 8 describes how this basic research was applied to improve the design of this intervention.

performance of Black girls was an example of conducting ex post facto research using a federal database.

Another type of ex post facto research is a ***natural experiment*** in which researchers take advantage of naturally occurring differences. For example, studying the differences in learning and behavior between identical twins raised together as compared to those raised separately would be a natural experiment to determine the relative effect of genetics and environment. The existence of different groups of identical twins was a naturally occurring phenomenon—one that occurred prior to the start of the research. We are now in a natural (but unfortunate) experiment in approaches to recovering socially and economically from a pandemic.

Most research in economics is conducted via natural experiments. For example, if you want to study the effects of implementing a minimum wage on employment, study two nearby similar states where one has just implemented one and another that did not—and study the changes in overall employment.

Another form of *ex post facto* research, even farther removed from real time, is *meta-analysis*. Generally, experimental studies of a similar issue will find varying amounts of differences between the experimental and control groups. ***Meta-analysis*** is a way of aggregating or pooling the results across all the experiments that studied the same type of intervention to determine a <u>single,</u> average overall difference between the groups across all the studies.

In organizing a meta-analysis the researcher will use specific methodological standards as to which studies will be included in the analysis. Unfortunately, meta-analyses rarely have information on the quality of the intervention and its implementation—so the results can easily under-estimate the real benefits of well implemented high-quality version of the intervention.[49] This is slowly starting to change. For example, the *meta-analysis* of reading development studies by Wanzek, et al. (2013) includes only studies of quality reading programs as evidenced by providing services to students for more than 100 days. (The results of this *meta-analysis* are contained in Case Study #1 at the end of this chapter) While the number of days is a very basic measure of the quality of the intervention in a study, it is a promising start. In addition, the authors analyzed the results separately for different grade spans. As you will see in the case study, the results are very revealing.

The simplest forms of quasi-experimental research involve just having a single group (with no comparison group), or an experimental and comparison group without a pre-measure—e.g., a post test. In the latter the researcher is just able to compare the final results for each group without knowing where they started from.

Ex post facto research can also consist of historical ***longitudinal*** and **cross-sectional research.** *Longitudinal research* tends to follow the same group or *cohort* over time,

---

[49] I once asked one of the researchers who had had a number of meta-analyses published: Why didn't you consider the quality of intervention, along with the quality of the research design, as a criterion for including studies in your *meta-analyses*? His response was that if he used both criteria there would not enough studies to conduct a *meta-analysis*.

while ***cross-sectional*** **research** studies how an outcome for successive *cohorts* of students at a specific grade level and subject area changed over time.

Examples of longitudinal research include:

- The National Education Longitudinal Study of 1988 - NELS:88/2000, which provides data about critical transitions experienced by a cohort of students who were in the eighth grade in 1988 over time; and

- Research on the sustained effects of Head Start and other early childhood efforts as the students enrolled in those programs transition to elementary school and beyond.

Examples of *cross-sectional* research include:

- Reports from state departments, or the U.S. Department of Education's National Assessment of Educational Progress (NAEP), that compare how the students tested most recently at a given grade level are doing compared with how students at those same grade levels did in the past; and

- Studies that examine whether high school students today know more geography or science than students did decades earlier.

While there are many examples of excellent and useful ex post facto research, there are times when the issue of whether research is real time vs. ex post facto can make a big difference. For example, according to Johnson (2014) a *meta-analysis* in 1997 by the World Cancer Research Fund found that diets loaded with fruits and vegetables might reduce the overall incidence of cancer by more than 20 percent. However, in 2007, a follow-up *meta-analysis* by the same organization reversed the earlier conclusion and found the evidence of a relationship between diet and cancer rates to not be convincing. What caused the change? The earlier studies were mostly *ex post facto* studies based on the recollections of individuals about their diets, while the more recent studies tended to be ones where researchers had individuals record their diet in real-time while the study was going on.[50]

At the same time, as the power of available computers and statistical programs increase, it is becoming easier for *quasi-experimental* research to control for the effects of the confounding effects of initial differences to the same extent as *true-experimental* design. Therefore, it is now possible for *quasi-experimental* research to be of very high quality—perhaps even more useful than *true-experimental* RCT research.

The primary method of controlling for possible confounding effects in quasi-experimental research is ***Analysis of Covariance*** (see Appendix A). Analysis of Covariance is typically used to weigh or adjust outcomes when there are significant

---

[50] While the inability of science to come to a conclusive decision about key matters such as the relationship between diet and cancer in a timely fashion despite decades of research is vexing, it puts into context some of the frustrations about the failure of educational research to provide convincing answers to some very fundamental questions. It also highlights how amazing and important it is when a research breakthrough does occur.

initial differences between the experimental and comparison groups on key dependent variables. *Analysis of Covariance* adjusts the final results in a way that takes into account the initial differences between the groups. So, for example, if the experimental group had a lower initial reading level, or had a higher percentage of students on free and reduced lunch, then this statistical procedure will weigh the gains made by the experimental group accordingly. This weighting will in effect raise the final scores of the experimental group relative to the comparison group.

Analysis of Covariance is sometimes even needed in a study where random sampling is used. While in theory random sampling reduces initial differences between groups on all relevant variables, that does not always happen—particularly when a smaller sample is used.

Another way to control for the effects of confounding variables in experimental research is to use hierarchical linear modeling (HLM). Much of the data in educational research is hierarchical in nature. Students are nested in classrooms, which are nested in schools. HLM enables the researcher to control for the effects of the school or classroom on student performance. (However, HLM methodology is extremely complex and discussing it further is beyond the scope of this book.)

Practical Tip

As a leader conducting an evaluation of a new program or process, or as a leadership student conducting action research, the chances are almost certain you will be conducting quasi-experimental research.

Table 6.1 below summarizes the relationship between the key approaches to research and whether they tend to be *true-experimental* or *quasi-experimental* research.

Table 6.1
Approaches to Experimental Research

Approaches to Experimental Research	True-Experimental	Quasi-Experimental
Real Time	✓	✓
Ex Post Facto		✓
Historical Longitudinal Research		✓
Cross Sectional Research		✓
Laboratory-based Research	✓	
Field-based Research	✓	✓
Basic Research	✓	
Applied Research	✓	✓

Sampling methods

As inferential research, the goal of experiments is to reach a conclusion that can be inferred to apply more broadly to a population. The **population** is all the students/teachers/schools/districts who exist in the category of who is being studied in the research. However, since only the NSA and the census bureau have the resources to study everyone, the majority of studies conducted in education and all social sciences involve the development of a *sample.*

*The **sample*** is the population subgroup of individuals or schools that are examined in a study. The researcher uses the result from analyzing the sample, usually the *Mean*, to infer the *Mean* of the population for the variable(s) being studied. For example, a researcher might want to infer the reading level of all fourth grade students nationally who declare their ethnicity to be Pacific Islanders (i.e., the *population*) from the reading scores of a sample of such students. Alternatively, a study of the effects of the strategy of reciprocal teaching from a sample of students, the researcher would ideally want to be able to infer that the effects from that sample are representative of what would happen everywhere else.

In an experiment, the goal is to have a large enough sample such that the *Mean* performance of the experimental group that has experienced an intervention will predict the *Mean* that the population of similar schools/classrooms/individuals can expect to achieve or experience if they adopt the same intervention.

The smaller the sample the less certain it is that the results of the research reflect the population of interest. Another way of saying this is that the smaller the sample, the greater the degree of error there will be in making any inference from the results of the research to the characteristics of the population—e.g., all voters, all schools (including yours), or all students/teachers.

One way to determine the *Mean* of the population is to conduct a series of the same study with different unbiased samples. Then the overall *Mean* of all the *Means* of each individual study will be about the same as the *Mean* for the population. Of course, in education we cannot realistically do successive studies. Fortunately, there are mathematical formulas for calculating the degree of ***sampling error*** for different size samples called ***power analysis***.

While the details of power analysis are beyond this book, the partial result is a *Mean* with a confidence interval—i.e., the range of possible outcomes for the population *Mean*—and the probability that the Mean lies within those boundaries. If the confidence interval is wide, and/or the probability is low, that is an indication that the sample size was too small. Results from too small sample sizes are usually useless for leaders. For example, knowing that there is a 60 percent chance that the expected reading growth for the overall population will be an average of .3 to 1.3 grade levels is fairly useless. Alternatively, if the result is a confidence interval such as being 95% certain that (a) 52% of voters favor candidate A, plus or minus 3%, or (b) the rate of student growth from intervention A is 1 year with a *confidence interval* of plus or minus 5 months, it is highly likely, but not certain, that Candidate A will win, and that students will probably achieve close to a year's growth.

A key issue in research is to avoid sample bias. ***Sample bias*** is where research relies on a sample that does not represent the population. Sample bias can result from drawing too small a sample, which will then be not as diverse in the same proportion as the population. Alternatively, you can have a large sample, but one that is selected in such a way that excludes certain types of individuals.

Sample bias can render the results of research to be misleading. For example, the classic case of *sample bias* is the Reader's Digest poll that sent out ballots to 10 million people it gathered from automobile registrations and telephone directories to predict the presidential election of Alf Landon vs. Franklin D. Roosevelt in 1936. Why was this poll wrong? It was wrong because it had a major sampling bias. The *population* was all those who would vote. However, the *sample* only represented voters who were relatively well off. (Only a minority of voters in 1936 had cars and telephones.) Biased sampling also led to the conclusion that Dewey would beat Truman to the extent that the headline in the Chicago Tribune November 3, 1948 was "Dewey Defeats Truman."

Sample bias has also been a major problem in medical research. Historically, the samples for medical clinical trials were composed primarily of white males. Finally, in 1993 Congress passed a law (PL 103-43) that *required* that women and minorities be included in clinical research, and in sufficient numbers to allow for valid analyses of differences that they may experience in the effects of medicines. However, this law largely affects government funded medical research, and sample bias remains a problem in industry funded clinical trials.

Sample bias can develop even if you start the research with a representative sample. In survey research those who respond may be different than those who do not. Another problem of bias creep is that in any longitudinal study some of the experimental and comparison students who started in the study will not be there when post-test data are collected. This is referred to as ***attrition***. The questions then become whether the *attrition* biased the results. For example, it may be that the highest poverty students were most likely to transfer out and there were more high poverty students leaving from one group than the other one in the study. This will bias the results as it may make the intervention look more effective than it actually was. So the question then becomes whether the remaining sample in each group is similar in characteristics to the one that started.

The worst type of sample attrition is where the researcher decides to drop some schools or students from the sample without adequate justification. This is actually a bigger problem across the disciplines than is realized as part of the phenomenon of what is referred to as p-hacking wherein the researcher makes a minor change in the sample to produce an outcome that is statistically significant (p-hacking will be discussed later in this chapter).

	When reviewing research check to see whether attrition occurred and the rationale provided by the researcher and see if it makes sense to you. If it does not, ignore the research findings.

Practical Tip | (There will be an example of inappropriate sample manipulation from an article published in a top research journal in Case Study #3 at the end of this chapter.) |

Conducting an experiment with a biased sample can produce misleading results. If there is a *biased* sample, the *Mean* of the result for the variables in the study will be different from the actual *Means* that exist for the population (and that will exist for your schools). Differential attrition and other forms of sample bias can make an intervention that is not effective appear to be effective, or vice versa.

154

Researchers consider the best type of sample to be the ***random sample***. In a *random sample* every member of the population has an equal chance of being selected for the sample in the study, and an equal chance of being in the experimental or comparison groups. As previously discussed, creating a random sample is central to conducting RCT experiments.

Creating a random sample that ensures that everyone has an equal chance of being assigned to the experimental group usually involves assigning numbers to all members of the population. For example, all students in a school can be listed alphabetically and given a number that represents their alphabetical rank. If there are 2,000 students in a school and you want to interview 60 to determine students' attitudes toward the school, the 60 students can then be randomly selected by having a random number generator produce a random sequence of 60 numbers between 1 and 2,000. You would then interview the 60 students with the generated numbers.

Practical Tip

Excel ToolPak has a random number generator. In addition, there are a number of random number/integer generators on the internet; e.g., random.org, randomresult.com, etc. (to find one just Google "Random Number Generator.)

However, even randomly assigning participants in a sample to the experimental and comparison groups can be problematic if the samples are too small. In that case not all confounding variables will be controlled for as the experimental and comparison groups can end up being different in some critical way. In addition, the problems of bias and attrition can create problems.

An example of a high quality, very large, random sample are the ones used in the clinical trials to test the efficacy of the COVID-19 vaccines. The Pfizer-BioNTech sample had 40,277 participants and Moderna had 27,817. Moderna had a smaller sample because its target population was smaller, 18+ years of age, while the Pfizer targeted individuals 16+ years of age. These random samples were large enough to account for all possible confounding variables—e.g., having individuals with diabetes equally represented in the experimental and comparison groups. The large size and randomization ensured that any reduction in COVID deaths was caused by the vaccine. In addition, great care was taken to minimize/eliminate sample bias. There was a substantial number of older participants since they were the most vulnerable to COVID, There was also major effort to recruit non-white participants. Blacks were only about 2.5% under-represented in the sample as compared to their percentage in the US population, while Hispanics were over-represented.

The sampling process at the other end of the spectrum from a random sample is a ***sample of convenience***. In such a sample the researcher selects individuals or schools that are easy to get access to. For example, the researcher may reach out to a group of principals with whom he/she is familiar to be part of the experiment. Similarly, standing on a street corner to try and get volunteers to fill out a survey is a sample of convenience. Clearly, the findings of this study could not be said to generalize to other principals or individuals who do not come to that street corner. Samples of convenience have the least generalizability of any formal sampling process.

An intermediate sampling method in experimental research is using matched pairs. A *matched pair* sample is where the researcher identifies potentially confounding independent variables and matches each individual or school with another that has similar characteristics. Obvious examples of independent variables that would be used to make matches of students would be Race and SES, and some independent variables to match up teachers would be Experience and Grade Level. If there is a large number of schools in the sample, researchers may match up schools with one another based on variables such as the Reading Scores, Percentages of Free and Reduced Lunch, Size, Grade Levels, etc. Once all the matches are formed the researchers then randomly assign one of the pair to the experimental group and the other to the comparison group.

Chapter 10 will discuss additional sampling strategies for conducting action research such as an evaluation of a program in your schools.

Validity of experiments

There are two main types of validity:

- External validity
- Internal validity

External validity is the extent to which the results of an experiment or any study generalize to other people, schools, districts, or the nation. In external validity, statistics infer the *Mean* of the outcome for the population—e.g., all schools—from the outcomes of the schools in a given study. The key, but not only, determinant of the degree of *external validity* is the nature of the sample. In general, the larger and more heterogeneous the sample is the greater the degree of external validity. An experiment with a large random sample will generally have the greatest external validity. Research that relies on a sample of convenience or a small sample will generally have the least external validity.

Another key determinant of the external validity is how well the study controlled for the effects of confounding variables. If confounding variables actually caused the results, when other schools implemented the tested intervention they would not get the same benefit—i.e., the results of the experiment would not generalize.[51]

Internal validity is the degree to which a study's design ensures that there are no *confounding* variables impacting the experiment so as to be able to conclude that the experimental treatment *caused* the outcome. RCT research with its random assignment to groups has higher levels of internal validity than quasi experimental research.

---

[51] An often overlooked confounding variable is the possibility that those who participated in the initial experiment were unusually talented or unusually motivated—akin to the Michael Jordan effect discussed earlier. Such experiments have low external validity.

While researchers and research journals are most interested in trying to maximize *internal validity* and establish causation, leaders are most interested in *external validity*. Leaders want to know that the results of a study conducted elsewhere will produce similar benefits in their schools—i.e. that the findings of an experiment will generalize to their schools.

Internal and external validity are not necessarily in conflict. However, given the problems previously described with respect to establishing causation and finding replication studies, the two types of validity often end up being in conflict. Unless available ex post facto research has very large, highly diverse samples, it is hard for leaders to extrapolate the extent to which the findings of the *Mean* of the population of schools are likely to benefit their specific schools. So in the absence of causation or replication studies with large samples showing BIG benefits, it is not clear that the results can be inferred to the population of schools or to the population of schools like yours with any precision or high probability—i.e., external validity is low.

Indeed, given the tremendous diversity within and between schools it is hard to envision that there is a single population, and/or that there can be a population *Mean* with a small confidence interval—i.e., a result from a study that would apply pretty much equally to all schools. At the same time, there are three situations where leaders are interested in the population *Mean*:

1. When they want to assess how their schools are doing in comparison to others in their state or region. In that case the state or region is the population;

2. When the population *Mean* suggests a problem that needs to be addressed. For example, suppose a national study found that the rates of inoculation for measles were lower for some subgroups than for others. If these subgroups exist in one's schools, it becomes important to determine the inoculation rates among one's students and take appropriate action.

3. When evaluating an intervention in some of their schools, all the schools in the district are the population.

At the same time, there probably are elements of teaching, learning, and leading that do lend themselves to high levels of generalizability—i.e., *external validity*—with appropriate research evidence.

Types of outcomes from experiments

1. Distal vs. proximal effects

    Research on ***proximal*** effects measures whether an intervention designed to improve something improves that specific "thing," while research on ***distal*** effects measures whether improvements in that "thing" leads to larger, more general benefits. For example, research on the *proximal* effects of a different approach to improving students' ability to solve math word problems would test whether there was an improvement in the experimental group's ability to solve those types of word problems relative to the control group. *Distal* research would measure whether there was an overall improvement in math grades or math scores on an end-of-year test as a result of that intervention, or whether it improved students' ability to solve other types of math word problems. Research on *distal* effects is related to the concept of *transfer*, i.e., that improving one thing can lead to improvements in others.[52]

Leaders tend to be more concerned with *distal* effects, while classroom teachers tend to be more concerned with *proximal* effects. Teachers want to know whether an approach will help their students learn a specific unit or a specific learning objective better, or whether it will produce an immediate improvement in behavior. Leaders, on the other hand, want to know whether an intervention will produce *distal* effects, such as gains on end of year tests or ongoing improvement in a school's culture.

It has been easier for research to find *proximal* benefits than *distal* ones—though the latter is the ultimate goal of school improvement and increasing equity.

2. Immediate vs. Sustained/Enduring Effects

    Immediate effects of intervention are those evaluated right after the conclusion of the experiment. In most cases, laboratory based research study immediate effects. Alternatively, research on **sustained/enduring** effects evaluates the results of an intervention after the experiment is over. Sometimes the time lag between the conclusion of the research and its evaluation can be several weeks, and at other times it can be several years—e.g., studies of the effects of early childhood education on later school success.

    A hybrid approach is to evaluate the effects of the intervention right after the conclusion of the research and to then repeat the evaluation at several subsequent times to determine both the immediate and *enduring* effects. This would constitute *longitudinal research*.

    Clearly, finding evidence that the benefits from an intervention are sustained after the treatment is ended is the ideal.

Formative vs. summative evaluation

A *formative evaluation* is done to make sure the experiment is proceeding as planned, and if not, to explain why not and what can be done about it. The *summative evaluation* is the formal analysis of results that is conducted at the end of the experiment.

Summative evaluations use a wide variety of statistical techniques that produce lots of numbers and tables that are then interpreted to determine the success, or lack thereof, of the experiment. (See Appendix A for a more specific discussion of statistical techniques.) A good *formative evaluation* is important for interpreting the *summative* results. For example, if the implementation of the intervention was of low quality,

---

[52] The issue of whether it is possible to produce transfer is controversial. However, finding a way to produce transfer would be a major breakthrough and a powerful tool for improving schools and increasing equity.

leaders and other researchers should NOT conclude that the intervention was ineffective if the summative results are poor. Further research would be needed to test the intervention with a higher quality implementation process before any conclusion could be made as to its effectiveness. If the summative results of the research were positive, then the *formative evaluation* tells us the conditions under which one can expect such results. In addition, the *formative evaluation* is often a qualitative analysis even when the *summative evaluation* is quantitative.

Section 2—Methods for Analyzing the Results of Experiments

Before explaining the simple way that leaders can determine the practical benefit of any experimental study, it is important to first understand how researchers determine the results of experimental studies. Therefore, this section will discuss:

- How researchers use statistics to analyze experimental data; and
- How conventional statistical analysis of experiments can mislead practice.

Differences between the *Means*

Analyzing whether an experiment demonstrated that an intervention was effective involves determining whether the *Mean* of the experimental group ended up being larger than that of the comparison group, and if so, whether that difference is an important one. Such analysis is essentially a two-step process.

Step 1 - A **statistic** is used to test for the difference in the post-test *Means* between the experimental and comparison groups (*independent* Means), or the difference between the pre- post- *Means* of a single group *(dependent* Means). There are a number of statistics in Appendix A for comparing the differences in *Means*—e.g., Independent t test, dependent t test, ANOVA, etc. Appendix A also provides rules for deciding which statistic to use.

The statistic produces a number.

Step 2 – A **statistical test** is used to determine if the resultant number indicates that the difference between the *Means* is a BIG/important difference. If the *Mean* of the experimental group is larger to the degree that the statistical test indicates a BIG/important difference, that is considered evidence that the intervention that the experimental group used was effective because of the large benefit it provided.

The two most widely used statistical tests to determine whether the results of the statistical analysis are important—i.e., indicate that the intervention was effective—are:

- ***Statistical significance*** (p-value, which is also used for relationship research as discussed in the previous chapter); and

- *Effect Size (ES)*, sometimes called **Standard Deviation Units** or just **Standard Deviation**. As a result, it will often be referred to as *ES* or (SD/U).

ES or (SD/U) is essentially a measure of the size of the differences between the *Means* of the experimental and comparison groups. It is sometimes referred to as *practical significance*.

Given the previously discussed problems with statistical significance or significance, this chapter will focus on analyzing the results from the statistical test of *ES* or *(SD/U)*. However, unlike statistical significance which is indicated with asterisks, the ES is a number, usually less than 1. How large should the ES be to conclude that the intervention in the experiment is effective? This will be a main focus of the discussion in this chapter.

The value of the *ES* will usually be indicated in a table or in the findings section of the study.

Adjustments to the *Means*, values, and outcomes

Published research tends to add sophisticated touches to the above two-step process in the form of three types of adjustments to the data.

1. **Adjusted *Means***

   If there are initial differences between the groups the statistic, **Analysis of Covariance (ANCOVA)** is used to control for that possible confounding factor. For example, if the experimental group has lower initial reading scores, ANCOVA takes that into account and adjusts the post-test *Means* of the experimental group to compensate for that initial disadvantage—in effect raising their outcome *Mean*. Similarly, if there were differences in the percentage of under-represented students in the experimental and comparisons groups, ANCOVA can similarly adjust the outcomes.

2. **Converting all the scores or values to z scores**

   There are times when it makes sense to convert all the scores or values from the initial raw scores of everyone in the comparison and control groups to z scores. As discussed in the previous chapter, z scores create a common denominator score across disparate ways of measuring a variable. For example, if a study involves schools or students from different states which have different tests, students' raw test scores can be converted to their score in relation to all the students who have taken that same test—i.e., converted to z scores. So converting all scores to z scores is useful in that such conversion enables researchers to compare scores from different state tests, or different tests of social-emotional outcomes.

   For example, suppose that the *Mean* scale score for 5th graders in State A is 256 (whatever that means), and the Standard Deviation is 20 points. So a student who gets a score of 246 (whatever that means) is .5 of a *Standard Deviation* below the

160

Mean. Therefore, that student would have a z score of -.5. Similarly, every student in the study from that state would have their actual score converted to z scores. The same would be done with the test scores in the other state. The *Mean* and *Standard Deviation* of all students in State B will probably be different that those in State A since the scales and raw scores would be different. However, a z score of -.5 for a given student in State B is considered the same as a student with the same z score in State A—regardless of differences in the raw scores of each individual.

Students' z scores from the different tests can then be combined into a single set of scores. The *z scores* of all the students in the experimental group drawn from the different states in the study can then be analyzed relative to the z scores of all the students in the comparison group. An analysis can then be conducted to determine which group has the higher z score *Mean*. If an *analysis of covariance* was conducted to adjust for initial differences in *Mean* scores or some other different characteristic of the groups, a statistical analysis would be conducted to determine which group has the higher adjusted *Mean* of *z scores*.

Huh? (At this point you have a right to be confused or concerned about all this data manipulation.)

So, for example, while such a study could conclude that the experimental group had a higher adjusted *Mean* z score of .15, what does that indicate in any real world sense? In order to try and communicate the finding in a way that would make sense to practitioners, researchers manipulate the result *yet again* by extrapolating the result to some other, more familiar, metric.

3. **Equivalent extrapolation of the result**

So, now after two manipulations of the data and results, differences will be expressed in arcane language such as *z scores*, **standard deviation units** (SDU) or just **standard deviation** (SD), or *effect size* (ES). What sense can school leaders make of such highly transformed data and arcane outcome? These outcome *Means* and differences are just abstract numbers that have no recognizable real-world meaning to practitioners or policy makers. The abstract *Mean* difference in such an analysis does not convey the actual benefit that the experimental group obtained from the intervention in any recognizable real-world metric.

In order to try and communicate to practitioners and policy makers what the results from comparing such abstract numbers actually mean, it is common practice in the research literature to do a final adjustment and convert the abstract numerical results into something familiar to practitioners and policy makers. This conversion process is referred to as **extrapolating** an **equivalence**—i.e., an equivalence is extrapolated between the *ES or (SD/U)* result to some metric that is familiar to leaders. The most common type of extrapolation is a conclusion such as:

> *The size of the effect favoring the experimental students is EQUIVALENT to moving students from the 50th to the 58th percentile on the Stanford Reading Test.*

161

Another common type of *extrapolation* is to convert the abstract difference in *Means* into an equivalence of extra days or months of learning. For example, the widely cited result from the CREDO (2013) study at Stanford University combined scores from 16 state tests to test whether students did better at charter or traditional public schools (TPS). This widely publicized study concluded that black and Hispanic students made 14 days of additional learning per year in charter schools as compared to TPS. This is an impressive difference that suggests that charters are superior.

Beware

However, keep in mind that both of these types of extrapolated equivalences are *hypothetical* because the researchers did not actually document that the students ended up at the 58th percentile or that an extra 14 days of learning occurred—nor is there an evidence-based method for doing so.

NOTE: If your instinct is to be confused at this moment you are being perceptive!

Remember

Keep in mind that we now have data that have gone through three transformations: Conversion to z scores, adjustment of the *Means*, and finally an extrapolated equivalent result. Each of these adjustments have statistical error associated with them, and as will be seen shortly, the extrapolated equivalence—i.e., the final step—will often have the biggest error.

What started out as a seemingly simple analysis to determine the experimental effectiveness of an intervention by comparing the outcomes of groups, has become so rife with allowed adjustments that it is starting to resemble a Rube Goldberg process.[53] The next section will describe how this analytic system can be even more problematic than what it appears to be on the surface, and how the resultant conclusions that a tested intervention was effective can, and often does, mislead practice.

Section 3—How Rigorous Statistical Analysis of Experiments can Mislead Practice—and Often Does

The standard form of analysis described above for claiming evidence of effectiveness can mislead practice on a large scale. Examples will be provided of research produced by top researchers at top research universities such as Stanford and Johns Hopkins that misdirected practice on a large-scale. It will be shown how some influential research—e.g., findings that "Success for All" was an effective reading intervention, and that charter schools promoted substantially greater achievement in students of color than traditional public schools—were artificially produced by taking advantage of the complexity of the above analytic process. This complexity leads to five common problems with how researchers analyze the data from experiments, and how they reach and justify conclusions. Each of these problems will be described. Unfortunately, the

---

[53] Rube Goldberg was a prolific Pulitzer Prize winning cartoonist who drew intricate chain reaction-types of machines intentionally designed to perform a simple task in an "indirect and overly complicated way." His name has become synonymous with any overly complex machine or process.

research community not only continues to support such problematic analysis of experiments, it often considers such techniques to be evidence of "rigorous" research.

Problem #1—Research that fails to report unadjusted *Means* or *Medians*

The overwhelming majority of experimental research reports differences between the *Means* of the experimental and comparison groups. But given the discussion of the power trio of statistics (*Mean*, *Median*, and *Standard Deviation*) in Chapter 4, there are times when the *Median* is a better measure of the overall performance of a group than the *Mean*—depending on the size of the standard deviation relative to the *Mean*. However, most of the statistics for analyzing differences between groups in Appendix A are designed to be used with *Means*, and research journals tend to prefer research that uses those statistics. So the basic question is whether the researcher reported *Medians* and *Standard Deviations*, and whether the *Mean* was in fact the most representative score for each group and what should be compared. If the latter statistics were NOT reported, and/or the *Median* was the more representative statistic and the research still compared *Means*, then the research is problematic.

An even bigger, more common problem occurs when the *Means* are adjusted through an ***Analysis of Covariance*** because of initial differences between the groups. How this statistic is calculated is not important to this discussion. What is important to understand is that if the starting *Mean* for the experimental group is lower on some measure, such as its reading level, this statistical procedure will bump up the final *Mean* of the experimental group. This means that the final *Mean* reported in the research is NOT the actual *Mean performance of the experimental group.*

Of course, if a school administrator bumps up students' scores he/she would be fired and perhaps sent to jail. At the same time, this weighting of scores is legal statistically, and helps make comparison between unequal groups fairer.[54]

However, such weighting schemes in research can skew results. There are general incentives for researchers in all disciplines to weight/adjust variables in ways that will favor the experimental group in the outcome. The academic reputation of a researcher is often enhanced by findings that favor the experimental group. Not finding a significant difference between the groups reduces the likelihood that an article will get published, a phenomenon known as *publication bias*. For example, research about the effects of "Success for All" never weighted for the fact that more money was spent for the experimental schools and/or that the experimental students spent more time reading—which would have bumped up the *Means* for the comparison schools. Unfortunately, reviewers and editors at the top research journals ignored these obvious confounding variables.

At the same time, there is nothing wrong with using a weighting procedure—as long as the researcher also reveals the *unadjusted* outcome *Means* for the experimental

---

[54] Indeed, states sometimes weight school performance based on key demographics such as the percentage of free and reduced lunch, the percentage of minority students, etc. Such weightings give a sense of how the performance of a given low-SES school would do compared to a more advantaged school if all things were equal.

group. Unfortunately, major research publications such as the journals published by the American Educational Research Association (AERA) do NOT require researchers to report the unadjusted *Means*. In such cases, consumers of the research do NOT know how the experimental students actually performed. So the final weighted results can show that the experimental group outperformed the comparison group—while masking the fact that the experimental students actually did poorly. Not reporting unadjusted *Means* was a major strategy for how researchers were able to make "Success for All" appear to be 'effective'.

Beware

While covariate analysis can be valuable if both the adjusted and unadjusted results are reported, ignore research that does NOT report unadjusted *Means* (or other measures). The researcher is probably hiding something.

Problem #2—Results that are necessarily contaminated by accumulated statistical error

Data Analysis Sub-principle #2.2 (Chapter 4) states that: *The more statistical procedures that are conducted in a study, the less trustworthy any one finding is, and the greater the statistical error.* While a process for analyzing the outcomes of experiments that uses adjustments and transformations as described above is elegant mathematically, it inevitably contains high levels of statistical error. The compounding of statistical error reduces the likelihood that the results are valid, and even if they are valid they are unlikely to generalize to benefits for your schools with any useful degree of predictability.

The problems associated with statistical error from highly manipulated analyses of results from experiments are magnified when the findings ultimately only demonstrate tiny benefits.

Problem #3—Claims of effectiveness that rely on tiny benefits and exaggerate their importance

The two main statistical tests used in experimental research to determine how important, or BIG, the benefit from the use of the intervention are ***Statistical Significance (p-value)***, and ***Effect Size (ES)***. When the p-value reaches a certain threshold (p<.05*) the result is said to be statistically significant, and when the ES reaches a certain level the result is considered to have ***Practical Significance***.

Historically, *statistical significance* has been the most widely used statistical test in experimental research, just as it has been in relationship research (Chapter 5)—and just as problematic. Carver (1978), Kirk (1996), Harlow, Mulaik, and Steiger (1997), and Hubbard (2015) center on:

a) The artificiality of positing a *null hypothesis* when the researcher is really expecting to see a difference based on prior research or theory;
b) Small differences between the groups that are of no practical importance can be *statistically significant* if a large sample is used; and

164

c) Large differences that are truly important can show up as NOT being *statistically significant* if a small sample is used—causing a potentially important finding to be rejected.

Indeed, when Harlow, Mulaik, and Steiger (1997) summarized the arguments for and against the use of *statistical significance* as a key evidentiary tool, the arguments in favor were primarily related to theory generation or philosophy of science as opposed to applied decision-making. Even the developer of *statistical significance* testing, Ronald Fisher is cited by Mulaik, Raju, and Harshman (1997) as having said that probabilities used in tests of significance "...do not generally lead to any probability statements about the real world" (p. 106). Indeed, physics' use of *statistical significance* is very different than how education and the social sciences use it.[55]

So, relying on *statistical significance* as a key evidentiary criterion often misdirects practice. Kirk (1996) noted that with significance testing "...the work of science does not progress as it should" (p. 753-54). Meehl (1978) noted that *significance testing* "is a terrible mistake, is basically unsound, poor scientific strategy, and one of the worst things that ever happened in the history of psychology" (p. 817). Schmidt and Hunter (1997) concluded that testing for *statistical significance* "...retards the growth of scientific knowledge; it never makes a positive contribution" (p. 37).

Allowing a statistical standard wherein researchers can claim that an intervention is effective, or that some clinical discovery has been made, has encouraged the process mentioned earlier of p-hacking, wherein researchers manipulate some small element of their research design in order to get their results over the hump and produce a finding of statistical significance. This process has misdirected evidence about effective practices in a wide variety of fields including education.

For all these reasons, as previously noted, the American Statistical Association called for abandoning the use of statistical significance as an indication that an intervention is effective.

---

[55] Sometimes physics does NOT use statistical significance for important scientific claims. For example, in a key test of Einstein's general theory of relativity, scientists concluded that light passing a massive body bent as much as this theory predicted without using any test of *statistical significance* (Schmidt & Hunter, 1997). On the other hand, when *statistical significance* is used it is applied in a much more demanding fashion. For example, when scientists wanted to confirm the recent breakthrough discovery in physics of the Higgs boson, the so called "God particle," they wanted to be completely sure that they had in fact observed the particle and it was not caused by some chance occurrence of one of the billions of particles produced by the powerful Hadron collider. So they did not use a p<.001, i.e., less than 1 chance in a thousand that what they observed was just some random event. Rather, they used the more rigorous standard of Sigma 5, which is about a one-in-3.5 million chance that the signal they saw was not a chance event—but that it was indeed the Higgs boson. Scientists set such a high bar of evidence because the existence of this particle was so fundamental to understanding how the physical world works, and because the particle itself is so small and elusive that they needed to be very very very sure.

However, if education or social science used such a standard for rejecting the *null hypothesis*, it would never be rejected and therefore all studies would conclude that their findings were not significant and were simply chance occurrences. There have been calls to use a more rigorous standard in social science by requiring a minimum value of p<.005 to establish significance, but that has not been adopted by journals (Kopf, 2017).

Unfortunately, the education research community, professional associations, and media continue to hype experimental research findings based on *statistical significance* as the next new thing, or new findings of "best" practice or an evidence-based practice. Sometimes such results are couched as being a "significant" finding, or significant impact, in summaries and abstracts of research, and media reports of research. As was true for relationship research, this use of the term "significant" is misleading to practitioners, as it has nothing to do with the colloquial use of the term. "Significant" only means that the *null hypothesis* has been rejected. It does NOT mean that there was a noteworthy difference between the experimental and comparison groups.[56]

As previously discussed, statistical significance, or a "significant" finding, *simply means that something other than nothing probably occurred.*

Practical Tip	Leaders should **ignore** evidence of effective practices based on "significant" results/differences in abstracts/summaries of research articles, media reports, and syntheses put out by professional associations. *Statistical significance* by itself has NO relevance for leadership decision-making.

Given the problems with statistical significance, the newer statistical test of ***Effect Size (ES) has gained*** popularity. Effect size is sometimes also referred to as ***Standard Deviation Units (SDU)***[57] or just ***Standard Deviation (SD)*** (hereafter referred to as (*SD/U*). *ES* has the benefit of being able to calculate the size of the difference between the experimental and comparison groups. In theory, *ES*, and its related concept of practical significance, make sense.

The big question is:

> *How BIG should the ES (SD/U) be in order to conclude that that the results indicate a sufficiently BIG difference in favor of the experimental group to conclude that the benefit constitutes practical significance—i.e., that the intervention was effective?*

---

[56] Why don't statistics test for the hypothesis that the experimental group will do substantially better and have a significance test for that—instead of relying on the *null hypothesis*? The answer is that "substantially better" is in the eye of the beholder. There is no objective statistical way to define what "substantially better" is, so there is no way to test the probability of whether the performance of an experimental group is "substantially better" than the comparison group. So while one can posit a directional hypothesis, and state that one group will do better than the other, most statistics do not produce results for such a hypothesis. (An exception is the one-tail t test—an option within using the t-test statistic.)

[57] In order to understand what an *SDU* is, consider for example, the distribution of IQ scores. On most tests of IQ the population *Mean* is 100 and the *Standard Deviation* is 15. So if an experimental group ended up demonstrating +1 *Standard Deviation Units* from the *Mean*, this would mean that they ended up with an IQ of 115, which would appear to be a large enough difference from the *Mean* to have *practical significance*. Similarly, -1 *SDU* would be a group IQ of 85. On the other hand, suppose the experimental group's IQ turned out to be +.1 *SDU* from the *Mean.* That would be an IQ of 101.5. Is that substantially different than the *Mean* IQ? Common sense would say "No." Even +.2 *Standard Deviation Units* from the *Mean*—i.e., an IQ of 103— would still be characterized by Cohen, and common sense, as a "small" difference.

This question is analogous to the process of setting a criterion of what level of blood pressure is normal (see Chapter 3). In the case of setting the blood pressure range considered normal is to establish a relationship between a given level of blood pressure and a measured clinical outcome—e.g., death rates. So the key corollary questions are:

How did education (and social science in general) researchers calibrate the desired level of ES or (SD/U) to conclude that an intervention was effective?

What clinical outcome was used—e.g., documented real-world improvement?

There are essentially two ways that researchers set the criterion for the desired size of an *ES (SD/U)*. The first way to determine the importance of an *ES or SD/U* is to determine its *statistical significance*. However, that just brings us back to the previously discussed problems with using *statistical significance* so that is a dead end.

The more widely accepted criterion for interpreting the size of an *ES* was set by Cohen (1988). Cohen (1988) recommended characterizing the *ES* magnitude of differences of the *Means* (averages) of two or more groups as follows:

.2 = small
.5 = medium
.8 = large

While you do not need to worry about how to calculate the value of *ES or SD/U*, the table below provides a concrete example of how different values of *ES* correspond to the difference between groups in terms of comparing the heights of girls at different ages. As *ES* increases, the amount of difference between the *Mean* height of the older and younger girls increases, and an increasing percentage of the older girls are taller than the younger girls. Clearly, 18-year old girls are going to be on average a lot taller than 14-year olds, and that difference will result in a high *ES*, but 15-year olds will only be a little bit taller than 14-year olds, and that difference will result in a low ES.

Table 6.1

The Relationship of ES and the Amount of Mean Difference in Girls' Heights[58]

Effect Size (ES)	Magnitude of Difference	Equivalent difference in height between the groups of girls	Percentage of the older group who are taller
.2	Small	*Mean* difference in average height between 15 and 16 year old girls (.5")	Average (or taller) 16 year old girls are taller than 57.9% of 15 year olds

[58] These criteria for small, medium, and large are for comparisons of *Means*. Cohen (1988) used different cutoff scores for other types of statistical comparisons.

| .5 | Medium | *Mean* difference in average height between 14 and 18 year old girls (1") | Average (or taller) 18 year old girls are taller than 69.1% of 14 year olds |
| .8 | Large | *Mean* difference in average height between 13 and 18 year old girls | Average (or taller) 18 year old girls are taller than 78.8% of 13 year olds |

It is important to understand that *Means* and *ES*s refer to general tendencies. They do not indicate that <u>all</u> the older girls are taller than the younger ones. There will always be cases where some of the younger girls are taller than the older girls. Indeed, for the "small" *ES* of .2, 42.1% of the younger girls are as tall or taller than the older girls who are at least average height. This is a very substantial minority and suggests that an *ES* of .2 does NOT indicate a widespread height superiority for the older girls, or a BIG superiority.

However, as *ES* increases, it becomes more likely that the older girls are taller than the younger girls, and that the older girls dominate in height more and more. For example, when the *ES* increases from .2 to .5, the percentage of older girls who are as tall or taller than the average younger girl increases from 58% to 70%. In other words, as *ES* increases, the distribution of individual scores on the key variable, in this case "height," shifts to the right—i.e., the *Mean* height of the older group of girls becomes increasingly larger and the percentage of taller girls coming from the older group increases.[59]

As a result, the difference of *Means,* or *ES,* between 18 vs. 14 year olds is obviously going to be larger (ES=.5) than the difference between the *Means* of 16 vs. 15 year olds (ES=.2). In other words, the larger the *ES,* the more confident we can be that the older girls are truly taller <u>on average</u> than the younger girls, and that a higher percentage of the older girls are taller than those in the younger group.

Clearly an ES of .8 (18 vs. 13 year olds) would represent even greater certainty that any given older girl is taller than the average younger girl, and that the difference in height is even more noticeable.

The same relationship between the size of the *ES* and the relative *Mean* advantage of one group just discussed in relation to girls' height also applies to measuring the effect of an intervention on student performance. In this case the experimental and comparison groups will not differ by *Age* but on whether or not they received the experimental intervention(s)—and the key outcome that is being examined will NOT be the *Height* of the students—but by how well experimental vs. comparison groups did on some educational outcome measure. However, the principle of the size of the *ES* and the relative advantage shown in Table 6.1 works the same (if the distributions

---

[59] The expression "shifting to the right" refers to the fact that when you draw a graph, the values on the horizontal axis, or x axis, increase as you move to the right. So if you put the distribution of scores for the heights of 18 and 14 year old girls on the same graph, or in this case a histogram, the shape of the distribution for the 18 year olds will in general be further to the right, though there will be some overlap.

are the same). If the intervention is effective, the students in the experimental group (analogous to the older girls) will do better than those who did not receive the treatment (analogous to the younger girls).

So how did researchers decide what minimum *ES* indicated a sufficiently BIG advantage to indicate *practical significance*? While Cohen (1988) warned that his cutoffs of .2, .5, and .8 are somewhat arbitrary, researchers have taken it to mean that when research finds an *ES* of at least .2 (i.e., a "small" difference) favoring the experimental group the results have *practical significance*. The bottom line is that this *ES* standard is arbitrary and not linked to evidence of some clinical/actual real-world outcome as is typically done in medicine when the FDA approves a drug. For example, to approve a vaccine the FDA generally want to see an efficacy rate of at least 50% in terms of actually reducing severe illness/death.[60]

KEY COMMON SENSE QUESTION #1: Keeping in mind that if the equivalent relative outcome at the *ES* level of .2—i.e., the extent to which 16 year old girls did better (i.e., were taller) than 15 year olds, would you be happy if the same percentage of average performing students in the experimental group did better than only 57.1 percent of the comparison students? Would you consider that to be a success?

<< …think for a minute… >>

If you would not consider that result to be a success, a decision I would agree with, you are essentially saying that an *ES or (SD/U)* of .2 does NOT indicate that the intervention was successful because not enough students benefitted. You are saying that you would want to see a larger *ES—i.e., more students benefitting* before considering implementing the new intervention in your schools.

So you would not be happy with researchers who concluded that an intervention was evidence-based if the resultant *ES* was .2 or even smaller. Indeed, researchers have gotten so fixated on using .2 as an indicator of success, that they have ignored how Cohen, the originator of the *ES* measure, characterized the cutoffs. This is his description of what the cutoffs mean:

Small *ES* (.2) — a difference that is "difficult to detect" (p. 25)

---

[60] Unfortunately, it now appears that even the FDA is moving away from requiring demonstration of clinical benefits from a new drug.—i.e., evidence that that the dug improves how a person feels, functions or survives— to approve it. Kesselheim and Avorn (2021) note many drugs are now approved based on what's called surrogate endpoints—i.e., changes in the body measured by lab tests without any evidence that this translates into actual improvements in patients. These authors note that the new drug to treat Alzheimer's disease, Aducanumab, received FDA approval based on changes in lab tests of its effect on brain tissue, which might be beneficial, without any clinical evidence that patients treated with the drug actually improved. While not requiring clinical evidence that patients benefitted will get the drug to market faster and at lower cost to the drug companies, these authors note that this is a diminution of research standards.

The bottom line is that the tension between using research standards based on clinical outcomes versus some other criterion is an ongoing tension even in medicine.

Medium *ES* (.5) — a difference that is "visible to the naked eye" (p. 26)
Large *ES* (.8) — a difference that is "grossly perceptible" (p. 27) [61]

KEY COMMON SENSE QUESTIONS #2, 3:

#2 Using these characterizations of small, medium, and large *ES*s—what would be the smallest value of *ES* that would influence you to consider adopting an intervention?
#3 Would research with a "very small" magnitude of difference impress you?

<< …think for a minute… >>

Your answer to the first of the above questions was probably that you want to see an *ES* or *(SD/U)* at least close to .5 (or higher), so that the benefit from the intervention would be visible to teachers and the community.

If you answered "no" to the second question, that means that you want an improvement that is larger than "difficult to detect"—i.e., an *ES* or *SD/U* result that is larger than .2 for you to consider adopting the intervention in the research. You probably want an intervention where the vast majority of students do noticeably better than those who did not receive it.

 It is clearly reasonable for leaders to want a new intervention to produce an improvement that is "visible to the naked eye" of teachers and the community— which is why up to this point this textbook has emphasized that a practical benefit is a noticeable one. However, when statisticians/researchers accept an *ES* or .2 or less as indicating success, they are in effect rejecting your common sense point of view and are advocating the use of interventions whose benefits are NOT visible.

 In order to understand how to interpret *ES* outcomes in a common sense way we will use the metric of .2 as an outcome whose benefit is "difficult to detect." That means that an *ES* of .1 indicates a benefit that is half of "difficult to detect"—i.e., infinitesimal.

Remember

In other words, an *ES* of .2 or .1 means that there was virtually no apparent difference in outcomes between the experimental and comparison groups. Leaders should NOT view such differences as important enough evidence to warrant spending time and money to implement the intervention. (Such findings only benefit the researcher who produced the result and the journal editor who published it.)

---

[61] In addition to the aforementioned example of "grossly perceptible" as being the difference between the height of 13 and 18 year old girls, Cohen also relates an *ES* of .8 to the magnitude of difference in IQ between the holders of a PhD and college freshman.

Beware

Unfortunately, as will be seen shortly, researchers not only use an *ES* of .2 to indicate a successful intervention, they are now using even smaller ones. This means that researchers are now claiming evidence of effectiveness based on benefits that are much less than "difficult to detect."

For now, the important thing to remember about *ES* or (SD/U) is that:

Remember

The larger the +*ES*, the following things generally occur:

- The superiority of the *Mean* performance of the experimental group(s) relative to that of the comparison group gets BIGGER; and

- The percentage of students in the experimental group doing better than students in the comparison group increases.

The smaller the +*ES*, the following things generally occur:

- The less likely the findings of benefits and effectiveness are true (see the discussion about BIGness in Chapter 3); and

- The less likely it is that your schools and students will experience any noticeable benefit if you adopt the intervention.

So both your common sense and Cohen's characterization of what .2 actually signifies, suggest that leaders should seek evidence from experiments in which the benefit in terms of the *ES* advantage for the experimental group should be greater than .2. How much bigger? Recommendations for size cutoffs will be made later on in this chapter. In the meantime, a good rule of thumb is that…

Practical Tip

Leaders should avoid considering any intervention in which the *ES* or *(SD/U)* is less than .35 —— unless it meets the criteria discussed later in this chapter.

So, while the idea of a measure such as *ES* and practical significance has potential, the fact that the minimum level of *ES* needed for an intervention to be judged as effective and having practical significance has been set at .2, renders most evidence based on *practical significance* to be highly misleading

Even worse, researchers continue to push for using ever smaller *ES* values to conclude that an intervention is effective. Kraft (2020) is the latest such effort. In a paper published in the AERA journal *Educational Researcher* (ER) he argues for using an *ES* as low as .05, or a quarter of "difficult to detect." The rationale put forth by Kraft and other researchers such Lipsey et al. (2012) for further lowering evidentiary standards is because educational research generally only produces small effect sizes that is what practitioners should accept.[62] However, this is researchers basically saying about practitioners—"let them eat cake."

---

[62] Another rationale for using small *ES*s in education is that the medical community approves the use of drugs, such as baby aspirin to prevent fatal heart attacks, despite tiny ESs. Aside from the obvious problem that the

Leaders vs Researchers

The use of tiny *ESs* serves the needs of researchers to get their findings published—but not those of leaders seeking to produce noticeable improvements and increases in equity. Sadly, this gap between the evidentiary needs of researchers versus practitioners for identifying effective practices seems to be getting wider over time. *This gap means that when leaders adopt an "evidence-based" practice the majority of the time they will NOT see any benefit—unless they check out the ES or (SD/U) values.*

Numbers matter—whether it is the percentage of oxygen in the atmosphere or the size of the *ES* or *(SD/U)*! In terms of the latter, *it is essential that leaders examine the actual size of the ES or (SD/U) reported in the research before making any decision as whether to trust the reported finding.*

Why are education researchers so hellbent on reducing the minimum *ES* standard even lower than the already inadequate *ES* level of .2? As previously noted, the research community is wedded to the ideal of the gold standard RCT methodology. However, Lortie-Forgeus and Inglis (2019) found that among all the 141 large-scale RCTs aimed at improving educational outcomes in grades K-12 funded by the UK and the U.S. National Center for Educational Evaluation and Regional Assistance, the average *ES* was a miniscule .06—*i.e., less than a third of difficult to detect.*

Unfortunately, the research community does not consider the possibility that the tiny *ES* results indicate that:

- The static approach of RCT research does not mesh with the dynamic ever changing reality of school environments; and

- That they should consider using an alternative scientific approach such as the one discussed in Chapter 8.

Instead, researchers and reporters …

---

functioning of the human body differs from the functioning of complex social organizations such as schools, there are also many other differences between using baby aspirin as compared to implementing a complex educational intervention. For example, baby aspirin costs pennies a day and does not require training or a learning curve. In addition, Carroll & Frankt (2015) note that if 2,000 people who have a 10% chance of a heart attack take aspirin for two years only one heart attack is prevented, and the other 1,999 are unaffected. Would practitioners agree that an expensive, time-consuming intervention that has no benefits for 99% of their at-risk students should be implemented? Probably not.

... continue to exaggerate the importance of the tiny ESs that their static methods can produce, and take advantage of the lack of understanding about what the seemingly arcane ES values actually mean.

I SWEAR IT WAS *THIS* BIG!

(Cartoon by Dana Fiorelli)

An example of researchers and reporters taking advantage of small *ES*s is he following headline in *Education Week* of the results of study of *Success for All*: "School Improvement Model Shows Promise in First i3 Evaluation" (Sparks, 2013, p. 8). This headline parroted the conclusion of the researchers. The conclusion of "promise" is based on the following results in kindergarten shown in Table 6.2 below.

Table 6.2
Effect Sizes for Kindergarten Reading Outcomes

Outcome	ES
Letter-Word Identification	-0.01
Word Attack	0.18

Why is such a result "especially promising"—especially for a program that had been around for decades? Given that the earliest grades are the easiest ones to produce big *ES*s it is surprising to see a negative effect size, which means that the "Success for All" students did a tiny bit worse. The one positive result is slightly less than "difficult to detect." The positive evaluation is based on the fact that the .18 for a single sub-skill is larger than Title I's overall effect size of .11. Thus, the program is mistakenly considered to be promising because its tiny *ES* or *SD/U* is bigger than a tinier one, and is approaching the level of "difficult to detect." The correct conclusion is that the program is NOT effective.

173

Another example where prominent educational researchers conclude in an AERA journal that half of "difficult to detect" is evidence of an effective practice is where Borman, Grigg, and Hanselman (2016) concluded that self-affirmation exercises are a good way to reduce the achievement gap in mathematics. Their research found *ES*s of .09 and .11 favoring the self-affirmation groups. They claimed that these low ESs demonstrated the effectiveness of the intervention because they were consistent with the *ES*s of other national reforms. In other words, the fact that their new trivial *ES* results were the same *as other* reforms (mistakenly) considered to be "successful," was considered to be evidence this new intervention was also effective. **The correct interpretation is that none of these reforms were effective.**

Beware

Pogrow (2018) has characterized this phenomenon of the research community accepting tiny *ES*s as evidence of effectiveness as ***ES-hacking***. As a result, practical significance is just as misleading as statistical significance in determining whether an intervention was effective.

The problem is not the *ES* test itself—but with how researchers have set the criteria for interpreting the results.

As a result, the next section will present a new statistical test—practical benefit.

Nor is the existing tendency to headline trivial findings from small *ES*s or *statistical significance* as important scientific evidence limited to evaluations of educational interventions. Evidence based on trivial outcomes/differences distorts even the most fundamental efforts to reduce social inequity and are used to rationalize maintaining and promoting inequity. Consider, for example, the claim of Harvard's president that women are underrepresented in science because their minds work differently and as a result they have less scientific ability. Lisa Randall (2005), the widely respected Harvard theoretical physicist, reviewed the evidence and reached the following conclusion:

> One of the more amusing aspects of the discussion was that those who believed in the differences and those who didn't used the same evidence about gender-specific special ability. How could that be? The answer is that the data shows no substantial effects. Social factors might account for these tiny differences, which in any case have an unclear connection to scientific ability. Not much of a headline when phrased that way, is it?

Dr. Randall's reference to the absence of substantial differences to warrant reaching a conclusion that there are differences in the mathematical ability of men and women is akin to seeking evidence of benefits that are BIG for adopting an intervention. Her conclusion illustrates the tendency of those who craft headlines, and/or advocate for a particular approach, to make much ado about research findings based on trivial outcomes because it reinforces an existing bias. In the case of "Success for All," the education research community wanted to believe that one of its own had crafted an evidence-based program that was uniquely successful. It is obvious what the bias was in the Harvard case.

174

Small *ESs* have even compromised the value of one of the most important methodological tools—i.e., meta-analysis. Gene Glass, the developer of meta-analysis, found that while in medicine the *ESs* of experiments tend to be large and stable across studies, in education meta-analyses the *ESs* are "relatively small" and their variation within a given meta-analysis is "great" (Glass, 2016). As a result, he argues that meta-analysis has not been as useful for informing policy in education as in medicine.

Beware

The only reasonable conclusion is that the research community emphasizes arbitrary statistical criteria—e.g., *statistical significance* or small *ES based practical significances*— that make it easier for researchers to claim discoveries.[63]

To be fair, the process if overhyping the significance of research findings is not unique to education. Hossenfelder (2018) reports that from 1974 to 2014 the use of the terms "unprecedented," "groundbreaking," and "novel" in scientific papers increased by 2500%.

Problem #4—Results based on invalid hypothetical equivalences that hype results

Now that you understand how to interpret ES/standard deviation units/standard deviation in experimental outcomes, let's revisit the CREDO (2013) study at Stanford University that combined scores from 16 states and concluded that black and Hispanic students made 14 days of additional learning per year in charter schools as compared to traditional public schools. This is clearly an impressive difference that suggests that charters are superior. However, the ES or SD/U of the difference produced by these two types of schools was only .02, or one-tenth of "difficult to detect."

> **QUESTION?** How much extra learning do you think a tenth of difficult to detect represents in a school year?

This is a case of where your guess is as good as mine.

My guess would be that it would be about a one hour difference. Such an undetectable difference would obviously NOT be anything close to 14 days of extra leaning per year.

How did CREDO come up with their conclusion about the 14 days extra days of learning? CREDO (2013) noted that their findings "…are only an estimate and should be used as a general guide rather than as empirical transformations" (p. 13). The CREDO researchers are essentially admitting that there is no real empirical basis for their published extrapolation. Maul and McClelland (2013) noted that CREDO's conversion of effect size into days of learning was "insufficiently justified" and that *there really was no substantial difference between the performances of the two types of schools.* CREDO's conclusion is a hypothetical extrapolation or equivalence since

---

[63] It is a bit ironic that while the research community pushes the practitioner community to use the research evidence it produces, it neglects to provide evidence that the statistical criteria that it uses actually predict real-word outcomes.

the researchers never actually measured the days of extra learning. Concluding that charter schools are better based on this result is a very misleading finding that magnifies the importance of a tiny difference dwarfed by large errors associated with major transformations. Unfortunately, this highly biased finding developed at Stanford University received a great deal of publicity and was widely cited.

Another type of popular extrapolation in the research literature is to claim that an outcome of .1 standard deviation (i.e., ES) is the equivalent of moving students from the 50th to the 58th percentile on a nationally normed test. This would be a large benefit if that had actually happened. However, this seemingly impressive improvement is only a hypothetical extrapolation of differences in adjusted z scores. We do not know whether the experimental students actually scored at the 58th percentile or the 18th. In these types of equivalent *hypothetical extrapolations* in research journals students may not have even actually taken the test mentioned or any nationally normed test. In addition, this type of extrapolation assumes that the distribution of scores for students at risk is the same as national norms—which is clearly NOT true for studies in high poverty schools.

Another common misleading hypothetical extrapolation that inflates the benefits of small ESs is the widespread belief by researchers that an ES of .1 is equivalent to an extra month of learning in a year. Such a benefit, if real, would be important. However, .1 which is half of "difficult to detect"—is in reality a much smaller amount of extra learning.[64] In addition, even if there actually was an increase in a month of learning, would anyone care if, for example, fourth graders ended up only 2.2 years below grade level as opposed to 2.3? Would you adopt the intervention that produced this result?

But it is likely that even this trivial benefit is not real. The convoluted process of using hypothetical equivalence to create an artificial result from highly manipulated numbers is a house of cards that exaggerates the importance of results. Indeed, such studies never document what the amount of extra learning actually is. That such a convoluted process is widely accepted as evidence of effectiveness in the top research journals simply makes it easy to produce misleading results either intentionally or unintentionally. Such results are the province of mathematics—not of practice.

The concern about convoluted sophisticated mathematical processes not representing the reality of education practice is similar to the concern expressed by Moosa (2019) about whether econometrics is relevant to real-world economics. His concern is that econometrics has become "…more and more abstract and highly mathematical without an application in sight or a motivation for practical use" (p. 4).

These exaggerations of research outcomes with tiny ESs via equivalent extrapolations do have real-world consequences. CREDO's unjustified equivalence mistakenly denigrated traditional public schools and its practitioners. The previously discussed education replication study by Boulay et al.'s (2018) study showed that the vast majority of interventions that met the federal *What Works Clearinghouse* minimum ES

---

[64] At best, the hypothesized gain of 1 month is at best only for a school with a *normal distribution* with a *Mean* and *Standard Deviation* near the national/state average, on a nationally normed test. If the samples in the study, or your schools, are below or above average, or some other type of test was used there is no evidence as to what the amount of actual additional learning would be.

of .25 (or less) mostly do not replicate or provide noticeable benefits—thereby misleading leaders looking for effective interventions.

Some researchers have indeed expressed skepticism about the more common types of equivalencies. In a personal communication (June 20, 2016) Gene Glass indicated that no one knows precisely what *ESs* or *SD/Us* generated from adjusted normalized relative data equate to in terms of actual days of learning or test scores for non-normed samples and non-normed measures such as most state tests. Baird and Pane (2019) concluded that converting effects sizes into years of extra learning is the *worst* way to interpret *ES* results because such "...translation can produce implausible results." (The same is true for parts of years such as extra months or days of learning—e.g., the unsubstantiated claim that an *ES* of .1 is equal to an extra month of learning.) However, these cautions are largely ignored because the current methods for analyzing the results of experiments are simply too useful to researchers and journals.

Practical Tip | Leaders should avoid considering any intervention in which the research findings are expressed as "...equivalent to..." or "...the equivalence of..."

Problem #5—Relying on relative results which can obscure that the experimental group actually performed poorly

Data analysis principle #6 states that you should NOT make decisions based on relative performance but should seek data on the actual end result before making a decision. However, the standard method for analyzing the results from experiments compares the relative performance of the group receiving the new intervention and a comparison group.

Indeed, relative data by itself is not sufficient and can be misleading. Consider the following questions:

1. Suppose you are thinking of buying a different car to get better mileage, but not sure if you should buy one now. You find out that Car A gets better mileage than Car B. Assume that both cars cost the same. What additional information would you need to decide whether to get rid of your car and buy Car A? What key piece of data about the actual end result would you need to make your decision?

<.....think for a minute.....>

Assuming that gas mileage was the primary basis for the decision, the key actual end result would be to determine what gas mileage Car A got, and then determine whether Car A got noticeably better mileage than your existing car. If it doesn't there is no reason to switch from your current car to Car A.

2. Suppose you find credible research evidence that students in reading program A did better than those in reading program B. Assuming that both programs cost the same and would require the same

implementation effort, what key piece of data about the actual end result related to reading would you need, and how would you use that to make your decision?

<…..think for a minute…..>

The key actual end result would be: How well the students in Program A ended up achieving, and then determine whether they ended up reading noticeably better than the students in your schools. If not, there is no reason to adopt Program A.

In both of these example, there is a common-sense two-step process to making the needed decision that involve additional information beyond the relative performance data:

a) What was the actual final performance of the experimental group or superior object? and
b) Was that performance noticeably better than the status quo.

If the answer to (b) is "yes" that supports a decision to change your car or reading program.

Remember

Of the information, in these examples, the performance of Car B/Reading Program B was not relevant to your decision, nor was the relative information on how better A was than B. Remembering this common-sense lesson is critical to appreciating the rationale for the alternative the statistical test of practical benefit described later on.

In other words, research analysis that simply reports relative data between groups is NOT providing sufficient information. In addition, just providing relative information can be misleading. Consider the following example of a conversation between a husband and wife planning a January getaway to a warm beach.

Wife:	*I cannot wait for our vacation in January. Let's go somewhere warm.*
Husband:	*Definitely.*
Wife:	*Where should we go?*
Husband:	*I just read that Greenland is warmer than Antarctica in January.*
Wife:	*That sounds great.*
Husband:	*Even better, due to climate warming Greenland will be warmer this year than last. Plus, it has 27,394 miles of coastline, so it will be no problem finding beaches.*
Wife*:*	*That's great. It will be wonderful to go somewhere where we can leave our winter clothes behind.*

While this couple made an evidence-based decision they are clearly in for a freezing surprise. Why?

They have made the mistake of confusing a comparative/relative measure of something, in this case temperature, with the actual, i.e., absolute, level of the temperature of the desired destination. The actual temperature in Greenland in January

178

averages -8 degrees Celsius with zero hours of sunshine. In other words, something can look good on a relative basis and actually be horrible on an actual/absolute basis.

Clearly this couple is not very bright. They are more likely to die from hypothermia in Greenland than they are to get a tan. However, their decision was in fact "evidenced based" and the differences were in fact BIG. They were simply looking at the wrong numbers/evidence.

This example illustrates that evidence-based practices based solely on relative data can be disastrous. The couple needed to incorporate a key piece of actual end result data—in this case the actual temperature. Indeed, their decision would have been better if they had just gotten a list of actual temperatures around the world in January than the relative comparison they did.

Practical Tip

Sole Reliance on Relative Data is Misinformation—for any type of research analysis, including experimental research. *Sole reliance on relative data is as likely to mislead practice as to inform it. The primary focus needs to be on the key piece(s) of absolute/actual end result evidence for the experimental subjects.* You need to know what the actual final (unadjusted) *Means* were for the experimental group (only). Then you can compare this end result to how your schools are already doing to determine whether it makes sense to adopt the intervention.

Indeed, trying to make sense of series of studies reporting just relative results is like trying to shop in a supermarket with all the price labels reading something like: *"The price of this is less than the one on the left but more than the one on the right."* Furthermore, suppose the items on the right and left, as well as every other item in the store, has the same type of price label. It would make shopping for food difficult if not impossible. You would not know the actual end result—i.e., the cost of each item—until you checked out or received the bill. Unfortunately, much of education research is based on such relative labeling. Indeed, the essence of experimental data analysis is a relative comparison between groups.

Unfortunately, before we make fun of the sun-seeking couple, we need to recognize that in the sophisticated analyses of experimental research, educational researchers often just report relative outcomes—even in the best research and practitioner journals. Indeed, all experimental research is a relative process that compares the results from one group with another—neither of which are from your schools. As a result, evidence from experiments creates the risk of the same type of evidence-based error as our hapless Mid-western couple.

The best way to minimize the problem of reliance on relative data is, as described in Problem #1 above, is to report the final unadjusted *Means, Medians,* and *Standard Deviations* for at least the experimental group. (See Chapter 3 for the discussion of the power trio.) This is the only way that practitioners can tell whether the experimental students actually performed well, and noticeably better than their schools.

Alas, reporting unadjusted results is NOT required by research journals and is NOT always done—which leaves leaders to make decisions based on the same type of data as our hapless couple. Leaving practitioners to rely solely on relative results has led to large-scale misdirection of practice in education.

Two examples of relative comparisons between groups misleading practice

1. *Success for All.* This schoolwide reading program became the most relied on reform intervention for more than two decades for improving the reading performance of high-poverty inner city elementary schools and for reducing the achievement gap. A large number of studies appearing in the most prestigious research journals over several decades seemed to document evidence of the unique effectiveness of the "Success for All" program. Based on this extensive research evidence this program received the most federal funding for dissemination than any other, and it was the most widely adopted intervention for urban schools undergoing reform over the past two decades.

    The most famous example of this program's evidence-based "success" involved the original experiment in Baltimore Public Schools in the early 90s. The research articles had lots of sophisticated statistical analyses and descriptions of the methodology. The relative criterion of *practical significance* showed impressively BIG *effect sizes* (*ESs*), particularly for the most at-risk students. Sounds good!

    However, there were two main problems with this conclusion. First, Venezky (1998) found that the special education students disappeared from the experimental sample, and all students who had not been at the school all 5 years of the experiment were dropped. This undisclosed methodological manipulation of the sample clearly exaggerated the final results for the *Success for All* schools—which called into question whether on a relative basis those schools actually performed better. The second problem was that the researchers did not reveal the actual end results for how the experimental schools actually performed.

    Fortunately, Venezky was able to obtain data on actual performance. Pogrow (1998, 2000) concluded from Venezky's analysis of actual scores that the experimental students included in the sample entered the sixth grade after 5 years in the program reading about 3.2 years below grade level. Had all students in the "Success for All" Baltimore schools been included, a reasonable expectation for a program that bills itself as a schoolwide model, the actual end results would have been even worse.[65]

---

[65] Another "success" claimed by "Success for All" in its i3 proposal was its use in all the high poverty schools (only) in Atlanta Public Schools. The actual result was a huge cheating scandal that made national headlines and that resulted in educators being given jail sentences. The superintendent who imposed the use of this intervention passed-on before she could be brought to trial.

I think that most would agree that such an actual end result is terrible and documents failure as opposed to success.[66]

Unfortunately, the actual end result was omitted from this published research (and subsequent research)—so no one knew how poorly the "Success for All" students were actually performing.

The published 'evidence' from the Baltimore 'success' continue to be used in research articles to document the program's effectiveness, and this 'evidence' was also used in the program's successful i3 funding request in 2010 that netted it a $50 million grant from the U.S. Department of Education (ED) to scale-up this program two decades later. It was also used to convince the *What Works Clearinghouse* to certify the program's effectiveness based on its meeting the highest level of research evidence criteria.

However, my research (Pogrow, 2002; Pogrow, 2008) showed that the published claims of success in subsequent major reform efforts around the U.S. based on relative *ES* results consistently masked the fact that the "Success for All" students were doing poorly. **Yet, the top journals continued to publish research claiming that this intervention was successful without any reviewers or editors checking to see if there was contrary evidence. The peer-review panels for funding programs such as foundations or the *What Works Clearinghouse* also did not check to see if there was any contrary published data.**

This misdirection of practice on a large scale is a perfect example of the previously stated principle that *"Sole reliance on relative data is misinformation."* This is equivalent to the research community and the U.S. Department of Education advocating that all educational leaders should vacation in Greenland in January to get a tan.[67] However, in this case the damage from relying on relative data was national in scope (thousands of high poverty schools) and spanned several decades.

Beware

It is simply too easy, and seductive, to cover up actual poor end results by providing only relative data. There is no excuse for not providing the unadjusted *Mean/Median* to indicate what the actual end performance of the experimental group was.

---

[66] An interesting question is why schools continued to adopt the program over several decades. It was a combination of superintendents not allowing research departments to release the embarrassing data of the program's failure, and press releases by the developer claiming that the program had not been successful because of politics or that the schools had not implemented the program properly. Once my articles connected the dots of what had happened across the country, the use of the program began to drop. However, in 2010 the federal government subsidized its dissemination yet again with a $50 million i3 scaling-up grant based in part of the program's "successes" in Baltimore (where the students were 3 years below grade level in reading) and Atlanta (with its cheating scandal).

[67] Indeed, to truly understand the damaging consequences of the federal government's and research community's support for this program that was used predominantly with the neediest students read Jonathan Kozol's (2005; 2006) description of the rigid nature of the program and what it's like for teachers and students in "Success for All" schools. He characterizes the use of this "evidence-based" program in high-poverty schools to a system akin to "apartheid."

Leaders who applied principle #5 would have avoided an expensive mistake. If they checked the research, and ignored all the technical detail but just searched for the final, unadjusted Mean/Median for the experimental group, they would have noticed that it was missing. They then would have made the correct decision to ignore this research evidence (and program).

2. *Math Pathways and Pitfalls.* This is an intervention that develops skills and understanding in the use of academic math language. Heller, Hansen, and Barnett-Clarke (2010) found that 30 hours of instruction with this math reform over two years in grades 4 and 5 produced significant gains in the standardized test scores of Latino and English learner students relative to those not receiving the instruction. This research is elegant, done with integrity, and the intervention is clearly substantive. These researchers then did the following three things that are often not done:

    - While most of the analysis was done on *proximal* gains, they also looked for *distal* gains in the form of standardized math test scores;
    - They also provided the intervention to the advantaged students in the schools and reported their distal gains as well; and
    - They provided *Impact Scores* on the actual/absolute progress of all the groups' distal scores.

These data show a different outcome than the initial more typical relative analysis. If you look inside the impact estimates on the standardized tests section, the impact coefficients of the program showed that the experimental at-risk students made NO progress, and that their relative advantage occurred because the comparison at-risk students fell further behind. Interestingly, the advantaged students who also received the intervention made progress. This means that providing the same high quality intervention to all students actually widened the achievement gap.

The difference between the evidence provided by relative analysis and the actual end result analysis in this case suggest very different leadership decisions. The relative evidence suggests that there would be a benefit to implement the program for all students. However, the actual/absolute end results indicated that such a decision would *decrease* equity—but that this might be a good program to implement just for at-risk students.

These examples of misdirection and the general critique of the inadequacy of relying on relative outcomes in experimental research raise the following questions:

- In how many other studies, or validated evidence-based practices, is the evidence obscuring the fact that the at-risk students actually performed poorly—i.e., how widespread is the problem?

- Why is the research community so blasé in terms of demanding evidence as to the actual unadjusted performance of the students (or others) in the experimental group in applied research? Is this not the number one issue that practitioners and parents want, and deserve, to know?

In terms of the latter, the actual end result of how experimental students performed on an absolute basis would seem to be the most important issue to address in evidence designed to inform practice.

This divergence between the evidence provided by so many studies means that leaders need to conduct their own independent assessment of experimental research evidence.

Practical Tip

Leaders should never adopt an evidence-based intervention without first examining the evidence to find the unadjusted *Means* for how the experimental group (only) performed and see if that appears to be a substantial improvement over how your schools are already doing. If you cannot find that simple statistic in the study, chances are that the experimental students did not actually end up doing all that well.

The problem of relying on relative data also applies to evidence provided by salespeople to document the superiority of their product. They will typically tout 1-2 studies in their promotional pitches. The studies that I have seen typically rely on relative data showing the superiority of the group that used the materials being peddled with lots of asterisks—i.e., statistical significance.

Practical Tip

When examining any sales material claims ask the salesperson for the actual end result of absolute performance data. For example, if it is a new reading program, ask the salesperson questions such as:

- What percentage of students of color in your program ended up reading at grade level?
- What was the final average reading level of the key subgroups of students using your reading program in this study—and were these unadjusted averages? Etc.

Chances are that the salesperson's face will change color. He/she will probably promise to get back to you with the requested info—and probably won't.

Being judicious and avoiding the problems

Leaders can use the knowledge in this section to easily spot analytic problems and ignore the resultant 'rigorous evidence'. They can thereby avoid adopting an evidence-based intervention or best practice that is NOT likely to improve their schools or increase equity.

The goal of this section is NOT to discredit experimental research. Experimental research is critical to improving practice. Rather the goals of pointing out the common problems in analyzing experimental research outcomes are to:

a) Enable leaders to focus their attention on those experimental studies whose findings are authentic; and

b) Set the stage for understanding the need for, and application of, the proactive, alternative methods for identifying authentic experimental research in the subsequent section of this chapter and the next one.

Most importantly…

Practical Tip

AVOID experimental research evidence that is based on…

- Relative results;
- Small *ES (SD/U)*—i.e., difficult to detect benefits such as .2 or the .25 standard of the What Works Clearinghouse;
- Statistical significance—e.g., p<.01 **;
- Adjusted *Means*; and
- A non-representative sample with a high attrition rate.

And above all, AVOID any combination of the above.

Section 4—Implications for Practice: How to Identify Authentic Experimental Research Evidence

New opportunities

While it is clear that the mathematical sophistication and methodological rigor researchers do not ensure that the results predict real-world outcomes or even provide the type of evidence that leaders need, the combination of problems in setting up RCT research and in analyzing the results of experiments can be thought of as good news in two respects:

1. If a substantial portion of research evidence is NOT useful, that quickly narrows the field of evidence and the evidence-based practices that you should consider—which makes it easier to focus on the most promising evidence; and

2. If the most mathematically rigorous methods and statistical analyses are the least useful and/or most problematic, that reduces the need to deal with the arcane technical aspects of experimental research—making it easier to focus just on the fundamental numbers.

It turns out that it is easy to determine the actual end result of absolute performance using junior high level basic math. In addition, the practical problems of establishing causation in the complex dynamics of schools with even the most rigorous gold-standard methodology opens the door to the possibility that there are alternative, less sophisticated methods for conducting, and analyzing evidence from, experiments that are far more useful for leadership decision-making. The next section will present an array of such methods.

While exaggerated, hypothetical, extrapolations of tiny abstract differences continue to be widely cited as evidence that interventions (or types of schools) are better, or "best-practice," or "evidence-based," leaders can easily identify that subset of experimental evidence that is authentic and beneficial for their schools.

Methods for Identifying authentic experimental evidence

While it would be nice to find replicated gold-standard evidence supporting interventions that produced BIG distal gains and high levels of *external validity*, that almost never happens. But then, most things in life are not perfect—and yet we often make good decisions that improve our lives. Similarly, leaders can indeed make use of clues within an imperfect body of experimental research evidence to identify practices that are likely to improve their schools and increase equity. And it is essential that they do so, given that reliance on qualitative or relationship research without confirming experimental evidence tends to lead to large-scale adoption of ineffective practices.

There is therefore a need for alternative quantitative methods that leaders can use to independently analyze the results of experiments to separate the wheat kernels of authentic evidence in experimental research from the chaff. By conducting their own independent assessment using the proactive methods in this section leaders can avoid going down the rabbit hole of adopting widely publicized "evidence-based" practices that in reality never actually worked in any practical sense. Such failure is even true for most of the interventions that the federal What Works Clearinghouse has validated as being effective. In addition, these new alternative analytical methods will also enable leaders to identify evidence that the research community has not considered as meeting its "rigorous" standards but that is very useful for leadership decision-making.

The following proactive methods for analyzing the results of experiments are designed specifically to meet the evidentiary needs of leaders while being intuitive and accessible.

Beware

These alternative methods bypass many of the "rigorous" traditional statistical standards. As a result, they will be criticized as non-rigorous by many traditionalists. However, these alternative methods are MORE scientific because they are more likely to accurately predict whether adopting the findings will improve your schools and increase equity—i.e., the methods are more authentic.

The four alternative analytic methods for identifying authentic research evidence from experiments are:

1. Implicit causation;
2. Eyeball comparison of *Means;*
3. Practical benefit; and
4. Potential practical benefit

The common element among all of these methods is:

185

- They do NOT require any statistical skills beyond the power trio (Chapter 3) and basic math; and
- They are initiated by setting improvement and equity goals.

So this section will first discuss the process of setting goals and then discuss in turn each of the four alternative methods.

Setting improvement and equity goals

The leadership process of using research evidence to improve your schools does NOT start with sophisticated statistical formulas, statistical tests, and research analyses. It starts with setting improvement and equity goals. The only way to determine whether research evidence is likely to produce an important outcome for your schools is to first determine what the current level of school/district performance is for a critical objective and then set improvement goals.

For example, suppose a district is trying to reduce suspensions. The first step for leaders before reviewing any research is to set a goal for how much improvement in a given outcome(s) is sought over the next two years that would cause the district to adopt a new approach. Keep in mind that the goals should be ones of substantial improvement expressed in quantitative terms. However, these goals should represent incremental progress. For example, it is not reasonable to set a goal of moving from 300 suspensions a year to zero.

Practical Tip

Goals are action statements that indicate what you plan to achieve. The goal should specify a specific numerical target with a specific timeline. You can set one goal for a high cost intervention, and another goal for a low cost one.

The setting of improvement goals is a fundamental exercise in human judgment and aspiration. There are no formulas or rules for how to set improvement and equity goals. No statistician can tell you what the goal should be. However, it is only after knowing where you are and where you want to get to that you can assess whether research outcomes are likely to provide sufficient benefit to achieve the desired goals—or at least make promising progress towards the goals.

Once you have established improvement goals you can proceed to implement the alternative data analysis methods below.

Implicit causation

The highest quality experimental methodology, RCT, with all of its technical wizardry simply cannot describe the reality of the myriad social and programmatic interactions within complex organizations such as schools or hospitals. The problems with relying on RCT experiments in an effort to establish causation were previously discussed—including a general failure to demonstrate noticeable benefit. It was also pointed out that leaders are more interested in evidence of replication and *external validity* than of causation.

So while experimental research remains essential for improving practice, it is time to conclude that relying on a single, very expensive, structured gold-standard study to try and prove causation, and then inferring that its result is applicable on a large scale, simply does NOT work for applied research on improving schools.[68] Fortunately, causation is not the only important scientific principle. There is an alternative approach to using experimentation to improve practice—one which in fact relies on the scientific principle of seeking replication.

The alternative is to conduct a series of less formal, lower cost, rapid prototyping experiments with fewer controls for confounding variables, in a variety of contexts. If it turns out that all the studies produce similar, important benefits from the use of an intervention—we can then ask the following question:

What is the likelihood that the benefit was NOT caused by the intervention?

So while there would be methodological problems with each of these studies, collectively they produce a replicated pattern of widespread notable benefit—which is exactly the type of evidence that leaders seek and need. In this scenario it is reasonable to conclude that the intervention was the source of the benefit. This type of approach to testing interventions will hereafter be referred to as ***implicit causation***.

Implicit causation is a less statistically formal method of proving the effectiveness of an intervention via repeated experience of its success in a variety of contexts/settings. The advantages of conducting a series of rapid prototyping studies to test for *implicit causation* are:

- Lower cost;
- Generate results quicker; and
- Flexible and adaptable—i.e., you can make modifications to the intervention based on early feedback.

While top education research journals do not (yet) publish this type of research, implicit causation is essentially the method successfully used in finding effective treatments in a variety of clinical disciplines—particularly for solving problems of practice in complex organizations such as hospitals or time critical problems.

Indeed, the belief that medicine only uses RCT methods is wrong. Consider for example Kolata's (2015) description of *precision medicine* as the newest federal initiative for improving medical care and discovering new and more powerful treatments for cancer. This new research effort as "unlike previous efforts that looked for small differences between a new treatment and an older one…researchers are gambling on finding huge effects" (p. 2). Kolata goes on to note that scientists are finding a patient response rate to the new drugs of 50-60% as compared to existing treatments that give a response rate of only 10-20%. One of the researchers notes that "When you are having a big effect, it is kind of jaw dropping."

---

[68] Gold-standard RCT methodology does remain essential for basic research to uncover fundamental principles of teaching, learning, social behavior, brain functioning, communication, etc.

In other words, precision medicine is finding BIG differences. Furthermore, precision medicine does NOT use randomized control groups or control groups of any kind. Rather, the actual end results are compared to a known threshold of performance. A finding of BIG consistent improvements over current tumor response rates is used by itself without randomized controls and sophisticated statistics to show that the benefits are real and are not happening by chance.

Remember

The principle and goal of precision medicine is completely consistent with the statistical test of practical benefit, which seeks BIG improvements over an existing threshold of performance; which in this case is the existing performance of your schools. The performance of an experimental comparison group is irrelevant.

Furthermore, the Food and Drug Administration (FDA) is planning to approve new treatments on the basis of BIG consistent improvements without randomized clinical controlled trials.

Chapter 8 will discuss this rapid prototyping approach without control groups which has come to be known as *Improvement Science*—along with its benefits for improving schools and increasing equity.

While there have been a few projects in education that have used the principles of improvement science to try and develop *implicit causation*, you are usually left to try and find a variety of experiments testing the intervention that is of interest. If there have been similar studies with different samples that have shown the same benefits, conducted by different *independent* researchers in different types of schools, that increases the likelihood that the intervention will work in your schools—even if the individual studies are not the highest quality.[69] You have thus established *implicit causation*.

If you can find a series of studies or reports that found similar types of BIG benefits, you can look for clues of *implicit causation* in those studies. The two most important clues are (a) the similarities of the findings, and (b) whether the subjects or schools in any of the samples resemble those in your schools. If there is a consistency of findings and some resemblance to your schools that suggests that the results might apply to your schools. Alternatively, the study may break out the results for subgroups within the sample, and one of the subgroups may be consistent with the students you are interested in improving in your schools. For example, the samples in the COVID-19 studies were large enough to break out the results for senior separately.

---

[69] It is important that the replication studies be conducted by independent sources—i.e., sources not affiliated with the individual who did the original research or with the development of the intervention. For example, there were lots of published studies showing the effectiveness of the *Success for All* reading program in a variety of top research journals. While this would seem to be replication and corroboration, in fact it was all produced by the developer or those associated with his center. It was not until 20 years after my first published reports of the program's ineffectiveness that there were evaluations of the program by independent evaluators who confirmed the program's ineffectiveness.

Two caveats for examining the characteristics of a study's sample:

1. The characteristics of the sample in any study will never exactly match your schools. In addition, the most important variable in my experience to match is the percentage of low-income students in the school. How close should the match be? Use your judgment.

2. My experience is that it is possible to successfully transplant practices used in elite schools to inner city high poverty schools. (See the description of the HOTS program in Chapter 8.)

If you cannot find confirming studies you can also seek evidence of replication from other leaders whose schools have adopted the intervention you are interested in. You can investigate the results they have found. While reports of effects from other leaders as to their findings understandably have little credibility in the research community, and indeed have low internal validity, if the other schools have truly experienced substantial *documented* positive results, that increases the likelihood that your school will similarly benefit from the intervention. However, beware....

Beware

…leaders who have adopted a novel approach will often exaggerate how well it is actually working for a variety of reasons such as ego, being paid by the developer, etc. Always get specific numerical data as to the extent of the benefit as opposed to just a testimonial.

Clearly, leaders should trust published research to a far greater extent than testimonials from other leaders. Hopefully, useful replication/confirming published research exists. However, if it does not, a leader should seek the best available evidence.

Eyeball comparison of unadjusted Means

As previously discussed, most of the statistics used in analyzing the results of experiments involve comparing the differences in the *Means* of the experimental and comparison groups and seeing if there is a "significant" difference in the *Means*. However, do you really need to use complex statistical procedures to see if there is an important difference between the *Means*?

Not really! You can simply eyeball the differences and see if the difference between them appears to be substantial to you. While statisticians will view this as being a biased judgment and prefer their "unbiased" methods, it is clear that their criteria for determining significant differences—be they statistical or practical significance—are constructed so that they can claim a discovery of a "significant" finding that does not represent any real-world practical benefit. These statistical tests are biased in favor of the needs of the researchers. In addition, we make decisions every day on the basis of numerical differences without calling on a statistician to tell us how to judge the numbers. Finally, while evidence can help leaders make decisions, most decisions in the end are fundamentally a judgment call.

So whenever students of mine engage in a statistical analysis, be it an original study or critically looking at published research, I insist that they eyeball the results before conducting any statistical test. I ask them to tell me whether in their opinion the difference in *Means* is substantial/important based on their judgment. Letting users of research make informed judgment about the magnitudes of performance in the research is consistent with theorists such as Gorard (2015) and Moosa (2019) who have argued for the use of human judgment and simple arithmetic to assess the importance of findings rather than statistical tests. Pearl and Mackenzie (2018) emphasize that there is a subjective element to even determining causal mechanisms "…that cannot be reduced to mechanical routines such as those laid out in statistical manuals." (p.88)

Indeed, I snuck in an eyeballing exercise of the difference between *Means* in Chapter 3's discussion of gap analysis. Specifically it was analyzing whether the reading gap between Black and White girls was systemic. Normally, such a comparison would not have been discussed in a chapter on descriptive research but would have been introduced in this chapter as an ex post facto study, and a statistic such as a t-test would have been performed to see if the difference was statistically significant. But that statistical analysis was not necessary. You were able to tell by eyeballing the *Means* of each group's reading scores that the gap was systemic.

Remember

There is a compelling theoretical, as well as practical, basis for using informed judgment and common sense basic math to analyze research evidence. This is particularly true when the current widely-accepted sophisticated, abstract mathematical, analyses, and mechanical statistical procedures do not accurately predict real-world improvement outcomes in schools.

While it is easy for students to make judgments about the extent of benefit by eyeballing the results in their own research, it can be more difficult for assessing the published research. The first issue is:

> Which *Means* are of interest? Data analysis principle #6 indicates that the key to determining the effectiveness of an intervention is NOT the relative difference between the groups. So the difference in the *Means* of the experimental group vs. the comparison group is not the key to determining whether the evidence is authentic—regardless of whether traditional statistical tests or human judgment are used. Which *Means* should be used?

The second issue in interpreting *Means* is what to do when they are abstract numbers such as adjusted z scores.

> Ideally, in research analyzing results for samples that span several states, the researchers would supplement the *z* score results with the actual *Means* for each state so that one can then easily judge the results for the state or states of most interest to them. However, if such intelligible data are not provided, what can you do?

In order to deal with these issues, and given the problems with the existing statistical tests of *statistical* and *practical significance*, a new statistical test has been proposed— practical benefit. Practical benefit provides a mechanism for judging the authenticity of research findings—i.e., whether research findings will translate to noticeable benefits in your schools if you adopt the recommended intervention.

Practical benefit

Given the problems with using relative comparisons discussed in this chapter, along with the problems of relying on statistical or practical significance, how can leaders determine the likelihood that a research finding that an experimental group at external sites did relatively better than a comparison group also at external sites will provide the same benefit at their school(s)?

A methodology for evaluating the authenticity of evidence from an experiment came from a conversation that I had many years ago with a principal in New Jersey. At the time all high poverty elementary schools in that state were being pressured to adopt "Success for All"—as opposed to several alternatives. I asked the principal why he did not adopt the recommended program. His response was:

I looked at their results and my students were already doing better than the students in the "Success for All" schools ended up doing.

BINGO! In other words, the principal's criterion was to compare the actual end result of the absolute performance of the experimental students (only) to the current performance of his students. He had no interest in how the comparison group in the research did. Similarly, if the hapless Midwest couple seeking a warm vacation spot in winter had compared the actual temperature in Greenland to the actual temperature where they lived and seen that it was even colder, they would have looked for another potential place to vacation.

This principal's insight also illustrates that there is a fundamental difference in the type of research questions asked by academicians and leaders.

Table 6.3
Differences in Key Questions Asked of Research Findings

Academicians/Researchers	Leaders
Did the experimental group in the research context do better than the comparison group, and was that difference statistically significant? What inference from that finding can be made to all schools? What are the implications of the findings for theory?	Was the actual end result of the experimental group (only) noticeably better than how my schools were already doing? If not, there is no reason to adopt the program.

This difference in perspective is not trivial. Indeed, the problem for leaders to extrapolate the likely outcome from the contexts in published research to their own school(s) is far more complex than generally acknowledged in methodology textbooks. (Keep in mind that we are talking about the findings of published research of experiments conducted at external sites. It is, of course, easier to extrapolate findings if the experiment was conducted in the leader's own schools as part of a program evaluation.) The bottom line is that the guidance provided by statistical inference in the typical study is much less helpful than researchers acknowledge—and looking for the needed clues in the data is easier once the unnecessary technical analyses are stripped away.

Most importantly, this principal's initiative and decision NOT to go down the state recommended rabbit hole of adopting a failed program also illustrates the following four points:

1. It is possible for a non-statistician to determine how the experimental students actually performed because he looked for the right numbers—i.e., the actual end result performance of the experimental students (only);

2. By taking the time to look into the actual research and investigate the key underlying relevant numbers this leader was able to avoid a bad decision that likely would have resulted in his/her school's performance declining;

3. The leader did not need to employ any sophisticated statistical methodology; and

4. This intuitively obvious approach enabled the principal to make a direct inference as to the likely benefit of the research finding to his/her school—better than any other method I have encountered.

What data and statistics did the principal use?

The return of the Power Trio to save the day

Chapter 3 introduced the importance of the power trio of statistics (Mean, Median, Standard Deviation) and discussed how they interact to determine the most representative value for a group of values and provide clues as to the nature of the distribution of values. In this case the principal determined the *Mean* result for the "Success for All" students and compared it to the *Mean* of his/her own students. *The principal ignored the performance of the control group.* While the performance of the comparison group is critical for most data analyses of the outcomes of experiments, it is of no value to that principal's decision as to whether the intervention is likely to produce a noticeable/BIG improvement, in his/her own schools.

But suppose the evidence was different, and the intervention did produce superior results as compared to his/her schools. In that case the principal would have to use the power trio to judge whether the advantage that the intervention provided to the experimental students versus the current performance was BIG enough to constitute *practical benefit*.

Determining the practical benefit of experimental research

Definition of practical benefit

The principal's insight provides the basis for defining practical benefit.

Practical benefit *for leadership decision-making is defined as whether the actual unweighted/unadjusted Mean/Median performance of the experimental group (only) in a study represents a BIG improvement over how your schools are already doing.*

This principal's experience suggests that it is possible for a non-statistician to take ownership for deciding how to use evidence to determine the *practical benefit* of research, and reach the correct decision by ignoring the conclusion of the researcher. However, determining the *practical benefit* of the findings of an experiment leads to the following questions:

> *What constitutes a BIG improvement/benefit for your schools? How is that determined?*

What is a BIG improvement/benefit?

There are some precedents in education policy for defining a BIG difference. One example of policy where BIG differences are required is in special education's use of discrepancy analysis to identify whether a student has a learning disability. In discrepancy analysis you look for the difference between a student's score on some cognitive measure and a lower performance on an academic test. This difference needs to be BIG in order to classify the student as having a learning disability. One state defines BIGNESS as a discrepancy of 50% (this is similar to the FDA standard for the desired minimum effectiveness of a vaccine). Another standard of BIGness in the literature is a difference of 1.2 to 2 *Standard Deviations*. (This is about 10 times the *ES* or (*SD/U*) standard that researchers have decided to use to identify a "significant difference." As already discussed, such differences are trivial.)

The point is that a trivial difference, e.g., one that is *statistically significant*, or .2 *Standard Deviations (SD)*, is not considered to be a BIG enough discrepancy to justify classifying a student as having a disability. Similarly, leaders should not accept trivial differences between experimental and comparison groups as evidence of effectiveness, but should seek a BIG benefit from adopting any new intervention.

What is a BIG advantage? The best conceptual definition of BIG was offered by a colleague, Christopher Tienken, associate professor of Educational Leadership at Seton Hall University. In a conversation he described *practical benefit* this way:

> Did the students or teachers in a study benefit so substantially that it makes sense for you the leader to commit a substantial part of your discretionary monies and time, and others' time, to implement the intervention in the study?

Operationalizing this conceptual definition in terms of a statistical test, the question becomes:

> *How large should an ES or benefit be for leaders to consider it to be BIG enough to adopt the intervention in that research?*

Human Judgment

The best measure of BIGness is human judgment. It is your judgment as to whether the unadjusted *Mean/Median* of the experimental group is in line with your improvement goals and substantially better than how your schools are currently performing.

Sorry. There is no magic formula or statistical test to determine whether the likely benefit is BIG enough to warrant your adopting the intervention. However, your improvement goals should be a baseline guide as to the amount of BIGness to seek.

In addition, all things being equal, the BIGger the advantage of the actual end result for the experimental group (only) is relative to your schools' current performance, the more likely it is that your schools will experience a noticeable benefit from adopting the new approach.

Of course, this assumes that the study was conducted with integrity in a setting that at least somewhat resembles your schools, and that there is some corroborating/replication evidence.

Good News

A major advantage of using *practical benefit* besides its intuitiveness, is that it enables anyone to easily critique even the most mathematically sophisticated experimental research study in the top research journals. You can ignore all the complicated statistics—just as the previously mentioned principal did in arriving at his/her decision. You can also ignore virtually all the technical terms you do not already know as they have little to do with determining the actual end result performance of the experimental group. You can even ignore the recommendation and conclusion of the researchers and determine on your own whether the results indicate a practical benefit.

Using the "three number method" to determine practical benefit

Ironically, the most important tools for determining the *practical benefit* of experimental research is the most fundamental form of quantitative analysis which gets the least respect—i.e., *descriptive analysis and the most fundamental of statistics, the power trio.*

Given that the mass of statistical analyses and the data presented in studies generally deal with the comparative analysis between groups, you can quickly wade through the article and the technical jargon and tables to find the few kernels of data that indicate the actual performance of the experimental group. Specifically you are just looking for three numbers: The unadjusted *Mean, Median,* and *Standard Deviation of the experimental group.*

The three numbers that describe how the experimental group actually did is usually found in just a single sentence, or in a single line in one of the many tables in the article. *The bottom line is that you can <u>ignore</u> all the other statistics, data, and technical jargon in order to find the unadjusted Mean or Median, to determine how the experimental students actually did.* This is akin to wading through the data about Greenland vs. Antarctica to find the single piece of info that matters the most—i.e., the actual temperature in January.

Usually, the *Mean* is some type of score expressed as a grade, scale score (e.g., attitude scale), or percentile. The *Mean* can also represent the average percentage of students achieving a level, e.g., basic or proficient, percentage of students/schools achieving success/failure, or the probability of students/schools achieving success or failure, e.g., probability of students being suspended or retained.

In theory it should be easy to find out how the experimental group actually did in applied published research since this is the most relevant data for leaders. Knowing the unadjusted/unweighted *Means* is also essential for ending the phenomenon in wherein an intervention is "proven" to be effective when in reality the experimental students actually did poorly. Fortunately, in many cases the unadjusted/unweighted final *Means* are provided and you can dig them out—and you can then determine the *practical benefit* of the research for your schools.

In other words, quantitative research increasingly provides tons of analysis about many things except how well the experimental students *actually* did. It should not be such a low priority in applied research to let non-researchers know how the experimental group actually did on an actual/absolute basis.

Hopefully journal editors and review panels will start to require researchers to include the *unadjusted/unweighted Mean, Standard Deviation*, and *Median* in their findings.

Suppose you are interested in using research to find a better way to try and reduce suspensions, and you set a goal of reducing them by 20% within a year. You find a study wherein an experimental group of schools had 25% fewer suspensions than the comparison group of schools. Such a result would probably be *statistically and practically significant*.

QUESTION: Based on this evidence (assuming it is true), would you adopt the intervention used by the experimental group? What other data would you seek?

ANSWER: NO!

The reason for this answer is in this footnote.[70]

---

[70] While at first glance the research appears to document a BIG rate of improvement, even higher than your target improvement goal, by now you realize that finding a 25% advantage is only relative data, and does not indicate what the actual end result of the experimental group was—i.e., what the *unweighted/unadjusted Mean* of the actual number of suspensions for the experimental schools was at the end of the experiment. It is only by knowing the end result that you can you compare the experimental schools' result to your schools' rate of suspensions. It

Once leaders have overseen the setting of improvement goals, the decision as to whether the performance of the experimental group represents a sufficiently BIG improvement relative to their schools' current level of performance, and whether it contributes substantively to their improvement goals, is a human judgment call. This is not a rejection of science, or of the use of evidence, or of statistical analysis. It is a scientific process that recognizes the key points when human judgment is necessary and better than a formula.

Good News

In other words, any leader can critique any published experimental research in terms of its *practical benefit* by simply extracting and then analyzing the three power trio numbers relative to their schools' needs and improvement goals.

However, while *practical benefit* is the epitome of an *authentic* method, what happens if the researcher has not provided the *unweighted/unadjusted* for the groups—only adjusted *Means* or no *Means* at all?

Why didn't the researcher report the actual *Means*/Medians? Is he/she hiding something? The bottom line is that if you do not know how the experimental students actually performed you CANNOT determine the *practical benefit* of the research. You can be suspicious about why the researcher omitted such results—or give the researcher the benefit of the doubt and contact him/her directly to try and obtain unadjusted results. If the researcher will not provide unweighted/unadjusted data—*be very very suspicious.*

Remember

These new methods collectively seek to replace the statistical tests of *statistical significance* and *practical significance* with that of **practical benefit**.

The bottom line is that at this point the best you can do is rely on relative information and reluctantly settle for finding a BIG relative difference of the adjusted *Means* between the groups—a statistical test hereafter referred to as **potential practical benefit**.

Determining *potential* practical benefit

If the research does not report the actual final unadjusted *Mean, Median, Standard Deviation* for the experimental group, you have to reluctantly rely on the relative *ES* or *SD/U* of the differences between the adjusted *Means* of the groups—and seek a big

---

may be that the suspension rates in your school(s) are already lower or about the same as those for the experimental group. In that case there is no reason to adopt the suspension reduction technique in the study.

How much lower should the actual suspension rate in any experimental study be relative to your schools' current rate before deciding that the results would represent a *practical benefit* and that the new intervention should be adopted? That is up to you and the other leaders and the school board to decide.

relative difference favoring the experimental group. This is highly problematic for all the reasons discussed in the previous sections.

The statistical test and criteria to determine whether *ES* or *SD/U* is BIG enough is ***potential practical benefit.***

However, potential practical benefit cannot be viewed as an indicator that the given evidence is authentic. Research that meets the recommended cutoffs of BIGness listed in the next section should only be considered as a "suggestion" that leaders should probably investigate the results further. Always keep in the back of your mind the vacationing couple vignette in which they selected Greenland for a getaway based on BIG relative differences, and educators who adopted "Success for All" based on BIG *ESs* of weighted *Means*. If the statistics do indicate a BIG relative difference between the groups, the most you can say is that there <u>may</u> be something here that warrants further investigation. In other words, relative BIGness—i.e., potential practical benefit—does NOT indicate that your schools will likely benefit from applying the research findings because you still do not know how the experimental group actually performed and whether it performed better than your schools are already performing.

While *potential practical benefit* is a new evidentiary standard, it uses the same statistical tests of *ES* or *SD/U* that the existing criterion of *practical significance* does. However, *potential practical benefit* sets a much higher bar for what the value of *ES* or *SD/U* needs to be for the findings to be considered noteworthy.

You can determine the *potential practical benefit* from an individual experimental study or from a meta-analysis.

Individual experimental study

How BIG should the *ES* or *SD/U* be to consider the evidence as having demonstrated *potential practical benefit*? Definitely bigger than .2 ("difficult to detect")! If we use Cohen's original cutoff scores and his descriptions of what they mean, most would agree that we should seek an *ES* or *SD/U* of at least .5 ("visible to the naked eye").

Another researcher, Hattie (2009), has recommended a flat *ES* cutoff point of .4. This recommendation is based on his review of all meta-analyses on education effects (more than 800 meta-analyses incorporating more than 50,000 studies). Hattie concludes that .4 means that there is a benefit over and above simply having a teacher in front of the class (which has *ESs* ranging from .2 to .4). In other words, schools should want to implement an intervention that is expected to produce value over and above what is generated from just having a teacher in front of the class.

While .4 is a relatively large *ES*, the good news is that Hattie estimates that almost 50% of the interventions/factors (66 out of 138) that have been researched met the criterion of an *ES* of at least .4. So Hattie argues that the goal is not to adopt something that has a benefit of simply better than doing nothing, but rather to adopt one that does better than the average intervention—hence he recommends that leaders should NOT consider an *ES* result less than .4. Finally, he argues that an *ES or SD/U* difference of

.4 is the hinge point at which "…we can notice real world differences" (p. 17). This is close to the suggested minimum of .5 based on Cohen's criterion.

Unfortunately, while Hattie's logic seems appropriate, his work did not link *ES* results to the different research contexts. In order to understand the importance of context, suppose Intervention A produces an *ES* of .8 and Intervention B produces an *ES* of .35. Which is better (aside from the issue of cost)? The principle of BIGness would suggest that Intervention A is more effective. However, suppose that Intervention A involved teaching a specific skill to early elementary children in a single day and testing them and a comparison group of students the next day on that single skill. This will always produce a very large *ES*. Suppose Intervention B tested the effects over the course of an entire year and reflected the results on an end-of-year test in the sixth grade. Given the differing contexts of the research, the result from Intervention B is probably more important and worthier of consideration.

Indeed, context is related to the size of *ES* as shown in the examples below:

- *ES*s for short-term research are generally higher than for longer-term research;
- *ES*s for younger students are generally higher than for older students;[71] and
- *ES*s for school developed tests are generally higher than for state end-of-year tests.

So, for example, we cannot tell from Hattie's analysis what the average *ES* across all meta-analyses that excluded very short-term studies was. It would probably be less than .4. Nor is there any indication as to what percentage of the studies incorporated into Hattie's analysis consisted of *proximal gains*—i.e., highly specific skills measured right after the conclusion of the experiment, as opposed to *distal gains* which tend to have lower *ES*s. The average *ES* for the latter types of studies would probably be less than .4. Nor is there information on what percentage of the studies focused solely on recall forms of learning as opposed to measuring higher-level learning outcomes.

Scammacca, Roberts, Vaughn, and Stuebing (2013) identified other types of key contexts that are related to the level of *ES* when they studied the effects of intensive reading interventions in Grades 4-12 over time. They found that the *Mean ES* for studies between 2005 and 2011 was about 50% less than for studies between 1980 and 2004. What happened? Did teachers and schools get worse? Are the more recent interventions poorer? There is no evidence for these interpretations for the anomaly of falling *ES*s. Rather the researchers attribute this to: (a) increased use of standardized test scores (which tend to produce lower *ES*s), (b) better research designs, (c) differences in student characteristics (lower overall ability), and (d) improvements in the "business as usual" methods used in the comparison schools.

---

[71] A counter example of where the *ES* is <u>higher for older students</u> is the effect of homework on academic achievement. Hattie (2009) found a negligible *ES* (.15) for elementary students and a medium effect (.64) for high school students.

So which minimum *ES or SD/U* criterion should we use in research and leadership decision-making?[72] This question has important implications for practice. Consider, for example, the combined *ES* across meta-analyses' *ES*s of the effect of providing special education services in the general education setting (previously called mainstreaming). Hattie (2009) calculated the overall *ES* of mainstreaming at .28. Putting aside for the moment that special education is the law of the land, and the possibility that the *ES* would be larger for some types of students with disabilities such as those at the early elementary level or with milder disabilities, is this level of *ES* sufficient for deciding that it has *potential practical benefit*? Under Hattie's criterion it would not be.

A contrasting example would be interventions to reduce disruptive behavior which has an *ES* of .53 (Hattie, 2009). Clearly, this intervention meets both Cohen's criterion for having visible differences and Hattie's cutoff. So it clearly has *potential practical benefit*. Developing meta-cognitive skills has an *ES* of .69, which clearly has *potential practical benefit*.

So where does this leave us? Given the many context factors related to the nature of the research that affect the *ES* or *SD/U* it appears that while .4 is a good starting minimum point, it probably does not make sense as a single criterion. In addition, we will usually want an *ES* or *SD/U* to be greater than .2 for *potential practical benefit* since we are usually not seeking "difficult to detect" improvements—particularly if an intervention is costly in money and/or time. While .4 seems small for a short-term intervention seeking proximal gains on researcher-developed measures at the early grade, an *ES* or *SD/U* of .3 at upper grade levels might be considered to have *potential practical benefit* if it is a longer-term intervention in a large high school with results on a standardized end-of-year test in a specific content area.

As a result, Table 6.4 below contains some suggested minimum *ES* or *SD/U* benchmarks for different types of research at different grade levels to be considered as having *potential practical benefit*. These are admittedly arbitrary.

However, there are two remaining issues that have to be addressed for the value and validity of the three-number system to be fully realized. They are:

- **BIG** is not always better and at times SMALL is beautiful, and

- **BIG**ness may not matter if the research's context is unique or very different than your school(s).

These issues will be considered later in this chapter.

---

[72] There are several other rule of thumb recommendations for minimum ESs for an intervention to be considered effective. Gall, Gall, and Borg (1999) recommend using a minimum *ES* of .33 for establishing practical significance (or what is being called here *potential practical benefit*). However, there is no statistical basis for this recommendation other than "…there is some consensus among practitioners and researchers" (p. 72) for this criterion. Fraenkel and Wallen (2011) recommend a minimum *ES* of .5.

Table 6.4

Suggested Minimum *ES* or *SD/U* for Considering Experimental Research to Have *Potential Practical benefit* by Grade Level and Type of Research

	Short Term/Proximal Gains & Researcher Developed Test	Longer Term Intervention with Distal gains	Longer Term Intervention that uses an end-of-year Standardized/Normed Test
K-3	.5	.45	.4
Upper elementary	.45	.4	.4
Middle school	.4	.4	.35
High School	.4	.4	.35
High school (Large) [73]	.4	.35	.3

Determining the potential practical benefit of a meta-analysis and mining its gold nuggets

Meta-analysis is a valuable form of research that scrunches the results from all the studies of the effectiveness of a given type of intervention into a single *ES* or *SD/U*. The advantage of meta-analysis is that if the results across the individual studies are somewhat consistent it offers a form of replication.

There are two problems with meta-analyses. The first is that while researchers conducting meta-analyses usually have strict standards as to the quality of the methodology used to select which studies they will include, they generally have no standards to the quality of the intervention or implementation quality in selecting studies. The meta-analysis in Case Study #1 at the end of this chapter is a notable exception in that it included only intensive interventions—i.e., studies where the intervention was at least 100 days, and analyzed the results separately for grades k-3 vs. 4-12. This *meta-analysis* was probably more focused on the quality of implementation of the interventions in the studies because the researchers were not only top methodologists, but also experts in the content area of reading.

The second problem with meta-analysis is that the resulting *ESs* in education are generally small with large variations in outcomes.

However, the "large variations in outcomes" offers an opportunity. Do NOT give up if a published *meta-analysis* of an intervention that you believe can help your school(s) has a low overall *ES* that does not constitute *potential practical benefit*. Look at the table of the individual studies that were included in the *meta-analysis*. There is a good chance, given the variation of results, that there will be an outlier study or two with an unusually high *ES* compared to the other studies. These high *ES* outlier studies are a potential gold nugget and should be mined; i.e., those high *ES* studies should be retrieved and looked at individually. One possibility is that the *ES* of these studies were

---

[73] The criterion is a bit lower for a large high school since there are more students who will benefit from the same *ES* since there are more students. So it is likely that as many students will benefit in a large high school when the *ES* is .3 as for a small high school when the *ES* is .35.

substantially higher because the intervention was of even shorter duration and an even more narrow skill outcome than the other studies. If these were the reasons why the *ES*s were higher then they may not meet the needs of your schools.

The other technical details have little implications for leadership decision-making. However, if the high *ES* studies had a more sustained, higher quality implementation of the intervention, along with a description of implementation parameters such as the nature of the training, materials used, intensity, etc., then leaders should consider implementing the specific form of the intervention used in those studies. It might even be useful to contact the lead authors of the unusually effective studies (within the *meta-analysis*) to get more details on the implementation of the intervention.

Exceptions to BIGness—When SMALL differences (*ES* or *SD/U*) may be important

While the recommended *ES* or *standard deviation/unit* outcomes for considering an experimental study to have demonstrated potential practical benefit are BIG, there are exceptions wherein SMALL outcomes—e.g., small ESs—can be very important. For example:

- A SMALL *ES* can at times actually indicate a highly effective, important finding in the unusual situation where both the experimental and comparison groups made BIG gains, i.e., both approaches were highly successful.[74] That would produce an *ES* of close to zero and would lead to the wrong conclusion that both approaches were ineffective. However, in reality both of the approaches were highly effective.

- A SMALL *ES* or *SD/U* or an experimental group doing worse than your school is already doing can be important if there was poor implementation of the intervention in the study. In other words, if a leader hears about an intervention that his/her personal theory of action suggests should be effective, but the research does not find either *practical* or *potential practical benefit*, the leader is encouraged to read the research to examine the context of the intervention in the study. Then if the leader has an idea as to how to implement a better version of the intervention, he/she can reasonably expect the possibility of larger benefits.

    Indeed, implementing a better version of a "failed" approach led my success with the HOTS program. This program developed general thinking skills in Title I and Learning Disabled students. However, general thinking development approaches were consistently shown in research to have a negative *ES*—i.e., students in the general thinking experimental group

---

[74] While a situation in which both groups do exceptionally well is rare, it actually happened to me around an intervention that I introduced into several schools. The district research staff found no *ES*, and concluded that the intervention had not worked. However, it turned out that in fact the students in the intervention had made enormous gains. The comparison schools happily made similar gains. News that more students are doing well is always good news. So the district appropriately gave schools the choice as to which approach to adopt.

201

ALWAYS did worse than those who were taught to think about specific content. However, the research NEVER examined the effects of *intensive* general thinking development—i.e., services sustained over an extended period of time. It turned out that when the general thinking development was sustained over the course of a school year it produced BIG benefits.[75]

Similarly, there are probably many other interventions with low ESs that could be made to be effective when implemented in a different way.

- There may be legal and moral factors that enter into a decision to adopt or reject an intervention regardless of the size of the *ES or SD/U*. For example, providing special education services in regular classrooms delivers lots of public social benefits that are not measured in the formal research. Conversely, one may choose to reject an intervention with a BIG difference on moral grounds.

- Leaders can choose to use a lower *ES* for a school that is already very high performing. Such schools benefit more from a small boost than schools near the bottom; and

- Leaders could decide to adopt and combine two or three interventions, each of which has a small ES or SD/U, into a single approach to determine whether the combination would produce substantially greater benefits than either one individually.

Summarizing Experimental Research

Experimental research is essential for:

- Conducting basic research on the nature of learning and social behavior;
- Describing the extent and nature of equity problems; and
- Determining which interventions are effective in the real world.

At its best, experimental research can unpack the nature of systemic inequities, and increase understanding of how the brain and social networks operate which provide insight on the problems that need to be solved and provide clues as to how to go about designing interventions to solve them.

---

[75] It turned out that the existing research with negative *ESs* for general thinking interventions only involved very short-term interventions with proximal outcomes and/or with samples that were far removed from at-risk students in grades 4-8 (e.g., university graduate students). As a result, existing research was NOT applicable—even worse, it was WRONG as applied to the population I was working with. This demonstrates that it is essential to look inside the studies, as opposed to simply relying on the abstracts or summaries, when considering their applicability to practice.

While the classical, rigorous methodologies for setting up experiments and the statistical methods for analyzing the results have been invaluable for the first two of the above uses of experimental approach, they have a spotty track record for producing evidence on best or effective practices that actually solve problems, improve schools, and increase equity. While gold–standard RCT experimental research is valuable for laboratory-based research it usually does NOT capture the complex shifting dynamics of schools or provide the types of information that leaders seek and need. In addition, the logistical complexity, expense, and cumbersomeness of establishing such research often does not produce:

- Useful knowledge for time critical goals in schools;

- An understanding of the extent to which observed benefits are scalable and the conditions under which they are; and, most importantly

- Valid results. The results and conclusions tend to exaggerate the actual benefit found in the research which misleads practice.

At the same time, experiments are critical for improving education. In addition, leaders should first seek out research that uses the most traditionally rigorous methods. However, when doing so leaders need to abide by a different set of rules for interpreting the results of experiments than those used by researchers. Most importantly, leaders should ….

- Independently interpret the results of rigorous experiments to determine if the outcomes are BIG enough to constitute practical benefit; and

- NOT reject findings of BIG, practical benefits in experiments that use simpler methodologies—particularly if there is some replication of the findings.

Remember

Practical benefit means that the results were BIG enough such that if leaders adopt the intervention, it is likely to produce noticeable improvements and/or increases in equity in their schools.

This chapter has provided simple rules/criteria that leaders can use to develop their own independent assessment as to whether an experiment is likely to improve their schools by introducing the two statistical tests of *practical benefit* and *potential practical benefit* to replace the tests of *statistical significance* and *practical significance*.

Practical benefit is by far the preferred test for generating evidence, as it most accurately predicts the likelihood of the intervention in the experiment improving ones' schools and increasing equity. In addition, it is easy for leaders to determine the *practical benefit* of research findings. Leaders simply need to find three key numbers, the unadjusted *Mean*, *Median*, and *Standard Deviation* of the end result for the experimental group only. They can then use judgment to determine whether the results are better than how their schools are currently doing and whether the results are consistent with their improvement goals.

In the end, it is not sophisticated statistical analysis that best predicts the likely benefit to schools from research evidence, but three numbers—i.e., the mighty power trio—and human judgment.

Practical Tip

Fundamentally, statistics aside, *practical benefit* is simply designed for leaders to determine on their own what they most want to know—i.e., how the experimental students actually end up doing once the statistical adjustments have been stripped away. Then they can determine on their own whether the experimental students end up performing noticeably better than their students are already doing—an outcome that the sophisticated relativistic statistics often obscure.

If the unadjusted power trio of numbers are not present, then leaders can, reluctantly, employ the simple rules for determining *potential practical benefit* by assessing the *relative* BIGness of the *ES (SD/U)* results. Because *potential practical benefit* only provides information about relative, as opposed to *actual,* BIGness, leaders cannot use *potential practical benefit* to directly predict whether the result will benefit their schools. *Potential practical benefit* does, however, provide a hint to leaders that the evidence and the intervention may be worth looking into.

So while the most desirable form of experimental evidence for recommending new practices for improving critical large-scale goals is *gold standard* quality research that (a) was replicated, (b) was conducted in actual school settings, (c) had high levels of *external validity*, and (d) produced BIG *distal* gains, the perfect methodology and best evidence should not be the enemy of good data and evidence. If one can find such perfect research—great! However, one can glean extremely valuable evidence from all the other types of experimental designs, analyses, and outcomes.

The final step in the process of analyzing the results of experiments occurs in Chapter 8 wherein leaders establish their own experiments, design their own interventions, and analyze the results, all using the principles of *improvement science*.

Case Study Challenges

The following six challenges provide an opportunity to critique published research articles. See the extent to which your analyses agree with those in the provided answer section.

CASE STUDY #1

The table below summarizes the results from two meta-analyses on the effects of intensive reading interventions on the performance of students with reading difficulties. The first meta-analysis in the table presents *Mean ES* for the early grades (k-3), and the second presents the *Mean ES* (Effect Sizes) for the upper grades (4-12).

The following is a table from a meta-analysis that summarizes the *Mean ES* for the effects of intensive reading programs in the early elementary (k-3) and upper grades (4-12) from Wanzek et al. (2013).

TABLE 4

Comparison of effect sizes in early elementary and upper grades for studies with 100 or more sessions

Study characteristic	Early elementary (Wanzek & Vaughn, 2007)			Upper grades (Current synthesis)		
	Mean ES	ES range	*N* of effects	Mean ES	ES range	*N* of effects
Comprehension outcomes	0.46	−0.12, 0.92	25	0.09	−0.23, 0.84	37
Reading fluency outcomes	0.34	0.00, 0.56	11	0.12	−0.01, 0.35	8
Word reading outcomes	0.56	−0.18, 1.33	53	0.20	−0.06, 1.02	22
Word fluency outcomes	0.56	−0.09, 0.91	18	0.16	−0.10, 0.48	23
Spelling outcomes	0.40	−0.18, 0.88	24	0.20	0.01, 0.39	5
Duration						
5–7 months	0.63	0.31, 1.11	32	0.07	−0.11, 0.35	28
8–9 months	0.45	−0.18, 1.33	57	0.14	−0.23, 1.02	55
More than 1 year	0.45	−0.12, 1.21	42	0.29	0.03, 0.70	12
Instructional group size						
Group instruction	0.35	0.05, .73	10	0.14	−0.23, 1.02	95
1:1	0.51	−0.18, 1.33	121			0

Note. ES = effect size.

Part A

Write one or two sentences (in your own words) summarizing the effects for the early elementary grades, and another sentence or two for the upper grades.

Part B

Download the article either from your university's library or from http://www.ncpeapublications.org/index.php/doc-center, and look at a few the high *ES* outlier studies included in the *meta-analysis* at either the early or upper grades to see if you can find a study that has results that you think have *practical* or *potential practical benefit* and an intervention that is worth considering.

CASE STUDY #2*

Table 4 below compares the Means and Standard Deviations for the *Mean* score (5 being the maximum) on a social studies AP exam, for the use of a Project-Based Learning Approach to the AP course in a high-achieving school, with the same approach in a moderate achieving school, with the performance of a traditional approach to an AP course in two moderate achieving schools.

Effect Sizes for the average score differences between the Project-Based Learning Approach and the traditional approach to teaching the AP course are presented in the text below Table 4 which is drawn from the study's summary.

Table 4
Means and Standard Deviations of AP Test Scores and Percentage of Students With High Pass

	Project-Based Learning AP High-Achieving School A	Project-Based Learning AP Moderate Achieving School B	Traditional AP Moderate Achieving Schools C and D
Average score (SD)	3.37 (1.27)	2.33 (1.15)	2.03 (1.07)
Students with high pass (4–5)	47.7%	16.8%	5.7%
Number of students	86	89	87

* Parker, W. et al. Beyond Breadth-Speed-Test: Toward Deeper Knowing and Engagement in an Advanced Placement Course *American Educational Research Journal, December 2013; vol. 50, 6: pp. 1424-1459.*

SUMMARY AP Test Results

The results indicate that it is possible to get the same or higher scores on the AP test with a PBL course. Table 4 displays the means and standard deviations of the AP scores of the students in the three groups. The table also shows the percentage of students with a "high pass" (score of 4 or 5) on the AP test. PBL-AP students scored significantly higher on the AP test than the traditionally taught AP students in both the moderate achieving PBL-AP school, $t(7) = 3.12$, $p = .018$, effect size (ES) = 0.25, and, with a greater effect size, the high-achieving PBL-AP school, $t(7) = 6.73$, $p = .001$, ES = 0.78. Also, because some colleges assign college credit for high scores (4–5) on the AP test, we compared these "high pass" rates. Significantly more students at the PBL Schools A (47.7%), $t(7) = 4.52$, $p = .001$, and B (16.8%), $t(7) = 2.66$, $p = .033$, achieved a high pass than traditional students at Schools C and D (5.7%).

QUESTIONS:

Using the *Mean*, *Standard Deviations*, and *ES*—

a) Do the results in the table indicate *practical benefit?* (Hint—Do not answer this by comparing the experimental and control schools)

b) Do you think that the use of the Project Based approach made a sufficient difference to be considered as having *potential practical benefit?*

c) Would you recommend that your schools switch to this approach? Justify your conclusion!

CASE STUDY #3

Use the information in this chapter to critique the following article:

Borman, G. D., & Hewes, G. M. (2002). The long-term effects and cost-effectiveness of Success for All. *Educational Evaluation and Policy Analysis*, *24*(4), 243-266.

Step 1. Download the article either from your university's library or from the following site: http://www.ncpeapublications.org/index.php/doc-center .

Step 2. Read the article as follows:

- **Read only pages 243-255, and the top half of the first column of page 256** (until the heading "The Cost of Success for All"). **Ignore the rest.**

- **Ignore <u>all</u> technical terms that you do not understand.**

Step 3. Critique the study.

On the surface this study looks like it provides compelling evidence as to the effectiveness of Success for All. But you are now skilled in looking at the evidence in terms of its *practical* and *potential practical benefit* and how well the context of the study is described and consistent with good practice.

In critiquing the study:

- Find the key pieces of critical evidence for determining the practical and potential practical benefit and decide whether the evidence indicates that Success for All is effective, i.e., whether the experimental students are actually doing better. Try to find at least two key pieces of evidence to critique.

- Critique 1 or 2 elements of the context of the research.

For those elements of the study you critique, refer to the page #, column #, and line # from the top where you found the data/info you are critiquing.

CASE STUDY #4

Given the results that were presented in this chapter for the Pathways and Pitfalls project materials, would you as a leader consider using it, and if so how, assuming it was affordable?

CASE STUDY #5

This case study is a marked contrast in many ways to the prior one. It is a study of the effectiveness of the Cognitive Tutor curriculum for improving student performance in Algebra I in both middle and high schools. Clearly, passing Algebra is a major hurdle for many students and is a gateway to developing the higher level math and science skills that are of increasing importance. In addition, increasing the passing rates in Algebra is a national priority that is critical for increasing equity. This curriculum combines traditional types of materials with the latest of technology, and an individualized intelligent math tutor.

Pane, J. F., Griffin, B. A., McCaffrey, D. F., and Karam, R. (2014). Effectiveness of cognitive tutor algebra I at scale. *Educational Evaluation and Policy Analysis*, 36(2), 127-144.

    Step 1. Download the article from your university's library.

    Step 2. Read the <u>entire</u> article but **ignore all technical terms that you do not understand**.

    Step 3. Critique the study by:

        a.   Listing the positives of the study's methodology,

        b.   Identifying what the key missing piece(s) of data are in the results provided, and

        c.   Assessing the results provided and whether you found it sufficiently compelling to consider adopting it for your schools—and explain why in terms of the specifics of the results.

CASE STUDY #6
(Regression standardized coefficients)

Download Kane et al.'s (2016) study of the effects of instructional implementation strategies on a school's performance on common core tests in math and English language arts from the Harvard Center for Education Policy Research. The study entitled: *Teaching Higher: Educators' Perspectives on Common Core Implementation,* can be downloaded at: https://cepr.harvard.edu/teaching-higher.

Take a look at the standardized regression coefficients in Table 6 on page 20 for the effects of different implementation strategies on test scores. Keeping in mind that a standardized coefficient is pretty much the same as an ES, which implementation strategies had a large enough effect to warrant leaders focusing in implementing them? In other words, which implementation strategy meet the criterion of *potential practical benefit.*

CASE STUDY #7

Castleman, Owen, Page, and Stephany (2014) found that sending an automated text message to randomly selected students about college application deadlines along with links to required forms and live counselors increased the likelihood of the students enrolling in college to 70% as compared to only 63% who did not receive the texts. One added piece of information is that the estimated cost of the intervention was only $7 per student. Do you think this is a BIG difference in general? Do you think that this is a BIG enough difference to warrant implementing this approach given the low cost?

Solutions to the Case Studies

Case Study #1

Early grades: Intensive interventions to increase the reading performance of students show small to medium levels of *potential practical benefit* on all reading skills using Cohen's criteria, and 4 of the 5 reading skill interventions demonstrate *potential practical benefit* using Hattie's criteria. It therefore appears that intensive reading interventions are effective at the early grades.

Upper grades: Intensive interventions to increase reading performance have much less effect than at the early grades. Only 2 of the reading skills interventions barely met Cohen's criteria, and none met Hattie's criterion. Therefore, a reasonable conclusion is that intensive reading interventions do not have potential practical benefit after the third grade.

Having said this, there was at least one study in the meta-analysis for the upper grades that produced a large *ES* of .84 for "reading comprehension," and another that produced an *ES* of 1.02 for "word reading outcomes." It would be worthwhile to "mine" these potentially gold nugget studies to see if there seems to be some reason or unique characteristic for the unusually high effect intervention in those studies that seem valuable and replicable for your school(s).

Finally, this is an important meta-analysis study because it considered two other *independent* variables for selecting and analyzing studies in addition to the typical quality of the statistical design. By using intensity of the intervention as a proxy for the quality of the intervention, and breaking out the studies by grade level, the results are far more illuminating than a meta-analysis that aggregated all well designed studies of reading intervention into a single result.

I would also note that the findings of this meta-analysis support the contention that I have made at several points in this book, based on my own research, that leaders need to adopt different types of interventions for the early grades as opposed to the later grades.

Solution Case Study #2

a) First let's examine the data in the table for the *practical benefit* of the outcomes. The researchers should be commended for separating out the outcomes for different types of schools.

While the table indicates that the experimental intervention seemed to produce better results in moderate achieving schools, you cannot determine *practical benefit* just from the table. If your schools are high- or moderate-achieving ones, you have to determine whether the results in the study are substantially higher than how your schools are already performing. If the results of the Project-Based Learning are close to what your schools are already doing there is no convincing evidence to suggest that you should adopt the intervention—i.e., there is no *practical benefit*. If, on the other hand, the results in the table are clearly superior to your schools' results, there is reason to consider adopting the Project-Based Learning approach—i.e., there is *practical benefit*.

Your decision on whether to adopt the intervention is further complicated if your school(s) is a low-performing one which is not included in the study. The only way to then make a decision is to try to find a school more similar to yours that is using the intervention and see what the results are there.

b) In order to determine *potential practical benefit*, you have to look at relative comparisons. The table reveals relative comparisons ONLY for moderately performing schools. Relative data are provided for average score (*Mean*) and the percentage of students with a "high pass" score. Do the differences between the *Means* of the moderately performing schools seem BIG from a common sense point of view? Eye-balling the data suggests that the experimental program produced a substantial advantage for the "high-pass" rate. The advantage for the *Mean* scores is not as clear. In addition, the relatively large *Standard Deviations* suggest that it is more appropriate to compare the *Median* scores which are not revealed.

In terms of the *effect size* results, an *ES* was reported only for the differences in the *Means* of the moderate achieving schools. That *ES* was only .25, which is below the recommended minimum for considering a difference to have *potential practical benefit*.

No *ES* is provided for the differences in the "high pass" rates in the moderate achieving schools. The "high-pass" differences are presented as "significant"—i.e., statistically significant only. At the same time, the differences in the percentage of students with a "high pass" score do seem convincing and important since a high score increases the likelihood that students will receive college credit which is an important consideration.

Of course, from an equity point of view, it is troubling that even the higher 16.8% "high pass" score rate in the moderate achieving experimental school is still substantially below the result in the high-achieving school.

c) Depending on whether you are able to draw a conclusion as to practical benefit, this research and intervention may be something worth exploring further by:

- Analyzing the complete study,

- Searching for other research on this intervention, and

- Contacting other schools that may be using this approach.

Solution Case Study #3

This study looked at students who started Success for All (SFA) in the first grade to determine the long-term effects as compared to comparison students in other similar types of schools in Baltimore. (Students were given a reading pre-test in Kindergarten.)

There were two types of studies. The first looked at how the experimental students were doing in reading and math at the end of the 8th grade. This analysis was first done for the full sample, and then a separate analysis was done on the low-performing students only. The second study was a transcript study that examined whether there were differences in the number of years in special education and retention in grade.

Table 1 (p. 250) shows that the reading scores at the end of kindergarten of the SFA students who remained in the sample group until the end of the study eight years later were initially lower, and differences in the initial age level of SFA students (for the full sample) were lower at the start. As a result, *Analysis of Covariance* was used to adjust/weight the final scores of the experimental students. (Please note that there was no initial difference in the reading scores of the low-achieving sample.)

The <u>key outcome data</u> for the reading and math scores for the (so-called) entire sample is on the first three lines of the second column on page 254, and the reading and math outcomes for those who were initially low performing (in kindergarten) are on page 255 in the second column starting 14 lines from the bottom of the page.

Problem 1. Aside from the fact that kindergarten scores are notoriously unreliable, the *Standard Deviations* of the initial *Means* in Table 1 of the CAT reading scores were very high—indicating that the *Median* scores should have been reported. Indeed, the *Standard Deviations* are higher than the *Means*. Were the initial *Median* scores different? Why aren't we being told?

Of course, if the *Median* scores were the same for both groups then the outcome scores should not have been weighted.

Problem 2. How was this final sample of Ns of 581 and 729 arrived at? There was some natural attrition from the initial sample, which is to be expected in a longitudinal study that spans 8 years. The researchers spend a lot of time showing that the attrition did not affect the outcomes. However, the researchers then slip in the information that they decided to drop a bunch of other students from the sample. Look at lines 2-6 in the second column of page 248 where we are told that 50% of the students that the researchers dropped from the study remained in the school system but were "missing data on one or more measures." What measures? Street addresses? Did the students who were dropped have post-test scores? If they had post-test scores they should not have been dropped. How many of those dropped had outcome post-test scores? We don't know. You cannot remove students from a study so casually. Did they drop students until the remaining sample had low initial test scores so that they could justify weighting/adjusting the experimental students' scores higher?

Problem 3. Let's look at the key final differences between the groups on outcome scores. The key outcome results are listed at the top of the second column on page 254. While it shows what appears to be a substantial difference in outcomes at the end of the 8th grade between the grade level performance of the SFA vs. control students, a difference of six months. There are four problems with this.

1. This seemingly large difference is in adjusted scores. What was the difference in the non-adjusted score? We are not told. Presumably, the unadjusted 8th grade scores of the SFA would have been lower without the adjustment.

2. We are not told what the post-test scores, adjusted or unadjusted are for <u>all</u> students for whom there were post-test scores.

3. Keeping in mind that by the end of the 8th grade students should be reading at about the 8.7 grade level. However, even with upwards adjustment the SFA students were only reading at the 5.7 grade level—or 3 years below grade level. Is that a success?

4. We are not told what the *Standard Deviations* are for the 8th grade outcome scores. Were the differences a result of a few outlier scores? Perhaps the *Median* results would have been more appropriate to compare.

The problem is the same with the results for the low-achiever (in kindergarten) subsample. The adjusted means of the SFA students in reading ended up being four years below grade level. Is that a success?

Problem 4. The SFA schools had a lot more money spent on them and the students spent more time reading than control schools. If the results were adjusted for this difference, then that would have substantially adjusted up the results for the comparison students. These are in fact more obvious variables to control for.

Problem 5. If you look at the data in Table 3 for the transcript outcomes, the results for special education and retention results have large SD (standard deviations) relative to the *Mean*. What were the *Median* differences?

Problem 6. There are ethical problems with the study. First, the literature review did not mention the studies with contrary findings, a number of which documented that the program in Baltimore had produced terrible results and was dropped as a result. Instead, the authors call the earlier results "impressive" (p. 246, column 2). In addition, the authors do not disclose that one was working for the SFA foundation and another had previously been the lead researcher for the SFA project.

When all is said and done, what looks like a very high-quality statistical study with lots of sophisticated statistical terminology in a prestigious research journal turns out to be Swiss cheese.

\

Solution Case Study #4

This is a close call. In terms of equity, at best it should only be used with the disadvantaged students. However, it only had the benefit of keeping them from falling further behind. While of some benefit, is that a sufficient outcome? Is there another intervention that would produce actual gains?

Solution Case Study #5

a. Positives:

A major positive of this study is that it has a high level of transparency and reflectiveness. The researchers clearly present the data in an impartial and open manner. They point out negative results for the intervention. There are also places where they point out that a conclusion of theirs can be interpreted differently. For example, in the first column on page 40, in trying to equate what an ES of .2 means in terms of national expected growth, when they note that it is comparable they also note that their ES did not include summer loss which the expected national growth did.

A second positive is that no members of the sample were dropped even when there was not all the information needed to perfectly match them. In addition, the sample seems to be large and diverse enough to make the study relevant.

A third positive is how they reported the outcome data. Like the study in the previous case study, the researchers adjusted final scores via *Analysis of Covariance*. They are clearly making such an adjustment more carefully. They openly discuss the problems associated with such an adjustment and try to use advanced techniques and three different methods of adjustment to minimize potential problems. Table 4 and 5 show that there is no difference in outcomes between the three different levels of adjustment (Models 2, 3 & 4).

A fourth positive is that they analyze the results separately for middle and high school. This makes it clear that there is no rationale for middle schools to adopt this intervention. As a result, the rest of the analysis will focus just on the high school results.

A fifth positive is that they conducted the study over two cohorts of students so that teachers were able to gain a year of experience, and indeed the high school results were better for Cohort II.

A sixth positive is that the researchers report both the unweighted results, i.e., the "no covariate" Model 1 in Table 4, and the fully weighted Model 4. They acknowledge on page 139 (column 2) that the treatment effects for the unweighted results were "substantially lower than for the models with adjustments." One minor criticism is that it would have been better for the researchers to simply state, "There was no significant treatment effect for the unweighted results."

As an aside, one interesting thing to note is that the researchers thought that the weighted high school results improved in Cohort II because the teachers reverted back to traditional approaches to teaching.

b. Problem:

There is one big problem. There is no data on the actual post-test performance of the experimental and comparison groups. Everything is once again a description of the relative differences. We do not know how well the students did in Algebra or on any math test. How many passed? How many moved on to the next level of math? Why are we not told how the students actually did on the Algebra Proficiency Exam in a non-standardized form? Why not tell us how many of the 32 items on the post-test each group got correct?

Instead, the researchers try to make the *ES* of .2 seem important by:

-   First indicating that it is equivalent to students moving from the 50th to 58th percentile. But that does not mean that anyone scored at the 58th percentile. Did they move from the 10th to the 18th? Did the lower performing students make any equivalent percentile gains?

-   Second, they compare this *ES* to typical achievement gains nationally in the affected grades. Not only was the *ES* reported in this study slightly smaller it did not include summer loss—so it is even smaller than what is typically achieved nationally.

In any event, this study continues the tradition of trying to make an *ES* at the smallest end of Cohen's range seem more important than it actually is.

Should you adopt the program?

c. Given that:

-   The program is expensive,
-   The intervention was not compared to traditional individualized drill and practice software,

213

- The progress was less than what students typically achieve nationally,
- The low ES that does not meet recommended minimums for potential practical benefit, and
- No absolute data on how the students actually did,

I would not recommend that anyone adopt this program based on this research.

Solution Case Study #6

While a few of the implementation strategy coefficients were statistically significant, none of the standardized coefficients (*ES*s) by themselves were large enough to meet the criterion of *potential practical benefit.* In other words none of the implementation strategies made a substantial enough of a difference by themselves to be made a priority. Unfortunately, the study did not explore the effects of a combination of these strategies and report the combined R^2.

Solution Case Study #7

There is no clear answer to this case. It would depend on the availability of funding. If ones' schools had a college enrollment rate lower than 63%, it might be worth considering. This is a case where human judgment is a critical element to the decision-making process.

However, it would probably be best to use this intervention as part of an overall plan to increase college enrollment. Chapter 9 will have an example of one successful multi-faceted approach to increasing college enrollment.

Chapter 7

Seeking Practical Benefit—Final Principles for Analyzing Quantitative Evidence

Chapters 4-6 discussed how to critically interpret and apply the following types of quantitative research for improving your schools and increasing equity:

- Descriptive analysis;
- Relationship research; and
- Experimental research.

Each chapter discussed the usefulness and problems associated with each type of research—and how to minimize the problems and take maximum advantage of their usefulness. Indeed, the first two types of research turned out to be more useful than generally acknowledged. These chapters also showed that not all evidence about effective practices can be trusted and that much of it relies on statistical criteria that never actually demonstrated noticeable or practical benefit and whose results are therefore misleading—even when published in the top research journals. At the same time, research evidence that demonstrates substantial benefits from a new intervention or relationship is critical to making progress in education. So what is a leader to do?

First, it is important to recognize that research that actually demonstrates real benefit is a precious resource for leaders and is worth searching for and utilizing. To find the invaluable pieces of research evidence leaders must be as judicious a consumer as he/she is in making a decision to consume any other product. You need to be skeptical about claims of "evidence-based" or "best practice"—but still be an interested, open-minded, and informed consumer. *Simply because research claiming effectiveness or a significant relationship has been published in a prestigious journal, widely advocated by a professional association, or highlighted by the press, does not necessarily mean that the intervention was ever actually effective.*

So, using research evidence is not the straightforward process portrayed by the research/academic community wherein practitioners are expected to unquestioningly apply the evidence provided to them. Rather, it is a two-step process in which leaders first have to assess which evidence can actually be trusted and then begin exploring the use of that subset of evidence. Most importantly, kernels of highly useful research do exist, and taking advantage of them requires separating these kernels from the chaff of available research evidence about "effective" or "best" practices. *In other words, leaders need to become research evidence detectives* who search for clues as to whether a given research finding is authentic for their schools.

215

It turns out that it's not difficult to be a research evidence detective. You do NOT need to know lots of statistics, mathematics or technical details. Indeed, the previous chapters have shown that generally the more sophisticated the statistical methods are, the less useful the resultant evidence is. The most important clues for whether the evidence is authentic—i.e., can improve performance and equity in your schools, is found in a few key numbers. In addition, straightforward guidelines for interpreting these numbers have been provided. And while no statistical procedure can guarantee that something will be effective in your schools, it is relatively easy to use these clues to eliminate those "effective/best practices" that probably won't.

So to become an astute evidence detective, you seek clues in a few numbers. But instead of looking at the best option for a home heating system by examining numbers for the "cost per kwh," or "mpg" in considering cars, choosing the best evidence for improving one's schools and increasing equity, involves looking for clues in the numbers for r, R, ES, sd, Mean, Median.

Chapter 1 started by talking about the power of numbers. We have now come full circle in chapters 4-6 which have prepared you to examine the key numbers in research evidence for clues to be used by you as an evidence detective.

Remember

It's making judgments about a few key numbers—not advanced statistics—that matters in making leadership decisions based on quantitative evidence.

This chapter summarizes the clues by presenting the final version of the principles of data analysis. But first, this chapter summarizes the differences between classical research methods and those that better meet the needs of leaders.

The Divergence Between the Evidentiary Needs of Leaders and the Evidence Provided by Researchers—Final Take

Table 7.1 below summarizes all the key methodological issues discussed in Chapters 4-6 that leaders need to be on the lookout for.

As can be seen from this table, there is far more divergence between the type of evidence provided and the needs of leaders than there is overlap. Therefore, while leaders need to be proactive in seeking authentic research evidence, they also need to be wary.

Table 7.1

Overlap and Divergence Between the Evidentiary Needs of Leaders and the Evidence Provided by Researchers

Evidentiary Need of Leaders		Evidence Provided by Researchers/ Statisticians
Importance of quantitative evidence		
Importance of the power trio of statistics		
Importance of the actual end result performance of the research subjects independent of other groups or history		Relative performance
Actual unadjusted performance/outcomes of research subjects in recognizable metrics	v	Outcomes that are adjusted and then often extrapolated to hypothetical recognizable metrics
Seeking BIG relationship	e	Small relationship
Large r or R > +/- .39	r	Statistically significant or significant r, R.
Practical benefit/potential practical benefit	s	Tiny benefit, statistical significance, practical significance ES (SD/U)
Large ES (SD/U) > .4	u	
Evidence that the benefits replicate	s	Evidence that the intervention caused the benefit
Implicit causation via rapid prototyping		Gold standard RCT methods
There is a role for human judgment in interpreting data		Unbiased analysis requires that all conclusions be made on the basis of formulas and statistical tests

Remember

Even within these differences, there is some tremendously valuable research available that can benefit your schools. **Go find it!**

(How to find evidence is described in the Literature Review section in Chapter 10.)

Final Principles of Data Analysis

As mentioned earlier, these principles apply equally to analyzing published studies and evaluation studies conducted by schools/districts.

Principle #1—Always seek replication/confirmation of a research finding.

Principle #2—The greatest threats to the validity of quantitative evidence are (a) researcher bias, (b) statistical error, and (c) confounding variables (Chapters 4-6).

Sub-principle 2.1—The more a single individual or organization is involved in all the different steps in a research study, the greater the degree of bias there is, and the less trustworthy the findings are.

Sub-principle 2.2—The more statistical procedures that are conducted in a study, the greater the error and the less trustworthy any one finding is.

Sub-principle 2.3—To determine *causation* it is important to eliminate the possible effects of (all) possible confounding variables (Chapter 6).

Sub-principle 2.4—Three techniques for controlling for confounding variables are:

- Homogenous sample, limiting the sample to only those (i) who do possess the confounding variable, or (ii) those who do not (Chapter 4)
- Three-way crosstabs table where one of the variables is a possible confounding variable (Chapter 4)
- Partial correlation (Chapter 5)
- Analysis of covariance (Chapter 6)
- Randomized sampling (Chapter 6)

Randomized large samples offer the best control of confounding variables.

Principle #3—The most convincing evidence that a practice is likely to improve your schools is research that demonstrated BIG benefits from its use.

Principle 3.1—Leaders should generally ignore evidence of effectiveness if the research only demonstrated a *small* benefit from the use of a practice—and should usually avoid implementing the practice analyzed in such research (Chapters 5, 6).

3.1.1—Findings with language such as "significant", "statistically significant", or "…equivalent to…" usually indicates an effort to exaggerate what is actually a small, if any, benefit.

Principle #4—The BIGness of the benefit found in experimental research is NOT determined by analyzing the results from the *statistics*—e.g., t-test, F-test, etc. Rather, the benefit is found by analyzing the *statistical tests* used to determine the importance of those results—e.g., p value and effect size.

The BIGness of a **relationship** is determined by the r and R values listed in Table 7.2 below.

Table 7.2
Criteria for Establishing the BIGness of Relationship Research (Chapter 5) *

		Minimum Recommended Cutoffs	
		r or R	R^2
Correlation	One-way	More than .39 Less than -.39**	.15 or 15%
Ordinary Regression	School Improvement		
	1 independent variable	.39	.15 or 15%
	2 independent variables	.49	.24 or 24%
	3 independent variables	.59	.35 or 35%
Logistic Regression	(Odds Ratio)	N/A	N/A

* The shaded area indicates the results that are likely to be the most helpful when you look at tables in research.
** The "–" sign indicates an inverse relationship wherein as one variable increases the other decreases. An example of a larger inverse correlation than the recommended cutoff would be -.48.

If the BIGness of relationship research meets the above criteria, it will be deemed to have *potential practical benefit*. It cannot be said to have practical benefit because in the absence of experiments, you cannot tell whether there will be any benefit from taking action based only on the relationship evidence.

The BIGness of the benefit in **experimental research** is best determined by *practical benefit* derived using the three-number method (Chapter 6). As a less desired alternative, BIGness can be determined by *potential practical benefit* by seeking BIG ES (SD/U) values (Chapter 6).

The methods for determining *practical benefit* and *potential practical benefit* are depicted in the graphic on the next page.

Principle #5—Always first examine the Mean, Standard Deviation, and (if needed) the Median of any distribution. These three statistics are fundamental and the *Power Trio* of statistics.

5.1—Rule of Mean-Median Differences: When the Mean and Median are very different, trust the Median, or at the very least explore the nature of the distribution of individual numbers using a histogram (Chapter 4).

The "Three-Number Method" for Determining Whether the Findings of Experimental Research Have *Potential- or Practical Benefit* for Improving Your Schools

Determining the Practical Benefit of Experimental or Quasi-Experimental Research

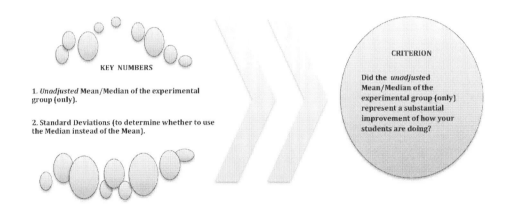

KEY NUMBERS

1. *Unadjusted* Mean/Median of the experimental group (only).

2. Standard Deviations (to determine whether to use the Median instead of the Mean).

CRITERION

Did the *unadjusted* Mean/Median of the experimental group (only) represent a substantial improvement of how your students are doing?

If you cannot find the unadjusted Mean/Median of post-test results, you have to rely on the *less reliable* relative measure of differences between groups, which is only...

Potential Practical Benefit

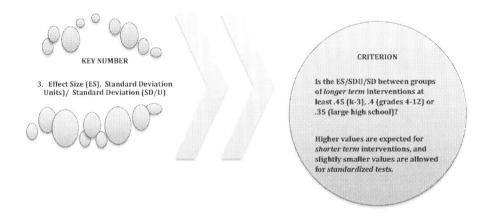

KEY NUMBER

3. Effect Size (ES), Standard Deviation Units)/ Standard Deviation (SD/U)

CRITERION

Is the ES/SDU/SD between groups of *longer term* interventions at least .45 (k-3), .4 (grades 4-12) or .35 (large high school)?

Higher values are expected for *shorter term* interventions, and slightly smaller values are allowed for *standardized tests.*

Ignore <u>all</u> the other numbers, tables, and technical terms in the research!

Principle #6—The *law of actual end result.* The only way to understand the authenticity of a research outcome for improving your schools is to know what the actual end result was for the research subjects (only) *at the end of study*—as opposed to a relative change over time for the research subjects, or a relative difference between groups or things

In other words, you have to know how the experimental subjects ended up actually performing/achieving by themselves at the end of the experiment—as opposed to:

- The degree of improvement of the experimental group;
- Adjusted or equivalent outcomes; or
- How the experimental group performed as opposed to the comparison group.

(Chapters 4-6 discussed how these three common measures can be misleading.)

The actual result for how the experimental group ended up achieving in the research can then be compared to how your schools are already doing, or to some state or national threshold of performance. Was the actual end result for the experimental group noticeably superior to these comparisons? If "yes," you should consider implementing the practice.

Rating The Authenticity of Studies

The forms at the end of this chapter can be used to determine the practical and potential benefit of a given experimental or relationship study.

Conclusion: You are now a Trained Authentic Evidence Detective

You are now ready to become an ace evidence detective. You are ready to find those gems of authentic research evidence and become a true leader who uses evidence judiciously and critically to improve your schools and increases equity.

When seeking the most authentic evidence, do not let yourself be overwhelmed by the arcane jargon in the research and the many tables overflowing with numbers. Seek out the few key numbers and flee if they are not there. Leadership in the use of research evidence means avoiding being sucked down the rabbit hole of following the herd in adopting practices that were never effective. If the principal in Chapter 6 was able to do that—so can you.

So, ultimately, the process of seeking research evidence and using it as a decision-making tool comes down to making sense of a few numbers, some knowledge of what those numbers mean, and human judgment. In other words, deciding what research evidence to adopt and apply to improve your schools and increase equity is similar in principle to the methods you use to make intelligent decisions about purchasing any other consumer product.

The next series of chapters extend the principles of data analysis to your research as students and/or leaders—or ideally both combined. Indeed, you may be the best one to generate new research evidence that solves a problem of practice in your, and others', schools. It happened to me so it could happen to you and your colleagues.

Rating Form for Assessing the Practical Benefit/Importance of an **Experimental** Quantitative Research Study

Study Name
                                                Intervention or Process being studied

What are the 2-4 key outcome numerical data results—be specific in terms of the numbers (e.g., *Unadjusted* Mean & Standard Deviation of Experimental Group, and/or ES or SD/U)?

What was the conclusion of the researcher(s) in terms of the study's findings?

What are your conclusions as to the practical (or potential practical) benefit of this study _strictly_ in terms of the magnitude of the numbers and whether relative or actual end results were presented using the principles of data analysis in this chapter?

How would you characterize the results in your lit review?
                         What action (if any) would the results suggest that you as a leader recommend for your organization?

On the back of this form note any commonsense (non-technical) concerns you have as to the nature of the sample or the context of how the research was carried out.

Rating Form for Assessing the Potential Practical Benefit/Importance of a Quantitative Study About the Relationships Between Variables

Study Name   Intervention or Process
                                                        being studied

What are the 2-4 key outcome numerical data results—be specific in terms of the Correlations/Regressions and their squares?

What was the conclusion of the researcher(s) in terms of the study's findings?

What are your conclusions as to the practical benefit of this study strictly in terms of the magnitude of the numbers presented using the principles of data analysis in this chapter?

How would you characterize the results?   What action (if any) would the results suggest that you as a leader recommend for your organization?

On the back of this form note any commonsense (non-technical) concerns you have as to the nature of the sample or the context of how the research was carried out.

Challenge Activities

1. Pick a quantitative or mixed method research article you are interested in that uses **experimental** research. Fill in the appropriate rating form in this chapter to characterize the statistical findings.

Article (Bibliographic reference) _____

_____

_____

Based on the results of your analysis, is this something you can recommend for your school(s)?

See if the evidence meets the criteria for either *practical,* or *potential practical, benefit.*

2. Pick a quantitative or mixed method research article you are interested in that uses **relationship** research. Fill in the appropriate rating form in this chapter to characterize the statistical findings.

Article (Bibliographic reference) _____

_____

_____

Based on the results of your analysis, is this something you can recommend for your school(s)?

See if the evidence meets the criteria for *potential practical benefit.*

Leader Initiated Action Research—Designing Innovative Practices and Analyzing School Data

The previous chapters showed how to find existing research evidence that can help solve a problem of practice in your school(s). But suppose you cannot find any existing research that you feel confident in applying to solve the identified problem at your schools—and you want to use an evidence-based approach—what can you do? The answer is simple:

Develop your own research evidence, either on your own, or ideally in collaboration with other leaders and/or experts.

Chapters 8-10 describe how you can develop your own quantitative evidence using the final principles of data analysis in Chapter 7. The emphasis is on quantitative methods that are simpler, and more intuitive, than the traditional "rigorous" methods of generating and analyzing quantitative evidence discussed in Chapters 5 and 6. Even better, these innovative methods are more appropriate for generating scientific evidence for supporting decisions in complex organizations such as schools.

In addition to these innovative methods for conducting research, there are many rich sources of primary source data available from a wide array of federal, state, foundation, and non-profit organizations that are summarized in Appendix B. Another source of evidence are data generated by individual schools and districts on their own to support an array of initiatives and program evaluations. Indeed, the quantitative data leaders initiate about the performance of their schools are at times the most useful and authentic evidence to support decision-making.

Therefore, key quantitative skills developed in Chapters 8-10 include how to make decisions about what data to collect, and how to organize systemwide data collection efforts.

Chapter 8 describes how, in the absence of convincing published research about a specific evidence-based effective practice to solve a critical problem of practice in one's schools, the best scientific method is to design an innovative approach using the techniques of *Improvement Science*—sometimes referred to as Design-Based Research (DBR) or Network Improvement Community (NIC). The data and evidence generated from such alternative design experiments can have widespread applicability, and can also result in BIG improvements in longstanding problems of practice. This chapter discusses the conditions that increase the likelihood of BIG improvements.

Chapter 9 deals with managing and applying the massive data flows that exist within schools and between schools and other governmental levels. It describes the different types of data that exist, the fundamental characteristics of data use for program evaluation, and the forms and uses of quantitative data about one's schools that provide the best evidence for basing an improvement strategy on. This chapter also discusses how leaders can use data about their schools as evidence to support decisions about how to improve practice and increase learning, and what the roles of leaders are in the generation, management, and application of data flows and uses about school practices.

Clearly, test scores are important forms of data. However, there are many other aspects of the functioning of a school that affect its test scores, which have their own data sets. Chapter 9 will discuss the other, more fine-grained quantitative measures, that are needed to truly understand the nature of a school's problems and/or opportunities to improve student success and equity on a variety of dimensions. In addition, this chapter will also explore the importance of generating and monitoring measures of social justice.

Chapter 10 will discuss how to apply the data analysis principles from Chapters 4-7 to conduct one's own research project—either as a leader conducting a survey or program evaluation or as a student conducting an action research project. The emphasis will be on the types of non-dissertation culminating projects used in educational leadership programs. These will include:

- Literature review; and
- Action research

Caveats:

- This part will only focus on using data to help schools better identify and meet students' needs. It will NOT deal with using data to establish punitive mechanisms for either staff or students.

- Technology and data systems are changing rapidly. Therefore, the discussion on systems for managing data will focus on what is desirable, possible, and state-of-the-art under currently widely available technological capabilities.

Chapter 8

Using Improvement Science to Design Solutions for Problems of Practice

🔔 Key Takeaways 🔔

To this point this book has focused on rethinking how to critically examine research evidence and how to apply the basic evidentiary criteria of *potential practical benefit* or *practical benefit* to determine whether an existing intervention or practice is so effective that leaders should consider it. However, suppose after diligently assessing all the available research on a specific topic you cannot find any experimental or relationship research that meets the recommended evidentiary criteria—what should you do?

This chapter describes how to engage in evidence-based decision making when there is no compelling evidence available on how to solve a key problem of practice. The fundamental question is:

> *How can I use evidence to make BIG improvements in my schools and solve a problem of practice if there is no trustworthy research evidence available?*

The answer to this questions is:

> *Innovate and apply the principles of improvement science to generate new evidence and practice!*

Improvement Science is a methodology for conducting experiments that is an alternative to RCT for designing and testing dramatically new interventions for solving major problems of practice that is:

- Based on an expanded view of science that is not limited by the need to demonstrate causation but that seeks to describe the nature of practice as it actually occurs;
- Seeks patterns of clearly noticeable improvements;
  Provides results more quickly via rapid prototyping and adaptation of newly designed practices;
- Less technically demanding; and
- Geared to directly addressing critical problems of practice in complex organizations such as schools (and hospitals) where traditional RCT methods were failing to identify effective practices.

Improvement science was developed because of the seeming inability of traditional research methods to solve many longstanding problems of practice in a wide variety of disciplines or to generate authentic evidence—leaving practitioners without any clear research on which to base action.

This chapter will describe in detail the processes used to design and implement several interventions developed via improvement science that addressed long-standing problems of practice and produced

BIG benefits for school improvement and increasing equity on a large-scale. The success of these interventions demonstrates that it is in fact possible to design interventions that are effective at scale and across a wide variety of contexts.

As importantly, the design and implementation of these interventions will be analyzed to find the key common elements for the purpose of deriving principles of effectiveness that leaders can use to design and implement their own interventions in their local schools. These methods include:

- Methods of design that do NOT rely (initially) on academic theory or evidence;
- Iterative experimentation; and
- Implicit causation that can be determined via the use of the power trio of statistics.

Remember

In other words, it remains possible, and important, to engage in evidence-based practice, even when there is no existing authentic evidence. There is an alternative scientific research process, improvement science, that leaders can engage in to develop evidence-based practices that can produce BIG improvements and increases in equity.

The methods of improvement science are not only powerful and more authentic, but are also more accessible to leaders and leadership students than the traditional scientific method with its emphasis on causation and their associated complex statistical methods.

Good News

Leaders can use the methods of improvement science to generate evidence and highly effective practices without major quantitative or methodological skills. All that is needed is a desire to improve their schools, good instincts, and a dash of creativity. The creative element comes into play in the design and implementation of new interventions and potentially more effective interventions.

This chapter will explore how and why the alternative, accessible, scientific method of improvement science is probably the best approach to generate authentic evidence on how to solve problems of practice in education that produce BIG improvements and increases in equity. It will describe:

- How to design and evaluate new interventions;
- **The characteristics of good design;**
- How the experimental methods of improvement science differ from traditional experimental methods, and why the improvement science methods are probably better for developing more effective interventions; and, most importantly,
- **The implications of improvement science for improving:**

  - ✓ **Applied research**
  - ✓ **Academic theory**
  - ✓ **Leadership programs;** and most importantly
  - ✓ **Leadership practice for improving schools and increasing equity.**

Introduction

The ideas in this chapter emerged from an experience I had about 30 years ago while teaching a class in using decision-making models in a leadership program. It was an innovative class which brought ideas from economics and business into education.

> The class project was to apply one of the decision-making models to available evidence about how to help Title I students and decide which approach to use. I was impressed by the cleverness and originality of this type of assignment until students started to complain that the assignment was impossible. The reason they gave was that they could not find any usable research to incorporate. My first reaction was—THAT IS NOT POSSIBLE. Then I checked. The students were right! I was stunned.
>
> In other words *there was no evidentiary basis for leaders to make any type of evidence-based decision as to how to improve the performance of students in the largest federal initiative for one of the great needs of our nation.*
>
> Shortly thereafter I was asked to work with a Title I school to improve its scores. We started with a blank sheet of paper, and created a new design for Title I programs that, to our surprise, turned out to be dramatically successful.

The approach that was developed together with key school leaders in one district evolved into the breakthrough, national Higher Order Thinking Skills (HOTS) project.[76] The blank sheet design process that we engaged is one that any leader can apply to any problem where the existing research does not provide adequate guidance.

At the same time, I want to make it clear that the methods used to develop HOTS were borne out of desperation to help students—as opposed to formally applying the principles discussed in this chapter because the methodology did not exist at the time. Fortunately for you, these techniques that we instinctively engaged in have now been detailed and systematized in the research and scientific literature.

These alternative scientific quantitative methods have come to be known as ***improvement science***.

This chapter discusses:

- The methods of improvement science;
- The characteristics of successful *improvement science based* interventions that produced BIG improvements in education and in medicine;
- The implications of improvement science for rethinking the nature of quantitative research methodology; and

---

[76] There is no conflict of interest when I draw on my experience with the HOTS program since it no longer exists.

- How to incorporate the *improvement science approach* into your leadership practice.

Overview of Improvement Science

Rationale for an alternative methodology

It is important to first search to see if you can find existing authentic evidence. Hopefully you will find some evidence that a given intervention is likely to result in BIG improvements in your schools. *However, you may not find any.* In such cases the only honest conclusion is that available research evidence has not to date produced a scalable solution to that problem.

Furthermore, there is growing evidence that the most rigorous ways of producing education evidence, RCT with its randomized control groups, may not be the best way to develop authentic evidence for improving complex organizations such as schools. There are many human endeavors in which it is not practical to conduct randomized experimental groups, such as:

- Testing parachutes;
- Rescuing people from collapsed buildings;
- Helping pre-mature babies (obstetrics);
- Heart surgery; and
- Many other examples, including (possibly) school improvement and increasing equity.

In these cases you need to respond in real time and cannot morally create a control group—or even get samples. How many of you would participate in a study where you were randomly assigned to a group that either received parachutes or didn't—and then you had to jump out of a plane? Other examples on this list involve complex interactive processes wherein it is impossible to isolate a single factor and test it for causal effects—e.g., trying to keep a prematurely born baby alive and healthy.

Please note that several of these bulleted examples where "rigorous" traditional experimentation is NOT used includes branches of medicine. So science is clearly involved—but an alternative type of science. Similarly, given the complexity of the ongoing interactions in schools which make it almost impossible to isolate a single factor, and the limited usefulness of RCT research in education to date (see Chapter 6), it is probably time to add school improvement to the above bulleted list. This would indicate that it is time for researchers and leaders to seek alternative scientific methods to solve the many seemingly intractable problems in education.

Indeed, some notable researchers have started to question whether available research methods have actually produced evidence of sufficiently powerful solutions—as opposed to blaming practitioners for not using research. Sandoval and Bell (2004) noted how others in educational psychology, the keepers of the flame for the scientific model for quantitative research, began to question the traditional model of quantitative research. They quote Lagemann (2002) as noting that "…the traditional paradigm of psychology has striven for experimental control at the expense of fidelity to learning as it actually occurs. Thus, although such claims might be scientific in one sense, they do not adequately explain or predict the phenomena they purport to address…" (p. 199).

The problem of relying on randomized controlled trials (RCT), i.e., gold-standard research designs, to inform educational practice is best summarized by Bryk, Gomez, Grunow, and LeMahieu (2015):

> …the on-average difference documented in an RCT tells us nothing about the conditions necessary for better outcomes to occur. Likewise, it tells us nothing about how an intervention can be effectively adapted so that good outcomes can emerge in different settings. This perspective brings different light to common understandings about "what works." At their best, the rigorous field trials summarized in the What Works Clearinghouse tells us *what can work*… However, these studies provide little or no information about *how to make it work* effectively in the hands of diverse individuals working under varied organizational conditions. Yet this is precisely what practitioners need to know as they seek to implement an intervention in their local schools… (p. 207-208)

These critics of the traditional quantitative methodology are NOT rejecting science or quantitative research. They are simply drawing on other traditions of science and knowledge generation that have not been applied to education research. The belief that we need to approach quantitative research differently to meet the needs of leadership decision-making is similar to the realization of Walter and Anderson (2013) that different quantitative approaches were needed to better understand indigenous populations.

As a result of this growing skepticism about the application of "rigorous" statistical methods to solve problems of practice, researchers began to explore the application of new methods to generate new evidence for how to solve key problems in education. They used some of the above examples as models, and started to ask:

- How did the above examples such as obstetrics and heart surgery make such dramatic improvements in practice over the past 50 years?
- What scientific process did the practitioners/clinicians in these fields use to generate evidence that produced such BIG improvements in outcomes—i.e., saving lives?

The most promising and widely applied alternative scientific methodology has been *improvement science*.

232

Origin of Improvement Science

Improvement Science was first developed to improve health care services in hospitals, which like schools is a complex organization.[77] Berwick (2008) and Plsek (1999) developed the idea that if medicine was to improve the quality of health care it had to develop and use new research methods that could take into account the social processes and context specific mechanisms inherent in delivering better patient care across institutions. They successfully argued that the gold-standard research methodology of *randomized controlled trials* (RCT) was inadequate for such analysis. For example, consider the following statement by Berwick (2008) in the prestigious Journal of the American Medical Association (JAMA):

> Changes in the current approach to evidence in health care would help accelerate the improvement of systems of practice…Educators and medical journals will have to recognize that, by itself, the usual… experimental paradigm is not up to this task. It is possible to rely on other methods without sacrificing rigor. Many assessment techniques developed in engineering and used in quality improvement…have more power to inform about mechanisms and contexts than do RCTs, as do ethnography, anthropology, and other qualitative methods. For these specific applications, these methods are not compromises in learning how to improve; they are superior.

This alternative method of scientific discovery and assessing evidence of effectiveness are now being used in networks springing up in medicine and other fields to try and solve heretofore-intractable problems. Improvement science has turned out to be particularly useful for solving problems that:

i. were time-sensitive—i.e., there was a limited window of time in which to solve the problem;
ii. occurred in complex organizations wherein there were constantly shifting social dynamics; and
iii. involved complex processes wherein multiple steps are needed to solve a problem as opposed to a single action such as administering a drug.

In all these three types of problems it is extremely difficult, probably impossible, to exert sufficient control to establish causation or wait years to obtain results. It turns out that the most intractable problems of practice in education meet all three of these criteria which make the techniques of *improvement science* ideal.

Remember

Improvement science still relies on conducting experiments—more often referred to as clinical trials. However, as you will learn, the methodology for conducting such experiments is very different from the traditional, rigorous, RCT methodology—even the opposite in some ways.

---

[77] The field of improvement science was inspired by the work of W. Edwards Deming (1986) in industrial settings which were then adapted to hospital settings.

Application in education

Improvement science was first brought to education as ***designed-based research (DBR)***. The start of DBR is generally credited to Ann Brown (1992) who came to realize that results from laboratory based research were inherently limited in their ability to explain or predict classroom learning and moved her research to the classroom; a process she called "design experimentation."

The DBR movement began to pick up steam as it moved from educational psychologists to a broader mix of educational researchers. In 2003 *Educational Researcher*, the journal that goes out to all members of AERA, had a special issue devoted to DBR (Kelly, 2003). According to Bell (2004) scholars from a wide variety of disciplines became interested in participating in DBR to: "… better understand how to orchestrate innovative learning experiences among children in their everyday educational contexts as well as to simultaneously develop new theoretical insights about the nature of learning" (p. 244). Sandoval and Bell (2004) introduced the concept of "embodied conjectures." These are conjectures, rather than formal hypotheses as generally used in traditional experimental research, about the possible effects of different educational designs.

The most important insight from the term design based research is that it combines "design" which is an artistic term, with "research" which is an analytical one. As early as 1992, Collins (1992) advocated that educational research be a "design science," like aerospace engineering that required a methodology to systematically test design variants for effectiveness. **In other words, DBR highlighted that *improvement science* combines the components of creative design and analysis.**

Unfortunately, the DBR movement has been co-opted by traditional researchers who pushed for academic theory to be the prime rationale/basis for design, and claimed success for their DBR projects based on small *ESs*.

More recently, the Carnegie Foundation developed the concept of ***networked improvement community (NIC)*** that built on the earlier *improvement science* work in medicine and health care. NICs engage in a series of iterative trials in a variety of schools/classrooms to test a new intervention's ability to solve a key problem. They learn by doing, and quickly modify and elaborate the intervention as needed to adapt to new settings and issues. The most desired form of evidence is consistently replicated levels of BIG improvement across sites. While it is harder to develop an intervention that works consistently across sites, as opposed to finding some small effect in a gold-standard study of a single sample that focuses on *internal validity*, the evidence required to show consistency of effects is simple and basic—and more useful. You simply need to:

- Demonstrate how much improvement occurred in each context as compared to the past or some existing state or national benchmark;
- Describe the adjustments needed for each new setting;
- Analyze the quality and parameters of implementation.

The goal of NICs and improvement science is to develop new and better interventions to solve a problem of practice that can be scaled with predictable and consistent improvements across a wide variety of contexts. The key methodological goal of an NIC is to demonstrate *replicated* effectiveness at scale. Demonstrating replication of results is consistent with Data Analysis Principle #1 (Chapter 7), and is more credible evidence for leaders.

Remember

Ideally, the improvements turn out to be BIG enough such that the benefits are clear to the naked eye and obvious to leaders, staff, and community.

In addition, NICs are different than the traditional reform network in education. In the latter networks, some type of reform is deemed to be effective and scientifically validated. Everyone is then pushed to adopt it. An example would be the NCTM math reform. Experts are identified who roam the nation or a given state, training everyone in how to implement the reform. Those who adopt constitute a network. In the end such networks generally have little or no effect, and it turns out in retrospect that the reform was (a) not sufficiently defined to take into account all the processes involved in trying to make it actually work, and/or (b) never actually effective to begin with.

An NIC is the opposite type of network. Its perspective is that the problem has NOT been solved because no one has yet figured out how to do it. As a result, the formation of an *NIC* is viewed as establishing a process wherein "…improvers can systematically learn by doing" (Bryk, Gomez, Grunow, & LeMahieu, p. 205). The establishment of the network is viewed as a way to speed up the learning process about how to take into account and adapt to the many social and context factors that affect the success of the intervention.

Designing a New Intervention

Using improvement science to solve a problem of practice starts with the design of an innovative intervention. Such design generally does NOT start with the traditional reliance on academic theory. While important, **academic theory is NOT evidence**. In addition, as discussed in Chapter 1, academic theories are seldom specific enough to provide the primary basis for designing a detailed intervention. **An academic theory is NOT an intervention**. Theory is an idea—while an intervention is a very specific set of procedures and materials. Indeed, Sandoval and Bell (2004) note that it has never been simple to translate theoretical insights into educational practice.

Fortunately, the assumption in education that the traditional model of research is universally how discovery is made in science is WRONG. Working from academic theory is but one of two approaches used in science. The other approach is characterized by Randall (2005a) as "model building" in which the researcher builds something from bits of available ideas and information and then tests it. The reality is that many of the important discoveries in science have occurred via such alternative pathways of discovery—and these alternative pathways lead to different designs for interventions which have the potential to produce better results than relying on existing prevalent theory.

Alternative pathways to scientific discovery

The most effective uses of improvement science tend to rely on designs and evaluation processes developed via alternative pathways to scientific discovery hinted at in the earlier discussions of "model building" and "embodied conjectures. This section shows how the alternative pathways of…

- Accident
- Metaphor
- Iterative clinical trial of prototypes—i.e., tinkering…

…have played major roles in scientific discovery.

Accident

The classic case of an accidental scientific discovery was Madame Curie discovering x rays because a photographic plate was left uncovered. The discovery was made because, unlike most people who might have dismissed it as a faulty plate, she was intensely curious as to what might have caused the shadow and was persistent in trying to find an explanation.

Nor is this a unique example of accidental discovery in science. Teflon was also discovered as a result of an accident. Chapter 4 described how a test for a drug to reduce smoking was accidentally discovered to promote weight loss. Nor is this an anomaly. Many important drugs, from Penicillin to Viagra were discovered by accident. Until Fleming's accident—wherein he left an uncovered petri dish in the open air—led to the discovery of Penicillin, humans were largely defenseless against bacterial infections. Similarly, scientists failed repeatedly in their efforts to crystalize RNA, a critical step in the effort to develop RNA vaccines. The breakthrough occurred when a sample was put in a malfunctioning incubator which cooked the RNA at a much higher temperature than intended (Isaacson, 2021). Perfect crystals.

Accidents also lead to breakthroughs in industrial scientific labs. In 2014 an accident at an IBM lab produced a scientific breakthrough in polymer materials that led to a new generation of super-hard and light plastics that are easily recycled (Long, 2014). Such material has wide potential applicability in industrial and consumer products. Markoff (2014) reported that this discovery occurred when a researcher who was mixing a traditional recipe of chemicals accidentally left one out and came back to find a mixture with unique properties. Until this "error," it had been widely assumed that all classes of polymers had been discovered, and this accident led to the first new class of polymers discovered in decades. The story concludes by a scientist noting, "Serendipity is the mother of invention."

Learning from accident only requires open-mindedness and curiosity to explore all options as to why something unexpected happened.

Metaphor

There are many examples in science where metaphor and intuition, not theory, led to major discoveries. The first manned flying machine was not developed by a theorist applying theoretical principles or research evidence. The key knowledge that ushered in aviation was discovered by a pair of bicycle builders and repairers. How did they succeed when everyone else before them had failed?

Their breakthrough design, the flexible wing, came to them by observing birds in flight. They noticed that when birds quickly changed direction they bent their wings. They were then able to use their knowledge of materials and pulleys to design a flexible wing. The wing was based on metaphor...not theory. While the concept of aerodynamics existed and the general concept of lift was known, it was not really developed. In addition, the Wright brothers' breakthrough came because they discovered that whatever data or predictions that existed about the nature of flight were wrong.[78] Only after manned flight was demonstrated did the theory of aerodynamics begin to evolve. In other words, *metaphor-based invention preceded the development of an elaborated, validated, academic theory.*

There are numerous other cases historically besides manned flight where major inventions emerged from intuitive leaps of the imagination as opposed to the scholarly application of academic theory. James Watts' "model building" which led to his inventing the steam engine is another example where invention and design preceded the development of theory—in this case the development of thermodynamics.[79]

Metaphor not only enables invention to precede theory, metaphor has also played a role historically in the conceptual development of some of the most important theories in science—what physics calls "thought experiments." The classic example is Einstein imagining what it would be like to travel on a beam of light which helped lead to the theory of relativity.

Iterative clinical trials of prototypes/tinkering

Many of the major discoveries in science and improvements in other fields were the result of iterative clinical tinkering. The classic case is Edison's invention of the light bulb. It was only his dogged tinkering with various combinations of materials that led to this and his many other discoveries. (James Dyson claims that it took 5,127 tries to develop a bagless vacuum cleaner that worked efficiently.) Most theorists and

---

[78] After relying initially on existing data about the characteristics of flight, the Wright brothers began to realize that the existing principles were wrong and built their own wind tunnel and did their own calculations.

[79] For a fuller discussion of how at times model building and tinkering produce important innovations without relying on theory, and whose demonstrated success led to the development of theory, see Ridley (2000).

scientists would argue that what Edison did was very inefficient and certainly not intellectually elegant. While that is true, Edison's way turned out to be far more efficient than waiting for science and theory to evolve to the point where it was obvious how to produce a light bulb.

How long would the invention of the light bulb have been delayed if not for Edison's "tinkering"?

Tinkering is in fact a warranted path to discovery in science—as well as in educational practice—*where there is insufficient evidence or theory.*

Indeed, it is only when theory has a very strong evidentiary basis that it becomes a more efficient basis for solving a problem than iterative tinkering. It can also be argued that trying to apply a variety of theories that cannot meet a strong evidentiary standard are themselves little more than iterative tinkering—albeit tinkering with ideas rather than physical models.

Of course, modern medicine would never resort to iterative tinkering. Wrong! Gawande (2007), in his book *Better: A Surgeon's Notes on Performance*, provides a powerful example of how clinical tinkering in medicine has saved lives. He argues that the single greatest improvement in medical practice in the past 50 years in terms of saving lives has been the tremendous reduction in the mortality rate of newborn infants. In the 1950s the mortality rate for newborn infants in the U.S. was 1 in 30. By 2000 only 1 baby out of 500 newborns died. Did this improvement occur from the application of theory, or from gold standard randomized experiments, or from the use of evidence-based practices? The answer to all of these questions is … NO!

While this life-saving improvement was occurring, obstetrics was ranked dead last among all medical specialties in the use of hard evidence from randomized clinical trials. Obstetrics was considered to be the scientific backwater of medical practice. Yet, obstetrics did a better job of improving practice—i.e., saving lives—than any other medical specialty. How did obstetrics do it?

The first "baby" step was the development and widespread adoption of a standard checklist to assess the baby's condition 1 and 5 minutes after birth. This common sense method has endured and is now referred to as the "Apgar score." The Apgar score provided an incentive to develop new practices to improve baby's health in the first 5 minutes instead of just leaving the health-challenged babies to die after delivery. How did these new life-saving—practices develop? Dr. Gawande describes it thus:

> In obstetrics…if a new strategy seemed worth trying, doctors did not wait for research trials to tell them it was all right. They just went ahead and tried it, then looked to see if results improved. Obstetrics went about improving the same way that Toyota and General Electric went about improving on the fly, but always paying attention to the results and trying to better them. Whether all the adjustments and innovations of the obstetrics package are necessary and beneficial may remain unclear…But the package as a whole has made child delivery

demonstrably safer…despite the increasing age, obesity…of pregnant mothers. (p. 189-90)

This is essentially crowd-sourced clinical tinkering across a network. Different hospitals tried new approaches and communicated what worked in real time to all other obstetricians. How many more babies and mothers would have died if not for the clinical tinkering of hundreds of doctors and nurses?[80]

Examples of successful application in education

Despite the dominant emphasis on the traditional conception of science research methodology in our field, some interventions that have been generated outside the traditional model have started to permeate and benefit education—e.g., KIPP Schools and the Kahn Academy. These two examples of *improvement science* networks were designed to solve a specific problem. Teach for America was designed to recruit top college graduates from a variety of disciplines to teach in inner city schools. The Kahn academy was designed to make math concepts more understandable to struggling learners and to make them available free via the internet.

Both use alternative pathways and emerged largely from outside the formal education academic institutions and funding sources. Indeed, the design approach of the Kahn Academy lessons violates most theories taught in colleges of education about how to apply technology in instruction and how to design effective instructional materials and user interfaces. Instead, Kahn used his intuition as an engineer to develop his tutorial lessons using a very basic, almost primitive, interface—that has been highly effective.

The Gates Foundation has also pivoted away from supporting traditional types of education reforms to establishing an improvement science network. The foundation's prior efforts that relied on traditional forms of research such as establishing small high schools and improving the measures of teacher performance had not been successful—despite the expenditures of large sums of monies, and hiring the best education experts to apply the best research. I was highly critical of these earlier initiatives and correctly predicted that they would fail because of reliance on research with small benefits.

However, Gates later funded the establishment of an improvement science network to convert an interdisciplinary college history course into a high school course called "Big History". The goal was to increase students' interest in, and mastery of, history by going "beyond specialized and self-contained fields of study to grasp history as a whole." According to Sorkin (2014), the course grew from an initial pilot in five high schools to approximately 1,200 schools in the first 3 years. This reform network is still operating and provides the curriculum at no cost to schools.

---

[80] Since the work of Dr. Atui Gawande's perspective on obstetrics is very prominent in this chapter, it should be noted that he has become one of the most influential voices nationally on rethinking health care in the US. In a recent New York Times OP-ED, Kocher and Mostashari (2014) refer to an article by Gawande (2009) as perhaps "… the most influential magazine article of the past decade." They further point out that "The article became mandatory reading in the White House. President Obama convened an Oval Office meeting to discuss its key finding…" Dr. Gawande's research became a major stimulus for developing some of the key policies of the Affordable Care Act and for building political support for them.

239

"Design" skills versus "research" skills

Improvement science is clearly the form of science characterized by Randall (2005a) as "model building." At the heart of implementing an improvement science process is the design of the novel intervention. Who should be qualified to design an educational intervention, and what should the qualifications be?

Few individuals are exceptional in both design and science/research—as each requires very different skill sets. Of course, there are exceptions. One would be Gaudi, the Spanish architect of the early 1900s. He was way ahead of his time in both the aesthetic and material science of creating unique structures. More current examples that come to mind are Steve Jobs of Apple and James Dyson of the Dyson Company.

In order to design a successful intervention using improvement science, we have to understand what science is and what design is. Fortunately, Chapter 1 in this textbook provided a good sense of what science is. So the key questions in trying to understand how to use improvement science to design an intervention become:

- What is design?

- What is good design in an education intervention?

- How does one "design" an educational intervention to improve practice?

- How does one blend the artistic, intuitive elements of design with the science?

The answers to these questions are important to all leaders seeking to develop better solutions to key problems they face—because at some point they will need to become leaders, or members, of a design team.

What is "design"?

Design is clearly a process that is increasingly critical to the success of a wide range of products and activities in our society. For example, the success of Apple products is partly based on the sophisticated use of design.

There are many elements to a good design, and there may not be one best definition. A good starting point in describing/defining "design" is that it is partly an artistic process with little reliance on "academic theory." In addition, design is not a purely engineering process. For example, much of the design of Apple products was based on the creative instincts and life-experiences of Steve Jobs, and a great deal of emphasis was placed on the aesthetics of how the screen and devices looked.

Surprisingly, the emerging scholarship about improvement science in education largely overlooks the aesthetic, metaphorical nature of design. Design in education is viewed as merely an engineering process—e.g., something in which specific procedures and formulas exist that can be applied. However, aesthetics and engineering are both critical and are not mutually exclusive. There are many examples of collaboration between aesthetics and science even in the physical sciences. For example, engineering can also include aesthetics. Such overlap is certainly true in

240

architecture. There is a very strong aesthetic element in the design of buildings, but then there is also the materials science and engineering to make sure the building will remain standing.

One classic example of combining aesthetic design and engineering is the iconic, Sydney Opera House. The design of Jørn Utzon won in a competition based largely on aesthetics. Once the design was selected the realization set in that there was no way to actually build it under existing knowledge and available technology. Fortunately, the decision-makers remained committed to the aesthetics of the design and waited for the science and engineering to catch up.

Another individual who has successfully combined artistic design and scientific engineering is James Dyson, the inventor of the bagless vacuum cleaner and the air hand dryer. His inventions have made him one of the richest people in England and earned him a knighthood. His initial background was as a student in the Bryan Shaw School of Art and the Royal College of Art where he studied architecture. Once he had the design skills he then studied engineering. Both Steve Jobs, who studied calligraphy, and Dyson had the combination of artistic design and scientific engineering skills that lead to breakthrough inventions. Dyson sees the engineering and design processes as separate but synergistic processes (Science Friday, 2014). The experience of these inventors implies that design is a more intuitive, creative process that is necessary but distinct from engineering—and that design does not depend on academic theory.

Practical
Tip
Since it is rare for individuals to have both the artistic and scientific sets of skills, the key for leaders seeking to implement an improvement science process is to understand the importance of forming teams that can integrate both types of skills.

State-of-the-art breakthrough interventions in education will increasingly require small teams consisting of a mix of individuals who…

- Are experts, or who have access to experts, in academic research;
- Have an intuitive sense of how students and teachers think and react;
- Can think creatively;
- Can create artistic works; and
- Are detail oriented.

The design part of developing more powerful interventions requires intuitive and creative leaps of thinking. In Dyson's case, the idea for using cyclonic action as the key to eliminating the vacuum bag and filter was happenstance. The idea came to him while walking by a junkyard and observing a huge cyclonic tower and wondered if a smaller version could be made for use in a vacuum cleaner (Science Friday, 2014). Metaphor strikes again!

So "design" seems to be more than just engineering. At the same time, it is critical to carefully engineer the fine details of the intervention—regardless of whether it is the materials of the bagless vacuum cleaner, or the details of a curriculum, staff development, student scheduling, etc.

241

(Additional elements of good design will also become evident as this chapter proceeds.)

However, the importance of design leads to the following questions:

- Can "design" skills be taught?

- If they can be taught, what is the best way to do it?

- How can it be incorporated into the curriculum of colleges of education?

- Should there be a department of design?

- What kinds of faculty can best teach "educational design"?

- How do you train individuals to become master designers?

- What would a design research center in a college of education look like?

- Indeed, what would a college of educational design look like?[81]

At this point there are no answers to these questions largely because most have not been considered in education. However, it is clear that being creative is a different skill than being a scholar (though there can of course be overlap)—and that both types of skills and individuals are needed, working cooperatively, if we are to make BIG improvements in education. Unfortunately, unlike physics that has a balance and divide between theorists and experimenters who systematically benefit from each others' contributions, education can probably be characterized as a field with too many theorists and hardly any designers.

I can say without false modesty that my real, and probably only, talent is that I am a master designer of educational interventions. To me, a master designer is someone who can think of new approaches and instinctively see in his/her head how diverse students will react to a new idea, or a new approach to teaching something. I suspect that the following are some key characteristics of a master designer:

- Immature and adventurous—yet organized,
- Gutsy/fearless,
- Tremendously imaginative with an over-developed sense of fantasy,
- Highly skeptical, and
- Insatiably curious about things in general and especially about how kids view life and their place in it.

---

[81] A good model for a multi-disciplinary design school is here is the Hasso Plattner Institute of Design at Stanford University—also called the d school. According to its website:

The d.school is a hub for innovators at Stanford. Students and faculty in engineering, medicine, business, law, the humanities, sciences, and education find their way here to take on the world's messy problems together. Human values are at the heart of our collaborative approach. We focus on creating spectacularly transformative learning experiences. Along the way, our students develop a process for producing creative solutions to even the most complex challenges they tackle. This is the core of what we do.

Remember

Clearly, having a good imagination and an imaginative personal theory of action is more important to being a good designer than having lots of degrees. I suspect that there are many leaders and teachers who have been, or have the potential to be, master designers.

Of course, this explanation of design is verrrrrry incomplete and verrrrry general. Indeed, it may be impossible to precisely define what design is or how to best apply it to educational practice. However, putting on my researcher hat, a question that is more helpful for understanding the nature of design that can guide leaders—that I can answer—is:

What, if any, were the common characteristics of the design process used by those who have used improvement science to develop highly effective interventions?

An effort will be made in the next several sections to explore the answer to this question by examining in more detail the design and implementation processes used by the successful Statway and HOTS interventions. Then the emergent similarities in the design and implementation processes used in these two projects will be used to recommend practices that leaders can use to establish an improvement science project in their schools.

Summary of the characteristics of improvement science

Pulling together the above discussion, improvement science methodology consists of:

- Identifying a key problem of practice to try and solve; . and structural impediments to improvement that exist;

- Identifying the key structural impediments to improvement, and trying to understand what the key causes of the problem are—though you will not always be able to do so.[82]

- Designing a novel intervention using conjectures and alternative methods of scientific discovery;

- Testing it out on a very small scale—e.g., one classroom, one or two schools;

- Learning by doing—i.e., evaluating how it is progressing and making adjustments on the fly (tinkering);

- Increasing the scale if the results are promising, and implementing the modified intervention in new contexts—i.e., new classrooms/schools; and

- Making additional adjustments to accommodate the new demands and problems as they arise in the new contexts.

Hopefully, the intervention will become one that consistently produces BIG benefits.

---

[82] It too about 10 years of experience with HOTS before we came to understand why the Title I students were struggling and falling behind academically after the third grade. But the program was successful because of the metaphors and conjectures used—even without knowing what the causal problem was.

The advantage of *improvement science's* form of experimentation is that it allows for flexible adaptation of the intervention in a variety of real-world contexts in real time as opposed to testing a static intervention in a highly controlled context in a single sample.

Two Improvement Science Projects That Produced BIG Improvement and Increases in Equity

This section discusses two recent examples of improvement science networks that solved a problem of practice and that produced BIG improvement. The first is the Carnegie Foundation's Statway initiative to collaboratively redesign the developmental math sequence at the community college level (Bryk, Gomez, & Grunow, 2011). The second is my Higher Order Thinking Skills (HOTS) intervention for students receiving Title I and mildly impaired learning disability (LD) services in grades 4-8 (Pogrow, 2004; Pogrow, 2005).

The next few sections explain the design process that Statway and HOTS used to produce BIG improvements in under-represented students' academic performance and in equity, and the results. (While I was the lead designer of the HOTS intervention, I also studied the design process that the Statway intervention engaged in.) The goal is to determine what, if any, the common design elements were across the projects.

The knowledge about the common design elements can then be used as a guide by school leaders seeking to initiate and lead an improvement science project in their schools to design new interventions to solve different problem of practice. And, while school leaders are not interested in scaling their interventions on a national scale, these similarities can help them scale a successful homegrown intervention across their own schools.

The longstanding problems of practice promoting inequity

Both interventions tackled historically long-standing problems that were major blockages to increasing equity in students' academic achievement—perhaps the biggest blockages.

Statway was established to improve upon one of the greatest systemic failures in American education. Approximately half the students who enroll at a community college (CC) are placed into a remedial/developmental math course sequence of at least a year which they must pass before they can enroll in CC credit-earning courses. In this sequence they are essentially asked to relearn high school mathematics. Bryk, Gomez, and Grunow (2011) cite national statistics that 60-70 percent of these students nationally fail to complete the sequence of developmental math courses and drop out without having had the opportunity to earn any CC credit. *This may be the highest dropout rate in American education.*

244

The HOTS project was established to solve the long-standing problem of at-risk students' academic performance declining after the first three grades—regardless of how much progress they made in these early grades. While achievement gaps stay stable or decline during the first three grades, the gaps start to rewiden in the 4th grade and by the eighth grade the gaps are large in all measured subject areas despite decades of reform. This post-grade 3 drop-off is one of the biggest impediments to equalizing education achievement.

In both CC developmental math and the post-grade 3 drop-off, the existing approaches were not working for those students who were the most vulnerable, and existing "effective" practices had failed to produce noticeable improvement for decades.

General approaches of Statway and HOTS

The Statway initiative designed and tested a new developmental math sequence that emphasized the statistical types of math knowledge that students need in CC coursework and the types of problems they will encounter in a variety of CC majors. This new curriculum replaced the traditional high school algebra based developmental coursework. The Statway curriculum was developed collaboratively by researchers, foundation scholars, and CC administrators and faculty.

The Higher Order Thinking Skills (HOTS) project started 30 years ago. HOTS replaced the remedial approach to supplemental services for students in grades 4-8 designated as Title I and mildly impaired LD with intensive general thinking development activities. The general thinking development was produced by combining a Socratic learning environment with the use of problem-solving challenges based on computer games and simulations. The activities were modeled on how gifted programs operated. So HOTS replaced ALL remedial activities with ones that treated students as intellectually gifted. In addition, HOTS was the only supplemental service provided to the Title I and LD students—all the other supplemental "help" services were eliminated.

The goal of both projects was to produce dramatic improvement. In both cases they did indeed produce dramatic improvement early on. This is critical for the initiative continuing and expanding across sites.

Results

Results from the small-scale field tests show that the percentage of students earning community college math credits increased from only 15% after two years of developmental math to 50% after only a single year of Statway developmental math.

From the beginning, HOTS students showed three times the growth in reading comprehension and twice the growth in math on standardized and state tests without extra "help" in those content areas as compared to students receiving extra instruction in those subjects. In addition, approximately 15% of the students made honor roll after only a year in the program. Students also made substantial social-emotional gains as evidenced by dramatic increases in verbalization.

HOTS was subsequently adopted in close to 2600 schools nationally and served close to ½ million Title 1 and LD students.

These results indicate that both projects produced BIG improvements and increases in equity in solving heretofore intractable problems—and did so from their very beginning. How did they achieve such results? The key is the nature of the design process both networks used.

The Design Processes of HOTS and Statway

However, to answer this question about common characteristics, it is necessary to first analyze the design processes used by each of these projects separately, and then determine what similarities existed.

The design of HOTS

When I got involved in a collaboration to design what would eventually become HOTS, I had what turned out to be a major advantage. My advantage was:

- I did not know anything about Title I, cognitive psychology, or theories of teaching reading; and

- I had no idea as to what "best" practice was or what the latest theories of the moment were.

So, out of necessity, what did drive the initial design process was the insight of the leaders and teachers who approached me to work with them. Their instinctual insight was that their Title I students were bright and they realized that the current remedial approaches were not working.

Based on that insight we decided to design an intervention suitable for "bright" advantaged kids. (This was technically illegal under the then existing Title I regulations.) *The first metaphor used to drive design was to consider our Title I students as individuals attending an elite private school.*

So we set out to design something that mimicked the type of education we felt that gifted and privileged students would receive—even if only for a small part of the school day. That led to the decision to focus on using an intensive Socratic approach.

Metaphor #2 was to think of the HOTS Title 1 intervention as replacing the conversation that students were not getting in the home. This intuition was later supported by the classic study by Hart and Risley (1995) that found that there is shockingly little conversation in low-income households with caring parents, and that

246

this appeared to have an effect on their children's cognitive development.[83]

Once the decision was made to create a conversation rich environment, the next design questions was:

What kinds of conversations should we create to stimulate cognitive development?

Well, the classic conversation in the home was dinner table conversation. Emulating key aspects of dinner table conversation was a logical extension of the second metaphor and it served to guide how we designed key aspects of the conversation, curriculum, and computer use activities. Since dinner table conversation is an ad hoc exploration of what happened in the context of recent life experience, we used experiences on the computer as a metaphor for life experiences.

Metaphor #3 was *to organize discussions that explored their experience on the computer in a manner that parents use to question and prod their children around the dinner table.* That is why, for example, we made the counterintuitive decision to not link the discussions back to the classroom content since parents in the home do not link their dinner table conversations to specific classroom content. This metaphor also provided some guidance for the design of the Socratic system.

But how could we design conversations to stimulate cognitive development?

This question was solved by *Metaphor #4—which was to think of the brain as a muscle and brain circuits as muscle fibers.* If athletes engage in building muscle via repetitive actions, could we structure the conversations so that students would repeatedly engage in verbalization that mimicked the physical structures of neural networks? I approached a series of cognitive psychologists and asked them:

> *"Which 3-4 studies, or researchers, have produced the best evidence (not theory) on how brain networks work for storing and retrieving information?"*

Note that I did not try to read all the research on brain functioning or survey all theories. I took the small set of research resources they provided me and found that the key experimental evidence was that learning and retention could be enhanced by increasing linkages between and among concepts. So the focus of all the curriculum and conversations in the intervention was to maximize the linkages between all the disparate experiences students had on the computer with each other and with their existing general knowledge base. (Ideas were linked across the computer contexts via organizing the curriculum around a set of linkage concepts.)

---

[83] The reality was that we did know of this study when we made the decision to focus on creating a Socratic environment. That decision was made solely on the basis that we felt that it was an enduring characteristic of elite education.

Remember

While we sought basic research experimental evidence about how the brain stores information, we were NOT using theory or research evidence as the basis of the design. Rather we were seeking traditional basic experimental research evidence that fit with, and informed, the chosen metaphor. So it was the metaphor that drove the design and the subsequent research evidence helped refine the engineering of the curriculum.

Another key design feature was to realize that no thinking program could work unless students decided to exert the energy to be thoughtful as opposed to being passive. In addition, by the fourth grade students had learned how to get out of verbalizing responses by either claiming "I dunno", or whispering a one-word answer and let the teacher fill in the blanks, etc. This required a way to motivate students to want to think and verbalize thoughtful responses. The methods HOTS used to increase student engagement was to…

- Tell students and their parents that this was a program for students who the school believes are very bright and is designed to help bring out that brightness;

- Use technology to provide game-based thinking and reading challenges to them every day;

- Provide challenges that were so difficult but engaging that they would struggle to succeed at them and then succeed on their own—i.e., controlled floundering; and

- Provide opportunity for HOTS students to share their ideas and discoveries.

While it is counterintuitive to have students fail initially, as long as they are motivated to want to succeed they can figure things out and then feel a tremendous sense of pride. After the first few times of success at figuring out truly difficult challenges they start to enjoy the process of outsmarting the computer. In addition, the HOTS students then choose to invite a classmate they always thought was brighter than them and discover that their classmates canNOT solve the problems they succeeded at.

HOTS students then tutor the "brighter" students—which increased HOTS students' self-belief, and earned the respect of their classmates. This subtle social engineering proved to be a key to HOTS' students' social-emotional development.

Developing a model for training HOTS teachers

In Socratic teaching the teacher never tells students whether their answers are right or wrong, or what the correct answer is. Teachers only ask questions. This required even the most veteran teachers to learn new skills in listening more carefully and analytically to what their students were saying and how to invent follow-up probes to enable students to come to an understanding on their own. How to develop those skills? I knew that it would require a special form of teacher training to develop these different behaviors and interaction reflexes. I knew that simply providing knowledge and theory about the nature of Socratic interaction would not change behavior—especially since all teachers believe that they already listen to what their students say. Good fortune led to the design of the training for HOTS teachers.

At the time I was living in the Los Angeles area and was hanging out with some actors. I was fascinated as to how individuals who did not know what day of the week it was could memorize and perform with great nuance scripts that could easily be more than 100 pages. How was this possible? I spent a sabbatical in the theater school at UCLA to learn how teaching and learning occur in the theater. It turned out that teaching and learning in the theater was virtually the opposite of how teaching and learning are done in schools. Actors learn their lines and how to perform them through the process of contextual familiarity gained from repetitive experience.

This led to *metaphor #5—which was to adopt the process of how teaching and learning occur in the theater as the basis for designing the HOTS teacher training.* The training was a 5-day experience in which each prospective HOTS teacher "taught" three lessons to their peers who played the role of students responding spontaneously to the questions and follow-up probes put forth by the HOTS teacher. It is through such experience and feedback from peers that these truly excellent teachers came to realize that they previously had not instinctively been listening to what their "students" were saying. They were not hearing responses other than the ones they were seeking— especially ones that were surprising. The peers then pointed out the rationale for their different responses, and all realized *that the responses made sense.* The participants then realized that they had routinely shut off creative responses from their real students. The trainees then became open to learning the very different listening and probing methods of the HOTS Socratic system. By the time they taught their third HOTS lesson in the training, the teachers listened and probed their "students" expertly.

Engineering the curriculum

All of the above key metaphors led to very specific decisions as to how to design the intervention. Someone working from a perspective of academic theory or research evidence on best practice, would have shaped the intervention differently. Indeed, 10 people looking at the same theory and evidence would probably come to 10 very different sets of decisions on key design elements. However, none of them would have come to the critical conclusion that the discussions should NOT be linked to classroom content...a critical decision that flowed naturally from the home dinner table conversation metaphor. That is why the other traditional model based reform efforts never produced anywhere near the BIG gains after the third grade that HOTS did.

But metaphors by themselves are not sufficient. Implementing the materials needed to support a Socratic intervention took lots of hard work, persistence, and open-mindedness on the part of all concerned. While I did not know what to expect, the open-mindedness of all the initial collaborators led to an expanding learning community as the number of HOTS sites increased. While I took the lead in the writing of the materials and the initial design of the workshops, the development process quickly developed a mind of its own. No one individual can make the myriad decisions that go into developing the day-by-day materials needed to support an intensive intervention.

As teachers began to use the materials they quickly started to make suggestions as to how they could be improved, ranging from small details to different conceptual

249

approaches to a given lesson. Suggestions came in from teachers all over the US. The creativity of their insights, as well as their suggestions based on their experience in teaching the lessons to their students were invariably better than the original conception. After a period of time a new iterated version of the curriculum would be issued as part of the iterative improvement process. Now when I look at the curriculum I have no clue as to which ideas were mine and which came from teachers.

The same iterative process occurred in the design of the intensive Socratic professional development. While the outlines of the initial training held up, the Socratic model underwent continuous tinkering to ensure that teachers were prepared for <u>all</u> the different types of situations they would encounter—especially the handling of surprising answers that may or may not represent thoughtfulness. Extensive teacher feedback of what they were encountering and how they were dealing with the situation, as well as extensive observations of classroom conversation, were used to make the needed tweaks in the Socratic model and training. Such iteration provided HOTS teachers with the probing strategies needed to deal with all of the types of student responses and challenges they would encounter—and still maintain a questioning environment to stimulate student verbalization as opposed to "telling" key ideas.

While some would consider this iterative process to be grunt work, it was in fact an amazingly intellectually rewarding process of idea sharing within a true learning community. The continuous flow of data about student outcomes and implementation processes were critical for improving the consistency of outcomes and increasing scalability to a wider variety of contexts. This iterative development process lasted about 12 years for the curriculum, Socratic model, and training before they were pretty much done. This iterative process is essentially the scientific process of "persistent clinical tinkering."

Of course no leader will embark on a process that takes 12 years to develop to solve their immediate problems. However, remember that the initial version of the intervention produced unexpectedly BIG gains from the very beginning—and the tinkering only improved the results at the margin and increased its ability to scale to very different contexts and maintain the benefits.

Remember

It should be expected that the intervention will produce BIG benefits from the first year of implementation. If it does not, move on to something else.

This iterative tinkering also helped develop the desired implementation parameters. *Implementation parameters* are the details of how to best implement an intervention. For example, it was important to determine the amount of HOTS experiences that needed to be provided in order for students to internalize the key thinking skills. How long should each HOTS period be, and how many periods per week? Too little will have no effect, too much and the students may get bored and/or the program becomes too costly. Which grade levels? Nothing works dramatically across all grade levels. These are fundamental parameters that HOTS, or any intervention, needs to establish in order to produce consistent effectiveness. Developing the specific implementation parameters via experience are what enabled HOTS to scale and continue to consistently produce BIG benefits across sites as varied as inner city Detroit, Bush Alaskan villages, Barrio schools, Navajo reservation, etc.

In summation, the critical processes in the design of HOTS were picking the right metaphors and the persistent clinical tinkering. Picking the right metaphors initially was partly luck—but it was also the result of the intuitions and personal theories of action of all involved—as well as the openness and creativity of the process.

Integrating traditional research evidence and academic theory into the tinkering process

Once the initial design was in place and the results of the initial pilots were promising, it then became possible to tap into some research evidence that could elaborate and extend the *initial* design. Some of the key work was Vygotsky's experimental data that were consistent with what we were seeing with HOTS students. His theory of the *Zone of Proximal Development* then became a guiding principle of subsequent iterative design and curriculum changes—and encouraged us to challenge the students at a much higher level than we would otherwise have dared. And the theory correctly predicted that the heretofore "low-performing" students would succeed.

So, some traditional research evidence and theory did come to play a role in the design of the intervention. However, their later application served to explain and extend the success of the initial metaphor based design. Academic theory following metaphor is the opposite of how academicians tend to think about the application of theory and evidence to improve practice. Indeed, now when I tell educational or cognitive psychologists about the brain as a muscle metaphor that was critical to the design of HOTS, they think that is "moronic". I tell them in response that… "It is not moronic but good design." At that point they generally turn and quickly walk away shaking their heads.

The design of Statway

I interviewed three of the original designers/conceptualizers of the Statway intervention to determine whether there were any similarities between its design process and that used by HOTS.

The development of Statway was funded by large external grants. This made it possible to hire lots of different groups to develop key elements of the project. In addition, the development process was sequential. First, the curriculum was developed over an extended period of time. Once the curriculum was in hand they began to design the teacher training. After some problems the project began to realize the need to rethink professional/staff development and research, and other individuals were then brought in to help organize instruction and create a more coherent whole. (In HOTS a small group designed all aspects of the intervention pretty much simultaneously.)

However, once the pilots started there were many similarities. Despite the extended development and subsequent fine-tuning that Statway underwent prior to the first pilot, it had a small core of individuals consistently involved in maintaining the original

251

design vision.[84] In addition, Statway established the very ambitious BIG improvement goal right from the very start of dramatically increasing the number of developmental students who quickly succeed in earning college credit in mathematics.

Most of those interviewed about Statway talked about "vision" as the key driver of the design. There was also a pragmatic basis for some of the design choices. For example, if they were looking for a different context to teach math they could have designed a course around robotics or measuring environmental changes as the alternative approach. However, they chose to teach math via a course in statistics. The rationales for choosing a statistics course as the alternative approach were the following pragmatic reasons:

- The course would be transferable to 4-year college credit,
- The bulk of mathematics needed for community college majors that are applied to the workplace is "statistics," and
- Statistics was already in the community college math curriculum so it would be easier to slip into the developmental course sequence.

There was no reference to metaphor in the design process until one of those interviewed described the design strategy to get students to buy into the curriculum and learning process and referred to the approach as "thinking of the brain as a muscle." It was reaffirming to see someone else independently applying the same metaphor.[85]

There was also a major emphasis on increasing Statway students' engagement in learning. The strategies used to increase engagement were:

- Telling them that what they were learning was "not math" or that it was "not high-school math,"
- Making sure that they experienced high levels of success initially, and
- Showing them how what they were learning was fundamental and linked to all their other courses and were critical job skills.

---

[84] It is possible that if Statway had used a more integrated design process, e.g., developing a single curriculum module and have teachers teach it, they would have been able to anticipate some of the problems with staff development and curriculum design earlier and been able to shorten the design and development process.

[85] The application of "the brain as a muscle" metaphor was used somewhat differently in the design of the two interventions. In HOTS it was used to have students constantly make linkages among ideas across different software environments. In Statway it was used to create a focus on getting students to consistently engage in mathematical reasoning successfully early on to train the brain to engage in such reasoning.

Lessons From the Success of HOTS and Statway

The processes of implementation and discovery

There are three distinct phases of implementation and discovery

Phase 1—Design and piloting

As has been described, the starting points of the design creation and the supporting frameworks emerge largely through creative intuition, trial and error. These initial frameworks then undergo some engineering as initial success and experience emerges. These initial design frameworks can also be said to be personal theories of action or working theories of what the designers hope will happen. They provide the base from which the supporting materials and processes are engineered. However, even this engineering process requires a great deal of constant creative invention.

However, at this point the frameworks are still largely guesses and hunches. The goal is to learn quickly from trial and error, with constant feedback, as to what is working and what is not. These feedback loops are critical to the ongoing iteration of the design.

Phase 2—Initial expansion

If the results from the initial pilots demonstrate BIG improvement, then some initial expansion is warranted. As more experience is gained and more data are received from the initial pilots and new sites, iterations to the initial frameworks become more formalized and elaborated—and design parameters, curriculum, and training are continually adjusted. The frameworks then become structures.

If the first phase was intuitive design, this phase is one of crafting—which is still a largely creative process with some elements of specific skills/knowledge/evidence being brought to bear.

It is very likely that the new sites will present new challenges and problems that need to be overcome, and those solutions become iterated improvements to the design. As more information is gathered it becomes more apparent what data and modifications are needed to the initial design.

In addition, the accumulated experience provides a basis for deciding what types of experimental basic research evidence are likely to be the most helpful. So, for example, experimental evidence of the importance of "inference from context" skills to academic learning caused it to be added as the fourth basic thinking skill in the HOTS framework a year and a half after its inception.

Phase 3-Scaling up

If there are consistent BIG benefits across the sites, then it is justifiable to further scale the intervention. At this point management, funding, and logistical issues rise to the fore and all components of the project and implementation processes need to be routinized. However, the feedback, evidence seeking, and iteration processes continue to further refine all components of the intervention. This cycle continues until the intervention has been sufficiently routinized to support *recognizable replication*.[86] The additional touches do NOT necessarily improve outcomes. Rather, they make the intervention more routine and robust—i.e., able to be successfully implemented on a larger scale and in a wider variety of settings, with consistent results for those who adhere to the implementation parameters.

In other words, this phase is largely one of *engineering* the finer and final details of all aspects of implementing the intervention so that it will be highly scalable going forward.

Remember

While leaders may not be interested in scaling the intervention beyond their targeted schools, they can play a role in helping others scale the intervention by sharing details and results through professional presentations, and/or being part of a sharing network with other leaders and researchers committed to using the same intervention.

Evaluating the interventions—seeking "implicit causation"

The goal of improvement science is to develop interventions that can demonstrate BIG benefits on a consistent basis across multiple, diverse, contexts. While it is not easy to design and develop such an intervention, when it occurs the consistency can be said to demonstrate *implicit causation*—i.e., it is NOT likely that the benefits were NOT caused by the intervention.

In addition, focusing on the replication of BIG benefits dramatically simplifies the evaluation of the intervention. No control groups or their attendant complex comparative statistical analyses are needed. The only comparison needed is to the existing, unsatisfactory, inequitable, level of outcomes that preceded the implementation of the intervention. The comparison benchmarks are how your schools performed previously, and/or existing average state/federal outcomes. Is the *Mean* or *Median* outcomes for the pilots clearly substantially better than what has occurred in the recent past or other existing benchmark? Does the actual unweighted performance of the experimental students clearly represent a BIG improvement compared to an existing performance benchmark? There is no need for further statistical analysis beyond answering these questions.

---

[86] The notion of recognizable replication is referring to a point between the extremes of trying to teacher-proof a curriculum, which is impossible, and the anarchistic extreme of simply putting forth an idea and leaving it up each practitioner to figure out how to implement the idea. For anything to scale with replicable results there needs to be a set of established research-based parameters that are adhered to while still providing space for individual interpretation and creativity. A good example is the theater. Performances of Macbeth allow for artistic interpretation while adhering to a script. The latter is a key implementation parameter that is adhered to across generations that enables audiences to recognize a classic story—while being moved by a variety of artistic flourishes and interpretations. Similarly, good design understands which aspects of an intervention need to be routinized and which need to left to individualized improvisation.

In phase 1, the initial pilots, the focus is on whether the results are surprisingly large. This can be done using descriptive statistics, especially the power trio (see Chapter 4). The goal is to determine whether the intervention produced BIG improvements in measurable outcomes relative to recent historical results.

And while by law Title I had to report test scores, from the beginning the HOTS project wanted to find simple, alternative measures of social-emotional development and even general thinking. The first alternative measure that was used was to measure pre- post the number of friends in school reported by the HOTS students. We then found a tool to teach metacognition, and turned that into a simple pre- post measure of metacognition.

But it was not till phase 2 that we discovered an even better way to measure social-emotional development—i.e., the growth in student verbalization.

It is also important to qualitatively monitor implementation for the purpose of fine-tuning the intervention's materials and adjusting many of the initial assumptions about how to best implement the intervention based on feedback. It is important for the design team to not be defensive and make the needed adjustments quickly.

If the benefits from the intervention are obvious then it makes sense to expand its use.

In phase 2, as the number of sites increases, variations in the process of implementation start to become apparent. This enables three types of evaluations to occur:

1) Which variations are the most effective and/or least effective;

2) What adaptations are needed; and

3) Whether the intervention continues to demonstrate BIG improvements on an absolute basis relative to an existing benchmark, such as recent local history, or statewide/national comparisons.

In addition, at this point the *consistency* of results becomes important. Consistency is measured by the *standard deviation*, one of the power trio statistics, of the improvements across the sites. As discussed in Chapter 4, a low *standard deviation* relative to the *Mean/Median* indicates that there is little variation in the average result across the sites—i.e., the results are consistent.

Remember

No external control groups are needed in these analyses. The summative quantitative evaluation uses the statistical test of practical benefit (see Chapters 6-7). In addition, consistency of BIG improvements demonstrates *implicit causation*—i.e., it is likely that the consistent improvement across diverse contexts results from the intervention.

While this methodology will seem simplistic and biased to statisticians, it actually gives a *better* sense of the effectiveness of the intervention in real-world practice. In addition, it was previously pointed out that the FDA is now approving treatments based on findings of BIG improvements relative to historical outcomes without clinical controlled experiments.

In phase 2, even as BIG improvements in test scores remained the primary criterion of success in terms of official reporting requirements, it becomes possible to refine and/or identify additional alternative measures of student success. In HOTS we began to see consistent increases in student verbalization. We even began to see patterns in how these verbalizations progressed qualitatively in terms of increased sophistication. We also observed anecdotally that these increases in the amount of verbalization were highly correlated with improvements in test scores and social interaction/behavior.

We also began to evaluate whether the increases in general thinking were transferring to improved content academic performance in the regular classroom. The measure used was the extent to which HOTS students were placed on the school's honor roll. There was typically a dramatic increase in such placement even in the first year of the intervention at a given school.

In phase 3, the process of scaling the intervention is intensifying. It now becomes critical to evaluate the implementation process and determine the *implementation parameters of effectiveness*. These parameters specify the specific conditions under which the intervention is effective.

Remember

Determining the parameters of effectiveness is equivalent to medical research that establishes a recommended dosage for an approved medicine. *This element of the research is critical in both medicine and education.* If the dosage recommendation is wrong, an otherwise beneficial drug can kill you. Too little help or professional development, or the wrong type, or the wrong target group, can render any education intervention ineffective.

Indeed, it is quite possible that many of the widely accepted research conclusions in education about what does NOT work is because the research was conducted with inadequate dosages/parameters of the approach. [87] *In other words, setting the parameters of effectiveness is a crucial, but generally overlooked, element of educational research*—largely because traditional experimental methodology is too static to determine the best parameters.

The design of any intervention involves making decisions about many parameters that can vary. How intensive does the intervention need to be—i.e., how much service does the intervention need to provide? Which students benefit—which grade levels, ages, subgroups, etc.? What kinds of professional learning/development, curricular strategy, technology support, etc. work best? Decisions need to be made around each of these issues. As the design team gets more experience in implementing the intervention, certain patterns of "what works best" begin to emerge. These patterns are then set as *specific* implementation parameters that all adopters of the intervention are advised/required to adhere to.

---

[87] A previously discussed example is how the research community "knows" that general thinking, the back bone of HOTS, does not work. However, all the previous research provided too little experience to students, and studied the wrong students—i.e., students who already had general thinking skills. The HOTS research has also identified a form of transfer, which the research community "knows" is impossible. The use of both general thinking and transfer could hold the potential to producing dramatic improvements in outcomes and equity.

Conducting traditional experimental research around each of these parameters would be impossibly expensive and take forever. Equally problematic is that traditional experimental research cannot realistically determine which of the infinite possible combinations of the parameters work most effectively together. That is probably one of the main reasons why RCT experimental research finds little benefit—i.e., it is necessarily testing incompletely-formed interventions.

Improvement science networks, on the other hand, discover the implementation parameters needed for consistent effectiveness via iterative clinical tinkering. If the intervention works in two schools but not a third, why not? What was the difference? How can you adjust the intervention to take this new factor into account? With enough experience the design team comes to understand the specific parameters and conditions of use under which the intervention is consistently effective. In other words, replicated successful experience replaces the need for most statistical controls.

And while there will be natural variations in the initial phase(s) of implementation, if the intervention is well designed, patterns of effective implementation begin to emerge. These patterns are then incorporated into the next version of the intervention. This process of changing parameters on the fly is the iterative improvement/clinical tinkering phase. It is critical that this iterative improvement process occurs quickly and that the resultant modifications be communicated to all sites using the intervention. Several rounds of iterative improvement will typically be necessary. Bryk, Gomez, Grunow, and LeMahieu (2015) refer to this as *practice-based evidence* and note that such improvement research "...is tied to the nature of the problem we are trying to solve—how to get quality outcomes to occur more reliably at scale" (p. 208).

For example, in the early phases of HOTS implementation, a few sites did not produce noticeable improvements. In those cases students were only exposed to the intervention 2-3 days a week. Thereafter, schools were required to commit to providing services 4-5 days per week. The same process was used when teachers decided to incorporate LD students into the program to determine how best to accommodate them.[88]

The point is that an iterative process of making sense of natural variation conducted over-time with increasing numbers of sites can produce very precise knowledge about expected effects and the implementation parameters of effectiveness—something that as a practical matter rigorous experimental research cannot provide.

As previously discussed, searching for consistent patterns of effectiveness through an iterative process is also a hallmark of precision medicine's approach to finding better cures for cancer. This approach seeks to determine which of the possible drugs can produce a BIG effect for one of the many types of genetic mutations that cause cancer.

---

[88] It quickly became evident that HOTS worked with most of the LD students—but not all. As a result of teacher surveys and discussions, we quickly came to realize that it provided little benefit to LD students who were below 80 verbal IQ. This meant that (a) it would benefit the vast majority of LD students, and (b) would enable leaders to predict which LD students needed an alternative intervention. Such a precise finding would have been almost impossible to figure out from traditional experimental research.

Kolata (2015) describes the approach as "basket studies," which is a trial and error process done with small samples of individuals to try and discover as many matches between drugs and benefits as possible.

Practical Tip

The best methodological approach for determining parameters of effectiveness where there are many possible combinations and permutations within the design of a single intervention, or a basket of possible interventions, is iterative trial and error without control groups—subject to the condition that the results provide a BIG improvement relative to existing performance levels. This is as true for improving student outcomes or for increasing cancer cure rates.

In phase 3, as the number of sites increases, the focus is on continuing to:

- Evaluate the consistency and size of the benefit;
- Use feedback to refine the materials and training; and
- Continue to refine and routinize the parameters of implementation.

In addition, once there is strong evidence that the intervention is successful, it becomes important to speculate on why it is working—and what the implications are for theory and improving leadership practice.

New knowledge and theory

As previously discussed, improvement science approaches are developed because of the absence of adequate evidence for solving a problem of practice. In addition, the resultant design is often at odds with the dominant beliefs of the academic community.[89] As a result, if the resultant intervention turns out to be consistently effective it will often lead to the development of powerful new theory.

Remember

While in the earliest phases of implementation the focus is on determining whether the intervention works consistently, once that has been established, and everyone breathes a sigh of relief, it becomes important to try and understand WHY it is working. At this point researchers/academicians can play a critical role in helping reflect on the implications of the success for new knowledge and theory—and communicating these insights to the field at large.

---

[89] I was amazed to find out that researchers had universally concluded that research had shown that general thinking development does NOT work, and that all thinking must be developed in the context of learning specific subject content—e.g., in the regular math and science classes/periods. But—general thinking was working for the HOTS students. It turns out that the existing research on general thinking had been conducted with university students who were already highly accomplished in learning the specific content of their major. What did that have to do with a 4th grader in Harlem or Appalachia who is 2 years behind in reading and math? Nothing. Other research that found general thinking to be ineffective had been conducted with prep-school students over the course of a few days. That tells you nothing about what will happen over the course of a longer time-span. In other words, the research and professional communities took an idea that they wanted to believe and treated it as gospel while ignoring the limited contexts in which it had been tested. The lesson here is that it is always essential to examine the context in which research was generated, and that widely accepted research findings will not necessarily extend to the contexts you are interested in.

The success of **HOTS** led to the following three critical theoretical insights:

1. The main reason that at-risk students stop progressing after the third grade is that the curriculum is becoming more cognitively demanding. At that point the students' main impediment is that "they do not understand what it means to understand"—though they clearly have the intellectual potential to understand and generalize;

2. A sense of understanding is developed through mediated Socratic conversation with the critical element being students' active, spontaneous verbalizing of increasingly sophisticated ideas; and

3 Continuing to focus on repetitive basic skills after the third grade inhibits the development of a sense of understanding.

These three findings led to the *Theory of Cognitive Underpinnings*.

Remember

Theory of Cognitive Underpinnings. In the absence of a sense of understanding students cannot benefit from quality content instruction to their full intellectual potential, or to the extent that students who do have a sense of understanding can. This gap in who benefits from quality content specific instruction occurs in all content areas.

The *Theory of Cognitive Underpinnings* is controversial in a normative sense—but is it good theory? If you recall the discussion in Chapter 1 about the characteristics of good academic theory, the best theory makes predictions that are substantiated, and it explains "why" things occur. This one theory predicts:

- Why progressive reforms to date to reduce the achievement gap have had such limited success after the third grade;

- The results reported in Chapter 6 around the Math Pathways and Pitfalls project which found that the experimental at-risk students did not make any progress while the advantaged experimental students made progress—from the same intervention; and

- That the common core's good intentions to increase the level of thinking development in reading and math curriculums will fail to reduce the achievement gap—and may, unfortunately, even increase it.

In all these cases, the theory predicts the "why" of the gap—i.e., these outcomes occur because those with a sense of understanding are better able to take advantage of these content-based interventions than students without a developed sense of understanding—despite the latter having equal intellectual potential and ability.

Most importantly, the "why" presented by the theory also provides a remedy for how progressive reforms CAN reduce the gaps.

259

The *Theory of Cognitive Underpinnings* predicts that progressive reforms can be made to be equally effective for both educationally advantaged and disadvantaged students by establishing the intermediary step of first providing the latter with intensive general thinking experiences. Thereafter, they will benefit equally from excellent content instruction and content specific reforms.

Similarly, the success of the **Statway** network led to a new theoretical insight as to why community college students who are smart, struggle so mightily with mathematics. Givvin, Stigler, and Thompson (2011) concluded that the CC students suffered from "Conceptual Atrophy". Stigler, Givvin, and Thompson (2010) define **conceptual atrophy** as "the willingness to bring reason to bear on mathematical problems lies dormant" (p. 15). This dormancy is viewed by the researchers as a result of prior mathematics instruction that failed to connect the intuitive sense that students have about mathematics to mathematical notation and procedures. The students have been conditioned to think of math as the application of rules. As a result, the Statway intervention became a "…reason focused mathematics class in which they [students] are given opportunities to reason, and tools to support their reasoning" (p. 15).

Much of what we think we know from the traditional approach to knowledge generation, academic theory, and personal theories of action—are wrong. This means there are lots of opportunities for skeptical, and creative people dedicated to social justice to develop better interventions and designs that increase equity.

No one had previously attempted to develop an intervention based on general thinking because everyone knew that the research had demonstrated that such an approach is not effective. Fortunately, I did not know that research[90]—or any research on how to teach reading. What I do know is that where we implemented the intervention, Title I students started thinking, verbalizing, and reading.

In addition to developing new theory, the process of trying to develop parameters of effectiveness as an intervention is scaling up, leads to new insights and surprising results. For example, I thought that no intervention would work cross-culture and in such disparate contexts. Fortunately, this turned out to be wrong. We saw the same student reactions in Soldatna Alaska, a small isolated bush village and on the Navajo reservation, as in inner city Detroit.[91]

---

[90] To be honest, it was fortunate that I did not know about the existing research on the superiority of thinking-in-content when it was decided to use a general thinking approach. Would I have gone ahead with developing the HOTS general thinking approach had I known about this research? I do not know. However, this illustrates that sometimes metaphor and personal theories of practice are more insightful than the existing state of research evidence.

[91] When I described the cross-cultural benefits in a proposal to the National Science Foundation, the reviewers accused me of being culturally insensitive. They did not understand that an intervention that worked cross-culture was a good thing—much as a medical treatment that can help with a variety of illnesses—e.g., aspirin—was a good thing.

Beware

If you start and participate in an improvement science project based on the hope that it will lead to theoretical insights, as opposed to trying to develop a solution to a practical problem, *it probably increases the likelihood of failure.* Keep the focus on the pragmatics of trying to solve the identified problem.

On the other hand…

Good News

…if the newly designed intervention results in consistent BIG improvement—it will probably lead to new and important, possibly/probably(?) controversial, theoretical insights.

To be fair, over time some academic theories do indeed become highly specified and should then be used as <u>the</u> basis for new proposed approaches or research efforts. Consider, for example, aeronautics. While the initial breakthrough in flight was driven by metaphor, today it would be folly to try and design the next generation airliner without basing the design on aeronautical theory and formulas given its maturation and high degree of specification. Hopefully we will get to the point in education where we also have more highly specified theories. In the meantime, the less formal methods of improvement science and the alternative paths of scientific discovery will potentially be the key to developing more effective interventions and more highly specified and valid educational theories.

In the meantime, the experimental methods of improvement science offer new opportunities to develop the multi-dimensional types of interventions that are most likely to produce BIG benefits. Such interventions designed by practitioners on the basis of intuition, metaphor, and personal theories of action are often likely to be far more effective than ones based on academic theory or rigorous research on "effective-practices."

Remember

Improvement science enables practitioners and researchers to go beyond simply asking whether any approach—e.g., bilingual education or culturally responsive pedagogy—is effective to efficiently determining the conditions under which any approach may be effective and scale via networked experimentation.

This more global analysis is made possible by moving from the traditional experimental methods that seek to isolate a single factor to the more flexible crowd sourced experimentation options of improvement science. This capability is significant because while each school and district has a variety of needs and problems, there are some fundamental, widespread problems that most experience—e.g., learning declines from (a) summer loss, (b) transition to middle school, and/or (c) transition to high school. These are problems that are crying out for more creative designs and for the sharing of promising ones. Applying networked improvement science approaches to each of these would produce major benefits for education.

Effective improvement science interventions can scale

Good News

While it is difficult to design an intervention that can produce consistent BIG benefits, the experience of HOTS and Statway indicates that it is possible to scale such interventions across very different contexts. This means that it is possible to develop a new generation of interventions and networks that enable education to make substantial progress on key problems at scale across diverse contexts.

Some argue that the notion that it is possible to scale-up interventions across contexts is a myth (Berliner & Glass, 2014). However, the examples of interventions they cite as never having been successfully scaled are invariably ones that never met the criteria for having *practical* or *potential practical benefit*. Perhaps the failure of "best practices" to scale is more a reflection of the process described earlier in this book of the academic community promoting as "best practice" interventions that only met the criterion of *statistical significance* or low *ES* effects—i.e., they never were actually effective so they couldn't scale.

Nor can you *develop scalable interventions in education using gold-standard randomized control trials (RCT) research methods for reasons already discussed in this chapter.*

The ability to scale an intervention is a function of whether:

- It provides a substantially better solution to a problem;

- There is access to funding;

- The implementation parameters are enforced/followed; and

- The approach resonates with practitioners and scholars (at that point in time).

In terms of the latter, policies and beliefs change in education as well as in all other aspects of life. HOTS scaled up very rapidly for 20 years, first with small development and dissemination grants and then as a self-supporting entity. HOTS began to decline around 2005 due to NCLB which caused the field to retrench into the basic skills mode of intervention, and the schoolwide use of Title I reduced interest in targeted, specialized approaches.

Good News

At the same time, the success of HOTS led to a change in the Title I law to require the teaching of "advanced skills" to children born into poverty. This change was the first time federal law recognized that students born into poverty should be challenged at a high level and that they had the capacity to succeed. This change made it legal to use Title I funds to provide interventions that provided the highest quality teaching and learning opportunities to students born into poverty in lieu of remediation.

Interventions can produce multiple BIG benefits

Should schools emphasize basic skills or thinking skills? Should math focus on teaching arithmetic algorithms or problem solving? Should reading emphasize decoding or comprehension—phonics or whole language? Should schools emphasize test scores or developing the whole child?

These "either-or" debates have led to warring camps within the profession and among parents. The success of HOTS has shown that it is possible to design interventions that produce multiple types of outcomes simultaneously. Indeed, an initial design specification was to produce gains in:

- Test scores:
- Higher order thinking: and
- Social emotional development.

This was accomplished.

We also showed that the same intervention that produced BIG gains with the vast majority of Title I students would produce similar benefits for the majority of LD students—and the criteria for identifying the minority of students for which it would NOT be effective and why.

In other words, rather than each side in the "either-or" debates trying to prove why the other is wrong, the reality is that neither side is wrong. Each has strong arguments as to why the educational approach that they favor *can* be beneficial.

Improvement science provides the potential to design interventions that simultaneously produces the type of benefit that each side desires. We can increase test scores and basic skills while also developing problem solving skills. All it takes is better, bolder, and more creative designs, and willingness of those in the warring camps to pool resources to support such designs.

Reforming Research and Development to Support Improvement Science

As previously discussed in Chapter 6, traditional researchers and theorists have focused on single element simplistic interventions that can fit into their rigorous RCT models to try and show causation—but with little success. As a result of this singular focus, researchers do not understand how to think about the design and evaluation of more fully developed, multi-faceted interventions developed by improvement science. Their attitudes and responses fall into two categories:

- Misdirected/unjustified concerns; and
- Outright, even irrational, resistance.

Misdirected/unjustified concerns

The following are a series of perceived methodological and theoretical shortcomings that have been put forth by traditional researchers and theorists—along with a rebuttal.

You do not know how much each component contributes to the overall success of the intervention.

That is true. But, why is disaggregating the effects of each component even a concern? Gavriel Solomon, formerly of Haifa University, would respond to this theoretical excess by pointing out that no one tries to determine how much the string section contributes to the audience's enjoyment of a symphony concert. In both the cases of the symphony and a multi-faceted intervention such as HOTS, the most important theoretical and research issues are NOT how much each part contributed, *but WHY the combination consistently produced the observed benefit.*

Findings establishing the parameters of how much of an activity is needed to produce a desired outcome is trivial information that has no scientific value.

The noted physics theorist, Lisa Randall (2005), would disagree. As previously noted in Chapter 1, she has defined theory as a…

> "definite set of elements and principles with rules and equations for predicting how those elements interact. When I speak about theories … I'll be using the word in that sense; I won't mean "rough speculation", as in the more "colloquial usage" (p. 66).

Determining that it takes an average of a year and a half of 35 minutes a day of Socratic interaction experience in grades 4-8 to develop a sense of understanding in a specific yet wide range of at-risk categories met Dr. Randall's definition of theory. Indeed, positing the interaction of these intervention parameters is in fact a theory in the purest tradition of science—plus it improves practice and helps kids. Conversely, it would appear that much (but not all) of what passes for theory in education falls into the category of "rough speculation."

Beware

Indeed, it is possible that in the absence of master designers involved in developing improvement science networks and detailed implementation parameters through iterative tinkering, we may not make progress in the development of real scientific theories in education and will continue to settle for constantly changing "rough speculations."

It is impossible to know whether an improvement science based intervention and its design has been optimized.

True! I do not know whether the implementation parameters for HOTS have been optimized, or whether it is the best way to develop the full potential of

Title I and LD students in grades 4-8. Hopefully, a better designer will develop an even better intervention. However, optimization is not a realistic goal of any complex intervention—regardless of whether it is education or obstetrics. Gawande (2007) noted that while obstetrics has developed their grab bag of clinical practices that have an excellent track record, they do not pretend to have optimized care or to know what the contribution of each component is. They just know, that in combination their grab bag, with the tried and true parameters of use, reliably saves lives across all the hospitals—and that is good practice and good science.

We can use the same methods that obstetrics did to produce BIG improvements in education—if allowed to. However, the above discussion indicates that traditional researchers and theoreticians continue to ask the wrong questions and are geared to pushing applied knowledge and methodology in a direction that is divorced from the needs of leaders to improve schools and increase equity. They are doing this in the name of science—but it is a very narrow view of science.

Remember

As discussed in Chapter 1, the fundamental process of science is to use systematic observations to make accurate predictions. When it is found that a grab bag of clinical practices save baby's lives, or that a grab bag of curricular and teaching materials and strategies consistently produce BIG benefits, such accurate predictions represent "real" applied science at its best.

Irrational resistance to the benefits of improvement science

Current conceptions of quantitative methodology, as well as criteria used by funding agencies in education, continue to be universally based on education's traditional model or science in the mistaken belief that it is the only way that true science can and must be conducted. The following personal experience indicates how hard it will be to change minds.

I met with a highly respected researcher at a top research college of education to try and convince him to adopt this textbook for his quantitative methods course. He was concerned that the recommendations were not sufficiently methodologically rigorous. I shared with him the above example from obstetrics about the importance of alternative pathways of conducting science. His expression suddenly changed, and softened. He recounted how his newborn daughter had recently undergone a life-threatening illness, and how the obstetrician had saved her. He then shared that the methods the physician used seemed to be a "blend of folk lore techniques." In other words, he did not view the techniques used to save his daughter as being real science.

The fact is that any other newborn with the same problems would have been treated similarly by other physicians with the same positive outcome. That the knowledge solved a major illness with a high level of predictability was secondary to him. It was NOT real science because it was not generated via RCT.

If he could not be convinced of the importance of these alternative pathways for solving problems of practice despite having benefitted from their power, then nothing will. To him and many others the methodology is the message—not the result and the predictive power of the research.

Moving forward—Recognizing improvement science as "real" and "better" applied science

My experience is that educational theorists tend NOT to consider theories produced from a successful improvement science intervention as "real" theories, and educational psychologists tend not to recognize the methodologies of improvement science as "real" science. Findings from such research tend to be ignored. However, such attitudes are shortsighted and represent a limited conception of the role and benefits of theory and science which limit the production of new knowledge and theories that can actually improve education and increase equity.

Indeed, suppose against all odds you actually succeed in using improvement science methods to develop an intervention in which a series of pilot studies demonstrate consistent BIG gains...what then? Alas, such research will not get published in any of the top education research journals—regardless of how good the results are.

Research funding suffers from the same delimited criteria. My applications to get funding to conduct a formal experiment of HOTS after large scale success were always denied on the basis *that the findings from the program could not possibly be valid.*

Accepting improvement science and its methods as "real" science with unique capabilities to develop interventions that can improve schools and increase equity will require non-traditional funding and publishing criteria.

Update research publishing and R&D funding criteria

When Einstein used metaphor as a basis for developing his theory of relativity, science recognized the importance of testing the results of thought experiments. It is time for education to take seriously the work and resultant theories of interventions designed via alternative pathways of scientific discovery when it leads to surprisingly successful results.

If education is going to move forward and overcome the resistance to what is a proven quantitative methodology, a number of things must happen.

- Top education journals need to further expand their current criteria to include quantitative research that does not rely on theoretical justification or advanced statistics to try and establish *causation* or complex relationships—but that can show large, replicated gains. In an applied field such as education, producing consistent BIG improvement is an important discovery worthy of publication in the best research journals.

- R & D funding needs to be available for individuals to try new ideas based on their newness—not on the basis of experimental evidence or of theoretical justification. The key is to demonstrate that it will be trying an approach to solving a problem of practice that has not been previously attempted.

Enacting such change requires establishing new types of standards to determine:

- How do you figure out whose designs have the greatest potential and should therefore be supported?

- If design is an artistic, intuitive, or "embodied conjectures" process, how do you determine whose artistic intuitions or conjectures should be supported? Why not yours?

Some will argue that publishing improvement science results and funding "conjectures" will open the door to fraud and the misdirection of practice. Clearly the potential for such misdirection exists. However, we can learn from other disciplines that have used improvement science effectively to improve practice. In addition, as was pointed out throughout Chapters 4-7, the existing rigorous traditional standards that were the hallmark of efforts to eliminate bias in quantitative evidence have often been used as tools to misdirect practice across the disciplines and in education.

Create a federal Center for Networked Improvement

Interventions improve practice at scale when a profession has an infrastructure to quickly network practices that demonstrate clear benefits. While it is possible for leaders to network their successes through contacts within professional associations, they are not in a position to sustain such networking beyond their own schools. Both HOTS and Statway had external individuals who organized and maintained a network capability to expand the use of the interventions. However, there are probably other highly effective interventions that were developed locally that were not networked or even sustained locally.

Therefore, there is a need for some national capability to provide networking support for promising improvement science interventions.

Beware	The networking of promising improvement science interventions should NOT be handled by the What Works Clearinghouse whose recommendations have been critiqued in Chapters 5-7. Rather, some new federal entity needs to be developed to network promising interventions—with a new form of staffing.

A federal initiative to support the networking of promising improvement science should be staffed by individuals within education and other disciplines who are expert in improvement science and who have a track record of developing successful innovations. There should also be representation from leaders to provide the perspective as to whether the reported benefits have real-world value.

Incorporate the methods of improvement science in graduate leadership programs

Masters and EdD programs should teach the methods of improvement science, and encourage/allow students to conduct culminating projects that involve improvement science.

Statistics courses should be converted into "quantitative methods" courses in which improvement science methods are taught along with traditional statistical analysis. The common statistical denominator across both research traditions is the power trio of statistics (see Chapter 4) which is critical to both. In addition, Pogrow (2021) provides suggestions for conducting improvement science EdD dissertations.

Implications of Improvement Science for Leadership Practice

Educational leaders can create grassroots improvement science interventions and networks on their own to improve outcomes and increase equity in their schools. All good educators are tinkerers who constantly redesign approaches when faced with problems. Over the years I have met many educators who had indeed designed a novel and wonderful approach to solving a problem of practice. This is an important source of innovation and a credit to our profession.

When faced with a seemingly intractable problem, and there is no research evidence that has *practical benefit* on how to solve it, leaders should think of themselves as designers. They should commit to organizing and participating in the design and implementation of a very different approach. The best guide for implementing an improvement science project is to emulate the key common design, implementation, and evaluation methods used by both Statway and HOTS.

Similarities between the design of Statway and HOTS

The 13 biggest similarities between the design processes for these two programs were:

1. Both improvement science efforts were focused on trying to solve a specific major problem of practice;

2. The initial design approaches were NOT driven by academic theory.[92] They were driven by metaphor, vision, instinct, and pragmatics based on the beliefs

---

[92] While in public presentations Carnegie officials claim that the design was based on theory, that was not what my research found. In follow-up conversations it turned out that they relied on what they called "normative" theories—i.e., expressions of values. Examples included the belief that it was important to increase the success rate of under-represented students. However, while I share the values that fueled the Statway project, most scholars do NOT consider normative theories/ideals to be academic theory (see Chapter 1's discussion of theory).

that (a) there was no point in trying to improve the existing failed approach, and (b) it was important to develop a very different approach if there was to be a "short-circuiting of the major problems that students were experiencing;"

3.   While both projects understood the scope and importance of the problem, **both projects did NOT really understand "why" the students were having so much trouble learning what they were being expected to learn and/or why the existing supports were ineffective.**

4.   Finding a way to increase student engagement by (a) pointing out to students how the approach was different, (b) presenting the curriculum as an advanced form of learning that they could master, (c) having them experience success early on in the intervention so as to build up their confidence, and (d) having them experience success in their other coursework;

5.   Both curriculums emphasized making explicit linkages across ideas and problem-solving contexts;

6.   All the aspects of the intervention—i.e., curriculum and training, had very clear and detailed specifications;

7.   There was extensive development and iterative improvement of all aspects of the intervention as the scale increased;

8.   There was extensive reliance on basic traditional metrics to constantly measure the degree of improvement that was occurring and extensive field-based observation to identify implementation problems;[93]

9.   The designers proceeded despite not having any idea as to whether the interventions would actually work. Once the initial design approach was established the philosophy was "let's try it out and see if it works";

10. There were BIG improvements right from the very beginning, and as the projects scaled-up new adaptations became necessary and possible;

11. It was only after the design was in operation and successful that research on student learning was brought to bear on solving problems or for enhancing the effects of the intervention;[94]

12. Both combined highly creative design elements as well as attention to detail, and a willingness to adapt on the fly;

---

[93] In the case of HOTS, the traditional metric was end-of-year test scores which Title I programs are required to report. The fact that HOTS students were doing much better on such a traditional measure means that it is possible to create a highly progressive environment that will consistently produce higher test scores while also simultaneously producing better outcomes that progressives care about such as emotional-social development.

[94] Some of the learning research/theory that was incorporated into the staff development/instructional techniques were (a) the importance of productive struggle, (b) explicit connection, and (c) deliberate practice.

13. Once it became clear that the designs were in fact producing BIG improvement across sites, there was an effort to understand why it was working—which led to new knowledge and theory about what the problem was in the first place.

In terms of item #10, it is important to see very promising results in outcomes right from the very beginning since improvement science networks cannot go through 5,127 attempts to get an approach right as Dyson did. Schools are not a vacuum cleaner—bagless or otherwise. I suspect that if the initial pilots do not produce major improvements there will not be major benefits down the road regardless of how many design iterations occur.

Practical Tip

If you do not see strong benefits right from the beginning it probably means that you are simply using the wrong metaphors/intuitions or tackling too general a problem.

While school leaders are not interested in scaling their interventions on a national scale, these similarities are instructive for thinking about how leaders can initiate and lead an improvement science project in their schools.

Initiating and leading an improvement science design in your schools

The most important steps in initiating an improvement science design in your schools are to:

1) Identify a specific problem along with specific metrics as to how you will measure improvement;
2) Create a design team;
3) Develop a design that:

   ➤ changes the approach you are currently using to try and solve the problem—i.e., simply doing more of the same is unlikely to solve the problem; and

   ➤ uses intuition/metaphor to develop a completely original, creative approach.

4) Create feedback loops between implementers and the design team;
5) Start small with 1-2 classes or 1-2 schools; and
6) Evaluate the initial pilot, and if there is dramatic improvement scale the intervention to more classrooms/schools and make needed adaptations.
7) If you do not see noticeable improvements in the first year or two go back to Step 3.

The role of the collaborative "design team" is to brainstorm possible interventions with everyone contributing and agreeing to move forward with the chosen design even though no one is sure what will happen. If academicians are part of the team it is important that they NOT serve as "the" expert bringing the gift of knowledge since there is no reliable existing evidence. Rather, they, along with everyone else, need to commit to problem solving and learning together.

Establishing an improvement science reform is different than the typical leadership practice of implementing a new approach in an organization. Typically the leader "sells" the idea to others and is a/the key persuader to adopt the new approach. To persuade others the leader needs to exude confidence that it will work. In the case of implementing the result of an intuitive improvement science designed intervention, the leader has to signal that it is okay to not be sure whether it will work, and that everyone is in it together to do their best to make it work without any finger pointing.

The leader needs to create a culture of trust and shared adventure and risk taking among the design team members in the hope that it will benefit their students and staff—with no one being blamed if this initial try at a solution does not work.

Anyone who has implemented an improvement science approach went into it with no idea as to whether it would work. I remember being shocked when the first set of data became available and it showed that HOTS students were dramatically outperforming the comparison Title I students—and then a feeling of overwhelming relief—then joy.

There is no reason why you and your design team cannot be the ones who invent a new highly effective intervention to solve a problem of practice.

The biggest significance of *improvement science* is a shift from the predominantly "downhill" flow of innovation from academicians and vendors to practitioners—to a more equal partnership for conceptualizing, designing, testing, and improving interventions. The shifts in the role of leaders under the traditional perspective and that of improvement science are described in Table 8.1 below:

Table 8.1
Key Differences Between the Traditional Approach to Leadership Decision-Making and Improvement Science

	Traditional Approach	**Improvement Science**
Who designs the intervention	Vendors, Academicians, policy makers	Practitioners (with or without Academicians),
Role of academician	Expert, bearer of the key knowledge the design will be built around, interested in implications for theory	Collaborator in a democratic process of idea generation, also hands-on participation in the feedback and design of new iterations

Design/Decision perspective	We know what works based on existing research.	We don't know what works, we need a creative, intuitive new approach that we should try to develop ourselves and test.
	Let's buy program X from vendor Y.	
Leadership perspective	This proposed new approach will work because…	This has not been tried before and we have no idea whether it will work, but it seems worth trying.
No measurable change in first year after initiating the intervention	Claim that there are non-measurable benefits	Cut your losses and move onto trying something else
BIG measured benefit	Rarely occurs	Scale its use

Key steps in designing the intervention

To the extent that problems persist despite decades of research means that there is a need and opportunity to discover better forms of interventions, and improvement science provides leaders with a methodology in which they can play a major role in designing such approaches.

Designing a new intervention for solving a problem of practice is an 8 step process. While the focus of the discussion is on instructional design, it will generally apply to other types of interventions as well.

Step 1: Identify a specific problem and try to identify the key structural impediments to improvement

Step 2: Design the intervention

The best design strategy is to invent something entirely new—either new for the district, or ideally, something that no one to your knowledge has tried before.

A creative example I came across several years ago was a novel solution to the falloff that occurs for many students trying to adjust to the increased academic demands and the new environment when moving from middle school to the freshman year of high school. The district decided to establish a camp for incoming freshmen who were deemed at-risk that started two weeks before the official opening of school. Students had some fun, received tutoring, orientation to the school, and were assigned mentors. The superintendent claimed BIG gains in the performance of the freshmen.

(The next chapter will have another example of a novel design to solve a problem—increasing the percentage of seniors attending 4 year colleges.)

One strategy for developing a creative approach is to first examine the reasons/excuses for why the problem exists. For example, it is easy to blame the home, or the failure of earlier schooling, lack of motivation, etc. If you can pinpoint what the specific blockage is you can then turn the blame into an innovative design approach.

A secondary design strategy is to explore providing a more intensive service if the initial approach has shown promise. However, this strategy has been largely ineffective for Title I students because remediation is the wrong approach. So simply providing more of the same has not been effective after the third grade—nor can it be!

Step 3: Identify the key strategy for engaging students (or others)?

How are you going to convince students that this is something different and beneficial for them that will give them a better chance to succeed, or that it will be more meaningful for them? *To be successful, a strategy to engage students needs to tap into how they view the world and their place in it—as opposed to how adults think about the world.*

At the same time, it is not enough to do something simply because students are interested in it. It has to be tied to solving a problem of practice. For example, it is not enough to teach about dinosaurs simply because students are interested in them. But you can design an approach to teach about dinosaurs that increases reading skills, and that links to the specific vocabulary building requirements of the existing curriculum.

Step 4: List the expected (ideally) multiple benefits.

Step 5: Decide how each expected benefit will be measured quantitatively.

There are a wide range of outcomes that can be measured besides test scores. You can measure a wide variety changes in behaviors and social participation by a variety of observational techniques and questionnaires, and you can also incorporate mixed methods research. Examples of a variety of alternative measures were provided in the earlier part of this chapter, and a social justice outcome will be described in the next chapter.

Step 6: Create the needed supporting materials for training curriculum, policies, etc.

While having an original, creative, insightful design idea is necessary, it is not sufficient. There need to be clear, detailed supporting materials.

Step 7: Logistics of implementation.

This involves assigning responsibility for the many implementation tasks, such as staff development, curriculum, reallocation of funds to support the intervention, etc.

Step 8: Determine how the quality of implementation will be monitored quantitatively (and qualitatively) and how problems and needed modifications will be communicated quickly?

Summary: The Value of Improvement Science

Improvement science provides a powerful alternative scientific experimental methodology for developing better approaches for solving problems where traditional research has not yet produced authentic evidence. Indeed, it is probably a superior experimental research methodology than RCT for solving ongoing problems of practice in education given the complex, intertwined, constantly shifting dynamics in schools. The many substantial problems of practice that remain in education portend a tremendous need and potential for applying improvement science methods.

A reliance on the use of RCT experimental methods to identify effective practices is likely to continue to NOT produce useful findings (see Chapter 6) because it reflects a misunderstanding of the nature of effective interventions. An effective intervention is not a single idea, theory, or ideal—but a combination of elements, each of which is critical and inseparable from the mix. On the other hand, the flexibility of improvement science, with its eclectic mix of creative insight and tinkering, makes it possible to engage systematic and detailed crafting and engineering of supporting tools *in real time during the course of the experiment*.

In addition, the flexibility of improvement science enables us to move beyond asking the traditional question as to whether an idea, ideal, or general approach—e.g., constructivism or culturally relevant pedagogy—is effective. Instead we can ask: Under what conditions do they become effective? We can then try to answer this question via crowd-sourced experimentation and iterative tinkering.

The experiences of Statway and HOTS and their resultant success indicate that it is possible to apply improvement science in education in ways that produce BIG benefits that scale across diverse contexts, and that can provide multiple benefits simultaneously. We can indeed solve problems of practice. However, harnessing the potential of improvement science requires rethinking some of the fundamental reflexes that have dominated applied educational research for decades. These include:

- Stop focusing on causation and switch to implicit causation;

- Expect interventions to show large actual end results in order to be considered "effective" or "evidence-based";

- Stop insisting that interventions be initially based on academic theory; and

- Respect the alternative scientific discovery methods of accident, metaphor, and iterative tinkering as important contributors to scientific knowledge and respect the educational theories that result from such endeavors when they produce BIG benefits; and

- Recognize the critical importance of research focused on establishing parameters of effectiveness. That is as important for educational interventions as it is for determining the appropriate dosages and schedule for administering Covid vaccines.

The bottom line for leaders is that since improvement science can produce BIG benefits they should NOT settle for the tiny, unreliable benefits that traditional research often uses to make claims of evidence-based practices. In addition, improvement science's less formal and technical scientific methodology means that any leader can engage in it without needing high levels of technical expertise. Any leader can initiate a process to design new interventions, and participate in generating original evidence (and theory). The key is for leaders to establish a design team tasked with developing an original design for solving a problem, and which then monitors implementation and adapts in real time as problems and unanticipated opportunities arise.

For leadership students, action research projects provide an opportunity for designing and/or implementing and/or evaluating a novel approach to trying to solve a problem of practice. Ideally they would have access to learning the principles of improvement science, and even a course on the design of new approaches.

Leaders and academicians should recognize that for the foreseeable future, improvement science represents the most promising approach to producing major breakthroughs in improving schools and increasing equity—and for generating new knowledge on how to do that. Leaders can, either individually or in groups engage in grassroots improvement science projects and network the practices and knowledge through their professional associations.

Chapter 9

Analyzing Your School's Data for Continuous Improvement and Program Evaluation

The fundamental focus of this textbook to date has been on the use of research evidence to improve practice. Chapters 4-7 focused on analyzing published research evidence in the search for an evidence-based practice that will lead to improvements and increases in equity, while Chapter 8 focused on designing new approaches on your own to try and solve enduring problems of practice. However, no improvement is possible without a dynamic organizational capability to generate, manage, and share quantitative data across one's organization. Such a capability is essential for both knowing where improvement is needed, and for monitoring whether it is occurring. The most successful organizations monitor the process of improvement continuously—which in turn requires an even more dynamic data management capability.

Ultimately, The most widely used quantitative evidence that leaders base their improvement decision on are data generated by, and maintained within, their own organization. This chapter discusses how to make decisions about how to generate and systemically apply quantitative data to support an organizational culture of evidence-based continuous improvement.

♔ Key Takeaways ♔

- Internal data are critical for supporting an organizational culture of continuous improvement. While continuous improvement is akin to the tinkering process in improvement science discussed in the prior chapter, it is a more general process.

- Establishing a process of continuous improvement to successfully improve practice at your schools depends primarily on (a) setting specific improvement goals, (b) data systems that share data and produce results in a timely and highly-focused-easy-to-understand fashion, and (c) creating a culture of reflecting about the use of data to make key decisions on how to improve.

- Applying results from modern data systems to improve school performance does not depend on sophisticated statistical analyses as much as it does on the design of key metrics and the creative reflection on the implications of key results for the collaborative design of a strategy for solving an emerging problem, and/or monitoring the progress and outcomes of an intervention.

- While program evaluation is important for determining the current status of the school and/or determining the effectiveness of a new approach, modern data systems need to go beyond just providing data to monitor the performance of the organization. They need to have the capability to provide proactive analytics that can be used as the basis of initiatory action to increase social justice.

- The best way to organize data systems to provide the greatest efficiency and to maximize the ability to quickly organize and retrieve data in easy to digest visual forms, is to have administrative applications that use a common database/data warehouse, and then link data visualization software to that database/data warehouse.

- Evaluating the improvement of your schools involves both relative growth measure and actual end result performance. In other words, it is important to share with your community and internally how much improvement has occurred. At the same time, it is still important to anchor presentations of improvement with data on the current level of actual performance as compared to goals and prior benchmarks.

- Effective use of internal data to support continuous improvement requires an organizational data infrastructure that goes beyond technical issues to include the political and social arrangements needed to support the sharing of data and related evidence-based interactions among individuals and data teams across the organization.

- The most important use of data is for leaders and teachers to be able to answer the questions of (a) how students, teachers, and schools are doing, (b) which students have started to slip, (c) which students should we be trying to provide additional opportunity, and (d) are we improving and if so in what ways—and where do we still need to improve?

- The key leadership skill for such evidence-based decision making is NOT the ability to conduct sophisticated statistical analyses. Rather, the key skill is the ability of leaders to establish a mindset that permeates an organization of basing decisions on the basis of data and a proactive, reflective mindset about the use of data to promote continuous improvement and social justice.

- In order to support a mindset of shared, reflective, proactive data use—the organization needs to have a data system capable of providing real-time data in highly flexible and visual manner.

Introduction

The most useful quantitative evidence is often the data you generate and store in your organization. This chapter is about the leadership skills needed to fully take advantage of the increasing amounts of such data to support the making of better decisions on how to improve and increase equity. These skills range from the design of a data management system, conceptualizing what data are in fact needed to monitor organizational performance and evaluate effectiveness of interventions, and creating a culture of sharing data and reflecting about the implications of the data.

Key Data Management Skills

Data use can be differentiated on the basis of whether the organization is a passive receptor of data that reports current performance, or whether it uses initiatory proactive analytics to continually monitor and reflect about what is going on in their school(s). In the passive receptor model, the schools respond to external demands for data by the state and federal governments, and rely on the reports that they receive back to assess their performance and progress. The focus of data use in the passive model tends to be on accountability. On the other hand, the initiatory, proactive uses of date focus on internally motivated uses of data to identify improvement needs and opportunities on an ongoing basis—with some predictive capabilities.

Given that, external mandates to provide and analyze data as the primary accountability tools to assess the quality of teachers, schools, and/or districts is fraught with a wide variety of moral, political, and technical issues, this chapter will NOT discuss the use of data for formal accountability purposes. Rather, this chapter will focus on how leaders can help schools/districts become initiatory proactive users of quantitative data from a variety of sources to:

- Address student learning problems and needs at the individual student and school levels;

- Expand learning opportunities; and

- Increase social justice.

Key roles for leaders are to:

- Develop a state-of-the-art system to provide the needed quantitative data and metrics in a timely manner; and

- Develop a culture of continuous improvement and stimulate everyone to engage in ongoing reflective data analysis as a key basis for making decisions about how to improve and increase equity.

The Evolution of Data Use in Schools

Quantitative data have traditionally been viewed as a valuable tool for teachers and leaders to improve instruction. Good teachers have always developed their own assessments based on their school's curriculum to provide information as to whether or how they should change their instruction. While teachers have always created their own tests to collect data on their students' performance, the tests used in schools are increasingly determined by external mandates from the state and federal governments. These mandates also determine what data will be collected, and what measures will be applied to that data to determine student, teacher, and school success.

Data use in schools and districts is increasingly driven by Federal and state assessment and accountability laws such as the former *No Child Left Behind* (NCLB) law of 2002, and the *Every Student Succeeds Act* (ESSA) of 2015.

External mandates are a relatively recent phenomenon. Until 1965 the primary data that schools/districts reported to the state were those that determined their funding such as (a) daily attendance, and (b) how many students were eligible for free lunch. A notable exception of a state mandating an end-of-year, or end-of-content, test was the New York State Regents exams which started in 1864.[95] The Regents exams are administered statewide to determine students' mastery of content in a wide variety of high school courses.

The dramatic expansion of federal monies to public schools with the initial passage of the Elementary and Secondary School Act in 1965 also dramatically expanded federal requirements for the amount of data schools/districts had to collect and report to the state and federal governments. However, much of that data remained essentially demographic reports of how many students were in each special category, such as Title I or special education, along with fiscal reports to show that the monies in each category were being spent for their intended purposes.

However, Congress began to be concerned as to the effects of this funding on student performance. The first national test, the National Assessment of Educational Progress (NAEP), was instituted in 1969. NAEP is administered to a sample of students in each state to measure their knowledge in a variety of content areas. A periodic NAEP report card is issued to compare student performance in different states. (A more detailed discussion of NAEP data is contained in Chapter 4.)

Congress then went further and mandated that evaluations be conducted on the effects of the major programs it was funding for helping key student subgroups—most notably Title I and special education students. Title I is the largest federal initiative and it is designed to provide supplementary help to disadvantaged students and thereby reduce the achievement gaps. These evaluations showed that compensatory programs such as

---

[95] An *end-of-year* tests is a test of grade-level mastery to that point in a general content area, most commonly in reading and math, while an *end-of-content* test is given at the end of a specific course—e.g., Algebra, American History, etc. to determine mastery of that content.

Title I were providing little or no academic benefit for the students they were serving. In addition, business interests began to complain about the poor skill levels of job applicants with high school diplomas. Others complained that today's students know less than previous generations about history and other content areas. Parents considering moving to a new community want data on the quality of its schools. Researchers wanted ways to examine the relationship between funding and school performance.

For all these reasons Congress enacted the No Child Left Behind Law (NCLB). NCLB mandated that starting in 2002 each state develop learning standards and end-of-year assessments in reading and math in grades 3-8, and once in high school. The latter was to assure that those who graduated had sufficient skills for careers or college. States were also directed to establish a cutoff score on each test such that those who scored above that level were deemed to be proficient. States were also mandated to establish a measure of Annual Yearly Progress (AYP) for schools. AYP was a specified growth trajectory wherein ALL students and subgroups of students would be proficient by 2014. There were strong accountability provisions with major penalties for those working in schools that repeatedly failed to make annual AYP progress.

The limited effectiveness of external mandates

Of course, there was NO WAY that schools were going to get ALL students to be proficient under any reasonable definition of proficiency. (*Proficiency* is usually defined as grade level performance.) It was also fallacious to assume that getting ALL students to be proficient could be achieved by simply imposing severe penalties for failure to meet AYP goals. This is equivalent to threatening to close all hospitals in 12 years that do not have a 100% cure rate for all cancer patients.

States began to develop standards and end-of-year assessments, along with data systems to report the results to the federal government and the public. Districts began to implement lists of detailed learning objectives along with interim or formative assessments linked to these objectives to better prepare their students for the end-of-year state tests. Companies sprang up to provide lists of objectives and diagnostic interim assessments.

At first it appeared that NCLB was working. Many states started reporting large increases in student performance in reading and math. Articles and books appeared highlighting turnaround schools and districts with rapidly rising scores in reading and math on their state's end-of-year test.

However, in many states gains on state test scores in reading and math were not reflected on NAEP. Many states reporting large gains in their test over time had stable NAEP scores, with large and widening gaps between their state test and their NAEP results (Fuller, Gesicki, Kang, and Wright, 2006). In other words, a wide gap between results on a state's test and their NAEP scores indicated a weak state test and/or the use of a low cut score in that state for rating students as being proficient.

There were clearly wide differences between states in the standards they had set. Most of the case studies of effective schools I examined at the time occurred in states with the simplest of tests. In addition, in the inexorable push towards staying on track to achieve each year's rising AYP performance goal, some states began to increase performance by lowering their cut score definition of proficient—i.e., students had to get fewer answers correct to be scored as proficient. It also became clear that in many states students who had been deemed to be proficient on the high school state test were not college ready and did not even have minimal basic skills. For example, Schemo and Ford (2003) found that passing the 10th grade Texas state test (TAAS) was the equivalent to scoring at the *5th percentile* (for real) on the Stanford standardized test. In addition, while Texas was proud that the achievement gap had declined on its state test, there was no such reduction on the Stanford test.

Given the widespread differences between state standards, and ongoing findings of U.S. students doing poorly on international assessments, political pressure built up to develop a uniform set of standards and tests for all states. This led to the development of the Common Core, a set of college- and career-ready standards for kindergarten through 12th grade in language arts/literacy and mathematics. Most states voluntarily committed to adopting the standards. The Common Core standards reduced the breadth of curriculum coverage typical in the NCLB era, and emphasized instead the depth of learning, and problem solving skills. For example, the math standards require not just solving routine problems but also demonstrating reasoning and sense-making.

States that adopted the Common Core standards had to transition from their prior end of year assessments to new ones based on the Common Core.[96] Time will tell how many states remain committed to the Common Core and the related tests, as well as whether the test providers will maintain rigorous cut score levels or lower them to boost sales—thereby defeating the purpose of the Common Core initiative.

Disadvantages of external mandates

External mandates always create unintended consequences—particularly if there are high-stakes accountability provisions with penalties for failing to meet the requirements. These unintended consequences can create perverse, counter-productive incentives. For example:

- When Congress mandated the medical reform of having patients rate hospital care as a component of determining how much hospitals would be reimbursed for services, physicians started to over-prescribe opioids lest their patients complain of inadequate pain treatment (Lembke, 2016).

- Measuring school success in terms of the percentage of students above a cut score provided an incentive for schools to use data to determine which students were on the bubble, i.e., closest to the cut score and then focus all resources on getting them over the hump while ignoring others further behind and needier.

---

[96] As this is being written there are two tests aligned to the Common Core standards: Smarter Balanced and the Partnership for Assessment of Readiness for College and Career, or PARCC. A number of companies also provide interim assessments aligned to the Common Core standards.

There are also cases of schools encouraging their low-performing students to take the day off on test day.

- If graduation rates are a key measure of success, there is an incentive for states to eliminate from the calculation those who drop out in the 9th grade, or count as a graduate someone who dropped out if he/she subsequently got a GED elsewhere. (The former also provides an incentive to NOT readmit students who dropped out in the 9th grade as those higher risk students would then count on that school's graduation rate calculations.)

One major dysfunctional consequence of the externally imposed accountability systems dramatically increased the amount of testing in the school year. A study by the Council of the Great City Schools (Hart, et al., 2015) found that students in urban districts were required to take an average of 112.3 required tests between pre-K and grade 12. (The actual number of tests is much higher if you also include optional tests, diagnostic tests for students with disabilities or English learners, school-developed or required tests, and teacher developed tests.) The average student typically took about eight standardized tests per year, e.g., two NCLB tests and three interim exams in two subjects per year. This study also found (a) no correlation between the amount of mandated testing time and NAEP scores, (b) a lot of redundancy in the testing, and (c) a lack of alignment between much of the testing and required state standards.

Clearly, this much testing is counter-productive. It puts students and educators under tremendous unjustifiable stress. It also produces more data than schools and teachers can use in a productive and timely manner to help students, and it takes too much time away from instruction.[97]

High-stakes testing also changes the nature of instruction. It narrows and homogenizes the curriculum and encourages a "teach to the test" mentality. This was particularly problematic under NCLB where state standards and tests focused primarily on basic skills as opposed to higher-order thinking and problem solving. As a result, teachers had to spend ever-increasing amounts of time drilling students on the basic skills that were being tested. This narrowing of the curriculum, combined with the unrealistic AYP improvement goals, and the threats of school closure and job losses for failure to meet those goals on the end-of-year exams for ALL subgroups was not sustainable.[98]

---

[97] The Hart (2015) study found that administering mandated eighth-grade tests took approximately 4.22 days or 2.34 percent of school time. (This does not include test preparation time, or optional tests or testing for special education purposes.)

[98] The narrowing effect of high-stakes testing had a dramatic and devastating impact on my own Higher Order Thinking Skills (HOTS) program for Title I students. The HOTS program got started in the earlier accountability period of the early 1980's. It thrived until the advent of NCLB type accountability. In the earlier periods it was easy to get school leaders concerned about the performance of their Title I program to implement the alternative thinking development approach of HOTS as a substitute for the traditional supplemental drill and kill approach. The key was that during the earlier accountability movement states could set their own progress goals and there were no major penalties if schools did not meet those goals. However, under NCLB repeated failure to meet AYP goals could result in school closures and the loss of jobs. Given the fear produced by this threat, schools' willingness to adopt any alternative non-basic skills direct instruction approach, including HOTS, evaporated despite decades of research on its benefits. Willingness to use a non-traditional approach or to experiment seemed

The "solution" to the problems of NCLB was the Common Core national initiative. A key goal of the Common Core standards was to emphasize thinking and problem-solving. The Common Core maintained a system of external data reporting mandates, but ones that provided more flexibility to schools.

However, the Common Core has fallen prey to some of the same problems that NCLB did including (a) the timeliness by which schools and teachers receive the data, (b) the sheer volume of data, (c) a lack of pre-service training in how to interpret data for both teachers and leaders, and (d) a lack of validated ways to improve some key forms of learning and learning objectives. In addition, despite the claims that the standards were evidence-based, it was previously noted in Chapter 1 of this textbook that none of the references cited by the developers in support of the standards were empirical studies. This raises questions about the validity or viability of the standards and resultant tests that schools were held accountable for.

Beware

In addition, the *theory of cognitive underpinnings* (Chapter 8) predicts that a sole emphasis on content-based problem solving will disadvantage students born into poverty and will *increase* achievement gaps and inequality after the third grade—unless they are provided with intensive support to develop and automate their general thinking processes.

Benefits of external mandates for data-based school improvement

Despite all the problems noted above, there have been some benefits from decades of external mandates and statewide tests. More is known about the performance of schools and what forms of learning most students struggle to master. There has been a change in political mindset from not revealing the performance of schools and districts to an acceptance that such data should be made public. Furthermore, there is growing acceptance of the importance of revealing how different subgroups of students are performing, and what the achievement gaps are—and whether progress is being made in reducing them. In addition, Rangel, Monroy, and Bell (2016) found that teachers have grown accustomed to reviewing the results of end-of-year test results.

In order to support implementation of NCLB, the federal government supported the improvement of state data systems. It spent close to $500 million in a 5-year period (NGA, 2012). As a result the data tracking and reporting capabilities of states have improved. States are now able to make a wide variety of data available to schools, researchers, and the public at large on the actual and relative performance of schools and districts. Many states are now able to track students who move from one district to another within the state, and are also able to report comparisons of schools' performance relative to their demographics. The latter indicates how a given school's and district's performance compares to others in the state with similar levels of poverty

---

to disappear from leadership decision-making. This is not a criticism of school leaders as much as it is a criticism of the unfair and counter-productive accountability situation that schools and leaders found themselves in.

and other key demographics. States are also breaking out results for special subgroups, such as special education students, Latino students, etc.

In addition, as it became increasingly apparent that it was impossible for schools to continue to improve at the accelerating rate that AYP required, states began to demand that they be allowed to use different, more realistic growth models. States and schools wanted to be rewarded for achieving demonstrable growth instead of being penalized if they did not reach the growth targets demanded by AYP. As a result, a variety of growth models were developed and implemented. Castellano and Ho (2013) identified seven fundamental types of growth models that either measure actual growth, or whether expected rates of growth based on some historical pattern are exceeded.

However, the latter tend to be complex mathematical models built on assumptions with built-in statistical error that can over-estimate growth and under-estimate the achievement gap. The problems with calculating expected rates of growth are somewhat similar to those of using hypothetical extrapolations to project the amount of extra learning from an *effect size* (see Chapter 6).

The Federal *Every Student Succeeds Act (ESSA)* of 2015 did away with the AYP measure of growth and the imposition of sanctions for failure to meet growth goals. States are now free to set their own growth measures/achievement targets, standards, and penalties. So while ESSA gave states flexibility to decide how to measure student performance, external federal mandates still require that states collect and report results for subgroups and identify their low-performing schools.

The Relationship Between District Data Systems and Data Use

As the number of reports required by external government agencies started to dramatically increase after 1965, districts began to establish increasingly complex data systems. District data systems consist of:

- Software applications for basic functions such as attendance, grading, and related data;
- Technology for storing, and communicating data; and
- General software for retrieving and reporting data.

The fundamental unit of data is a data element, such as "student name". The collection of data elements is usually referred to as a *database* or a *data warehouse*.

Of course, the existence of detailed data from external and internal sources about one's schools does not mean that it will necessarily be used—or that it will have any impact on improving student performance or increasing social justice.

How teachers use data

Teachers typically use data to (a) change student groupings, (b) determine which students need extra help, (c) what topics need to be retaught, and (d) refer students to needed services. In addition, Rangel, Monroy, and Bell (2016) found that high school teachers' use of data did not vary by subject area. Science teachers used the same basic forms of assessment as everyone else. Aside from such basic uses, Datnow and Hubbard's (2015) review of the literature concluded that little is known about how teachers actually use data to improve instruction, and what impacts these practices have on student performance.

Researchers lament that there is no evidence that teachers use data to re-examine their basic approach to instruction and to change their strategies. Marsh, Bertrand, and Huguet (2015) concluded that the use of coaches within professional learning communities could lead to changes in practices based on data. However, this was based on the perceptions of those interviewed, and no effort was made to determine whether the perceived changes actually occurred or what actual effect the changes had on students' learning.

Nor is there real evidence on how teachers should actually change instruction based on data results. Hamilton, et al. (2009) concluded that research does not provide clear evidence on how to use data to make instructional decisions that improve student achievement.

At the same time, we can surmise the conditions under which leadership can enhance or inhibit the systematic use of data in ways that provide the potential to improve instruction, learning, and social justice throughout their school(s). Two essential components of a proactive and effective data-use strategy are for leaders to:

- Develop a state-of-the-art data system: and
- Create a proactive culture of shared evidence-based continuous improvement.

The evolution of data systems

It is easy to criticize how teachers do or do not use data, or to discuss the importance of using data to inform instruction. However, if data systems do not provide data in a usable and timely fashion, the opportunities to use it to improve instruction are limited. Indeed, one of the problems with the above research on teacher use of data does not take into account the nature of the data that are available to them—which is a function of the nature of the district's data systems.

We are now in the era of real-time mobile applications where everything from data entry to results happens in a completely individualized way at the speed at which one can think and enter data. Indeed, we can even envision a point in the future, perhaps the near future, wherein...

- Students in a class will have wearable devices that monitor their micro facial expressions as they listen to instruction, that will immediately inform the teacher as to which students did not really understand the concept and require further individualized help.

- Students will wear devices that provide real-time biofeedback that indicate whether they understand what is being taught and their level of stress. Leaders will merely speak their data requests into an electronic device and the result will appear.

- Tests will be administered and scored electronically and provide instantaneous results (and new forms of cheating). Artificial intelligence will be used to score student essays and higher-order open-ended questions.

In between the past and this future there are desirable characteristics of data systems that currently make it possible for school personnel to easily gain access to the types of quantitative information they need to make better decisions on how to improve schools in a timely, proactive fashion—and increase social justice.

The following section will first discuss the problematic nature of first generation data systems, and then discuss how districts and leaders should design their data systems under current technological capabilities. Finally, it will discuss how to use their data system as a basis for creating a culture of continuous improvement.

First generation systems for managing instruction

Systems were traditionally incorporated into school management for facilitating basic record-keeping functions such as attendance, grade reporting, and financial management. When the pressures for accountability started building up in the late 1980's and early 90's, districts began to create more elaborate systems for tracking student performance.

The accountability systems were formed around large lists of learning objectives for each grade level, and large Excel spreadsheet reports on which students in each classroom were achieving mastery for each objective. This was tracked across numerous interim assessments. I remember being at a meeting with urban superintendents who started bragging to each other as to who had more learning objectives in place, who tested the most frequently, and who generated the most reports to "inform" leaders and teachers as to how their students were doing. Principals and teachers were given these extensive reports numerous times during the school year. It was left to humans to make sense of this huge mass of data. Of course, all that happened was that the spreadsheets and the massive amounts of data overwhelmed everyone to the point that it was hard for anyone to find useful patterns in the data that would help improve instruction.

To make matters worse, there were large time lags between the times that students took the tests and schools received the results—particularly the end-of-year tests.

First generation systems for school administration

The limited capabilities of early computers limited the degree of automation and integration that the management systems could offer. Each application came with its own standalone data set, and its own set of programs. Data elements, such as a student's name, had to be entered separately into a registration, attendance, and grading system. In addition, entering the data into a computer would require several manual steps, such as teachers filling out a grade report sheet that was sent to the office where someone would enter that information into the computer. All changes to the system, or new reports, had to be done by the programming staff. Such changes were highly technical, time consuming and expensive.

Such data accountability and management systems created as much work as they saved. In what was probably the first evaluation of education administrative software, Pogrow (1985) showed that from the very beginning there were major differences in the extent to which computerized management systems in education automated and linked key processes—but that none of the systems were fully integrated.

Characteristics of state-of-the art data systems

The key to using quantitative data to improve student outcomes in state-of-the-art systems is to consider it to be a highly fluid organizational resource that flows across applications and individuals on an as-needed basis. Data need to flow throughout the organization, much as water circulates through pipes throughout the district to where the demand/need is. Like any valuable resource, data use needs to leveraged and applied in as efficient a manner as possible.

Modern data systems make it possible for data to flow and be shared throughout the organization and across applications. Access to data and its use can and should be leveraged as widely as possible throughout an organization—as long as individual privacy concerns are not violated. Modern systems enable data can be input in real time by those who originally collect/generate the data, and retrieved by those involved in decision-making in a highly flexible manner. Those involved in using data can create metrics that the system uses to display visually the patterns of those who are not meeting the metrics so that action can be taken in a proactive fashion.

So, for example, in a state-of-the art system, a principal dealing with a student infraction can enter that information directly into the system as he/she is interacting with the student. That way the system automatically notes the time that the issue was dealt with which then provides the opportunity to look for patterns in the types of infractions occurring at different points in time in the school day, the teacher involved, and repeat offenders. If that data are then available to the counselors and social workers, they can take proactive coordinated action as soon as a student's problem exceeds an agreed upon metric— e.g., more than three referrals in a month. In addition, a report that highlights the patterns of the time of day that infractions occur can be useful for developing approaches that eliminate a key cause of these infractions. (See Case Study #1 at the end of this chapter.)

Much of the progress in data systems over the last decade has been in the following three areas:

- Increased interactivity among management applications in their ability to share data. For example, Heitin (2017) describes the participation of Gwinnett County Schools in Georgia in the IMS Global Learning Consortium, a non-profit consortium, that has developed inter-operability standards for vendors that sell management systems to schools to follow. This enables the data from one vendor's system, say attendance, to also be accessed by another vendor's application, say grade reporting—eliminating the need to enter the same data, such as student names, into all the applications.

- Individual application software built on top of a common database with general database capabilities so that there is a single data reservoir/warehouse, with the capability to easily retrieve any combination of data elements. This makes it relatively easy for non-technicians to query the data and extract needed information in new ways and develop new reports. So, for example, it becomes relatively easy for non-technicians to ask the database/data warehouse software to integrate attendance, grade, and registration data elements to generate a report on the relationship between attendance and GPA for different student subgroups.

- The use of data visualization software, such as Tableau or Microsoft Power BI. Such software has the ability to capture data from a variety of databases/data warehouses and integrate it to create:

  ➢ New metrics. A *metric* is a quantitative measure that is used to track and assess the status of a specific process that is usually a key indicator of organizational performance; e.g., graduation rate, the number of students chronically absent, etc.

  ➢ New dashboards. A *dashboard* is a data visualization tool that displays the current status of metrics and usually consolidates several related metrics on a single screen—much like the information on a car's dashboard where you can simultaneously see the car's speed, distance driven, outdoor temperature, fuel remaining, etc., all in a quick glance. Similarly, teachers can see in a single glance attendance, grades, referrals, scores on assessments, as well as trends.

  ➢ Produce visual representations of patterns and outcomes in the data. Data visualization software reduces the technical requirements for retrieving data in highly flexible new ways in the forms of graphical output. Rather than producing spreadsheets or typical reports, data visualization software makes it relatively easy to produce results in a variety of graphical forms such as (a) graphs to show trend and patterns, and (b) color-coded symbols to indicate progress or declines instead of numbers which makes it easier to determine where improvement is needed.

These new technological capabilities dramatically increase the potential usefulness of data for making better decisions, and democratizing evidence-based decision-making within an organization. They are particularly useful for creating teamwork in the entering, sharing, and analyzing data. **Data visualization software** makes it relatively easy for anyone to design new metrics and analyze patterns within the data and see the exceptions—e.g., which students are not making sufficient progress as opposed to reporting on all students.

In continuous improvement, the key applied quantitative skills for leaders are (a) conceptualizing what data elements are needed to monitor progress relative to an improvement goal, (b) designing a dashboard to indicate the current status and rate of improvement, and (c) creating an improvement metric.

The ability to flexibly set metrics and retrieve information in graphical form makes discussions about interpreting results less intimidating and provides all members of a data team with new opportunities to participate around the use of data in a much deeper and more meaningful way than previously. Everyone can now bring their expertise to discussions about how to design new strategies for improvement based on the easier to understand graphical display of results. In addition, if a data team discussion highlights the need for a different report or metric, they can be generated very quickly.

In other words, a state-of-the-art data system with all the formal applications built around a common database/data warehouse, with a data visualization program such as Tableau or Microsoft Power BI, provide the efficiency and flexibility to maximize an organization's ability to quickly organize and retrieve data in easy to digest forms to support a team approach to:

- Evidence-based decision making: and
- Shared tinkering to adjust improvement and social justice strategies in real time.

Types of Analytics: Passive, Predictive, and Proactive

These integrated system capabilities make it easier to NOT rely on passive analytics— i.e., the preset, standard reports from the state or vendor. Rather, leaders can establish teams to proactively set up the types of reports and data analyses that they deem to be the most useful—including predictive analytics. **Predictive Analytics** is the ability to use forecasts of future events to intervene in the present. One of the best examples I have seen is when Los Angeles Unified School District developed a system that was able to predict on the basis of results in one year at a given school what students will struggle with the following year at the next grade level.[99] Alas, this required highly specialized statistical expertise that few districts have.

However, there are other areas where predictive analytics can help. For example, Heitin (2017) describes Gwinnet County's development of a system that used results in the first semester at the school to predict which secondary school students were most at-risk for dropping out, and why. These results were used to establish timely, targeted, interventions.

Modern systems now make it possible to create new forms of proactive analytics. **Proactive analytics** make leaders aware of changes in school system performance as soon as they happen so that they can make improvements in real time. This is a form

---

[99] The method could only produce predictions by grade level at a given school—not by individual classrooms.

of early warning system that a new problem/opportunity has emerged. Williamson presents the process of using data as:

> ...practices that do not just generate those data, but also order, manage, interpret, circulate, reuse, analyze, link and delete them according to the normative, political, and technical imperatives and choices... (Attributed to Rupert, et al., 2015)

This description of data use akin to a waterworks process is the hallmark of proactive analytics. Proactive analytics, combined with a commitment to taking quick action as soon as a problem manifests itself, is the key to creating a culture of continuous improvement and for using data systems to increase social justice.

Creating a Culture of Continuous Improvement

While modern technology systems create the potential for organizations to share real time data, and create and share proactive and predictive analytics to support evidence-based decision making, it is up to leaders to create a culture that values cooperative reflection around the use of evidence to support decisions related to continuous improvement.

In other words, once the technology is in place, the hard work starts—i.e., culture shaping. It takes an organizational culture of an expectation that everyone will use the sharing of reflections about data to inform key decisions as a cornerstone of a culture of continuous improvement. Relatedly, Williamson (2017) presents the concept of organizational *data infrastructure* as:

> ...a complex socio-technical system...consists of more than the data system...itself...to include all of the technical, political, social and economic apparatuses that frames their nature, operation and work. (Attributed to Kitchim & Lauriault, 2014)

Using a data infrastructure to create a culture of continuous improvement requires a shared commitment to continually determine what the current state of practice is and seek ways to improve it at all levels of the organization and for all aspects of performance. It is easy to say "all kids can learn", and to be an advocate for all students learning to their full ability. It is easy to produce a vision statement about the school having "high expectations" for all students.

However, developing a culture of continuous improvement represents a commitment to produce measured and noticeable improvement on an ongoing basis in all aspects of school performance. It requires a marshalling of all the technical, political, and social capabilities of the organization to generate, flow, and analyze data as the basis of key decisions on how to improve and increase equity. It requires leaders to encourage everyone to:

- Participate in the processes of creating dashboards and metrics to monitor progress;

- Provide input about the type of graphical representations that will be the most helpful; and, *most importantly,*

- Reflect about the implications of the results for organizational improvement and increasing equity.

Setting improvement goals

The key first step is to set specific numerical improvement goals. There is no statistical procedure for setting goals. Rather, it is a process wherein leaders, together with input from teachers, staff, and community, set improvement targets and develop initial strategies for trying to meet them. The improvement goals should reflect a commitment to produce noticeable, and ongoing numerical gains over a period of years. For example, Hamilton et al. (2009) discusses developing a plan around a schoolwide goal of increasing the percentage of students reading on grade level 5 percentage points per year, to reach 75% in five years.

Evaluating school and program performance

The key to evaluating the effectiveness of interventions is whether they are meeting improvement goals that have been established and whether the performance has noticeably increased as compared to the prior year. (For all the reasons discussed in Chapters 4-7, you do NOT want to rely on *statistically significant* differences.)

There is also one major difference between evaluating school performance and the types of relationship and experimental analyses discussed in Chapters 4-7 of this textbook. In these earlier chapters relative comparisons were criticized as being misleading. However, this critique was for research conducted at *external* sites. In external research the most useful data for determining the practical benefit of such research for your schools was considered to be the actual performance of the experimental students (only). On the other hand, when doing *internal* comparisons in one's own schools, relative improvement becomes important. Evidence of relative progress should be presented to the community and internally. At the same time, it is still important to also ground such results in some measure of actual end result performance of the students—as opposed to the description about Denver Public Schools in Challenge Question #4 at the end of Chapter 4 that presented only relative data.

Creating a culture of monitoring performance and improvement strategies

Once an organization has a data system capable of providing real-time data in highly flexible and visual manner, the next step in developing a culture of continuous improvement is for leaders at all levels to establish and maintain ongoing conversations about how to link the use of data to decision-making, and to develop a data reflection skill/mindset culture that permeates the organization as a key component of creating a data infrastructure.

The expectation that everyone is expected to have the mindset of continually engaging in reflective group discussions about the implications of data for developing better strategies for helping students needs to come from the very top of the organization. Cho and Wayman (2013) found that district leadership is critical for setting the right tone as to how data will be used and generated. A laissez-faire attitude by the superintendent towards the use of data, and/or a failure to understand the extensive on-going conversations that have to occur around the use of data and instructional strategies at all levels, will prevent a culture of continuous improvement from taking hold. District leadership has to (a) signal that ongoing conversations linking discussions about data, instruction, and improvement strategies are critical and expected, (b) put in place a process of ongoing cooperation between the system designers, technical staff, teaching and counseling staffs, and (c) make the investment to build a start-of-the art data management system and staff.

There are six additional important keys to creating a culture of using data as an ongoing process to improve student learning and increase equity:

1) Do NOT treat the accessing of data as a primarily technical issue. Workshops for teachers on how to access and analyze data have little impact. First of all, if accessing data and making sense of it is overly complex, few will use it regardless of how much training is provided. Instead, technical complexity should be viewed as an indication that the system needs updating. Instead of formal training, Marsh, Bertrand, and Huguet (2015) recommend that it is important to have discussions about retrieving and using data embedded into dialogues about instruction. Jimerson and Wayman (2015) recommend:

    ➤ Purposefully embedding professional learning for data use in ongoing organizational routines; and

    ➤ Doing away with separate training on using computer systems and focusing on professional learning on how to turn data into action.

    While technical staff should be involved in such meetings and answer technical questions as they come up, the focus of the discussions about data use should ALWAYS be on how to improve organizational goals.

2) Maintain a relentless focus on evidence as the basis for making decisions about what needs to be improved, and which strategies are most likely to result in noticeable improvement (Bocala & Boudett, 2015). This helps keep reflections on track and avoid blaming people or having the ones with the most political power impose their personal favorite ideas.

3) Treat data use as two-way conversations. Consistently seek feedback from users.

4) Consistently create opportunities to talk about data, and on the problems, successes, and possible improvement strategies that are indicated by the latest results.

5) Constantly innovate interventions (see Chapter 8) and metrics to improve results by supporting collaboration by all the groups involved in providing related services—including metrics to improve socio-cultural and emotional needs. An example of improving emotional needs is overcoming the effects of early trauma.

6) When and if improvement goals are not met, rather than be defensive, an effort is made to solicit new ideas and approaches and recommit to meeting the goals in the next round of assessments.

A culture of continuous improvement requires periodic assessments and data teams at each school to monitor progress and communicate such progress or lack thereof. The data teams which are key components of a data infrastructure also need to engage everyone at the school in looking at the data and discussing emergent problems and soliciting suggestions for overcoming them. Such reflection needs to be an ongoing process. Principals need to set aside time in the school calendar for such meetings and also participate in data assessment and strategizing meetings (Schildkamp & Portman, 2015). Similarly, someone(s) at the superintendent level should be involved with training and encouraging principals to make staff-wide discussions about data a priority.

While there is no evidence on the best way to organize data teams, or the optimal number of interim assessments or systemic reviews of student progress, common wisdom seems to be that they should probably occur at least quarterly. Hamilton (2009) and Boudett & Murnane (2013) provide recommendations on how to organize data teams and data-based planning. David Priddy, former Chief Academic Officer, recommended a series of formative assessments developed jointly by teachers in a Professional Learning Communities (PLC) organized by grade level or content area— and all teachers in a given PLC used the same tests. This gave teachers buy-in to the assessment process.

However, Bambrick-Santoyo (2010) warns that all will be for naught if the district uses inferior interim assessments, provides delayed results, and tries to maintain secrecy. In addition, as described earlier, experience has shown that too much testing defeats the value of testing.

Proactive Data Use to Increase Social Justice—The Case of Fresno Unified SD

The major goal of administrative systems is to maintain daily operations and monitor performance. However, it is also possible to envision a more activist role for school data systems that goes beyond monitoring performance to one of also promoting social justice. Clearly, reasonable people can disagree about how to define social justice and what it would look like in practice. There are many ways to approach it.

One notable example of using continuous improvement to promote social justice is the work of the Equity and Access unit in Fresno Unified School District (FUSD) in

293

California. A key Equity and Access' social justice goal was to develop a system to increase post-secondary opportunities for disadvantaged students. This initiative was enacted in conjunction with its regional University of California campus (UC Merced) and the local California State University (CSUF). The goal was to give all students an equal opportunity to graduate with the greatest number of post-secondary choices from the widest array of options.

This initiative was first reported by Haxton and O'Day (2015) which prompted me to conduct follow-up interviews with the leaders of the initiative.[100] Key structural features of the effort were that…

- A new unit entitled *Equity and Access* was formed in FUSD at the Associate Superintendent level. This separate staff was established apart from the district's existing systems group that handled the key management systems and applications for the district. This was done to minimize interference with ongoing administrative applications;

- The staff of the Equity and Access unit were not programmers. Rather, they were individuals skilled in understanding the types of raw data elements that needed to be integrated in order to produce the desired metrics and dashboards, and on how to set up interactive filters on the warehouse data that made it easy to query the data and drill down to individual schools and students; and

- Special profile tools were created to enable counselors, social workers, teachers and administrators to see which students were making the desired progress towards graduation and postsecondary application and which were not. These profiles were used to identify students who needed interventions and encouragement to apply for postsecondary institutions.

Low income students were encouraged to also apply to top-institutions outside their geographic area and to apply for scholarships. Supports were also extended down to the earlier grade levels to have everyone involved in keeping students on track—including making sure that elementary students whose first language was not English were on schedule to be redesignated as being able to learn academic content in English. The system provided the potential for everyone to be on the same page as to which students needed help, as well as the actionable recommendations that had been made and the types of help they had received.

The integration of the systems between the school district and its regional post-secondary institutions made it possible for the district to certify which students should not be placed into developmental math and English at the community college level. This ensures that students are not accidentally misplaced in ways that reduce their chances for academic success.

---

[100] Many thanks to Jorge Aguilar, former Associate Superintendent for Equity and Access for Fresno Unified School District (FUSD), Vincent Harris, from FUSD's equity and access unit, Angel Sanchez, Vice President for Institutional Effectiveness, California State University, Fresno, and David Jansen, the Executive Director of Data Science and Software Systems, for providing insight into FUSD's equity use of data.

The initiative was successful. The district reported that the number of students applying to the California State University (CSU) system doubled over a five-year period, and the number applying to University of California (UC) institutions almost tripled. Admittances were up approximately 50% at CSUs, and almost tripled at UC campuses. Equally impressive was that the applications to all UC campuses throughout the state increased. While, unfortunately no end result data were provided, the relative improvement data suggest that there was a noteworthy improvement in the social justice goals of the initiative.

Evaluating Programs and Improvement

A common form of data analysis is program evaluation. A program evaluation involves determining whether performance in the school(s) using the new approach is noticeably better relative to an alternative program or past performance in the same schools. If professional evaluators conduct the evaluation they will tend to report results in terms of the traditional criteria as to whether the improvements are statistically significant or have practical significance—i.e., an ES or SD/U of .2 or more). While reporting a finding that the program provided a "significant" benefit may be useful politically, it is no more valid than it was in reporting the findings of external research (see Chapters 5-7). Indeed, there may not have actually been any noticeable benefit.

Practical Tip

It is therefore important for a leader to form his/her own opinion of the success of an approach by examining the super trio of statistics—Mean/Median/Standard Deviation (see Chapter 4). A leader should examine the average differences in performance on his/her own and use the eyeball test to characterize the degree of improvement and whether it justifies scaling the approach. The benefits of a highly effective approach should be obvious and not require statistical analysis beyond the power trio.

Beware

Social justice concerns mandate that it is not sufficient to judge improvement based solely on overall *Means/Medians*. It is also important to look at how the distribution of results changed—i.e., who improved and benefitted. For example, if a new program increased the overall average but only a small percentage of students benefitted, is it effective? Is a program effective if the average went up but none of the students below average progressed? If overall improvement goals were met but achievement gaps widened is that acceptable?

It is therefore critical to examine the distribution of scores (see Chapter 4). A large *standard deviation* of the students' improvement relative to the *Mean* is an early warning sign that the benefits were not equally distributed.

The equitable distribution of improvement can also be determined by analyzing improvement results in terms of thirds, i.e., what happened to students who had been in the top, middle, or lower third. It can also be done by analyzing results in terms of quarters and fifths.

Determining the degree of equitable improvement can also be determined by monitoring the changes in achievement gaps between subgroups.

Conclusion

Establishing a process of evidence-based continuous improvement requires both a modern data system and leaders committed to developing a culture of shared reflections about the implications of real time data and assessments for making decisions about how to stimulate overall improvement and increase equity.

A modern data system enables data to be a highly fluid and flexible organizational resource that flow across applications and individuals in real time and that can be input and retrieved in a highly flexible, easy to understand, manner. It is now possible to implement data management systems that, when combined with a culture of continuous improvement and a data infrastructure, go beyond just monitoring school and student performance. Data systems can also be tailored to proactively provide early warning signals of emerging problems at the school or individual student level, and help facilitate collaborative reflections among the different professional groups in a school to develop approaches to accelerate improvement.

However, even the best data system merely provides the potential to use data more effectively. Developing a culture of continuous improvement requires a shared commitment to ongoing real-time assessment and adjustment, and using data in a reflective manner as the basis of action. The real-time dissemination of data and analytics in an easy to understand and digest format, and ongoing group reflection about how to apply the numbers, is more important to improvement than sophisticated statistical analysis. At the same time, it can be expected that as AI becomes more widely available in educational applications, sophisticated mathematical algorithms will increasingly be embedded into software to provide predictive analytics. However, even under existing technology it is possible and critical to create a proactive culture of continuous improvement and evidence-based decision-making.

Challenge Questions

1) In schools A & B, 75% of the student referrals occur within the hour before lunch, and in schools C & D they occur an hour after lunch. What do such data tell you about possible different causes of student discipline problems at the schools, and what ideas can you generate for possible solutions at the different schools.

2) Find an area in your school(s) that you want to see improve. Bring in some key descriptive data that you feel can be used as the basis of developing an improvement strategy.

   (a) Set an improvement goal, and

   (b) Develop an improvement strategy and indicate how the data suggest the recommended approach.

1) Design a social justice *metric* by:

   - Identifying a social justice objective;

   - Set a goal;

   - Indicate what data you would track; and

   - Indicate some decision points you would use as warning signals to determine when and if immediate action is needed to keep things moving forward.

Chapter 10

Students' Final/Capstone Projects: Lit Review and Action Research

Many leadership programs have some type of final/capstone project. At the doctoral level, EdD students are typically required to produce a dissertation. Techniques for developing an EdD dissertation, including an improvement science dissertation, are described in the other authentic methodology text by this author:

> *Authentic Quantitative Analysis for Leadership Decision-Making and EdD Dissertations,* published by ICPEL.org

However, this chapter discusses capstone projects more typical for a Masters leadership program. These include:

- Literature review; and
- Action research project.

The literature review is sometimes a standalone project or a component of an action research project.

Action research projects usually involve working with data that you generate from your own schools, while the critical literature review examines the existing research evidence generated by others for solving the problem of practice you are interested in.

The action research project differs widely across Masters programs in terms of the types of studies expected and the standards for conducting them. Some programs require mixed methods while others leave the methodology up to the individual student and professor. Action research can either be an individual project or a collaborative one among several students—with each studying the same issue across several schools or different aspects of the same problem.

Action research projects span a wide range of research projects including, among others, conducting:

- A program evaluation;
- An analysis of key school/district outcomes, sometimes in relation to goals or to other similar schools;
- A study of the perceptions of stakeholders with respect to an issue;
- Classroom observations;
- A gap analysis of school outcomes by race, economic status, or gaps between improvement goals and outcomes; and
- An historical analysis of previous policies, reform efforts, community aspirations and makeup, etc.

All these action research projects tend to involve leadership students identifying a problem of practice in their schools, and using the evidence from this research to try and improve their schools.

This chapter differs from the others in that instead of discussing and critiquing the methods in others' research, this chapter discusses the quantitative methods you should use in your own research. This chapter is about how you should collect and analyze data for a problem that you have identified in your schools. At the same time, your data analysis process should be based on the same data analysis principles developed in Parts I and II of this textbook—particularly Chapter 7.

Remember

You should apply the same principles for thinking about your research and analyzing your data as discussed in the earlier chapters—e.g., Do your findings indicate a practical benefit? As a result, much of the discussion in this chapter about conducting and analyzing your own quantitative action research methods and findings refers back to discussions in chapters 4-8.

Literature Review

Types of literature review

The three main types of literature reviews are:

- Annotated review;
- Synthesized/analytical review;
- Synthesized /analytical *critical* review.

An annotated review simply contains a short description of each of the studies that are being reviewed. There may be a summary at the end, but each study is described discretely.

While the annotated literature review is easier to produce, it is not recommended for graduate-level work. First, it is counterproductive for leadership decision-making since it does not actually try to reach conclusions about the current state-of-knowledge or try to resolve differences in findings. Second, the annotated literature review does not make any attempt to critique the conclusions of the researcher and merely reports them as fact—as opposed to trying to determine whether the reported findings are exaggerations, as per the discussions in Chapters 4-7.

Rather than conducting an annotated review, it is suggested that you make brief notes about each study on a set of index cards, and then you can organize them into piles of studies that are related on some dimension, and then each pile becomes a synthesized paragraph.

The difference between the two versions of the synthesized literature review is whether students are encouraged to critique the conclusions of the researcher or accept them as provided. Clearly, the emphasis of this textbook is that it is possible, and necessary, for leaders and leadership students to critique research findings to support authentic decision-making that is likely to benefit their schools. As a result, the following discussion focuses on conducting a synthesized/analytical *critical* literature review.

How to find relevant research evidence

The importance of constructs/sub-constructs

Constructs are the basis of a good literature review. Constructs and sub-constructs are the variables that scholars use to break complex, general ideas into their constituent parts so that they can be analyzed and formally researched. The reason why constructs/sub-constructs are so important is that they are the portal into the existing research. Constructs are what enables a student with a general concern, such as student discipline, to link that concern to the specific ways that researchers have studied it and thereby provides access to the existing base of research and discourse.

Scholarly constructs are important because the social and psychological processes that educators are interested in are so tremendously complex that it is difficult to even begin to think about how to study them—e.g. concepts such as:

* Culture;
* Behavior;
* Motivation;
* Learning;
* Etc.

Over time, scholars figure out how to break off pieces of these processes that they can study. The researchers hope that if they can understand enough of the sub-processes of a psychological process that will help them understand the bigger picture—similar to learning how atoms work by discovering all of their constituent parts and the properties of each. These pieces of processes are called constructs, and these may get broken down even further into sub-constructs.[101] So constructs are essentially how scholars have previously defined and studied aspects of the phenomena/ideas that educators are interested in.

Consider, for example, trying to understand human engagement—particularly how student engagement affects their ability to succeed in school. Over time, scholars studying student engagement identified and studied three different constructs, or sub-constructs, of student engagement. Fredricks, Blumenfeld, and Paris (2004) described them as: behavioral, emotional, and cognitive engagement. If one tries to base a literature review on the construct of "Engagement" without breaking it down to the sub-constructs, chances are that it will be a superficial literature review. It is more realistic to conduct a literature review on the sub-construct of greatest relevance to the problem you are addressing.

---

[101] At times it is difficult to tell whether something is a sub-construct or a construct so the two terms will be used interchangeably. However, the guiding principle is that you want to analyze research at the most fundamental level of detail.

Of course, researchers will often use very different, technical language to describe a construct/sub-construct of culture or behavior than what leaders use. However, once you start to review literature you can quickly uncover the technical terms used for a key construct or sub-construct, and thereafter search on the key technical term. For example, the case study below describes how a principal started searching on the very general term of "discipline" and then discovered the subconstruct of the "prosocial classroom" that was a bullseye on her primary interest.

Delimit the search by types of schools, grade levels, and/or individuals

Another way to delimit the literature review is to focus on specific types and levels of schools, and/or types of students or adults you are most interested in. For example, if you search on the keyword "principals," you will find lots of studies. However, if you are most interested in Latina principals you will find a more manageable number of potential studies for your literature review.

Search methodology

The following discussion explains the methods for conducting a successful search for research evidence via a case study. A case study is used to illustrate key elements of the search process because it is a highly intuitive process that involves on the fly adjustments to the search terms you are using.

This case study involves a former student who had been the first Black high school principal in a large district and who had compiled an enviable record of success. She strongly believed that her success in an inner city school was because of improved discipline in the classroom with an emphasis on teachers using more respectful language towards students. She wanted to know if there was any supporting research.

I served as her "grad assistant." Here is the step by step search process we engaged in with Google Scholar in terms of describing the search terms and the number of references (HITS) that showed up. Typically, the first search will yield far more HITS than you can possibly consider so you need to get more specific.[102]

(Step 1) Basic search on the term *discipline*

Search Term	# of HITS
Discipline	4,090,000
Classroom discipline	1,960,000
"Classroom discipline"	29,600

---

[102] This example is for simply illustrating the effect of different techniques for reducing the number of HITS when conducting a search. You do NOT need to use all these steps in sequence. Every search process is different.

Key Finding: Adding quotation marks around multi-word phrases dramatically reduces the number of hits. This limits the search to examples with the complete phrase, as opposed to finding any reference with just one of the words—e.g., just "classroom."

(Step 2) ADD Descriptors, AND OR, to refine criteria

Search Term	# of HITS
"Classroom Discipline"	22, 800
"classroom discipline" AND "high school",	15,100
"classroom discipline" AND "high school" OR "grades 9-12"	15,200
"classroom discipline" AND "high school" AND poverty	11,200

Key Findings: Adding additional specific criteria using **AND** or **OR** substantially reduces the number of hits as the focus is delimited to high schools—especially schools with a high percentage of students born into poverty. (Use capital letters for AND, OR)

OR is necessary where different terms are used by different researchers to describe something—e.g.,

Latino OR Latina OR Latinx OR Hispanic
"Culturally relevant pedagogy" OR "Culturally responsive teaching" OR ????

If you search just on Latino you will miss out on important studies where the author used a different term.

OR is also used to describe a combination of elements. For example, if you are looking for studies that were conducted at middle schools or high schools, you would enter:

"middle school" **OR** "High School"

(Step 3) Add the scholarly term (Construct) found in abstracts

In looking through some abstracts the term *prosocial* kept showing up. The student got very excited because that sociological term dealt with the language used in the classroom which was exactly the element of discipline that she was interested in. To her this was the most relevant sub-construct of the general process of establishing discipline in classrooms.

In addition, we added search terms that further described the types of high schools she was interested in such as "hi-poverty" ones.

Search Term	# of HITS
prosocial AND "classroom discipline" AND "high school"	874
prosocial AND "classroom discipline" AND "high school" AND "high-poverty" OR "Hi-poverty"	184

Key Findings: Adding a commonly used scholarly term, in this case prosocial, dramatically reduced the number of hits.

(STEP 4)   Search for studies that contain "*outcomes of*" or "*effects of*" to find empirical studies

Search Term	# of HITS
prosocial AND "classroom discipline" AND "high school" AND "high-poverty" OR "Hi-poverty" AND "effects of"	187
prosocial AND "classroom discipline" AND "high school" AND "high-poverty" OR "Hi-poverty" AND "outcomes of"	104

Key Finding: Adding these terms not only reduces the number of hits, but the hits are more likely to be studies as opposed to pure philosophy/ advocacy pieces.

(Step 5) Add in *experiment* or "*experimental design*"

These additional keywords delimit the search to studies that used an activist form of research—i.e., experiments—where the idea/concept is actually tested relative to a comparison group.

Search Term	# of HITS
prosocial AND "classroom discipline" AND "high school" AND "high-poverty" OR "Hi-poverty" AND experiment	134
prosocial AND "classroom discipline" AND "high school" AND "high-poverty" OR "Hi-poverty" AND "experimental design"	39

Key Finding: The fewest studies tend to be the ones that incorporate experimental design

303

These step together took an initial search with 4 million hits down to a manageable number of 39. That does not mean that all 39 studies are useful but this a viable starting point.

Keep a record of the types of search terms you used in each step and the number of hits you received as this is important data for describing the methodology you used to select the final group of studies.

Once you have narrowed the search down to a reasonable number of studies, check the abstracts. Then,

1. Based on the description in the abstracts, identify those studies that seem to be the most useful;
2. Then try to get the full text of those studies.

You may be able to download the studies directly from Google Scholar. However, in most cases you will probably need to access the studies through a university library and its databases. To have such access through a university database you will generally need to be a student or employee of that University. If you are currently not a student, try to get a faculty member or student you know, obtain the articles for you.

Once you have made the final selection of studies to include in your literature review, and read them, you are now ready to produce your literature review.

Writing the literature review

Preliminary steps

Once a set of studies has been selected for inclusion in a literature review, there are three additional steps that students can take to increase the quality of their literature review.

(1) The ideal literature review contains a balance between a variety of types of sources, including philosophical/theoretical treatises and empirical studies. Within empirical studies you want a mix of qualitative and quantitative studies (and mixed method studies).

As a first step to organizing the studies, I ask students to prepare a bibliography of the studies they have selected for their literature review, and to then code each entry as follows:

P/T (Philosophical or theoretical)
Q/MM (Qualitative or Mixed Methods)
QS (Quantitative Survey)
QE (Quantitative Experimental—testing the effects of an intervention or practice.)

This coding provides a sense of the balance of sources within the literature review. I emphasize the importance of having at least some experimental studies (assuming that they exist). If they do not exist, then it is important for students to temper their conclusions about the state-of-the evidence in accordance with the discussions in Chapter 6.

(2) A second step is to examine a high quality literature review to get a sense of the academic writing style typically used. It is especially important to note how the findings of similar studies are synthesized within a paragraph as opposed to writing a separate paragraph for each study.

The best source of such reviews is the AERA journal, *Review of Educational Research* (RER). While students should not feel that they need to emulate what are essentially professional literature reviews that are developed by specialists over an extended period of time, students can draw some key lessons from such studies about how to shape their own literature review. A simple starting point is to mimic the outline of the literature review.

It is ideal if you find an RER literature review geared to your topic which you can update with more recent studies.

(3) Finally, once you have decided which studies you intend to include in your literature review, you should organize those studies into baskets of related studies using categories that make sense to you—e.g., qualitative articles, articles that found positive benefits, theoretical articles, experimental studies, etc.

There are also more fine-grained ways to organize the studies based on the methods used. For example, there may be differences in how studies analyzed the key construct. Perhaps some studies measured the pro-socialness of a classroom by analyzing how often the teacher raised his/her voice to a student of color, while others may have analyzed whether the teacher's language was threatening and/or disrespectful, and some may have analyzed both.

Each cluster of articles can then be synthesized into 1-2 paragraphs.

General writing style tips:

- The most important tip is to use well written synthesized paragraphs with appropriate general topic sentences for each paragraph;
- Paragraphs should usually not be longer than 5-7 sentences; and
- One idea per sentence—and if the sentence is longer than 3 lines it probably has more than one idea and will confuse the reader.

Academic writing tips:

If your program requires the use of a formal writing style such as APA or MLA, the best resource is owl.purdue.edu, then click on the appropriate style guide.

Analyzing the evidence

It is critical to only consider the evidence provided by *primary* source research, with a priority on finding peer-reviewed research. If a researcher in one article cites another's study and findings, access and read the original study and use the results you glean from the original study in your literature review.

As previously noted, it is critical that in this section you view yourself as a judge—not a lawyer. You are NOT building a case to support a point of view that you like or hope is true. Rather, you are weighing the competing evidence and rendering a decision as to what the quality of evidence is supporting any position, and which possible position is best supported by the preponderance of evidence.

Review **all** research, not just that which is convenient for your beliefs or which you agree with. Many breakthroughs result from considering research that come to unexpected conclusions to modify one's own initial conceptions, and/or figuring out how to resolve apparent differences in the literature. Consider the following example from a review of the literature on social promotion (i.e., promoting students to the next grade who have not done passing level work) by Muschkin, Glennie, and Beck (2014) that highlights conflicting findings in the research:

> Much of the research generated by the social promotion debate focuses on the effects of retention on the academic performance of students who have not mastered skills at their present grade level and are either made to repeat a year of school or are promoted despite their academic shortcomings. A substantial body of research offers varying conclusions about the academic effects of retention, including significant negative effects (Alexander, Entwhistle, & Kabbani, 2001; Babcock & Bedard, 2011; Pagani, Tremblay, Vitaro, Boulerice, & McDuff, 2001), mixed or no effects (Jacob & Lefgren, 2004; Reynolds, 1992; Roderick & Nagaoka, 2005), and significant positive effects (Jacob, 2005; Jacob & Lefgren, 2007; Lorence & Dworkin, 2006). (p. 2)

The good: This paragraph is an excellent summary of the existing literature on the effects of retention on academic performance in terms of both its conciseness, synthesis, and the lack of bias. It does not shy away from an apparent conflict in research findings. Indeed, there is usually a conflict in research findings on any topic.

The bad: Unfortunately the authors of this review did not try to understand why such conflict exists. For example, perhaps the studies that found benefits for retention were conducted at the earliest grades, and studies that found negative results from retention were at higher-grade levels. This would have major leadership implications and would be a major contribution to knowledge. Perhaps the studies with positive effects had poorer research designs or differed in some other way. Perhaps none of the studies reported findings that were of any *practical benefit* and as such the conflict was of little concern. Perhaps there were differences in the nature or size of the samples, Perhaps... Perhaps...

In other words, one of the most important things you can do in a literature review is to resolve such conflicts to see if there are any patterns of findings within the conflict—rather than simply pointing out that a conflict exists.

Above all, it is critical to cite all the studies, even if they have inconvenient outcomes. Then examine each in detail and see if you can find a pattern that explains the difference in findings. Try to figure out ways to explain these different/seemingly contradictory findings and state your conclusion.

Recommended Outline of a Quality Literature Review

Your Title
e.g., A Review of the Literature on...<Your Topic>

Part I—Methodology of the Literature Review

List of Keywords Searched {Peer Reviewed} Use AND & OR in searches e.g.,
Latinx or Latina OR Hispanic
developmental math AND community college AND reform AND effect

The Databases Used to Access Relevant Studies—e.g., Google Scholar, JSTOR

Overview/Scope of the Review

> **Criteria for selecting sources for the review.**
> **Key constructs/sub-constructs guiding the review.**

Part II—Review of the Literature

Definition and Measurement of Key Constructs/Sub-constructs

Description of Key Theories/Philosophic Issues

Analysis of the Primary _Empirical_ Research Evidence (*focus on efforts to solve the problem*) Empirical research can be either qualitative or quantitative. The focus is on studies where the authors collected the data being analyzed.

> **Basic analysis of the evidence (stage one).** Synthesized summary of empirical findings.

> **A critical analysis of the evidence (stage two).**

> > ➤ For *qual* research, how unbiased and comprehensive is the analysis
> > ➤ For *quant* research, what is the numerical size of the positive effect/benefit/ relationship? Using the data analysis principles in Chapter 7, are the results BIG enough to have practical benefit/be important?

Did a Preponderance of the Evidence Convincingly Support or Refute the Key Theory(ies) Discussed (if any)? *Did any of the evidence point to an effective improvement strategy/intervention?*

Reconciling/Summarizing Conflicting Findings (If Any)

Limitations of the Existing Research—what are the gaps in the knowledge base?

Part III—Summary Table(s) of Empirical Research *(optional)*

Part IV—Conclusions and Needed Research

Action Research Project

Nature of action research

There are many definitions as to what constitutes action research and the preferred methodology. However, the original impetus for action research was the belief that when practitioners conduct research on how to solve problems of practice in their institutions, that increases (a) the likelihood that the findings will be put into practice, and (b) the credibility and validity of the research than research produced by outsiders (Corey, 1953).

However, in a break with how action research has traditionally been described, it is recommended that for teachers aspiring to be leaders, that they NOT conduct their action research just in their own classroom. The action research project for aspiring leaders should study a problem in a broader fashion. This is in recognition that becoming a successful leader requires adopting a more global perspective that thinks holistically about the overall school/district.

The scope of the action research can be dealing with a personal problem of practice, one that is limited in scope to a few classrooms or grade levels, to a problem in a single school, or to a districtwide systemwide problem—e.g., how to improve services and outcomes for homeless students.

Common types of action research:

- Program evaluation—i.e., evaluating a practice that others have already initiated;
- Establishing a practice to solve a problem and testing its effects;
- Historical analysis to determine the extent of a problem over time, or the approaches that had been tried in the past and the degree of success; or
- A test of a personal theory of action (see Chapter 1).

However, the goal of any action research is to test an action, and (ideally) develop a plan of action, to facilitate improvement.

Institutions differ in terms of the requirements for an action research project. For example, some allow students to choose whether they will use quantitative methodology or a qualitative one, while others require a mixed method study—i.e., some elements of both methods. While mixed method research is always the best way to get a deep understanding of what is happening in classrooms, schools, and districts, this section will focus on the quantitative aspects of the research. In addition, a general outline for the research project will be presented.

Most importantly, any quantitative analysis in your action research should adhere to the recommendations and principles in the earlier chapters. (Review the final data analysis principles in Chapter 7 before conducting any analysis of your research findings.) For example, keep in mind that:

- The simplest statistics (e.g., power trio) are the most important analytical tools, and the most meaningful to practitioner and community audiences;
- Seek large benefits/relationships in your findings and do not settle for statistical significance; and
- It is important to exercise critical human judgment in interpreting results—e.g., eyeballing the differences in the *Means* between the experimental and comparison groups.

The best topics for action research are ones that:

- Can be conducted within a limited time frame;
- Are likely to be valuable in subsequent leadership practice;
- You can get permission to conduct the research; and
- You have passion and dedication to pursue a solution to that particular problem.

The writing style tip are the same as the ones discussed earlier for the literature review.

Getting permissions

There are two types of permissions generally needed. The first is from your school/district, and the second is from the Institutional Review Board (IRB) of your university.

If you are going to be collecting data from, or about, your school or district you will probably need to get approval from your school district. Most districts of any size have a research approval committee. If you are already a school administrator **it** is probably easier **to get district permission** than if you are a teacher. If you are a teacher try to get your principal to handle the district permission process.

Institutional review boards are generally concerned with making sure that your subjects:

- Are participating voluntarily;
- Are not being placed at risk physically or psychologically, or making their lives more difficult in any way inside school or outside; and
- Will remain confidential.

Typical risks include a principal trying to recruit his/her teachers to be research subjects, or including undocumented or homeless student as research subjects. In addition, it is harder to get permission to interview students as opposed to adults. In the former case, parental permission will **probably** be required.

Data collection

Your study will have a series of variables. For example, if you are studying the prosocial nature of classrooms, you will probably also be collecting data about the teacher e.g., race and sex, and perhaps the demographic makeup of the classroom. It is pretty clear how to measure most of these variables. But how would you measure the variable of pro-socialness? Indeed, there are probably several different aspects of a classroom's pro-socialness—each of which is probably a separate variable. In addition, if you are seeking to determine the relationship between the prosocial variable(s) and student outcomes, you may be adding additional variables such as discipline referrals, reading scores, etc. That expands the list of variables.

Once you know what your variables are, the next step is to determine how you will specifically measure them. This is referred to as operationalizing the variables. *Operationalizing* a variable indicates the specifics of how you will measure it and what data you will collect.

Operationalizing variables and collecting the data

In trying to figure out the best way to measure any variable, the first step is to ask: How have others measured it? This should have been discussed in your literature review. For example, if you are studying the prosocial classroom, previous studies would have identified the key variables and provided techniques for measuring each of the variables. Alternatively, if there are no validated measures on what you are studying, you may have to develop one.

The most common ways to collect data to measure variables are to:

- Use an instrument—e.g., tests, psychological inventories, surveys, questionnaires, etc., that are already in existence or that you develop;
- Use existing historical or current primary sources—e.g., minutes of school board meetings, school/district records, or external primary source data (see Appendix B); and
- Observe classrooms or meetings with some sort of checklist, rubric, or protocol.

The most common way to collect data about a variable is to use an instrument such as a test, interview protocol with a list of closed and open-ended questions, or a questionnaire. The most common type of survey instrument is a questionnaire with Likert items. A Likert item typically has 5 ordered levels of response (7 levels are better for statistical reasons) where the respondent is asked to rate a statement, ranging from strongly agree to strongly disagree, typically coded from 1-5.

You may be able to find an instrument that has previously been used in research that meets the needs of your study. In such a case make sure that you can get permission to use it as it may be copyrighted and/or a commercial product that you have to pay for. However, if you are researching something new, you will probably have to develop your own instrument to measure at least some of the variables in your study.

Some constructs or variables are not measured by tests or other instruments, but rather by collecting existing data from records such as census data on levels of poverty, or data maintained by the state or district—such as suspension rates, report cards, or health records. Historical artifacts such as minutes/videos of school board or district executive committee meetings, or newspaper clippings, can be valuable tools in studying the history of improvement efforts.

Another way that data are collected for measuring a variable is by observing classrooms, meetings, etc. and systematically recording relevant observations. The problem with observing phenomena is that your presence can impact what is happening in the setting. If you enter a classroom to observe students will wonder: "What is he/she doing here?" If you videotape or film a classroom, students and teachers may change their normal behaviors and interactions to look good.

Because of the problem of the observer impacting what is being observed, there was interest a while back in the concept of "*unobtrusive measures*" (Webb, Campbell, Schwartz, & Sechrest, 1966). *Unobtrusive measures* are indirect methods of collecting data about the remnants of social behavior. The classic case is measuring the relative popularity of a painting in a museum by observing the amount of wear on the floor next to each painting.

Unobtrusive observation is my personal favorite type of research. For example, I can get a very good sense of the academic quality of a school by walking through the halls of a middle or high school and peeping in the windows of classrooms 10 minutes before the end of a period and seeing whether students have been allowed to switch into social time, and how many classrooms that has occurred in. If the percentage of classrooms in this mode is high it means that there is insufficient focus on utilizing available instructional time. If while cruising through the halls of such schools I also see that most of the clocks are way off, that suggests to me that there is also a lack of attention to logistical details in school leadership. If I wanted to measure "Teacher Satisfaction/Morale" I would sit in the teacher room and check every time I hear a complaint as opposed to a proactive comment. I suspect that this will be a more valid measure of "Teacher Satisfaction/Morale" than data obtained via interviews or teacher rating scales.

At the same time, there are ways you can minimize the distorting effects of the act of observation even when you are being obtrusive. Once students have seen you in their class 3-4 times they tend to settle back into their routine. Intensive observation over an extended period of time is referred to as *ethnographic* research or *ethnography*.

Observation is the form of action research that may have the greatest potential to produce new knowledge. For example, measuring the pro-social environment of a classroom would probably best be done by observing the teacher-student dynamics in real-time with a checklist to record each occurrence of the key variables—such as a teacher's use of inappropriate language, yelling at a student, etc.

In general, there are two main advantages for observational work in action research. First of all, observing a teacher's instructional practice or leadership behavior will often produce very different and more valid data than asking teachers or principals to rate their own behavior. As someone interested in higher order thinking, I would get very different results from asking a teacher whether they tended to ask questions that required students to verbalize thoughtful responses, as opposed to observing them teach and recording the number of one-word answers that they elicited and the percentage of overall student responses that were one-word or recall answers. The second reason why observation is a particularly useful strategy for action research is that practitioners/leaders often (a) have original insight about how to observe and interpret behavior that professional researchers do not have, and (b) can gain access to records or observation opportunities that professional researchers cannot. This provides the opportunity for practitioner-based action research to observe and record new phenomena that have not previously appeared in the research literature.

Reliability and validity of measures

However, a key concern when deciding how to measure a variable is the potential for *measurement error*. **Measurement error** is the degree to which the measuring instrument is not accurate. We deal with measurement error in our everyday lives anytime we buy things that are weighed. We hope that the scale in a store is accurate. Chances are that the scale is not completely accurate as it is susceptible to changes of temperature, humidity, constant use, etc. The fundamental problem in measurement is that we do not measure most things directly but by its impact on something else. So when we measure temperature, we are not really measuring heat which occurs at the atomic level. We are measuring the physical effect of heat—i.e., the extent to which it pushes mercury up a thin column. Physicists looking for new sub-atomic particles observe the traces their movement leaves in a cloud chamber but do not view the particles themselves.

The problems of measurement are compounded when we try to measure social phenomena, knowledge, and emotion—e.g., teacher satisfaction or student self-esteem. We cannot see the operation of the brain so we do not know how many facts are stored there. We cannot see the changes in electrical charge moving across the brain synapses that produce emotional responses. All we can do is create tests to measure knowledge, intelligence, and questionnaires to get at the emotional state of an individual—e.g., their motivation, anxiety etc.

Another problem is that the act of measuring something can itself change what is being measured. For example, high stakes testing changes what and how teachers teach. The change from nationally normed standardized tests to criterion tests based on standards with cutoff points resulted in schools shifting supplemental funding from helping the lowest performing students to helping those on the bubble move up to the next level.

Over time there tend to be improvements in measuring devices. We now have MRI machines that can provide precise images of brain activity, and education tests now make provisions for special needs. Trying to understand people's hidden emotional reaction to a situation or question has evolved from studying body language to analyzing "facial micro-expressions", which are fleeting subconscious changes in the face that can last for as little as 1/15 of a second. It takes a high-speed camera to capture and study such changes.

For those of us who do not have access to MRI machines or high-speed cameras, we have to settle for published tests, observation protocols, psychological scales, and questionnaires to try and measure key constructs of learning and behavior.

The two key measures of the quality of a test or an instrument, be it a scale or a psychological test, is its *reliability* and *validity*. **Reliability** is the degree of consistency that the instrument maintains over repeated use. A scale that produces two very different measures of weight for a bag of the same groceries one minute apart is not a very good scale. There is no consistency of measurement. The *reliability* of such a scale would be close to zero and we would not trust it. The same would be true for a test of knowledge or intelligence. If the same test was administered to a student two days apart and produced very different results we would similarly conclude that the test was not reliable and should not be used.

Validity is the extent to which an instrument actually measures the construct that it claims to measure. For example, questioning whether aptitude tests actually measure students' aptitude to learn, or whether they are measuring their SES and what they already know, is questioning the *validity* of the test.

Clearly, if a test is not *reliable* it cannot be *valid* since it is not really measuring anything specific. At the same time, a test can be reliable but not valid. This test is measuring something specific in a consistent fashion, but not necessarily what it claims to measure.

The *reliability* of a measure can range from 0 to 1, and a general rule of thumb is that you should try to avoid any instrument whose *reliability* is less than .7 (Fraenkel & Wallen, 2009). If there are two options you should pick the instrument with the higher *reliability*. The best resource on the *reliability* and *validity* of commercially available tests is the *Mental Measurements Yearbook* (Spies & Carlson, 2010) published by the Buros Institute, hereafter referred to as "*Buros*", which is published every three-four years.

Beware

Just because an instrument has been previously used in published research does not mean that it has high *reliability* and *validity*. Check to see if the researchers report what the reliability and validity is. If not, use face validity (described below) to decide if you want to use it or develop your own.

At the same time, there is a good chance you may need to develop your own instruments—e.g., questionnaire or observation protocols—because you have not been able to find an existing one in the literature that meets your needs. In such cases you will probably have to rely on *face validity*—i.e., a common-sense estimation of whether the instrument or interview questions that you develop appear to measure what you intend. You can always empower a panel of researchers to make such a judgment.

Creating questionnaires

While describing good practice for developing and validating questionnaires is beyond the scope of this book, there is one thing to avoid like the plague. The biggest problem with student-developed questionnaires is that they contain a large number of questions/items—and then each is studied independently to see which ones are significant. However, while the error rate for each question may be p<.05, these error rates accumulate and increase the more items you have. Therefore, if you have 20-30 questions there is a very high probability that any finding of significance for any one question is merely a result of accumulated statistical error and in fact happened by chance and cannot be trusted.

To avoid such accumulated error the best practice is to try and group related questions into 3-4 categories, and then develop a total score for each category. These total scores are called **Scales** or **Indexes**. You are then examining whether 3 or 4 scales/indexes are significant as opposed to 20-30 individual items. As a result this increases the likelihood that findings of differences between groups on a given scale/index, or a strong relationship involving a given scale/index, are real and not primarily a result of statistical error.

Developing samples

Now that you know what data you are going to collect and how you are going to collect it, the next question is:

Who are you going to collect this data from?

Answering this question describes the sample for your action research. The key to developing an appropriate sample is to ask:

Who am I interested in studying?

The answer should be as specific as possible. Are you interested in studying all students? Are you interested in studying only students in high poverty schools? Are you interested in studying Latino students in grades k-3 in highly segregated schools, and comparing their performance to similar students in highly integrated schools?

314

For <u>experimental research</u> a random sample is the preferred type of sampling strategy as it is the most likely to eliminate confounding variables. (Chapter 6 described the method for drawing a random sample.) However, drawing a random sample tends to require more time and participants than are typically feasible in an action research project. The same is true for Stratified or Cluster sampling that involves randomly selecting from within groups or subgroups.[103]

A more feasible sampling strategy in experimental research is using matched pairs. A *matched pair* sample is where the researcher identifies potentially confounding independent variables and matches each individual or school with another that has similar characteristics. Obvious examples of independent variables that would be used to make matches of students would be Race and SES, and independent variables such as Experience and Grade Level would be used to match teachers. If there is a large number of schools in the sample, researchers may match schools based on variables such as the Reading Scores, Percentages of Free and Reduced Lunch, Size, Grade Levels, etc. Typically once all the matches are formed the researchers randomly assign one of the pair to the experimental group and the other to the comparison group.

However, it is most likely that in action research you will be conducting your research with what Blair, Czaja, and Blair (2014) call a *sample of convenience*. A sample of convenience consists of individuals most accessible to you and who are willing to participate. Unfortunately, such a sample is NOT likely to be representative of the population, since those you know, and/or those willing to participate, may not be the same as everyone else. At the same time, this sampling process may be the best you can do under the time and budgetary constraints for conducting your action research— *though always try to draw from as wide a pool of potential participants as possible.*

One can also consider *purposive sampling*. Purposive sampling is more intentional than a sample of convenience. In purposive sampling you seek participants with a specific characteristic. If your sample consists of teachers or administrators, you may choose individuals with specific experience related to a problem—e.g., special education teachers who serve severely autistic children. If you are studying students you may choose to study those with a special characteristic that you are interested in—e.g., students who recently arrived from Afghanistan in grades k-3.

How large should the sample be? In quantitative research there are statistical formulas to determine the size of the sample needed to minimize error. A simpler method is to use conventional general rules of thumb for the minimum size of samples depending

---

[103] *Stratified sampling* can be used where you have distinct homogeneous subgroups. Participants are randomly selected from each subgroup in proportion to their size within the overall population. For example, suppose a district with 600 elementary teachers wants to survey a sample of 30 teachers to find out what their morale is and what their suggestions for improvement are. If 400 teachers (2/3) are female and 1/3 are male, then 20 (or 2/3) of the sample will be randomly selected females and 10 (or 1/3) will be randomly selected males. In the above high school example, you may want to stratify students by grade level, race, etc. In *cluster sampling*, you randomly select some of the existing clusters in the population. Suppose a district has 20 schools. In cluster sampling you would select several schools to be in the sample. *Cluster sampling* tends to be lower cost, but is considered to be less accurate than stratified sampling.

on the type of study. For example, Fraenkel & Wallen (2009) suggest the following minimum size of samples:

- Descriptive/survey research   100
- Correlational research   50
- Experimental research   30 per group
- Random assignment experimental research   40 per group

Blair, Czaja, and Blair (2014) note that small *samples of convenience* are appropriate for exploratory studies—which is what many action research projects are. They recommend that you should use a sample of 5 to 15 when piloting a questionnaire, while Blair and Conrad (2011) found that using 15 as opposed to 5, avoided twice as many potential problems. This is probably good advice for testing any questionnaire or data collection instrument.

Some statistical tests such as Chi-Square have their own sample size requirements. Chi-Square expects each cell of "expected outcomes" to have at least five cases. So, for example, if you were to analyze students' math scores and wanted to break out the results by Sex (M/F) and Race (Black, White, Latino, and Asian Americans) you would end up with eight cells so you would need to have a larger sample. You would probably want to start the study with a sample of at least 80 students to increase the likelihood that there will be at least 5 in each cell. (While you would probably end up with different numbers of individuals in each cell—that is okay.)

All things considered, *the best rule for a Masters action research project is probably to create as large a sample as you can.* Larger samples are better for reducing sampling error and increasing the generalizability of the findings.

Practical Tip	A practical strategy for increasing the size of the sample is for several students to collaborate on an action research study, with each contributing their schools/classrooms/students to generate a larger overall sample.

If you find a BIG benefit from your research it is likely to be of interest to others who could also potentially benefit from your findings. This can be thought of as your research having a *generalizable potential benefit*. The smaller the sample, the less generalizable the results are—and the greater the care that must be exercised in delimiting any claim that the findings apply beyond the immediate sample. At the same time, the more specialized a purposive sample is, the smaller the sample that is needed for your findings to be of interest to others and potentially generalizable.

Preparing for the data analysis

Now that you are collecting your data, it is time to start planning how you will analyze the data. Preparing to conduct the data analysis involves the following key steps.

Step 1   Identify which of the three categories of research you will primarily be engaged in.

Is your research primarily descriptive (Chapter 4), relationship (Chapter 5), or experimental (Chapters 6,8)—or a combination? Indeed, almost any research you are conducting will probably have a descriptive component. If you will be using a combination, indicate which category of research will be used for what specific component of the research.

Step 2   Identify which statistic you will use for each analysis.

Appendix A describes the steps for determining what statistic you need to run to analyze your data, depending on the type of research, the level of data (interval, ordinal, or nominal), and whether the distribution of a given variable is normal.

Step 3   Review the discussions in Chapters 4-6 about the specific category of research and the specific statistic you will be using. These discussions include the appropriate uses of that analysis, and whether Excel provides the capability to analyze that statistic—and if so under which function name. If Excel does not provide the needed function, consult a faculty member for advice on the best way to proceed.

Step 4   Search for resources to help you learn how to run the Excel program to analyze your data.

The two main resources are the web and faculty. If you search the web you will probably find a variety of instructional videos—e.g., How to perform a Pearson correlation in Excel.

Analyzing the data

General procedures

Step 1   Study the nature of the distribution of the values for each of your key variables by developing a histogram. Is it a normal (bell shaped) distribution—e.g., intelligence? Are most of the values at the extreme ends—e.g., the percentage of high poverty students in schools across the US? Are there extreme values at one end of the distribution—e.g., the prices of recent home sales—a distribution which is skewed by a few very expensive mansions?

Step 2   Present the (unadjusted) power trio of statistics for each of the variables and groups (see Chapter 4). Which is the most representative value—the *Mean* or *Median*—for each variable and group?

Step 3   Create some initial descriptive basic tables with several variables that describe how they interact. Such tables may describe some outcome broken down by some demographic variable. An example could be:

Average student performance by race

(Note that the word "by" is often used to describe the variable whose values are in the table.)

For the purposes of highlighting inequity, you can also create a table that limits the cases included in the table to the top quartile—i.e., the top 25%—and the bottom quartile to highlight the differences at each end of the distribution. An example of such a table could be:

Average student performance for the highest and lowest SES schools.

Such basic tables can be an effective way to provide a rationale for the more detailed statistical analyses to be included in your study.

---- At this point you have only used descriptive analysis (Chapter 4). *Often that is sufficient.* **However, if you are taking your research to the next level of relationship or experimental research, continue on to the next steps. ----**

Step 4   (*Experimental* research only) Eyeball the differences between the Means/Medians of the groups (whichever statistic is more appropriate—see Chapter 4) and make a determination of whether the difference seems substantial.

(*Relationship* research only) Produce a scatterplot, and determine whether there is a distinct linear or non-linear (i.e., curving) pattern of dots. The clearer the pattern of dots, the stronger the relationship.

If the pattern is generally linear, determine whether it is a positive or negative relationship—i.e., does the imaginary line connecting the most dots slope upward or downward as you look from left to right. If it is non-linear, do not use the linear measures of r and R—e.g., Pearson r. At that point you would need to consult a statistician about how to analyze curvilinear relationships. The one exception—i.e., a curvilinear relationship that you can easily calculate—is where the dots form a circular pattern. This pattern indicates a correlation of zero (see Chapter 4).

Step 5   Conduct statistical analyses by:

- Applying the appropriate statistics;
- Applying the appropriate statistical test to the results; and
- Correctly interpreting the leadership implications for action based on the results of the statistical test and your eyeballing of the results.

If you are using Excel, keep in mind that at this point in time its statistics only report the statistical significance of the results—which you should ignore—and take the following additional steps:

For *relationship* research, you should make your own judgments about the importance of the r and R values produced by Excel—i.e., the correlation and regression coefficients—using the data analysis principles of Chapter 7. *To conclude that the relationship has potential practical benefit, you are seeking values that are greater than .39, or less than -.39.*

For *experimental* research, determine whether there is practical benefit by examining where the experimental group ended up performing—using the power trio of statistical outcomes (Chapter 4) produced by Excel —relative to some existing benchmark in your schools or statewide.

The best way to calculate *potential practical benefit* is to:

- Eyeball the differences in the *Means/Medians* between the experimental and control groups and make a judgment as to whether the difference appears to be substantial; and/or
- Calculate an *ES* by using the power trio statistics (Chapter 4) produced by Excel to obtain the *Means*, and then entering those values into one of the free effect size calculators on the web.

The most common *ES* is *Cohen's d* which measures the difference between *Means* for interval data (see Appendix A), with the desired cutoffs discussed in Chapters 6-7. Search your browser for: "Free calculator for Cohen's d." When you find one you can enter the Means and Standard Deviation for each of the groups, and the calculator will produce the *ES*.

Most statistics have an associated *ES* that can be calculated for the results. For example, if you are using Chi-Square—i.e., nominal data—Cohen (1988) describes an ES measure called *W* with the following cutoffs: .10 = low, .30 = Medium, .50 = High. To find W, search on Google for: "Free Effect Size Calculator for Chi-Square."

For ordinal data you can find the *ES* for the *Signed Rank* statistic (listed as *Sign* in the flowchart in Appendix A) that Cohen (1988) refers to as **g,** with the cutoffs of: .05 = low, .10 = Medium, .25 = High. You can then use an "effect size calculator for g" from the web.

For both *W* and *g* use the *Medium* cutoff value as the basis for indicating *potential practical benefit*.

Examine the values of **the power trio,** r, R *(for relationship research),* and ESs *(for experimental research)* that the statistics have produced. (Ignore the p values produced—i.e., ignore findings related to statistical significance.)

If the results are for *relationship research*, decide whether *r* or *R* are large enough (as per Chapter 7) to constitute potential practical benefit—i.e., that the relationship is large enough to provide some useful predictiveness.

If your results from experimental or relationship research are NOT large enough to meet the cutoffs in Chapter 7, you should conclude something like:

It appears that despite the fact that my findings were statistically significant the relationship is not large enough to provide...

- Useful predictability of expected improvements; and/or
- Potential practical benefit to be derived from using this relationship as the basis of leadership action.

If there IS a large *r* or *R*, then your conclusion should still be cautious but more positive—especially given the problems associated with expanding interventions at large scale based solely on relationship research as discussed in Chapter 6. The conclusion should be something like:

The correlation is large enough to suggest implementing an intervention that reflects this relationship, but to do so on a small scale until an experimental study documents the hoped for practical benefits for the intervention.

If you have conducted an *experiment* with a sample of convenience to evaluate a new approach, the first step is NOT to examine the *ES*, but to first ask the questions of whether the end result of where the experimental group ended up...

- Is consistent with the school's/district's improvement goals?
- Represents a major improvement over how students performed in the past?
- Noticeably reduced gaps?

The last question is for equity purposes. It is important to break out the end result data by key subgroups, including by race/ethnicity and disability status. If most of the overall benefit was derived by the advantaged students then the "success/ improvement" would have exacerbated existing inequities. However, if the results indicate that these conditions were met, you can conclude that the intervention (a) has practical benefit, (b) is effective, and (c) is worthy of being scaled if there were no obvious confounding variables.

If the evaluation was conducted with a more rigorous sample such as a random or stratified sample that systematically eliminated most confounding variables, then the comparison group and the relative measure of *ES* becomes useful. And while judgments about the end result of the experimental group remain important, if the *ES* is larger than the cutoffs in Chapter 7 in favor of the experimental group, then the intervention has *potential practical benefit*.

However, in all cases you can use the highly non-technical "*Eyeball*" test. In the *Eyeball* test you look at the statistically significant results and see if the differences between groups or in the observed results seem to you, or a selected panel, as sufficiently compelling for them to seriously consider taking action based on these results.

While the eyeball test is subjective, it may be more valid as an authentic measure of BIGness for predicting whether the intervention will in fact produce noticeable benefits in your schools than relying on small *ES*s. In addition, the eyeball test usually works just as well, if not better, for determining whether the differences in *Medians* in experimental research is BIG enough to demonstrate potential practical benefit as it is for the differences in *Means*.

When using a small sample of convenience you should be especially cautious in making any claims of benefit from your findings, and recommend a slower, more cautious process of scaling up the practice in your action plan, than if you had used a more rigorous sampling technique.

Any generalizable BIG benefit from your research can benefit your own school as well as others. There are a variety of professional mechanisms to make your findings known that include professional presentations and articles based on your research.

General structure of an action research study

You are now ready to write up your study. While different institutions have different formatting requirements **for how to structure the formal study**, they will probably be some combination of the following components:

- Title;
- Abstract describing the study, results, and recommendations (Max 250 words);
- Description of the problem and the context;
- Research questions;
- Review of the Literature;
- Methodology;

  - ➢ Description of the variables
  - ➢ How they were operationalized
  - ➢ How the data were analyzed

- Results (presentation and discussion); and
- **Action Plan**—Recommendations for leadership action (and future research)

While it is normal to hope that the intervention you are interested in turns out to be highly effective, it is important not to overhype the results and claim to have found an important benefit or relationship based on a finding of statistical significance. You need to be cautious in your conclusions. Do NOT claim that you have proven anything. Use language such as: *It appears likely that if my schools adopt this intervention they will see a noticeable benefit.* If possible, delimit the conditions of expected success—e.g., which grades, which types of students, what implementation parameters, etc.

When using a small sample of convenience you should be especially cautious in making any claims of benefit from your findings, and recommend a slower, more cautious process of scaling up the practice in your action plan, than if you had used a more rigorous sampling technique.

In addition, play devil's advocate with yourself as to whether there is an alternative explanation for the outcome of your findings—in either direction. For example, finding that an intervention was not successful *as implemented* is an important finding which does NOT mean that it would be ineffective if implemented differently. So, if you do NOT find any practical benefit from the use of the intervention, or potential practical benefit from a relationship, speculate as to why it was not effective/important, and how to possibly implement it differently to increase its effectiveness. This will provide a guidepost for either a new experiment for leaders to consider, or subsequent action research by another student.

Such speculation is important because, as described in Chapter 8, the HOTS program used the approach of general thinking, which research had conclusively shown was ineffective. Fortunately, general thinking development turned out to be highly effective when implemented in a more intensive fashion. Finding an alternative pathway for your initial idea could similarly lead to a highly effective intervention and create new knowledge.

Having said all of this, hopefully your action research does find:

- An intervention that turns out to produce substantial improvement with increases in equity; or

- An important relationship that you can use to design a new intervention that exploits that relationship.

Any generalizable BIG benefit from your research can benefit your own school as well as others. There are a variety of professional mechanisms to make your findings known that include professional presentations and articles based on your research.

Ideally, practitioners and leadership in your school/district will be willing to evaluate your new approach in the pursuit of continuous improvement.

Above all, it is hoped that you found the experience of conducting action research—and developing findings and an action plan that can benefit students, improve your schools, and increase equity—to be a rewarding one.

Appendix A

Selecting the Right Statistics for Your Research

What statistic should you use for the research you are conducting? The flow chart in the following pages illustrates the decision-making process for selecting the appropriate statistic—and includes all of the key statistics you are likely to need to choose from.

There are three key determinants as to what statistic is appropriate for your research:

- The level of the data you are collecting;
- Whether you are analyzing relationships or differences between groups—and if the latter, how many groups?; and
- Whether the data form a normal (bell shaped) distribution.

How to Select the Right Statistic

Level of the data

The level of data is a critical determinant of what statistic will be used for analyzing the data. The *level of data* is whether the data for a given variable are *interval*, *nominal*, or *ordinal*.

Interval data (also called scale or continuous) is a measure that uses regular numbers. Examples of *interval* data are individuals' actual height and income, or the actual (raw or scale) score on a test.[104]

Ordinal data are when the values of the measure are expressed as the rank of someone or something in relation to all the others in the sample. Examples of *ordinal* data are the academic rank of a given school as compared to all schools in a state, and where a student's test result is scored in terms of its percentile rank. However, if instead of giving a rank score, the result is presented in terms of the percent of individuals who scored higher, such percentage data can be considered *interval* data (though that is controversial). So, if one is ranked #31 in a law class that is ordinal data. However, if one's score on the SAT is 400 that value is considered *interval* data.

---

[104] Some differentiate *interval* data into **ratio** data which has a true zero such as temperature and height, and **scale** data which are arbitrarily created numbers, such as GPA. However, while this is a valid differentiation, it will be ignored in the interest of simplicity unless there is evidence that such a distinction produces a major change in the outcome of research.

Nominal **data** are when the values of a variable are categories, particularly when the categories do not have an order. An example of a *nominal* variable would be "race" or "sex". However, consider the variable of SES. If the dataset contains actual incomes, that clearly is *interval* data. However, suppose all you know is whether each individual's SES is *poor*, *middle class*, *upper class*, or *one-percenter*. In this case the data are in categories—but there is a clear order to the categories. Some argue that where the categories have a natural order, once you assign an arbitrary value to each category; e.g., ranging from 1 (poor) to 4 (one-percenter), the result can be considered *ordinal* data.

A special type of a *nominal* variable is where there are only two categories. Measures that contain only two possible categories are referred to as **dichotomous**. Examples of **dichotomous** data are where SES is measured in terms of whether students do or do not receive free and reduced lunch, or where Academic Achievement is measured as whether students do or do not graduate in four years.

Interval data are more precise than *ordinal* data, and *ordinal* data are more precise than *nominal* data. As a result, you should try to operationalize your variables in a way such that you are using *interval* measures. However, sometimes you have no choice—e.g., if your research uses Sex as a variable. That is *nominal* data by definition.

You can convert results from a higher to a lower level, but not vice versa. For example, you can take an actual test score (*interval* data) and convert it to a percentile rank number (*ordinal* data), and further convert it into whether the score is below basic, basic, proficient, or advanced (which can be treated either as *nominal* data or as ordinal if the rank of each category is coded). A person's height can be converted from the actual height in inches (*interval* data) to a rank in terms of how tall that individual is in relation to others if everyone lines up from shortest to tallest (*ordinal*), or to a category such as tall, medium, short. The latter can either be treated as *nominal* or you can code the categories in terms of its logical rank order, e.g., 3,2,1, and treat the result as *ordinal* data. However, you cannot go in the opposite direction, e.g., from nominal to interval. In other words, if you know that someone is short, you cannot tell from that information his/her exact height (*interval*).

Therefore, you should avoid dropping data to a lower level whenever possible since when you do so you lose precision. However, as you will see in the upcoming section on "Choosing Statistics", sometimes you have no choice but to drop one of the variables down a level.

Sometimes the level of data can be a bit ambiguous. For example, consider letter grades—A,B,C,D,F. These are clearly discrete categories (nominal), but the categories have an order (ordinal). Where possible treat it at the higher level: i.e., as ordinal data.

Most, but not all, statistics are designed for a single, specific level of data. For example, the *Mean* and *Standard Deviation* discussed extensively in Chapter 4 of this textbook are only used with *interval* data. For *ordinal* data you would use the *Median*, and for *nominal* data you would use the *Mode*.

Level of Survey/Questionnaire Data:

When using a Likert scale, the result on a single item/question is *Ordinal* data. However, as previously discussed in Chapter 10, you should construct an *index* of a sub-construct that combines the results from a series of related Likert items. For example, suppose you determine that there are seven critical aspects of the measure of "teacher satisfaction", and you construct a Likert item for each. The resultant *index score* for each teacher surveyed can range from 7 to 35, and this combined or *index* score can be considered *interval* under certain circumstances.[105]

If the questionnaire is filled out on a computer, you can use a sliding bar wherein the respondent slides a pivot along the length of the bar to indicate where his/her response would be relative to the extreme of "strongly agree" to "strongly disagree", or some other divergent outcomes such as "Love" and "Hate", or "Freezing" and "Boiling." (This is called a Track Bar scale.) The computer can then measure precisely (to as many decimal points as you wish) how far the pivot point has been moved along the continuum of the bar. Such a response for each item is then also considered *interval* data.

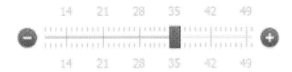

In order to determine which statistic to use for analyzing your data, you need to focus on these five things.

1. Are the *dependent* and *independent* variables in the analysis *interval, ordinal,* or *nominal* data?

2. Since most statistics require that all the data for the variables be of the same level, do I have to convert any variable from a higher level to a lower one?

3. There are several situations where you can mix levels of variables in the same statistical analysis. For example:

    *   You can mix data level types in *Regression Analysis, Discriminant Analysis, and Logistic Regression Analysis.* You can use both *interval* and

---

[105] The most widely cited condition for allowing an index from a combination of Likert items to be considered as *interval* data is if the index score of all the individuals in the sample form a *normal distribution*.

nominal data in the *independent* variables. *Nominal independent* variables; e.g., "sex", are called **dummy variables.**[106])

- You will often mix interval and nominal data when analyzing the difference of Means between groups such as the t-test. You may be examining the differences in the *Means* of boys vs. girls (nominal) on reading test scores (interval).

4. In experimental research, are you comparing the ***independent Means***, i.e., *Means* from different groups which means that the members of the experimental and control groups are independent of the other, or are you comparing non-independent *Means*. (***Non-independent Means*** is research with a single group where you are tracking the change of the pre- and post-test *Means* of the <u>same</u> group, or from matched pairs.)

5. Is the distribution of scores for a given variable a "*normal*" distribution—i.e., the classical bell-shaped curve? An example of a *normal* distribution is the "Intelligence Scores" of the population, which is a bell-shaped curve where the average score is the most frequently occurring one. A non-normal distribution is one where the scores are skewed to one end of the range of scores. As previously discussed, an example of a non-normal distribution would be "the number of minutes before a movie that individuals arrive." Most would usually arrive shortly before the movie started, so the most frequently occurring value would be at the low end of the distribution. If the distribution is extremely skewed you should usually switch your data to a lower level.

The statistics used when the data are derived from a known distribution such as a *normal* distribution are referred to as ***parametric. Non-parametric*** statistics in education are used with data that are not from a *normal* distribution and are usually used with ordinal or nominal data. However, just because data are *interval* level does not necessarily mean that you use a *parametric* statistic—unless the data come from a *normal* distribution. If the distribution is very non-normal, then it is recommended to convert *interval* data to *ordinal* and use *non-parametric* statistics.

There is also a unique characteristic of the t test. There is the option of a *two-tail* or *one-tail test*. The ***two-tail t test*** is for experimental studies that use the traditional null hypothesis; i.e., that there is no difference between the groups. The *t test* also has the feature where you can make a directional hypothesis: e.g., that the experimental group will do better than the comparison group. The ***one-tail version of the t test*** is used to test the *statistical significance* of the directional hypothesis.

You are now ready to apply the flowchart on the next page to determine which statistical procedure to use. Where there are several possible statistics listed for a given situation, the first one listed is usually the more widely used statistic.

---

[106] As illustrated in the following flowchart, *Regression Analysis* is used when the *dependent* variable is interval, *Discriminant Analysis* is used when the *dependent* variable is *nominal*, and *Logistic Regression* is used when the *dependent* variable is *dichotomous*; i.e., there are only two categories such as pass/fail.

Remember

While the flowchart is helpful in quickly navigating the impressive array of available statistics to select the one that is most suitable for your research—keep in mind that these statistics generally only directly test for statistical significance. That means that by themselves they cannot determine practical or potential practical benefit unless you go the extra step and determine the associated *ES* using calculator tools from the web as discussed in Chapter 10.

Good News

Most of the statistics you are likely to need are available in Excel, and in many cases you can find online tutorials on how to use Excel to apply them.

In any event, do not worry about what all these different statistical tests are or how they work. View them as automated tools, and your job is to choose the right automated tool for your research, and then assess the results that it produces on your printouts.

In order to help you practice selecting the right statistic, decide what statistic you would use for the following 10 challenge practice problems (note that there can usually be more than one correct answer).

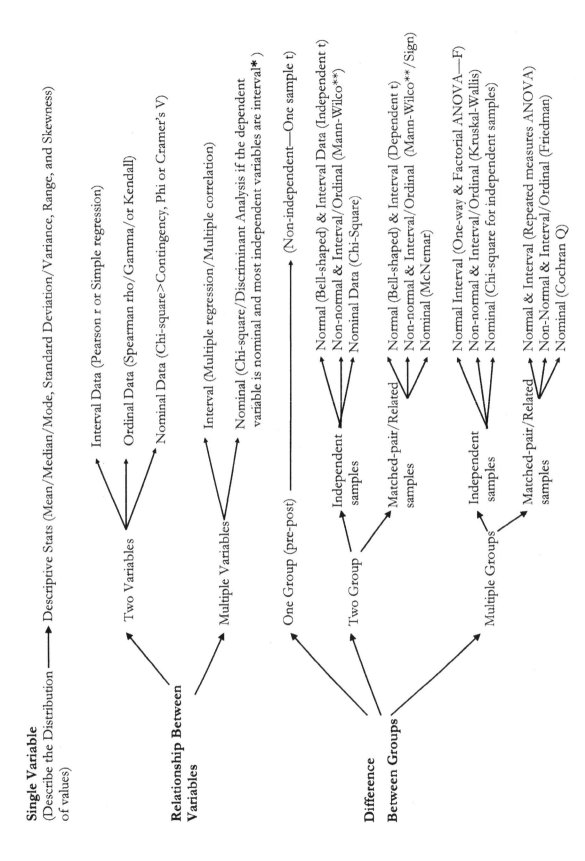

*If the dependent variable is a dichotomous nominal variable (i.e., only two possible values) use Logistic Regression instead of Discriminant Analysis

**This refers to the Mann Whitney U or Wilcoxon which are basically the same test.

Challenge Practice Problems for Selecting the Appropriate Statistic

(Solutions are at the end of this chapter)

Using the flowchart, and assuming that the *interval* level variables come from a *normal* distribution, what statistic would you use to determine:

1. The relationship between income and GPA (assuming GPA is numerical)

2. The relationship between Citizenship Status and GPA (assuming GPA is numerical)

3. Whether there is a relationship in the Statewide Rank of a School and its Percentage of Special Education students

4. Whether there is a difference between the final GPA (as a number) of individuals by race

5. Whether there is a difference in the change in GPA (as a number) according to household income

6. Whether students who enroll in experimental program x the first year make significant gains in their GPA (as a number) between the first quarter and last quarter of their first year

7. Whether students who enroll in experimental program x the first year make significant difference in their GPA (as a number) between the first quarter and last quarter of their first year as compared to students in program y

8. Whether there is a difference in completion status (e.g., did not complete, obtained Associate Degree, transferred to 4 year institution) by age of admission to the community college

9. Whether there is a difference in completion status as by race

10. What effect did Race, GPA (as a number), and Household Income have on whether or not students obtained an Associate Degree (Y/N)

Solutions to the Challenge Practice Problems

(The answers below are not necessarily the only possible answers)

1. This is correlation between two interval variables, so the statistic would be Pearson r or Simple Regression.

2. This is a correlation between a nominal variable and either an interval (if GPA is expressed as a number), in which case it has to be converted to a nominal measure, or it can already be a nominal measure if a letter grade system is being used. In either case, it is a correlation between two nominal variables, and the appropriate statistic is Chi-square, Phi, or Cramer's V.

3. This is a correlation between an ordinal measure and an interval one. You would therefore convert percentage of special education to an ordinal one, and then use the correlation statistic for two ordinal variables, which is Spearman rho, Gamma, or Kendall.

4. This is a relationship between an interval and a nominal variable, so the interval variable would be converted to nominal, and the analysis would be the relationship between two nominal variables, which is Chi-square, Phi, or Cramer's V.

5. This is a relationship between two interval variables so it is a Pearson r or Simple Regression.

6. This is an experimental "difference between groups" question with one group pre- post-test design, so the statistic is a one-group t test also called the t test for non-independent *Means*.

7. This is an experimental "difference between the groups" with two groups so it would be an Independent t test.

8. You can code the variable of "completion status" as an *ordinal* variable. (It would not be wrong to consider it as a nominal variable but that is a lower level than *ordinal*.) The preferred approach is to change the interval level variable of "age" to ordinal and treat this as the relationship between two ordinal variables, so this is Spearman rho, Gamma, or Kendall. (You can have ranks of ages, e.g., 1 for the youngest group, and 4 for the oldest.) You can also treat this as a relationship between a nominal variable and an interval one, so the latter needs to be changed to a nominal (e.g., for community college you might use the age categories of teenager, 20-29, 30 and older), and the relationship between two nominal variables is Chi-square, Phi, or Cramer's V.

9. This is a relationship between an ordinal and a nominal variable, or two nominal variables, so this would be a Chi-square, Phi, or Cramer's V.

10. This is a relationship between a dichotomous dependent variable, i.e., whether an associate degree was obtained, with several interval independent variables, so this is a *Logistic Regression Analysis*—However, given the problems with interpreting the odds ratios of *Logistic Regression*, as discussed in Chapters 3 and 4, you may want to use *Discriminant Analysis*.

Primary source data are used to assess educational progress and gaps at the national, state, and local level. Leaders can use such data at the local and state level to see how their schools compare to others, as well as the progress that their schools and students are making—and for identifying areas that need improvement.

Primary data are the original data that are produced by a research study. Secondary source data is what someone refers to that original data and makes claims as to what the original data demonstrated. Secondary sources are far less reliable than going to the source of the original research—i.e., the primary source—and seeing for yourself what the actual data of interest were. Leadership students in particular should always be suspicious of secondary claims of what the original study showed and should go to the primary source of the data and research and cite it directly from the source.

(Chapter 4 provides an example of accessing primary source data.)

This appendix lists the major sources of primary data, and suggestions for how to access them.

Federal Sources of Primary Data

I. K-12 (mostly) and Post-secondary

National Center for Educational Statistics (NCES) nces.ed.gov — This is one of the best *primary* sources for data on current and historic trends of achievement gaps and for general demographic data nationally and for each state. Unlike the rest of the ED website, NCES works very hard at not being influenced by political pressures. The three most valuable sources of *primary* data at this site are:

- The National Assessment of Educational Progress (NAEP) is also referred to as The Nation's Report Card.
- A set of longitudinal studies that can be accessed by selecting one of the tabs under the column <Surveys & Programs>, then select the student level or type of study you are interested in, then review the available studies, and select the one you are interested in.
- A series of annual reports that can be selected under the column <Publications & Products>, then select "Annual Reports".

The NAEP is administered to a national sample periodically in a variety of content areas for grades 4, 8, and 12 every 4 years. NAEP also has extensive stats on the achievement gaps on a wide range of variables such as Race, Sex, Disability, School/District Type, etc.

There are 5 types of NAEP studies:

- *Long-term Trend* NAEP, which tracks results in reading since 1971 and math since 1978. This test is periodically administered to students ages 9, 13, and 17, and is the best measure for showing historic trends.
- *Main* NAEP, which provides the most current results in Reading, Math, Writing, and Science, and that compares progress going back to a much shorter time span than *Long-Term Trend* NAEP.
- *Urban* NAEP (TUDA), which provides results for 13 of the largest urban districts (as opposed to all the other NAEP studies that only break down data to the state level).
- *High School Transcript Study (HSTS),* which contains data on the course taking patterns of 12th grade students who graduated high school and its relationship to their achievement.
- *National Indian Education Study (NIES),* which describes the condition of education for American Indian and Alaska Native students. (There is also a breakdown of results by ethnicity in the other NAEP studies.)

(Chapter 4 provides detailed instructions on how to access NAEP data and how to generate custom reports to analyze gaps and any other detailed information of interest to you.)

There are also <u>other longitudinal datasets and studies</u> at the NCES site, each of which has a rich trove of *primary* data and analyses. These can also be accessed under <Surveys & Programs> on the NCES website, and are organized by grade level, e.g., Early Childhood, Elementary Secondary, or postsecondary. Examples in the first two categories include:

- <u>Beginning Teacher Longitudinal Study - BTLS</u>;
- <u>Early Childhood Longitudinal Study - ECLS</u>, which followed a national sample of kindergarten students through the 8th grade;
- <u>Education Finance Statistics Center - EDFIN</u>;
- <u>Education Longitudinal Study of 2002 - ELS</u>, which is following 10th graders in 2002 into the world of work;
- <u>High School and Beyond - HS&B</u>, which describes the activities of seniors and sophomores in 1980 as they progressed through high school, postsecondary education, and into the workplace through 1992;
- <u>High School Longitudinal Study of 2009 - HSLS:09</u>, which follows a cohort of more than 25,000 9th graders through their high school, postsecondary, and early career experiences;
- <u>Middle Grades Longitudinal Study of 2016–17 - MGLS:2017</u>, which follows students as they enter and move through the middle grades. There is a special focus on socio-emotional and executive function measures, as well as successful transition to high school and later education and career outcomes;

- National Education Longitudinal Study of 1988 - NELS:88/2000, which provides trend data about critical transitions experienced by an 8th grade cohort in 1988 as they develop, attend school, and embark on their careers;
- National Household Education Survey - NHES;
- National Longitudinal Study of the H.S. Class of 1972 - NLS-72, which describes the transition of young adults from high school through postsecondary education and the workplace. The data span 1972 through 1986 and include postsecondary transcripts;
- National Teacher and Principal Survey - NTPS;
- Rural Education in America - Rural;
- School Survey on Crime and Safety - SSOCS, which among other things includes data collected on such topics as frequency and types of crimes at school, frequency and types of disciplinary actions at school, perceptions of other disciplinary problems, and descriptions of school policies and programs concerning crime and safety;
- Schools and Staffing Survey - SASS;
- Urban Education in America - Urban.

These datasets are a rich trove of data collected from a wide variety of sources with lots of demographic information about the participants, which makes an almost infinite variety of analyses possible. A significant percentage of published research in recent years has involved using advanced statistical methods to analyze the relationships among various combinations of the many constructs measured in each of these datasets.

The annual reports on the NCES website are also helpful. The most useful one is the "Digest of Educational Statistics".

Clearly, there is a ton of *primary* data in the NCES website, both for K-12 and post-secondary. It may seem overwhelming, but NAEP is generally a good place to start.

Another rich source of online federal equity related databases is the data center of the Office of Civil Rights (OCR) in ED. (The current URL is ocrdata.ed.gov). Among its many types of data, it contains data on disciplinary practices, and whether any race is disproportionately disciplined.

Finally, other government agencies also have relevant data. If you are doing research on science, technology, engineering, and math (STEM) issues, you should look for relevant primary source data from the National Science Foundation (NSF) website—www.nsf.gov. Indeed, a student who was interested in the percentage of doctoral degrees awarded to first generation students found such data on the NSF site.

In addition, many of the national education associations have descriptive data sets that are excellent sources of primary data.

Stanford Education Data Archive (SEDA) — This resource provides current and trend data in reading/language arts and math for grades 3-8, starting from 2008, broken out by school, district, county, and state. This dataset equates the results from the different state tests and converts them to grade level equivalents, which can then be further broken down by key socio-economic and demographic variables. SEDA provides an interactive graphic data explorer https://edopportunity.org/explorer/. It also provides the capability for individuals to download the data files themselves to conduct original data analyses using statistical software https://edopportunity.org/get-the-data/.

II. Federal Census Data

This has lots of demographic data on wealth, housing, educational attainment which can be linked to geographic areas such as school boundaries.

The best sources for getting census data by school district is a guided or advanced search through the census at: https://data.census.gov/cedsci/

NCES also has some of the census data by school district available on its site and provides some nice maps and tables at: https://nces.ed.gov/programs/maped/ACSMaps/ The census website also has access to other data, mostly economic, but some related to housing and social indicators. data.gov has a lot of federal and local data available, but it can be overwhelming. For even more detailed census analyses check https://ipums.org/ which also provides trainings, webinars, and a support team.

State Sources of Primary Data

While federal datasets will usually break out data by state, many states are now maintaining their own statewide databases that anyone can access. Such databases typically contain data on student performance on state tests, along with key demographic data, organized by school and district.

For example, the *California State Department of Education* maintains a series of data files that can be accesses that provides data on school/district demographics and performance at https://dq.cde.ca.gov/dataquest/

> (It also maintains the California Longitudinal Pupil Achievement Data System (CALPADS) but that is only available to identified school officials.)

Some states also have non-profit research and policy organizations that conduct original research on the status of education in that state and make the results available free. An example is Edsource in California, www.edsource.org. In addition, a number of universities maintain education research centers. Some conduct research specific to the state they are in and others conduct national research. Examples of centers that are national in nature include:

- National Center for Research on Evaluation, Standards, and Student Testing at UCLA, cresst96.cse.ucla.edu/index2.htm,

334

- UC Linguistic Minority Research Institute at the University of California at Santa Barbara, http://lmri.ucsb.edu

III. Community College

- The Community College Research Center at Columbia University http://ccrc.tc.columbia.edu/

- Institutional studies at your institution or community college district

- State Community College Chancellor's Office datasets

  California has Datamart, which has state-wide, district, college, and some program data, go to this link: http://www.cccco.edu/ChancellorsOffice/Divisions/TechResearchInfo/MIS/DataMartandReports/tabid/282/Default.aspx. Datamart is also available as a link on the left if you go to the CCCCO homepage: http://www.cccco.edu

  LaunchBoard provides data on the progress, success, employment, and earnings outcomes for California community college students. https://www.calpassplus.org/LaunchBoard/Home.aspx

- The U.S. Department of Education also has a post secondary data set in the National Center for Educational Statistics: http://nces.ed.gov/ipeds/ The center has released a study on: On Track to Complete? A Taxonomy of Beginning Community College Students and Their Outcomes 3 Years After Enrolling: 2003-04 through 2006 http://nces.ed.gov/pubsearch/pubsinfo.asp?pubid=2009152

IV. College

The National Center for Education Statistics (NCES) in the US Dept of Education provides lots of data on college graduation participation and graduation rates.

Other Federal agencies provide statistics on graduations in that particular field. For example, the National Science Foundation provides data on college and graduate degrees in STEM fields.

Higher Ed professional associations, such as the American Council on Education also has research studies.

Other Sources of Primary Data

V. Using Published Empirical Research

There are also scholarly sources of *primary* data. Many academic articles and books often contain studies that have generated *primary* data. It is *primary* source data if the authors are the ones who collected the data. Such *primary* data can be quantitative, historical, qualitative, anthropological, etc.

VI. Institutional/Local Research

There are many studies produced by local research groups, or research offices in school districts and post-secondary institutions. The studies and summaries of research can be used if they are reporting data and analyses that these organizations conducted themselves. However, if they are reporting results that others produced that is a secondary source.

VII. International

OECD Data hub https://data.oecd.org/

UN stats hub for international (and US) data
https://unstats.un.org/unsd/demographic-social/index.cshtml

BIBLIOGRAPHY

AbuAlRub, R. F. (2004). Job stress, job performance, and social support among hospital nurses. *Journal of nursing scholarship, 36*(1), 73-78.

Achilles C.M., & Finn, J.D. (1999). Tennessee's class size study: Findings, implications, misconceptions. *Educational Evaluation And Policy Analysis, 21*(2), 97-109.

Anderson, C. R. (1976). Coping behaviors as intervening mechanisms in the inverted-U stress-performance relationship. *Journal of Applied Psychology, 61*(1), 30.

Anderson, T., & Shattuk, J. (2012). Design-Based Research: A decade of progress in education research? *Educational Researcher, 41*(1), 16-25.

APA. (2010). *New edition: Publication manual of the American Psychological Association: Sixth (6th) edition.* American Psychological Association.

Ary, D., Jacobs, L.C., & Razavieh, A. (1979). *Introduction to research in education.* Holt, Rinehart, and Winston.

Augier, M., & March, J.G. (2011). *The roots, rituals, and rhetoric of change: North American business schools after the second world war.* Stanford CA: Stanford University Press.

Babo, G., & Elovitz, L.H. (2015). *Quantitative data analysis using Microsoft® Excel: A school administrator's guide.* NCPEA Press.

Baird, M. D., & Pane, J. F. (2019). Translating Standardized Effects of Education Programs Into More Interpretable Metrics. *Educational Researcher,* 0013189X19848729.

Bambrick-Santoyo, P. (2010). *Driven by data: A practical guide to improve instruction.* John Wiley & Sons.

Bocala, C., & Boudett, K.P. (2015). Teaching Educators Habits of Mind for Using Data Wisely. *Teachers College Record,* 117, 040304.

Baker, B. (2103). The Value Added & Growth Score Train Wreck is Here. Retrieved from https://schoolfinance101.files.wordpress.com/2011/11/slide5.jpg.

Begley, C. G., & Ellis, L. M. (2012). Drug development: Raise standards for preclinical cancer research. *Nature, 483*(7391), 531-533.

Bell, P. (2004). On the theoretical breadth of design-based research in education. *Educational Psychologist, 39*(4), 243–253.

Berkson, J. (1942). Tests of significance considered as evidence. *Journal of the American Statistical Association, 37*(219), 325-335.

Berliner, D.C., & Glass, G.V. (2014). *50 myths & lies that threaten America's public schools: The real crisis in education.* NY City: Teachers College Press.

Berwick D.M. (2008). The science of improvement. *JAMA,* 299(10), 1182-1184.

Bishop, W., Clopton, P., & Milgram, R.J. (Downloaded 2012). A close examination of Jo Boaler's Railside report. Downloaded from *ftp://math.stanford.edu/pub/papers/milgram/combined-evaluations-version3.pdf,* December 4, 2012.

Blair, J., & Conrad, F. (2011). Sample size for cognitive interviewing pretesting. *Public Opinion Quarterly.* 75(4), 638-658.

Blair, J., Czaja, R.E., & Blair, E.A. (2014). *Designing surveys: A Guide to decisions and procedures (3rd Edition).* Sage, Los Angeles CA.

Boaler, J. (2006). How a detracked mathematics approach promoted respect, responsibility, and high achievement. *Theory into Practice,* 45(1), 40-46.

Boaler, J., & Staples, M. (2008). Creating mathematical futures through an equitable teaching approach:

The case of Railside School. *Teachers College Record*, 110 (3), 608-645.

Borman, G. D., & Hewes, G. M. (2002). The long-term effects and cost-effectiveness of Success for All. *Educational Evaluation and Policy Analysis*, *24*(4), 243-266.

Boote, D.N., & Beile, P. (2005). Scholars before researchers: On the centrality of the dissertation literature review in research preparation. *Educational Researcher*, 34(6), 3-15.

Borman, G. D., Grigg, J., & Hanselman, P. (2016). An effort to close achievement gaps at scale through self-affirmation. *Educational Evaluation and Policy Analysis*, *38*(1), 21–42. https://doi.org/10.3102/0162373715581709

Boudett, K.P., & Moody, L. (2005). Organizing for collaborative work. *In Data Wise: A step by step guide to using assessment results to improve teaching and learning*, Boudett, K.P., City E.A (eds). Cambridge MA, Harvard Education Press, pp. 1-28.

Boudett, K. P., & Murnane, R. J. (2013). *Data wise: A step by step guide to using assessment results to improve teaching and learning*. Harvard Education Press. 8 Story Street First Floor, Cambridge, MA 02138.

Boulay, et al. (2018). *The Investing in Innovation Fund: Summary of 67 Evaluations. Final Report.* Institute of Education Sciences: U.S. Department of Education.

Bracey, G.W. (2006). *Reading educational research.* Portsmouth NH: Heinemann.

Brookings. (1998). *The black-white test score gap.* Jencks, C., & Phillips, M. (eds). Washington DC: The Brookings Institution.

Brown, A. L. (1992). Design experiments: Theoretical and methodological challenges in creating complex interventions in classroom settings. *Journal of the Learning Sciences*, 2(2), 141–178.

Bryk, A.S., Gomez, L.M., & Grunow, A. (2011). Getting ideas into action: Building networked improvement communities in education. in *Frontiers in Sociology of Education*, Maureen Hallinan (ed), Springer Publishing.

Bryk, A.S., Gomez, L.M., Grunow, A., & LeMahieu, P.G. (2015). *Learning to improve: How Americas schools can get better at getting better.* Cambridge, MA: Harvard Education Press.

Burdumy, J.S., et al. (2009). *Effectiveness of Selected Supplemental Reading Comprehension Interventions: Impacts on a First Cohort of Fifth-Grade Students.* Mathematica Inc., Presentation at IES research conference, June 8. Downloaded from http://www.mathematica-mpr.com/~/media/publications/pdfs/education/ies_readcomp_james-burdumy0609.pdf, October 15, 2014.

Buttram, J. L. (2014). Survey of EdD and PhD educational leadership programs. *UCEA Review*, 55(2), Summer.

Campbell, D. T., Stanley, J. C., & Gage, N. L. (1963). *Experimental and quasi-experimental designs for research* (pp. 171-246). Boston: Houghton Mifflin.

Carpenter, W.A. (2000). Ten years of silver bullets. *Phi Delta Kappan*, 383-389.

Carey, B. (2015, June 15). Science, now under scrutiny itself. *New York Times,* Downloaded 7/10/15 from http://www.nytimes.com/2015/06/16/science/retractions-coming-out-from-under-science-rug.html

Carey, B. (2015, August 27). Many psychology findings not as strong as claimed, study says. *New York Times*, retrieved from http://www.nytimes.com/2015/08/28/science/many-social-science-findings-not-as-strong-as-claimed-study-says.html

Carroll, R. (1978). The case against statistical significance testing. Harvard Educational Review, 48(3), 378-399.

Carroll, A. E., & Frakt, A. (2015, February 2). How to Measure a Medical Treatment's Potential for Harm, *New York Times*. Retrieved from http://www.nytimes.com/2015/02/03/upshot/how-to-measure-a-medical-treatments-potential-for-harm.html

Caroll, A. E. (2015, March 30). Red meat is not the enemy. *New York Times*. Downloaded from http://www.nytimes.com/2015/03/31/upshot/red-meat-is-not-the-enemy.html?hp&action=click&pgtype=Homepage&module=mini-moth&region=top-stories-below&WT.nav=top-stories-below&_r=0&abt=0002&abg=1.

Carroll, A.E. (2018, July 23). What if a Study Showed Opioids Weren't Usually Needed? *New York Times,* Downloaded from https://www.nytimes.com/2018/07/23/upshot/what-if-a-study-showed-opioids-werent-usually-needed.html.

Carver, Castleman, B. L., Owen, L., Page, L. C., & Stephany, B. (2014). Using text messaging to guide students on the path to college. In *Center for Education Policy and Workforce Competitiveness Working Paper No. 33.* University of Virginia Charlottesville, VA.

Castellano, K. E., & Ho, A. D. (2013). A Practitioner's Guide to Growth Models. *Council of Chief State School Officers.*

Cho, V. & Wayman, J. C. (2013). District leadership for computer data systems: Technical, social, and organizational challenges in implementation. In *Proceedings of the UCEA Convention, Indianapolis, IN. Retrieved from http://www. vincentcho. com/uploads/9/6/5/2/9652180/ ucea_2013_co_data_systems_final. pdf.*

Cohen, J. (1988). *Statistical power analysis for the behavioral sciences.* Hillsdale, NJ, Lawrence Erlbaum.

Collins, A. (1992). Toward a design science of education. In E. Scanlon and T. O'Shea (Eds.), *New Directions In Educational Technology* (15–22). New York: Springer-Verlag.

Collins, J., and Porras, J.I. (2004). *Built to last: successful habits of visionary companies.* New York, NY: Harper Business.

Comer, J. P. (1988). Educating poor minority children. *Scientific American, 259*(5), 42-48.

Connolly, P. (2007). *Quantitative data analysis in education: A critical introduction using SPSS.* Routledge.

Cook, B.G., & Cook, S.C. (2001). Unraveling evidence based practice in special education. *The Journal of Special Education.* 47(2), 71-82.

Cory, S.M. (1953). Action research to improve school practice. New York: Teachers College Press.

CREDO. (2013). National charter school study. Center for Research on Education Outcomes. *Stanford University,* Stanford, CA. Retrieved from http://credo.stanford.edu/documents/ NCSS%202013%20Final%20Draft.pdf

Creighton, T.B. (2007). *Schools and Data: Second Edition.* Thousand Oaks, CA: Corwin Press.

Creswell, J.W. (2011). *Educational Research: Planning, Conducting, and Evaluating Quantitative and Qualitative Research* (4th Edition)**.** Boston: Pearson Education.

Creswell, J.W. (2013). *Research Design: Qualitative, Quantitative, and Mixed Methods Approaches.* Thousand Oaks, CA: SAGE Publications.

Datnow, A., & Hubbard, L. (2015). Teachers' use of assessment data to inform instruction: Lessons from the past and prospects for the future. *Teachers College Record, 117*(4), n4.

Davis, S.H. (2008). *Research and Practice in Education: The Search for Common Ground.* Roman & Littlefield Education.

Dee, T. S., & Penner, E. K. (2017). The causal effects of cultural relevance: Evidence from an ethnic studies curriculum. *American Educational Research Journal, 54*(1), 127-166.

Deming, W. E. (1986). *Out of the crisis.* Massachusetts Institute of Technology. Center for advanced engineering study: Cambridge, MA.

Donker, A. S., De Boer, H., Kostons, D., Dignath van Ewijk, C. C., & Van der Werf, M. P. C. (2014). Effectiveness of learning strategy instruction on academic performance: A meta-analysis. *Educational Research Review, 11,* 1-26.

Drucker, P. F., & Drucker, P. F. (2007). Innovation and entrepreneurship: Practice and principles. Routledge.

Finkelstein, N., Hanson, T., Huang, C. W., Hirschman, B., & Huang, M. (2010). Effects of Problem Based Economics on High School Economics Instruction. Final Report. NCEE 2010-4002. *National Center for Education Evaluation and Regional Assistance.*

Finn, J.D., & Achilles, C.M. (1999). Tennessee's class size study: Findings, implications, misconceptions. *Educational Evaluation And Policy Analysis*, 21(2), 97-109.

Fishman, B., Penuel, W.R., Allen, A., & Cheng, B.H. (2013). Design-based implementation research: Theories, methods, and exemplars. National Society for the Study of Education Yearbook (vol. 2), New York, NY: Teachers College Press.

Flexner, A. (1910). *Medical education in the United States and Canada: A Report to the Carnegie Foundation for the Advancement of Teaching.* New York, NY: Carnegie Foundation for the Advancement of Teaching.

Ford, I., & Norrie, J. (2016). Pragmatic trials. *New England journal of medicine*, 375(5), 454-463.

Fredricks, J.A., Blumenfeld, P.C., & Paris, A.H. (Spring 2004). School engagement: Potential of the concept, state of the evidence. *Review of Educational Research*, 74(1), 59-109.

Frey, B.B. (2015). *100 Questions (and Answers) About Tests and Measurement.* Los Angeles: Sage Publications.

Fraenkel, J. R., Wallen, N. E., & Hyun, H. H. (2009). *How to design and evaluate research in education* (Vol. 7). New York: McGraw-Hill.

Fraenkel, J., Wallen, N., & Hyun, H. (2011). *How to Design and Evaluate Research in Education.* New York: McGraw Hill.

Frakt, A. & Carroll, A.E. (2015). Can this treatment help me? There's a statistic for that. *New York Times*, Jan 26.

Friedman, R.A. (2014). Why can't doctors identify killers? *New York Times*, OP-ED May 27. Downloaded from http://www.nytimes.com/2014/05/28/opinion/why-cant-doctors-identify-killers.html?ref=opinion.

Fuller, B., Gesicki, K., Kang, E., & Wright, J. (2006). Is the No Child Left Behind Act Working? The Reliability of How States Track Achievement. Working Paper 06-1. *Policy Analysis for California Education, PACE (NJ1).*

Gall, J.P., Gall, M.D., & Borg, W.R. (1999). Applying educational research: A practical guide. New York, NY: Addison Wesley Longman.

Gall, M.D. (2001). Figuring out the importance of research results: *Statistical significance* versus Practical Significance. Paper presented at the 2001 annual meeting of the American Educational Research Association.

Gardner, H. (1983). Frames of mind: The theory of multiple intelligences. New York, NY.: Basic Books.

Garet, M.S., et al. (2011). *Middle School Mathematics Professional Development Impact Study: Findings After the Second Year of Implementation.* Report prepared for the Institute of Education Sciences by the American Institute for Research and MDRC.

Gawande, A. (2007). *Better: A surgeon's notes on performance.* New York, NY: Metropolitan Books.

Gawande, A. (2009). The cost conundrum: What a Texas town can teach us about health care. *The New Yorker.* June 1, downloaded 9/25/14 from http://www.newyorker.com/magazine/2009/06/01/the-cost-conundrum.

Ginsburg, A., & Smith, M. S., (2016). Do randomized control trials meet the "Gold Standard"? A study of the usefulness of RCTs in the What Works Clearinghouse. *American Enterprise Institute.*

Glass, G.V., & Smith, M.L. (1979). Meta-Analysis of research on class size and achievement. *Educational Evaluation and Policy Analysis*, 1(1), 2-16.

Glass, G. V. (2016). One hundred years of research: Prudent aspirations. *Educational Researcher*, 45(2), 69-72. https://doi.org/10.3102/0013189X16639026

Givvin, K. B., Stigler, J. W., & Thompson, B. J. (2011). What community college developmental mathematics students understand about mathematics, Part II: The interviews. *The MathAMATYC Educator*, 2, 4-16.

Gopal, S., & Schorr, L.B. (2016, June 2). Getting "Moneyball" right in the social sciences. *Stanford Social Innovation Review*. Stanford, CA.

Gorard, S. (2015). *Rethinking 'quantitative' methods and the development of new researchers*. Review of Education, 3(1), pp. 72-96.

Gorman, J. (2014). All circuits are busy. *New York Times*, 26 May. Downloaded from http://www.nytimes.com/2014/05/27/science/all-circuits-are-busy.html?module=SearchandmabReward=relbias%3Aw%2C%5B%22RI%3A8%22%2C%22RI%3A15%22%5D.

Grimes, D. A., & Schulz, K. F. (2008). Making sense of odds and odds ratios. *Obstetrics & Gynecology*, *111*(2, Part 1), 423-426.

Hakim, A., et al. (1998). Effects of walking on mortality among nonsmoking retired men. *New England Journal of Medicine*, 338(2), 94-99.

Hamilton, L., et al. (2009). Using Student Achievement Data to Support Instructional decision-Making. United States Department of Education. Retrieved from http://repository.upenn.edu/gse_pubs/279.

Harlow, LL., Mulaik, S.A., & Steiger , J.H. (eds.) (1997). *What if there were no significance tests?* Mahwah NJ: Lawrence Erlbaun Associates.

Harris, R. (2017). *Rigor Mortis: How Sloppy Science Creates Worthless Cures, Crushes Hope, and Wastes Billions*. Hachette UK.

Hart, C. (1999). *Doing a literature review: Releasing the social science research imagination*. London: SAGE.

Hart, B. & Risley, T.R. (1995). *Meaningful differences in the everyday experience of young American children*. Baltimore, MD: Brookes Publishing.

Hart, R., et al. (2015). *Student Testing in America's Great City Schools: An Inventory and Preliminary Analysis*. Council of the Great City Schools, Washington, DC.

Harwell, M. R., & LeBeau, B. (2010). Student eligibility for a free lunch as an SES measure in education research. *Educational Researcher*, 39(2), 120–131.

Haskins, R. (2015). Social programs that work. *New York Times*, January 1, A17.

Hattie, J. (2009). *Visible learning: A synthesis of over 800 meta-analyses relating to achievement*. Florence, KY: Routledge.

Haxton, C. & O'Day, J. (2105). Improving equity and access in Fresno: Lessons from a K12 higher education partnership. American Institute of Research.

Heath, S. B. (1983). *Way with words: Language, life, and work in communities and classrooms*. Cambridge UK: University of Cambridge Press.

Heitin, L. (2017). Ga. District puts data to work. *Education Week,* Spotlight on Data-Driven Decisionmaking, 3-4.

Hojat, M., & Xu, G. (2004). A visitor's guide to effect sizes–statistical significance versus practical (clinical) importance of research findings. *Advances in Health Sciences Education*, 9(3), 241-249.

Holcomb Jr, W. L., Chaiworapongsa, T., Luke, D. A., & Burgdorf, K. D. (2001). An odd measure of risk: use and misuse of the odds ratio. Obstetrics & Gynecology, 98(4), 685-688.

Hossenfelder, S. (2018). Lost in math: How beauty leads physics astray. Basic Books.

Hubbard, R. (2015). *Corrupt research: The case for reconceptualizing empirical management and social science*. SAGE Publications.

Ioannidis, J. P. (2005). Why most published research findings are false. *PLoS Med*, 2(8). https://doi.org/10.1371/journal.pmed.0020124

Irwin, N. (2014). Why the middle class isn't buying the talk about a strong recovery. *New York Times*,

August 22, p. B3.

Isaacson, W. (2021). *The code breaker: Jennifer Doudna, gene editing, and the future of the human race.* Simon and Schuster.

Jacobson, N.S., & Truax, P. (1991). Clinical significance: A statistical approach to defining meaningful change in psychotherapy research. *Journal of Consulting and Clinical Psychology*, 59 (1), 12-19.

Jimerson, J. B., & Wayman, J. C. (2015). Professional Learning for Using Data: Examining Teacher Needs and Supports. *Teachers College Record, 117*(4), n4.

Joan I. Heller, J.I., Hanson, T., & Barnett-Clarke, C. (2010). The Impact of Math Pathways and Pitfalls on Students' Mathematics Achievement and Mathematical Language Development: A Study Conducted in Schools with High Concentrations of Latino/a Students and English Learners. A report prepared for the U.S. Department of Education. Institute of Education Sciences, Washington, D.C.

Jennings, P.A. & Greenberg, M.T. (2009). The prosocial classroom: Teacher social and emotional competence in relation to student and classroom outcomes. *Review of Educational Research, 79*(1), 491- 525.

Johnson, B. (2001). Toward a new classification of nonexperimental quantitative research. *Educational Researcher, 30*(2), 3-13.

Johnson, G. (2014). An apple a day, and other myths. *New York Times.* Downloaded 1/24/15 from http://www.nytimes.com/2014/04/22/science/an-apple-a-day-and-other-myths.html.

Johnson, R.S. (2002). *Using data to close the achievement gap: How to measure equity in our schools.* Thousand Oaks CA: Corwin Press.

Kahan, D.M. (2014). Climate science communication and the measurement problem. *Advances in Political Psychology*, Forthcoming.

Kahneman, D. (2011). Thinking Fast and Slow. New York, NY: Farrar, Strauss and Giroux.

Kane, J. T., et al. (2016). Teaching higher: Educators' perspectives on common core implementation. Center for Education Policy Research, Harvard University.

Kelly, A. E. (Ed.). (2003). Special issue on the role of design in educational research [Special issue]. *Educational Researcher*, 32(1).

Kesselheim, A.S. & Avorn, J. (2021, June 15). The F.D.A. has reached a new low. *New York Times*, retrieved from: https://www.nytimes.com/2021/06/15/opinion/alzheimers-drug-aducanumab-fda.html?action=click&module=Opinion&pgtype=Homepage.

Kirk, R. E. (1996). Practical significance: A concept whose time has come. *Educational and Psychological Measurement,* 56(5), 746-759.

Knaflic, C. N. (2015). *Storytelling with data: A data visualization guide for business professionals.* John Wiley & Sons.

Kocher, B, & Mostashari, F. (2014). A health care success story. *New York Times*, OP-ED, September 23, Downloaded 9/25/14 from http://www.nytimes.com/2014/09/24/opinion/a-health-care-success-story.html.

Kolata, G. (2015). A faster way to try many drugs on many cancers. *New York Times*, Downloaded 5/12/2015 from: http://www.nytimes.com/2015/02/26/health/fast-track-attacks-on-cancer-accelerate-hopes.html?_r=0.

Kolata, G. & Mueller, B. (2022). Halting progress and happy accidents: How mRNA vaccines were made. New York Times, retrieved 1/15/22, https://www.nytimes.com/2022/01/15/health/mrna-vaccine.html.

Kopf, D. (2017). An error made in 1925 led to a crisis in modern science—now researchers are joining to fix it. *Quartz*, Retrieved 9/1/17 from https://qz.com/1055287/an-error-made-in-1925-led-to-a-crisis-in-modern-science-now-researchers-are-joining-to-fix-it/.

Kozol, J. (2005). Confections of apartheid: A stick-and-carrot pedagogy for the children of our inner-city poor, *Phi Delta Kappan*, 87(4), 265-275.

Kozol, J. (2006). Success for All: trying to make an end run around inequality and segregation, *Phi Delta Kappan*, 87(8), 624-626.

Kraemer, H. C. (2016). Messages for clinicians: Moderators and mediators of treatment outcome in randomized clinical trials. *American Journal of Psychiatry*, *173*(7), 672–679. https://doi.org/10.1176/appi.ajp.2016.15101333

Kraft, M. A. (2020). Interpreting effect sizes of education interventions. *Educational Researcher*, 49(4), 241-253.

Krugman, P. (2020). Trump's Stalinist Approach to Science: Bully and ignore the experts, and send in the quacks. Retrieved from https://www.nytimes.com/2020/09/24/opinion/trump-science-coronavirus.html?searchResultPosition=2.

Kuhn, T.S. (1970). *The structure of scientific revolutions*: 2nd edition. Chicago, IL: University of Chicago Press.

Lagemann, E. C. (2002). *An elusive science: The troubling history of education research*. Chicago: University of Chicago Press.

Langer, E. J. (1989). Minding matters: The consequences of mindlessness-mindfulness. *Advances in experimental social psychology*, *22*(12), 137-173.

Langer, E.J., & Roth, J. (1975). Heads I win, tails it's chance: The illusion of control as a function of the sequence of outcomes in a purely chance task. Journal of Personality and Social Psychology, 32(6), 951-955.

Langley, Langley, G. J., Nolan, T., Nolan, K., Norman, C., & Provost, L. (1996). *The improvement guide: a practical guide to enhancing organizational performance*. San Francisco, CA: Jossey-Bass.

Lee, A. S., & Mohajeri, K. (2012, January). Linking relevance to practical significance. In *System Science (HICSS), 2012 45th Hawaii International Conference on Systems Sciences*, IEEE, 5234-5240.

Lee, I. M., et al. (2019). Association of step volume and intensity with all-cause mortality in older women. *JAMA internal medicine*, *179*(8), 1105-1112.

Lee, K. Talwar, V., McCarthy, A., Ross, I., Evans, A., & Arruda, C. (2014). Can classic moral stories promote honesty in children? *Psychological Science*. June, 1-7.

Lembke, A. (2016). *Drug Dealer, MD: How Doctors Were Duped, Patients Got Hooked, and Why It's So Hard to Stop*. Baltimore, MD: Johns Hopkins University Press.

Levine, A. (March 2005). *Educating school leaders*. Washington, D.C.: Education Schools Project.

Lipsey, M. W. (1990). *Design sensitivity: Statistical power for experimental research* (Vol. 19). Los Angeles CA: Sage.

Lipsey, M. W., & Wilson, D. B. (1993). The efficacy of psychological, educational, and behavioral treatment: confirmation from meta-analysis. *American psychologist*, 48(12), 1181-1209.

Lipsey, M. W., Puzio, K, Yun, C, Hebert, M. A., Steinka-Fry, K., Cole, M. W., Roberts, M., . . . Busick, M. D. (2012). *Translating the Statistical Representation of the Effects of Education Interventions Into More Readily Interpretable Forms*. U.S. Department Of Education. Institute of Education Sciences. Retrieved from https://ies.ed.gov/ncser/pubs/20133000/

Lipska, K. (2015). When diabetes treatment goes too far. *New York Times*. Downloaded 2/4/15 from http://www.nytimes.com/2015/01/12/opinion/when-diabetes-treatment-goes-too-far.html.

Long, T.E. (2014). Toward recyclable thermosets. *Science*, 344(6185), 706-707.

Lortie-Forgues, H., & Inglis, M. (2019). Rigorous Large-Scale Educational RCTs Are Often Uninformative: Should We Be Concerned?. *Educational Researcher*, 48(3), 158-166.

Ludwig, D.S., & Friedman, M.I. (2014). Increasing adiposity: Consequence or cause of overeating? *JAMA*. Published online May 16, 2014. Downloaded 5/18/14 http://jama.jamanetwork.com/article.aspx?articleid=1871695

March, J.C., & March, J.G. (1978). Almost random careers: The Wisconsin school superintendency, 1940-1972. *Administrative Science Quarterly*, 22 (1977), 377-409.

March, J.C., & March, J.G. (1978). Performance sampling in social matches, *Administrative Science Quarterly*, 23, 434-453.

March, J.G. (2014). Personal communication.

Marcus, G. & Davis, E. (2014, April 6). Eight (No, Nine!) problems with big data. *New York Times*, Downloaded 10/26/2014 from http://www.nytimes.com/2014/04/07/opinion/eight-no-nine-problems-with-big-data.html?module=Search&mabReward=relbias%3Ar%2C%7B%221%22%3A%22RI%3A7%22%7D.

Markoff, J. (2014). Error at IBM lab finds new family of materials. *New York Times*. Downloaded 7/26/14 from http://www.nytimes.com/2014/05/16/science/error-leads-ibm-researchers-to-a-new-family-of-materials.html?module=Search&mabReward= relbias%3Ar%2C%7B%221%22%3A%22RI%3A9%22%7D.

Marsh, J. A., Bertrand, M., & Huguet, A. (2015). Using Data to Alter Instructional Practice. *Teachers College Record, 117*(4), 1-40.

Maul, A., & McClelland, A. (2013). *Review of the national charter school study*. National Education Policy Center. Boulder, CO: University of Colorado.

McKenney, S., & Reeves, T.C. (2013). Systematic review of design-based research progress: Is a little knowledge a dangerous thing? *Educational Researcher*. 42(2), 97-100.

Meehl, P.E. (1978). Theoretical risks and tabular asterisks: Sir Karl, Sir Ronald, and the slow progress of soft psychology. *Journal of Consulting and Clinical Psychology*, 46, 806-34.

Mingfong, J., Yam San, C., & Ek Ming, T. (2010). Unpacking the design process in design-based research. In *Proceedings of the 9th International Conference of the Learning Sciences* (Volu. 2).

Moosa, I.A. (2019). Is economics relevant to real world economics?. *Real-World Economics Review*, 88, 2-13.

Mulaik, S. A., Raju, N. S., & Harshman, R. A. (1997). There is a time and a place for significance testing. In *What If There Were No Significance Tests*, Harlow, Mulaik, & Steiger (eds.), 65-115.

Murphy, J. (2014). Of questionable value: The EdD dissertation—An essay. UCEA Review, Winter, 27-28.

Muschkin, C. G., Glennie, E., & Beck, A. N. (2014). Peer contexts: Do old for grade and retained peers influence student behavior in middle school? *Teachers College Record, 116*, 040305.

Muse, L. A., Harris, S. G., & Feild, H. S. (2003). Has the inverted-U theory of stress and job performance had a fair test?. *Human Performance, 16*(4), 349-364.

NGA (2012). *Using Data to Guide State Education Policy and Practice*. Issue Brief, National Governors Association. Washington, D.C.

NIH (2013). *Monitoring adherence to the NIH policy on the inclusion of women and minorities as subjects in clinical research. comprehensive report: Tracking of clinical research as reported in fiscal year 2011 and fiscal year 2012*. Department of Health and Human Services National Institutes of Health. Downloaded 2/4/15 from http://orwh.od.nih.gov/research/inclusion/pdf/Inclusion-ComprehensiveReport-FY-2011-2012.pdf.

Olson, K., & Clark, C.M. (2009). A signature pedagogy in doctoral education: The leader–scholar community. *Educational Researcher*, 38(3), 216–221.

Open Science Collaboration. (2015). Estimating the reproducibility of psychological science. *Science, 349*(6251), aac4716-1—aac4716-8.

Osborne, J.W. (2015). *Best Practices in Logistic Regression*. Thousand Oaks, CA: Sage.

Pane, J. F., Griffin, B. A., McCaffrey, D. F., & Karam, R. (2014). Effectiveness of cognitive tutor algebra I at scale. *Educational Evaluation and Policy Analysis*, 36(2), 127-144.

Pearl, J., & Mackenzie, D. (2018). *The book of why: the new science of cause and effect.* Basic books.

Perrin, R. (2014). *Pocket Guide to APA Style.* Independence, KY: Cengage Learning.

Perry, J. A. (2012a). What history reveals about the education doctorate. In *Placing Practitioner Knowledge at the Center of Teacher Education: Rethinking the Policy and Practice of the Education Doctorate.* Latta, M.M., & Wunder, S. (eds.).

Perry, J. A. (2012b). To Ed.D. or not to Ed.D.? *Phi Delta Kappan,* 41-44.

Peters, T.J., & Waterman, R.H. (1982). *In search of excellence, Lessons from America's best-run companies.* New York, NY: Harper & Row.

Pew Research Center. (2013). *Public's Views on Human Evolution.* Downloaded from http://www.pewforum.org/files/2013/12/Evolution-12-30.pdf, 7/6/14.

Plsek, P.E. (1999). Quality improvement methods in clinical medicine. *Pediatrics,* 203 -214.

Pogrow, S. (1985). *Evaluations of Educational Administration Software.* Allyn & Bacon (1985).

Pogrow, S. (1998). What is an exemplary program and why should anyone care? A reaction to Slavin and Klein. *Educational Researcher,* October 1998, 22-29.

Pogrow, S. (2000). The unsubstantiated 'success' of Success for All. Implications for policy, practice, and the soul of the profession. *Phi Delta Kappan,* 596-600.

Pogrow, S. (2002). Success for All is a Failure. *Phi Delta Kappan,* 463-468.

Pogrow, S. (2004). The missing element in reducing the gap: Eliminating the 'Blank Stare'. *Teachers College Record,* Feature Article, (www.tcrecord.org/Content.asp? ContentID=11381).

Pogrow, S. (2005). HOTS Revisited: A thinking development approach to reducing the learning gap after grade 3. *Phi Delta Kappan,* September, pp. 64-75.

Pogrow, S. (2008). Rebuilding New Jersey school reform to reduce the literacy gap: Moving away from Success for All and hyper-remediation. *New Jersey Journal of Supervision and Curriculum Development.* January 2008.

Pogrow, S. (2017).The failure of the US education research establishment to identify effective practices: Beware effective practices policies. *Education Policy Analysis Archives,* 25(5). http://epaa.asu.edu/ojs/article/view/2517/1864.

Pogrow, S. (2019). How effect size (practical significance) misleads clinical practice: The case for switching to practical benefit to assess applied research findings. *The American Statistician,* a journal of the American Statistical Association.

Pogrow, S. (2021). *Authentic Quantitative Analysis for Leadership Decision-Making and EdD Dissertations* (Version 3.0), ICPEL.

Pong, J. (2017). *Effects Of A Comprehensive Array Of Dropout-Prevention Interventions: Responders vs. Non-Responders.* Unpublished EdD dissertation, San Francisco State University.

Powers, J.M. & Glass, G.V. (2014). When statistical significance hides more than it reveals, *Teachers College Record.* ID Number: 17591, Downloaded: 7/10/2014 from http://www.tcrecord.org.

Randall, L. (2005a). *Warped passages: Unraveling the mysteries of the universe's hidden dimensions.* New York, NY: Harper Collins.

Randall, L. (2005b). Dangling particles. *New York Times,* OP-ED, September 18. Downloaded 7/27/14 from http://www.nytimes.com/2005/09/18/opinion/18randall.html?pagewanted= all&module=Search&mabReward=relbias%3Aw%2C%7B%221%22%3A%22RI%3A5%22 %7D

Rangel, V. S., Monroy, C., & Bell, E. (2016). Science teachers' data use practices: A descriptive analysis. *Education Policy Analysis Archives,* 24, 86.

Reardon, S.F. (2013). The widening income achievement gap. *Educational Leadership,* 70(8),10-16.

Ridley, M. (2020). *How innovation works: And why it flourishes in freedom.* New York: Harper.

Russell, J.L., Jackson, K., Krumm, A.E., & Frank, K.A. (2013). Theory and research methodologies for design-based implementation research: Examples from four cases. *National Society for the Study of Education Yearbook,* 112(2), 157-191.

Sandoval, W. A., & Bell, P. (2004). Design-based research methods for studying learning in context: introduction. *Educational Psychologist*, 39(4), 199–201.

Sarid, O., Anson, O., Yaari, A., & Margalith, M. (2004). Academic stress, immunological reaction, and academic performance among students of nursing and physiotherapy. *Research in nursing & health*, 27(5), 370-377.

Scammacca, N. K., Roberts, G., Vaughn, S., & Stuebing, K. K. (2013). A meta-analysis of interventions for struggling readers in grades 4–12: 1980–2011. *Journal of learning disabilities*, 0022219413504995.

Schemo, D. J., & Ford, F. (2003, December 3). A miracle revisited: measuring success; gains in Houston schools: how real are they? *New York Times*, Retrieved from http://topics.nytimes.com/top/reference/timestopics/people/s/diana_jean_schemo/index.html

Schildkamp, K., & Poortman, C. (2015). Factors influencing the functioning of data teams. *Teachers college record*, 117(4), 1-42.

Schmidt, F. L., & Hunter, J. E. (1997). Eight common but false objections to the discontinuation of significance testing in the analysis of research data. In *What If There Were No Significance Tests*, Harlow, Mulaik, & Steiger (eds.), 37-64.

Science Friday (2014). Downloaded from http://sciencefriday.com/segment/01/24/2014/james-dyson-failures-are-interesting.html, 10/12/14.

Serra-Garcia, M., & Gneezy, U. (2021). Nonreplicable publications are cited more than replicable ones. *Science advances*, 7(21), eabd1705.

Shulman, L.S., Golde, C.M., Bueschel, A.C., & Garabedian, K.J. (April 2006). Reclaiming education's doctorates: A critique and a proposal. *Educational Researcher*, 35, 5-32.

Sorkin, R.S. (2014, September 5). So Bill Gates has this idea for a history class. *New York Times*. Downloaded, 10/7/2014 from http://www.nytimes.com/2014/09/07/magazine/so-bill-gates-has-this-idea-for-a-history-class.html?module=Search&mabReward=relbias%3Ar%2C%7B%221%22%3A%22RI%3A6%22%D.

Sparks, S. D. (2013, October 30). School improvement model shows promise in first i3 evaluation. *Education Week*, 33(11), 8.

Spies, R. A., & Carlson, J. F. (2010). *The eighteenth mental measurements yearbook*. University of Nebraska-Lincoln, NB: Buros Institute of Mental Measurements.

Stigler, J.W., Givvin, K.B., & Thompson, B.J. (2010). What community college developmental mathematics students understand about mathematics. *MathAMATYC Educator*, 1, 4-18.

Storey, V.A. & Hesbol, K.A. (2106). *Contemporary approaches to dissertation development and research methods* (Advances in Knowledge Acquisition, Transfer, and Management) 1st Edition. IGI Global.

Sue, V. M., & Griffin, M. T. (2015). *Data visualization & presentation with Microsoft Office*. SAGE Publications.

Swaab, R.I., Schaerer, M., Anicich, E.M., Ronay, R., & Galinsky, A.D. (2014). the too-much-talent effect: Team interdependence determines when more talent is too much or not enough. *Psychological Science*. June, 1-11.

Tang, J., Tang, Z., Marino, L. D., Zhang, Y., & Li, Q. (2008). Exploring an inverted U-Shape relationship between entrepreneurial orientation and performance in Chinese ventures. *Entrepreneurship Theory and Practice*, 32(1), 219-239.

Theobald, R., & Freeman, S. (2014). Is it the intervention or the students? Using linear regression to control for student characteristics in undergraduate STEM education research. *CBE-Life Sciences Education*, 13(1), 41-48.

Thompson, B. (2005). *Foundations of behavioral statistics: An insight based approach*. New York, NY: The Guilford Press.

Tienken, C.H. (2011). The Common Core State Standards: An example of data-less decision making. *AASA Journal of Scholarship and Practice, 7*(4), 3-18.

Tienken, C.H., & Wolfe, A. (2014). *Three-year predictions of grade 5 state test results using community census data.* Presentation at the annual conference of the National Council of Professors of Educational Administration. Channel Island, CA.

Tulliss, T. (2014). How game theory helped improve New York City's high school application process. *New York Times.* Downloaded 2/4/15 from http://www.nytimes.com/2014/12/07/ nyregion/how-game-theory-helped-improve-new-york-city-high-school-application-process.html.

Turabian, K.L., Booth, W.C., Colomb, G.G., & Williams, J.M. (2013). *A Manual for Writers of Research Papers, Theses, and Dissertations,* Eighth Edition: Chicago Style for Students. Chicago, IL: University of Chicago Press.

Venezky, R. L. (1998). An alternative perspective on Success for All. *Advances in educational policy*, Wong, K. (ed.) Greenwich, CN: JAI Press. 4, 145-165.

Vygotsky, L.S. (1978). *Mind in Society: The Development of Higher Psychological Processes.* Cambridge MA: Harvard University Press.

Walter, M. & Anderson, C. (2013). *Indigenous statistics: A quantitative research methodology.* Walnut Creek, CA: Left Coast Press.

Wanzek, J., Vaughn, S., Scammacca, N. K., Metz, K., Murray, C. S., Roberts, G., & Danielson, L. (2013). Extensive reading interventions for students with reading difficulties after grade 3. *Review of Educational Research.* 163-195.

Webb, E. J., Campbell, D. T., Schwartz, R. D., & Sechrest, L. (1966). *Unobtrusive measures: Nonreactive research in the social sciences* (Vol. 111). Chicago: Rand McNally.

Williamson, B. (2017). *Big data in education: The digital future of learning, policy and practice.* Sage.

Willingham, D.T. (2007). Critical thinking: Why is it so hard to teach. *American Educator*, Summer, 31, 8-19.

Wilson S.J., Tanner-Smith, E.E., Lipsey M.W., Katarzyna S.F., & Morrison, J. (2011). *Dropout Prevention and Intervention Programs: Effects on School Completion and Dropout Among School-Aged Children, and Youth.* Retrieved from campbellcollaboration.org.

Wolcott, H.F. (1973). *The man in the principal's office: An ethnography.* Toronto, Canada: Holt Rinehart and Winston.

Zaporozhetz, L. E. (1987). *The dissertation literature review: How faculty advisors prepare their doctoral candidates.* Unpublished doctoral dissertation. Eugene, OR: University of Oregon.

Ziliak, S.T., and McClosky, D.N. (2004). Size matters: The standard error of regressions in the American economic review. *The Journal of Socio-Economics*, 33(5), 527-546.

Ziliak, S.T., and McClosky, D.N. (2008). The Cult of Statistical Significance: How the Standard Error Costs us Jobs, Justice, and Lives. University of Michigan Press: Ann Arbor, MI.

Index

A

Academic theory, 17, 18, 19, 20, 22, 24, 25, 26, 28, 29, 240
    advantages of, 18
    definition of, 17
    limitations of, 18
Achievement gap, 11, 13, 100, 245, 331
Action research, xii-xv, 46-48, 57, 77, 152, 156, 226, 227, 298, 299, 308, 309, 312, 314, 315, 316, 321, 322, 339
Actionable variable, 115, 116, 129, 131, 133
Analysis of Covariance, 151, 152, 211, 213
    purpose of, 160
Analysis of Empirical Evidence
    critque of, 307
ANCOVA
    see Analysis of Covariance, 211
Applied research, 42, 43, 44, 47, 49, 50, 140, 141, 182, 187, 195, 345
    definition of, 154
    as applied to Covid vaccines, 43
At-risk students, 182, 202, 259, 260
Attrition
Average, 64

B

Bandura's Social Cognitive Theory, 22
Basic research 20, 42, 43, 140, 141, 148, 149, 187, 202, 248, 253
    as applied to Covid vaccines, 43
    definition of, 42
Binary, 130

C

Carnegie Foundation
    developers on the Statway NIC, 234
Categorical Data
    Definition of, 63
Causation, 23, 52, 53, 54, 61, 62, 79, 84, 94, 95, 99, 101, 108-112, 116, 120, 124, 132, 134, 135, 138, 140, 142, 144, 145, 146, 148, 149, 151, 155, 156, 157, 165, 184-188, 217, 218, 228, 229, 233, 236, 253-255, 262, 263, 266
    as opposed to relationship, 109
    definition of, 144
Chi-Square, 316, 319
Class size, 20, 21, 340
Cluster sample
    definition of, 315
Cohen's d, 319
Common Core, 11, 40, 41, 208, 281, 283, 347

Conceptual atrophy
    definition of, 260
Confidence interval, 130, 153, 157
    definition of, 37
Confounding variables, 53, 54, 61, 82, 83, 85, 94, 95, 99, 101, 108, 109, 113, 116-118, 124, 131-133, 136, 138, 139, 144, 146, 147, 152, 155, 156, 163, 187. 217, 218, 315, 320
    definition of, 53
Constructs, 300, 307, 311, 313, 333
    definition of, 300
Continuous improvement, xii, xiii, 39, 276-278, 285, 286, 289, 290, 291, 292, 293, 296
Correlation, 42, 103-119-125, 128, 131-133, 134-136, 138, 146, 218, 219, 282, 318,-320, 330
    one way, 117
    partial, 124
    two-way, 117, 118, 133
    definition of, 104
    difference between correlation and causation, 111
    Multiple. *See* Regression analysis
    negative, 104
    partial, 103
    positive, 104
Correlation matrix, 105
Correlational research
    definition of, 101
    types of, 103
Cosmic inflation theory, 4
Counter-intuitive
    conclusion, 10, 118
CREDO
    study that mistakenly concluded that charter schools were better, 162, 175
Cross sectional research, 151
Cross-sectional research
    Definition of, 151
Culture of continuous improvement,290, 296

D

Dashboard
    definition of, 288
Data infrastructure, 290, 291, 293, 296
    definition of, 290
Data visualization software, 288
Data warehouse, 277, 288, 289
    definition of, 284
Database
    definition of, 284
Datasets, 12, 332, 333, 334
DBR, 226, 234, 266

348

350

Made in United States
Orlando, FL
26 May 2024

47220902R00202